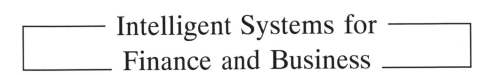

Intelligent Systems for Finance and Business

Intelligent Systems for Finance and Business

Edited by Suran Goonatilake and Philip Treleaven

JOHN WILEY & SONS

Chichester • New York • Brisbane • Toronto • Singapore

National   01243 779777
International (+44) 1243 779777

Other Wiley Editorial Offices

John Wiley & Sons, Inc., 605 Third Avenue,
New York, NY 10158-0012, USA

Jacaranda Wiley Ltd, 33 Park Road, Milton,
Queensland 4064, Australia

John Wiley & Sons (Canada) Ltd, 22 Worcester Road,
Rexdale, Ontario M9W 1L1, Canada

John Wiley & Sons (SEA) Pte Ltd, 37 Jalan Pemimpin #05-04,
Block B, Union Industrial Building, Singapore 2057

Library of Congress Cataloging-in-Publication Data

Intelligent systems for finance and business / edited by Suran
    Goonatilake and Philip Treleaven.
        p.   cm.
    Includes bibliographical references (p.   ) and index.
    ISBN 0-471-94404-1 (cloth : alk. paper)
        1. Industrial management — Data processing — Case studies. 2. Ind-
ustrial management — Decision making — Data proces sing — Case
studies.   3. Finance — Data processing — Case studies.   4. Artificial
intelligence — Case studies.   5. Neural networks (Computer science).
6. Fuzzy systems.   7. Expert systems (Computer science).   8. Genetic
algorithms.   I. Goonatilake, Suran.   II. Treleaven, P. C. (Philip C.)
HD30.2.I554   1995   95–19808
658'.0563 — dc20   CIP

British Library Cataloguing in Publication Data

A catalogue record for this book is available from the British Library

ISBN 0-471-94404-1

Typeset in 10/12pt Times by Laser Words, Madras
Printed and bound in Great Britain by Biddles Ltd, Guildford, Surrey

This book is printed on acid-free paper responsibly manufactured from sustainable forestation, for which
at least two trees are planted for each one used for paper production.

Contents

List of Contributors

SURAN GOONATILAKE
Department of Computer Science, University College London, Gower Street, London WC1E 6BT, UK
&
SearchSpace Ltd., 85 Charlotte Street, London WC1P 1LB, UK

ROBERT S. DIDNER
American Express, Tower C, World Finance Centre, New York, NY 10285, USA

R. WALKER, E. W. HAASDIJK and M. C. GERRETS
Cap Volmac, Daltonlaan 400, PO Box 2575, 3500 GN Utrecht, The Netherlands

DAVID LEIGH
44 Harvard Lane, Commack, New York 11725, USA

PETER FURNESS
Senior Principal, AMS Management Systems UK Ltd., 1 Angel Court, London EC2R 7HJ, UK

RICHARD WEBBER
CCN Marketing, Talbot House, Talbot Street, Nottingham NG1 5HF, UK

EARL COX
Metus Systems, 1 Griggs Lane, Chappaqua, New York, NY 10514, USA

STEVE MOTT
Cognitive Systems, 880 Canal Street, Stamford, CT 06902, USA

JOHN MAJOR and DAN RIEDINGER
5GS, The Travelers, 1, Tower Square, Hartford, CT 06183, USA

COLIN TALBOT
Lloyd's of London, Systems Development, Gun Wharf, Chatham, Kent ME4 4TU, UK

A. N. REFENES, A. D. ZAPRANIS, J. T. CONNOR and D. W. BUNN
London Business School, Sussex Place, Regent's Park, London NW1 4SA, UK

SHUN'ICHI TANO
Systems Development Laboratory, Hitachi Ltd., 292 Yoshida-cho, Totsuka-ku, Yokohama 244, Japan

JAE K. LEE. HYUN SOO KIM
Dept. of Management Information Systems, Korea Advanced Institute of Science and Technology 207–43 Cheongryang, Seoul 130–012, Korea

JOHN KOZA
Consulting Professor, Computer Science Department, Stanford University, Margaret Jacks Hall, Stanford, California 94305–2140, USA

PAUL TAYLER
Department of Computer Science, Brunel University, Uxbridge, Middlesex, UB8 3PH, UK

PETER ALLEN
International Ecotechnology Research Centre, Cranfield Institute of Technology, Cranfield, Bedford MK43 OAL, UK

PHILIP TRELEAVEN
Department of Computer Science, University College London, Gower Street, London WC1E 6BT, UK

Foreword

Across all business sectors and across all industries, business professionals today are seeking a modern-age philosophers' stone. The philosophers' stone was thought by alchemists to be the key ingredient in changing base metals into gold. Today, business professionals are performing a kind of alchemy of their own. Faced with mountains of raw data, they are trying to change these data into useful information by which their companies can profit. Stated in another way, the alchemy being performed is the attempt to turn base data into gold.

The alchemists did not have much luck. And, until recently, business professionals had limited success in applying scientific and mathematical methods to everyday business problems such as predictive modeling. The shortcomings in these methods were that they employed linear techniques such as regression to solve problems of a world that seldom behaves in a linear fashion. Human decisions of a mass scale, the type that most often affect the course of a business, are too erratic and too discontinuous to oblige an analyst with simple linear tools.

In contrast to the alchemists, business professionals today are finding a good deal of success with the use of intelligent systems that can find complex non-linear patterns in large data-sets. The systems have been used to solve a wide variety of common but extremely critical business problems. These include the ability to predict consumer behavior accurately, to detect fraudulent transactions, and to capture corporate knowledge within a system and to use it effectively.

Visa knows first-hand the power of these types of systems. Visa has deployed intelligent systems to provide member banks and Visa cardholders with the highest level of service that is possible with leading-edge technologies. Visa's global payment network, VisaNet, processes over 6 billion transactions annually with a sales volume of over US$550 billion. With the vast amount of transaction data — processed at an average rate of over 16 million transactions a day — Visa has enlisted the use of neural network technology to combat credit-card fraud.

Visa's neural network applications for fraud detection have proven very successful, and have helped turn the tide against what was an annually rising level of credit-card fraud. Finding the small percentage of fraudulent transactions out of an average 16 million on a daily basis is no small task — it is very similar to finding a needle in a haystack since fraudulent transactions closely resemble legitimate transactions.

Historically, the task of finding these needles was done on a manual basis, which was a painfully labor-intensive process. Most people are familiar with the type of fraud that affects cardholders, where a card or card number is stolen and used to obtain merchandise or services fraudulently before the theft is detected. Less familiar to the public is another type of fraud that directly affects financial institutions. Fraudulent transactions at a merchant location can result in significant losses to financial institutions due to fraudulent and abusive credit practices or improper merchant procedures.

The most critical factor in combating both types of fraud is time — the faster the fraud is uncovered, the more money is saved. Visa's application of neural networks to detect card fraud has proven to be not only extremely fast but, more importantly, also far superior at spotting patterns of fraud than previous manual processes. As an additional benefit, neural-network technology lends itself to being retrained to adapt to ever-changing global and regional fraud patterns.

This book provides real-life examples of intelligent systems at work in financial and numerous other business environments. For those individuals who would like to help their companies analyze data in order to understand the future and not just the past, I invite you to study this collection of chapters and determine which of these systems may be most applicable to your own business.

Cathy Basch
Senior Vice President
Visa International

Acknowledgements

Firstly, we would like to take this opportunity to thank all of our contributors for their time and effort in preparing their chapters. Many thanks to the staff at John Wiley for making the book possible, especially to Richard Baggaley for his patience and guidance throughout the project. A special thanks goes to Alison Mead for her tireless effort in the production stages of the book.

We also like to acknowledge the Department of Computer Science at University College London and our colleagues in the Intelligent Systems Group, for providing a stimulating environment for our explorations into financial and business applications of intelligent systems.

About The Editors

Suran Goonatilake is a research fellow at University College London and a co-founder of SearchSpace Ltd., a London-based company that specializes in applying intelligent systems in finance and business. Dr. Goonatilake is an authority on automated fraud detection and risk assessment, and has consulted for leading financial institutions including American Express and the London Stock Exchange on using intelligent systems for discovering patterns in business processes. A regular speaker at international conferences, he holds a PhD in Computer Science from University College London and a bachelors degree in Computing and Artificial Intelligence from the University of Sussex. Suran is also the co-editor of the book, 'Intelligent Hybrid Systems'.

Philip Treleaven is Pro-Provost and Professor of Computer Science at University College London. He is an authority on Intelligent Systems and in the organisation of government research programmes to help industry, such as Japan's FGCS project, the European Community's ESPRIT Programme and the UK's ALVEY/IED Programmes. Prof. Treleaven has published over 100 papers and serves on the UK Office of Science & Technology Foresight Panel for Retail.

The editors can be contacted at:

S. Goonatilake@cs.ucl.ac.uk
http://www.cs.ucl.ac.uk/staff/S. Goonatilake

P. Treleaven@cs.ucl.ac.uk
http://www.cs.ucl.ac.uk/staff/P. Treleaven

1
Intelligent Systems for Finance and Business: An Overview

SURAN GOONATILAKE

1 BACKGROUND

Companies are gathering ever-increasing amounts of data. Each time a person draws money from a bank teller machine, shops at a supermarket, sells a stock, or makes a telephone call, details of that transaction are recorded in a company database. Innovative companies are now treating the mountains of data they hold as potential treasures which can be 'mined' to find important, perhaps fundamental, patterns and relationships that can transform business practices.

Intelligent systems are a category of computing devices that can find patterns and discover relationships in large amounts of data. These systems encompass a repertoire of techniques including neural networks, genetic algorithms and fuzzy systems. They are now automating several areas of business decision making that were previously performed by experienced humans. Typical applications in the retail sector include discovering consumer spending patterns and in the financial sector, insurance risk assessment and currency price prediction.

The range of applications is increasing rapidly (see Figure 1.1) and companies are now using intelligent systems even to automate parts of their *core business*. Countrywide Funding, the largest originator of mortgages in the USA, uses an adaptive rule-based system to underwrite its mortgages. Visa International has a

Intelligent Systems for Finance and Business. Edited by S. Goonatilake and P. Treleaven
© 1995 John Wiley & Sons Ltd

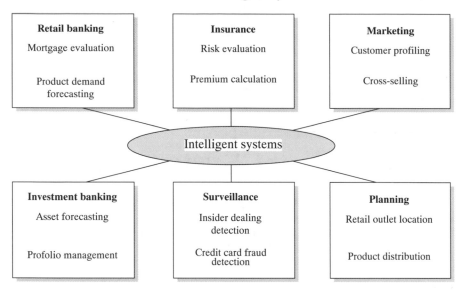

Figure 1.1   Application areas for intelligent systems

neural network system to detect fraudulent use of credit cards and Fuji Bank uses fuzzy systems for bond trading.

In all these companies the motivating factors for using intelligent systems have been similar — increasing the quality of their service and reducing costs. At American Express, for example, they have helped to reduce the cost of certain credit approval transactions from $15.00 to $1.40 (see Chapter 2 for details). At Visa International the saving due to the use of neural networks for credit-card fraud detection is estimated to be $40 million over a six-month period. Such savings are made possible because of the low running costs associated with intelligent systems after the initial development and installation.

In terms of increasing the quality of service, intelligent systems can produce more accurate and more consistent decisions than human operators (see Chapter 2). They are also faster and tireless, working 24 hours a day 7 days a week. Further, they can be used to provide services that are more focused on a customer's needs. For example, intelligent systems are being used to learn the detailed behaviour patterns of individual customers (e.g. product preferences and buying patterns). When armed with such knowledge, companies can offer niche tailor-made services which match a particular customer's preferences.

A common theme in intelligent systems is their mimicry of nature. Neural networks, for example, are inspired by the functionality of nerve cells in the brain. Like humans, neural networks can *learn* to recognize patterns by repeated exposure to many different examples. They can be used to recognize patterns or salient characteristics whether they be handwritten characters, profitable loans or good trading decisions. Just as humans have the capability to recognize handwritten characters produced by different people who have very different styles, neural networks can also learn to recognize patterns in data that are inexact and incomplete.

Neural networks are now being applied to problems that were previously solved using techniques such as linear regression and in tasks which were performed by experts with years of experience. For example, neural networks are used in direct marketing to identify the characteristics of people most likely to respond to a direct mail campaign. They learn the relationship between customer attributes such as income, profession, age and the likelihood of the customer responding to a mailing of a particular product advertisement (see Figure 1.2). This is done by repeatedly presenting the network with pairs of information consisting of the independent variables (e.g. income, profession, etc.) and the dependent variable (customer response to mailing — yes/no). A neural network finds this relationship through a *learning* cycle where many hundreds of past customer records are presented repeatedly to the network. At each cycle the network attempts to make finer refinements of the

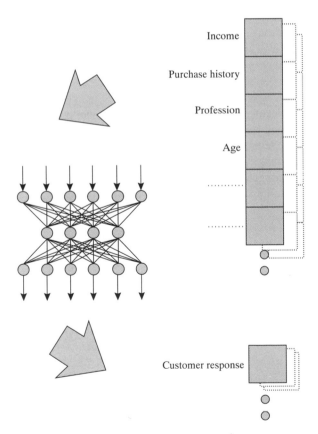

Income

Purchase history

Profession

Age

Customer response

Figure 1.2 Neural networks in direct marketing

relationship it holds. Once a neural network has successfully learnt the relationship, details of a new customer (e.g. income, profession, etc.) can be presented to the network and it will then make a decision as to whether the person is likely to respond to the mailing or not.

While the inspiration for neural networks is the functioning of the brain, the inspiration for another type of intelligent systems, Genetic Algorithms (GA), is the mechanics of biological evolution. Genetic algorithms are based on the Darwinian principal of 'survival of the fittest'. The main idea behind a genetic algorithm is the evolution of a problem's solution over many cycles of processing. At each cycle, known as a *generation*, refinements are made to *candidate solutions* with the aim of producing better solutions.

For example, a genetic algorithm used to learn the rules for evaluating credit will start with a set of random rules. At each generation the rules will be assessed as to how well or 'fit' they are at solving the task at hand. In a credit-evaluation task, a rule that makes fewer errors in classifying creditworthy customers (evaluated against hundreds of past records) will have a higher 'fitness' than a rule that makes more errors. New rules are created in the genetic algorithm by a process that mimics biological reproduction — constituent parts of rules are swapped with other rules. If the new rules are fit, then they have a higher chance of surviving to the next generation. Over many generations the genetic algorithm can yield good rules for evaluating credit.

This book shows how leading companies are using genetic algorithms, neural networks, fuzzy systems, expert systems and other intelligent techniques to solve complex financial and business problems. Applications are drawn from key industries in the service sector where these methods are having a dramatic impact on productivity and savings. The main application areas covered in the book are credit evaluation, direct marketing analysis, fraud detection, financial market prediction, and economic modelling. The book aims to provide readers with a critical assessment of these technologies and to help identify business areas that are most suitable for intelligent systems applications.

The next section evaluates the defining properties of intelligent systems with respect to their application in business. Section 3 introduces the basics of five main types of intelligent techniques. Section 4 discusses potential areas of future development and Section 5 describes the overall organization of the book.

2 INTELLIGENT SYSTEMS IN BUSINESS: THE KEY FEATURES

We now discuss five key features of intelligent systems which make them particularly attractive for solving financial and business problems. These are: learning, adaptation, flexibility, explanation and discovery. It should be noted that not all intelligent techniques exhibit all these features. Each different intelligent technique has particular strengths and weaknesses and cannot be applied universally to every type of problem. The relative assessment of different techniques is an issue that we shall return to in Section 3.

2.1 Learning

Arguably the most important feature of intelligent systems in business is their ability to learn decisions or the tasks they have to perform, directly from data. That is, they can derive a *model* of business practices purely by trawling through hundreds or thousands of past transactions. Typically such operational knowledge is only held by personnel in organizations who have had many years of experience in performing particular business tasks.

Intelligent systems such as neural networks and genetic algorithms have the capability to learn such models of business processes from past data. These learning techniques contrast sharply with an earlier generation of intelligent systems, expert systems, where the knowledge required to perform tasks had to be specified manually by a human expert. Knowledge elicitation, the process of specifying knowledge for expert systems, is time consuming, expensive and potentially unreliable (Evans, 1988). Experts find it difficult to articulate 'intuitive' knowledge (Partridge, 1986) and are sometimes unwilling to participate in lengthy knowledge-elicitation procedures.

Some professionals such as financial traders and insurance risk assessors have a very high premium on their available time and therefore the capability to learn directly from data without human intervention becomes very important. A learning approach can also help to overcome the limitations that are inherent in human professionals including the possible existence of *gaps* in an expert's knowledge and the correctness of an expert's knowledge (Jackson, 1986). Further, as different practitioners often have different views on the way to perform a particular task, 'objective' learning methods have advantages with respect to consistency.

2.2 Adaptation

Business is constantly changing. A specific business process may become quickly outdated because of a variety of reasons including changes in the macro-economy, changes due to new competitive pressures, or changes due to government regulations. For example, the pattern of consumer spending, say as reflected in credit-card usage, is significantly different during a recession from what it is in a booming economy. Intelligent systems used to support decisions in business (e.g. systems for deciding spending limits on credit cards) should therefore ideally have the capability to adapt to such changes in the business environment. It is not sufficient for an intelligent system to learn the initial knowledge needed to perform a task, it also has to monitor its performance constantly and revise its knowledge according to changes in its operating environment.

In some domains the ability to adapt to quick changes may be more important than in others. As financial traders know, the characteristics that define a particular market can change significantly over a relatively short time period. For example, for a few months, rises in interest rates may strengthen a currency, while it is possible that in following months, rises in interest rates may actually weaken it (Ormerod et al., 1991). Because of these changes of character in financial systems, an intelligent system used for trading should, ideally, have the ability to adapt to such changes and be able to make successful trading recommendations before and after them. In order for this to happen, the system should have the capability to *learn continuously* from the market (Goonatilake & Feldman, 1994).

2.3 Flexibility

When humans make decisions there is an inherent flexibility. Humans can make decisions even when the available information is imprecise and incomplete. For example, people who evaluate credit can make lending decisions even if there are a few minor details missing in an application form, and financial traders almost always make decisions with incomplete information.

While humans have such flexibility, traditional computer programs do not. Most programs work on strict yes/no, 'black and white' logic which does not permit shades of grey. For this reason, traditional computing systems are not *robust* in their operation — they fail to function even if a single condition is left unspecified or misspecified.

In contrast, intelligent systems such as neural networks and fuzzy systems have the capability to make decisions in a flexible manner that is similar to human decision making. They can reason with incomplete information and recognize patterns in conditions that they have not encountered before.

In a system used for 'profiling' customers, say, in a profitability analysis task, it is necessary to group *similar* customers together. An intelligent system such as a neural network used to learn such groupings or clusters will use past customer records and assess similarity based on customer attributes such as length of account, frequency of service usage and average revenue. Once these clusters are learnt, new unseen customer records can be presented to the system, and it will then make a decision as to which type of cluster (highly profitable, least profitable, etc.) a new record belongs.

The system will form such groupings using customer information which is usually incomplete or inconsistent. It is very common to find errors in large customer databases due to data entry mistakes. Some of the data entries may be incomplete because it is too costly to collect all the relevant data (e.g. ratings from a credit agency). Nevertheless, an intelligent system used to learn such groupings can *generalize* from the *majority* of records it has seen before and can offer a flexibility in its reasoning in a manner similar to the way professionals use and produce such groupings.

2.4 Explanation

While intelligent systems have the potential to automate many different decision-making tasks, there are organizational and legal reasons why the decisions they reach should be understood by humans. In the area of credit evaluation, for example, it is now a legal requirement in some countries to give detailed explanations to a customer in the event of an application being unsuccessful. When using intelligent systems in such tasks, the final decisions in an accept/reject format alone are not sufficient — the decision-making procedure has to be *transparent* and should be understood by other personnel in the company and by its customers. While some intelligent systems such as expert systems provide explicit explanations, other techniques such as neural networks have difficulties in explaining their decisions.

There are still further organizational reasons for having intelligent systems that can explain themselves. In portfolio management where the decisions involve very large amounts of money, sometimes the life savings of customers, reassurance as to the soundness of the decision-making procedure is needed. The ability to cite the exact conditions and reasoning of a trading decision is therefore often required by senior managers in fund management companies.

It is also important to have an understanding of the reasoning process in order to improve intelligent systems. If an intelligent system ceases to produce correct decisions due to some reason, it can only be corrected if the reasoning processes are understood by a human. On the other hand, if an opaque or 'black-box' decision system ceases to make good decisions, then it will be very difficult to understand what has caused the system to behave in that manner.

Transparency of intelligent systems is also important to allow interaction with human experts. There is evidence to suggest that under certain conditions expert revisions to quantitative decision models can improve the quality of their results (Bunn & Wright, 1991). These advantages are particularly evident under special circumstances such as in the case of extraordinary competitive developments or political events. In such circumstances it is only a human who can 'interface' with the external world (e.g. by reading news reports) and understand the impact of such developments. In order to allow such expert revisions, intelligent systems should provide access to their core knowledge and reasoning mechanisms in a format that humans can understand.

2.5 Discovery

Not only can intelligent systems automate tasks that are currently performed by humans but they also offer the possibility of *discovering* new business processes or relationships that were not known previously. Knowledge discovery, or *data mining* as it is popularly known, can be defined as the 'nontrivial extraction of implicit, previously unknown, and potentially useful information from data' (Piatetsky-Shapiro & Frawley, 1991). There are several intelligent techniques that can trawl through large databases and find relationships and business patterns that were previously unknown. Genetic algorithms, for example, have been used to find patterns in supermarket checkout data and they have found previously unknown purchase patterns such as the relationship between weather fluctuations and the sales of fruit.

However, checks must be made to validate whether the discovered relationships are truly representative and not merely statistical flukes. Considerations such as the integrity of the data on which the pattern was discovered and the size of the data sample are important factors in such validation exercises. Because of these reasons, it is important that relationships discovered by an intelligent system be verified by a human expert before they are used in an operational context.

3 INTRODUCTION TO INTELLIGENT TECHNIQUES

This section aims to provide the reader with an introduction to five main types of intelligent techniques:[1] neural networks, genetic algorithms, fuzzy systems, expert systems and intelligent hybrid systems. For each technique the basic operations are introduced and the strengths and weaknesses of the technique are assessed. Finally, for each technique two representative business applications are described.

3.1 Neural Networks

Neural networks (Beale & Jackson, 1990; Aleksander & Morton, 1990) are computing devices inspired by the function of nerve cells in the brain. They are composed of many parallel, interconnected computing units. Each of these performs a few simple operations and communicates the results to its neighbouring units. In contrast to conventional computer programs where step-by-step instructions are provided to perform a particular task, neural networks can learn to perform tasks by a process of *training* on many different examples.

Typically the nodes of a neural network (denoted PE for processing element in Figure 1.3) are organized into layers with each node in one layer having a connection to each node in the next layer. Associated with each connection is a *weight* and each node has an activation value. During pattern recognition, each node operates as a simple threshold device. A node sums all the weighted inputs (multiplying the connection weight by the state of the previous layer node) and then applies a (typically non-linear) threshold function (see Figure 1.4).

It is the values of the weights that determine the types of patterns a neural network can recognize. A *learning algorithm* is a procedure used to find the values of these weights for a given task. A popular neural network learning algorithm is the *back-propagation algorithm* (Aleksander & Morton, 1990; Wasserman, 1989). The back-propagation algorithm adjusts weights by presenting example training pairs of input-target patterns (e.g. a handwritten *A* with a perfect **A**). An input pattern is presented at the input layer and is propagated through all the processing elements in the network to produce outputs at the output layer. This output pattern is then compared with the 'ideal' target pattern, and an *error* is propagated back

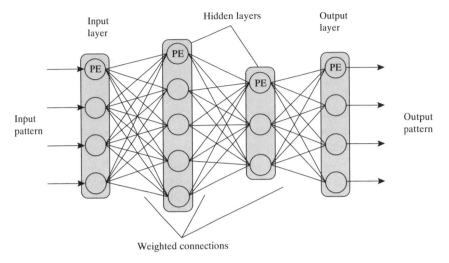

Figure 1.3 Multilayer neural network

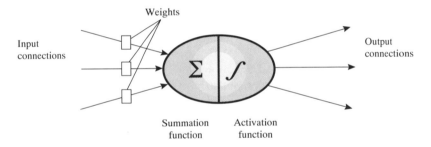

Figure 1.4 A typical artificial neuron

through the network. The propagated error is used to adjust the weights of the connections. This training process is then repeated with a new training pair, and a new error is propagated backwards. This process is repeated many times with many example pairs of patterns until the error is small, at which time the network has been trained.

However, when using any learning technique care has to be taken so that it does not learn patterns that are too specific to its training data. The relationships learnt should be truly representative of the business task in general and not merely reflect properties contained in the training data which may be statistically unrepresentative. If a neural network is allowed to 'overtrain', it would only be able to recognize the patterns in the training data — it would not be able to recognize patterns outside the training set which means it would not have the flexibility or generalization capabilities that business problems demand. In order to avoid this situation all neural networks (and other learning systems such as genetic algorithms) should be thoroughly validated on 'out-of-sample' data — data outside the training set. There are several methods to determine when a learning system has the 'correct' level of training, and the reader is pointed to Weiss & Kulikowski (1991) for an excellent introduction to this area.

Strengths and Limitations

Neural networks provide a relatively easy way to model and forecast non-linear systems. This gives them an advantage over many current statistical methods used in business and finance which are primarily linear. They are also very effective in learning patterns in data that are noisy, incomplete and which may even contain contradictory examples. The ability to learn and the capability to handle imprecise data makes them very effective in financial and business information processing. A main limitation of neural networks is that they lack explanation capabilities. They do not provide users with details of how they reason with data to arrive at particular conclusions.

Neural networks are therefore best suited for applications requiring pattern recognition in noisy, incomplete data, and for tasks where experts are either unavailable or where clear rules cannot be easily formulated. They are not suitable for applications where explanation of reasoning is critical.

Business Applications of Neural Networks

There are now many operational neural network systems in the retail and finance sectors. Here we describe two representative examples.

Visa International have an operational neural networks-based fraud-detection system which has been used in five Canadian and ten US banks, covering some 40 million card holders (Fraudwatch, 1994). The neural network is trained to spot fraudulent activity by comparing legitimate card usage with known cases of fraud. By looking at patterns such as the time of transaction and merchant type against a model held for each individual card holder the neural network can raise an alert for potential cases of abuse.

An example is the practice of checking the validity of cards at automated pumping stations without buying petrol. If a card is stolen, for example, there is window of a few hours before it is reported, and unmanned petrol stations provide a convenient way to check whether the cards are still valid before they are used at shops. The neural network is used to spot such transactions and reports them with a score from 0 to 999, with the highest score indicating the highest chance of fraud. This system, called Cardholder Risk Identification Service (CHRIS), has already saved Visa an estimated $40 million over a six month period (Holder, 1995). An additional benefit of the system has been the ability to spot both credit runaways and spending patterns that predict bankruptcy.

Dutta & Shekhar (1988) describe the use of neural networks to predict the ratings of corporate bonds. Bonds issued by a company are given ratings (e.g. AAA, AAB) by independent organizations such as Standard & Poors and Moody's according to their perceived risk. They assess the ability of a company to repay these bonds at a given time at the agreed interest rate. The methods the rating agencies use to make such assessments are kept strictly confidential.

If a method is found to predict the ratings of corporate bonds using public information such as company balance sheet data, then it can be used as a guide to make investment and lending decisions to that particular company. There have been many attempts to produce models of corporate bond ratings using regression analysis. Models constructed using these techniques have an average accuracy of about 60%. Dutta & Shekhar used a neural network to predict the classification of corporate bonds with 10 input variables describing various aspects of the financial status of the company. These variables included cash and assets, debt proportion, profit/sales, working capital and growth rates. The neural network achieved a prediction accuracy of about 82%.

3.2 Genetic Algorithms

Genetic Algorithms (GAs) (Davis, 1991; Holland, 1987; Goldberg, 1989) are efficient problem-solving mechanisms that are inspired by the mechanisms of biological evolution. They reward candidate solutions that contribute towards solving a problem at hand and penalize solutions that appear unsuccessful. GAs have produced very good solutions for complex optimization problems that have large numbers of parameters. Areas where these have been applied include electronic circuit layout, gas pipeline control, and job shop scheduling (Davis, 1991).

The main idea of a genetic algorithm is to start with a *population* of solutions to a problem, and then attempt to produce new generations of solutions which are better than the previous ones. This is a direct analogue of the Darwinian principle of the 'survival of the fittest' — i.e. let good solutions survive and cull bad solutions. GAs operate through a simple cycle consisting of the following stages: population creation, selection, reproduction and evaluation (see Figure 1.5).

The starting point for a genetic algorithm is the creation of a *population* of 'members' which represent *candidate solutions* to the problem being solved. These members can be encoded using a variety of schemes including binary strings (e.g. 011011, 11000, 01000), real numbers (e.g. 2.43, 101, 78) or rules (e.g. if condition X and condition Y then Z).

In the subsequent explanation we demonstrate the use of genetic algorithms as a rule learning mechanism. The reader is referred to Davis (1991) for their use as general-purpose optimization algorithms.

An example rule from an insurance risk assessment task will have the following form:

```
IF max-speed [91-100] AND age-of-car [11-15] AND age-of-driver [31-40] THEN risk [3]
```

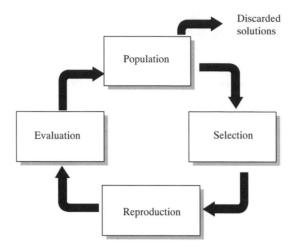

Figure 1.5 The genetic algorithm cycle

The rule is read as 'If the maximum speed of the car is between 91 and 100 (mph) and the age of the car is between 11 and 15 years old and the age of the driver is between 31 and 40 then the risk rating (between 1 and 5) is 3'. The population of members (rules) are firstly initialized with random values. That is, values from a given variable's permissible set of states are chosen randomly. For example, a variable such as age-of-car may have five possible states (1–5, 6–10, 11–15, 16–20, 21–25) and one state (11–15) is chosen randomly. At this initialization stage the rules are usually not at all good at solving the problem at hand.

In the selection stage, members are selected from the population to produce new 'offspring'. The chances of particular members being selected for the reproduction stage depend on how 'fit' or well adapted they are in solving the task at hand. This 'fitness' value is always dependent on the specific problem that needs to be solved. We shall detail the fitness assessment procedure later in this section.

New members or rules are created in the reproduction stage through the application of genetic operators, *crossover* and *mutation*. The *crossover* operator takes two members and swaps the constituent parts of the members to produce new members. This is analogous to sexual reproduction in nature where new chromosomes are created by the swapping of genetic material. For example, the condition part of one rule may be replaced with a condition part of another rule to create a new rule which may solve the problem better than either of the previous two rules.

Consider the two rules C1 and C2 which are members of a genetic algorithm population:

```
(C1)
IF max-speed [121-130] AND age-of-car [11-15] AND age-of-driver [31-40] THEN risk [3]
(C2)
IF max-speed [91-100] AND age-of-car [1-5] AND age-of-driver [51-60] THEN risk [2]
```

Crossover between rules C1 and C2 occurs by swapping the attributes in the condition related to max-speed and age-of-driver, thereby creating two new rules C3 and C4. The condition points at which crossover occurs is chosen randomly.

```
(C1)
IF max-speed [121-130] AND age-of-car [11-15] AND age-of-driver [31-40] THEN risk [3]
           ⇑ ⇓                                                    ⇑ ⇓
(C2)
IF max-speed [91-100]  AND age-of-car [1-5]   AND age-of-driver [51-60] THEN risk [2]
```

which results in,

```
(C3)
IF max-speed [91-100] AND age-of-car [11-15] AND age-of-driver [51-60] THEN risk [3]
(C4)
IF max-speed [121-130] AND age-of-car [1-5] AND age-of-driver [31-40] THEN risk [2]
```

The other genetic operator, the mutation operator, causes small random changes in the members. This allows the algorithm to introduce variation in the search process (Davis, 1991). For example, in C4 the age-of-driver attribute has been changed from 31–40 to 41–50 resulting in a new rule C5.

```
age-of-driver [31-40]    ⇒    age-of-driver [41-50]
```

```
(C5)
IF max-speed [121-130] AND age-of-car [1-5] AND age-of-driver [41-50] THEN risk [2]
```

After the members (rules) have been changed by the crossover and mutation operators, the new rules are then evaluated by the fitness function. This assesses the degree to which the new solutions are good at solving the given problem. The value returned by this fitness assessment will be used to select members for the next generation (cycle) of solutions.

Consider the following assessment of fitness. Let us assume we have a selection of records from past insurance claims as shown in Table 1.1 and that we have two candidate rules A and B.

```
(A)
IF max-speed [131-140] AND age-of-car [1-5] AND age-of-driver [21-30] THEN risk [5]
fitness: 0.75
(B)
IF max-speed [101-110] AND age-of-car [11-15] AND age-of-driver [41-50] THEN risk [3]
fitness: 0.5
```

Table 1.1

max-speed	age-of-car	age-of-driver	risk
91–100	1–5	51–60	3
131–140	1–5	21–30	5
131–140	1–5	21–30	5
101–110	11–15	41–50	4
91–100	1–5	51–60	3
91–100	1–5	51–60	2
131–140	1–5	21–30	4
91–100	1–5	51–60	2
131–140	1–5	21–30	5
101–110	11–15	41–50	3

If one evaluates the probability of rule A being correct, it is correct three out of four times in explaining the data in the table. If we take our fitness to be this simple measure of probability, then rule A's fitness value is 0.75.[2]

Rule B is correct two out of four times and its corresponding fitness is 0.5. Rule A therefore has a higher fitness (i.e. explains the data better) and has a higher chance of being selected for the production of new offspring rules than rule B has.

In the next stage of the genetic algorithm the current population is discarded and replaced with a population consisting of the new offspring. Then, at the next selection stage of the cycle, rules that are fit are chosen for the reproduction process to produce the next generation of members. This genetic algorithm cycle is repeated until a satisfactory solution (a good rule or number of rules) to the problem is found.

Strengths and Limitations

Because of their inherent parallel structure, genetic algorithms have proved to be very effective at efficiently searching very large data sets (Goldberg, 1989). This search process also has another advantage in being highly suitable for parallel computer implementations. They have had particular success in large optimization problems including job-shop scheduling, timetabling and portfolio optimization (Davis, 1991; Deboeck, 1994). Genetic algorithms can learn complex relationships in incomplete data-sets and they can be used as 'data mining' tools to discover previously unknown patterns. They can adapt to changes in their operating environment and they can provide explanations of the decisions they produce in a format that humans can understand.

A limitation of genetic algorithms is that the setting of parameters such as the crossover and mutation rates is problem dependent and is a time-consuming trial and error process. Further, the performance of a genetic algorithm is affected by the representation scheme that is employed. The selection of an appropriate scheme may require extensive experimentation.

Business Applications of Genetic Algorithms

The business applications of genetic algorithms is growing rapidly with successful applications in financial trading, credit evaluation and fraud detection. They have also been used for predicting corporate bankruptcy (Kingdon & Feldman, 1995). When granting a loan or credit to a company, an assessment as to the company's ability to repay its debt is a fundamental consideration. If one believes there is a possibility of the company going bankrupt, then the lending organization may not grant such a loan or may charge a very high level of interest to compensate for such risk. Currently the primary method of predicting bankruptcy involves linear modelling techniques, principally multiple discriminant analysis.

Kingdon and Feldman (1995) have used genetic algorithms to infer rules for bankruptcy prediction using financial ratios obtained from company balance sheets. Examples of financial ratios used in the rule-learning process are sales/total assets, current assets/current liabilities and income/sales. On average the genetic algorithm method was 15% better in classification accuracy than the currently used multiple discriminate models and was roughly comparable in performance to a neural network used on the same data. However, the genetic algorithm approach was favoured by the end-users (an Italian credit agency) over the neural network solution because of its easy-to-understand explanations (rules) of corporate failure.

Packard (1990) describes the use of genetic algorithms in budget allocation. Here the task was to assist a state government in making budget-allocation decisions among its offices. There were 730 offices in this study, each of which goes through a decision procedure to spend its money at the beginning of the financial year. To assist this process, every year each office fills out a questionnaire detailing the types of items that they wish to spend their money on. The questionnaire has 19 questions each of which could have up to 12 different answers. The genetic algorithm was used to find rules that indicate the best allocation decisions based on several years of data contained in these questionnaires. It found combinations of particular answers that led to maximal efficiency (money spent divided by money allocated) and compared favourably with other competing approaches to the problem.

3.3 Fuzzy Systems

Fuzzy logic (Cox, 1994; Zadeh, 1984; Kosk, 1992) is designed to handle imprecise 'linguistic' concepts such as *small*, *big*, *young*, *old*, *high* or *low*. Systems based on fuzzy logic exhibit an inherent flexibility and have proven to be successful in a variety of industrial control and pattern-recognition tasks ranging from handwriting recognition to credit evaluation. There are now several consumer products including washing machines, microwave ovens and autofocus cameras that use fuzzy logic in their control mechanisms. Japan is the leading country for the application of fuzzy logic techniques, with a national research programme devoted to fuzzy systems.

Central to the flexibility that fuzzy logic provides is the notion of a *fuzzy set*. In conventional set theory an item has a clear boundary or demarcation. For example, in a marketing application we might classify the price of a particular product, say the price of a pair of shoes, into two distinct sets: cheap and expensive (see Figure 1.6).

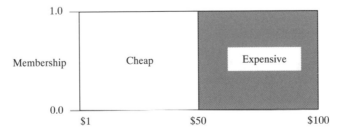

Figure 1.6 A conventional set

As can be seen from Figure 1.6, there is a clear-cut, abrupt change from cheap to expensive when the price is $50. In other words, when the price is $49.50 it is considered cheap and when it is $50.50 it is considered to be expensive, although there is only a $1 difference between the two prices. However, such clear-cut or 'crisp' distinctions do not correspond to our daily experience of what we consider to be cheap or expensive. If we consider $49 to be cheap, then $51 will also be cheap, but with a lesser degree of 'cheapness'. It is this *varying* degree of measurement of language constructs such as 'cheap', 'expensive', 'high', 'medium', 'fast' that fuzzy logic attempts to capture.

A more realistic representation of the above pricing phenomenon is that of a fuzzy set where there is a gradual decline in the strength of the cheap set and a gradual increase in the expensive set as the price increases. This is represented in a fuzzy membership diagram in Figure 1.7. The range of a given variable's values (prices of shoes in our example) represented along the horizontal axis of this diagram is referred to as the *universe of discourse*. The *fuzzy membership value*, which is the degree to which a particular price belongs to the two fuzzy sets, is represented on the vertical axis. The range of the fuzzy membership values is typically between 0 and 1. For example, when the price of the shoes is $1, then the value in the fuzzy set 'cheap' is 1.0 and the value in the fuzzy set 'expensive' is 0.0. Conversely when the price is $100, then the fuzzy set 'expensive' has a maximum value of 1.0 and the corresponding value of the fuzzy set 'cheap' is 0.0.

Usually the shapes and ranges of the fuzzy memberships are defined by a human expert. Once the fuzzy membership functions are defined, new data items can be classified into their corresponding fuzzy values. For example, as shown in Figure 1.8, a shoe with a value of $35 will have a membership of 0.8 in the fuzzy set cheap and a membership of 0.2 in the fuzzy set expensive. Data that have been converted into fuzzy membership functions are referred to as having been 'fuzzified'.

Fuzzy *inference rules* specify the relationships among the fuzzy variables. The fuzzy rules are in the familiar production rule (If/Then) format. These rules are

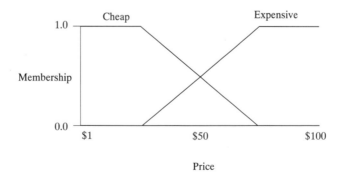

Figure 1.7 A fuzzy membership diagram

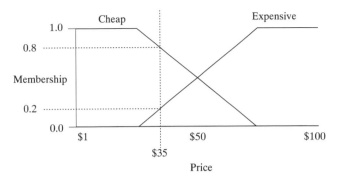

Figure 1.8 Fuzzy data classification

also usually specified by a domain expert. An example rule is:

IF prices are *high* AND industrial production is *low* THEN low market share

Fuzzy reasoning is the process of deriving conclusions from a given set of fuzzy rules acting on fuzzified data. In contrast to conventional rule-based systems where only one rule is activated in response to its conditions being true, in fuzzy inferencing *all* rules in a fuzzy rule-base (a collection of fuzzy rules) whose conditions match or partially match will contribute to the final result. That is, the final result of a fuzzy system is derived by *aggregating* the hypotheses of all the rules in the system. This resulting aggregation process is the key principle behind the ability of fuzzy systems to display an inherent flexibility when dealing with incomplete and inconsistent data.

Strengths and Limitations
One of the main strengths of fuzzy logic compared with other schemes to deal with imprecise data, such as neural networks, is that their knowledge bases, which are in a rule format, are easy to examine and understand. This rule format also makes it easy to update and maintain the knowledge base.

As for the limitations of fuzzy logic, the main shortcoming is that the membership functions and rules have to be specified manually. Determining membership functions can be a time-consuming, trial-and-error process. Further, the elicitation of rules from human experts can be an expensive, error-prone procedure. Additionally, they cannot adapt automatically to changes in the operating environment — new rules have to be manually altered if business conditions change.

In Section 3.5 we shall examine the use of intelligent hybrid systems for overcoming these limitations of fuzzy systems.

Business Applications of Fuzzy Logic
Fuji Bank in Tokyo has a fuzzy system for short-term bond trading (McNiel & Freiberger, 1993). The system has been in daily operation for the last two years

and has approximately 200 fuzzy rules which are based on popular technical trading strategies. In financial trading good rules have a limited life-span and therefore the fuzzy rules are regularly updated by traders. The system provides tools to help traders define their rules and allows traders to test their rules against historical data. This fuzzy trading system is estimated to earn Fuji Bank $770 000 per month (McNiel & Freiberger, 1993).

A growing area of fuzzy logic application is *fuzzy database retrieval*. Conventional database retrieval does not allow the flexibility that human operators wish to have. If a company wanted to find which of its young employees showed promise, it might issue a request like 'List salespeople under 25 years old who sold more than $40 000 worth of goods last year'. This search would miss the 26-year-old who sold $100 000, as well as the 19-year-old who sold $39 000 (McNiel & Freiberger, 1993). A more useful request would be 'List the *young* salespeople with a *good* selling record' which is the type of request that a fuzzy database can handle. A fuzzy database uses fuzzy memberships to describe the entities it holds. Instead of storing age as 20 years old, it might express it as *old* with a fuzzy membership of 0.2 and sales of $60 000 as good sales with a fuzzy membership of 0.6.

In conventional database retrieval, items are retrieved only if *all* the conditions specified are matched. Fuzzy database retrieval allows a mechanism to retrieve items that *partially* match the given criteria. So when searching a corporate database for companies that have an annual profit of $10 million with over 1000 employees, a fuzzy database can also identify a company with a profit of $9 million and 1200 employees, however, with a lower degree of match.

3.4 Expert Systems

Expert systems represent the earliest and most established type of intelligent systems. There are many hundreds of operational expert systems in domains ranging from fault diagnosis to commodity trading. As the name suggests, they attempt to embody the 'knowledge' of a human expert in a computer program. The process of acquiring the knowledge from an expert — knowledge elicitation — typically involves a series of interviews and the careful recording of observations when the expert is performing tasks.

Once the knowledge is acquired it is *represented* in a format that can be manipulated by the computer. There has been much research into finding good knowledge-representation schemes that are efficient and easy to use. Among the most widely used knowledge representation schemes are *production rules, frames* and *semantic networks* (Waterman, 1985; Jackson, 1986).

A production rule has the following format:

IF ⟨condition_1⟩ **AND** ⟨condition_2⟩ **THEN** ⟨action_A⟩ **AND** ⟨action_B⟩ ...

A typical collection of rules in an expert system for portfolio management might contain:

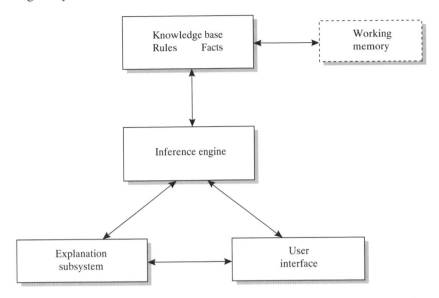

Figure 1.9 Expert system organization (adapted from Harmon & King, 1985)

IF client requires risk-free investments **THEN** consider government bonds
IF client requires maximum capital growth **THEN** consider multimedia companies
IF maximum capital growth **AND** country preference is USA **THEN** select shares of XYZmedia Inc.

The main components of an expert system are illustrated in Figure 1.9. The knowledge base contains the *rules* and the *working memory* contains the current facts known by the system. Lastly, the *inference engine* is the control mechanism that drives the reasoning process of the system. If the conditions of the production rules are matched with the elements in the working memory, then the rules are activated. Execution of a rule's actions cause the data elements in the working memory to be updated.

Strengths and Limitations

A great strength of expert systems is the explicit representation of knowledge, so that the knowledge contained in the programs is relatively easy to read and understand. Also, expert systems can generate *explanations* of how they arrived at a particular conclusion.

As for the limitations of expert systems, one of the main drawbacks is that they have no mechanisms for automatic learning of the rules they use. Further, they cannot adapt or learn from changes in the business environment in which they operate.

In some areas, experts describe their actions as being fuzzy and intuitive and have difficulty in translating their expertise into simple expert-system rules which usually have strict binary-logic definitions. In these domains knowledge-representation schemes such as fuzzy logic which are more flexible are needed.

Business Applications of Expert Systems

Applications of expert systems to finance and business are extensive (Feigenbaum et al., 1988; *IEEE Expert*, 1987; Leinweber, 1988). Institutions that have applied this technology successfully include American Express, Citibank, Manufacturers Hanover Trust, Yamaichi Securities and National Westminister Bank. They have used expert systems in personal loan evaluation, portfolio management, and in forecasting financial markets.

California-based Countrywide Funding uses a large expert system to underwrite its mortgages. The business aim of developing the expert system was to handle mortgages in a more efficient way with the capability of processing up to 50 000 applications a month (Intertek group, 1994). Countrywide first evaluated several other intelligent technologies including neural networks but decided to adopt expert systems because of their decision-explanation capabilities.

Traditionally the process of mortgage evaluation is performed by skilled underwriting personnel who evaluate up to 150 data items including such details as the applicant's creditworthiness and the value of the property. On average, the manual underwriting process takes approximately 50 minutes. The expert system now used at Countrywide, called CLUES, has approximately 1000 rules and processes an application in 1 to 2 minutes (Intertek group, 1994). It approves 55% of loan applications automatically and fails to approve any loan that an underwriter would reject. If the system recommends an application to be rejected, then that application is forwarded to a human underwriter for further evaluation.

In the insurance sector, Continental Canada has developed a very effective insurance underwriting system that is now in daily use (Pilote & Fillion, 1991). The system contains hundreds of underwriting rules elicited from experienced insurance underwriters. For example, there are specific rules to assign higher risk for older vehicles and young drivers. The system processes all incoming applications and (as in the Countrywide system) only if particular 'caution' rules are fired are the cases passed on to a human underwriter. Continental Canada claims that this system has had a dramatic effect on its business, cutting overhead expenses by 55% and boosting profits by 30%.

3.5 Intelligent Hybrid Systems

While intelligent systems as discussed above are being applied successfully in a variety of tasks, certain complex business problems cannot be solved by a single approach alone. Each intelligent technique has particular strengths and limitations that make it suitable for particular applications and not for others. As mentioned previously, while neural networks are good at recognizing patterns, they are not good at explaining how they reach their decisions. Fuzzy logic systems can explain their decisions but they cannot automatically acquire the rules they use to make those decisions. These limitations have been a central driving force behind the creation of *intelligent hybrid systems* where two or more techniques are combined to overcome the limitations of individual techniques (Goonatilake & Khebbal, 1995).

For example, when using a fuzzy system for loan evaluation, an expert in loan evaluation has to specify all the rules needed for the system to make a decision. Neural networks with their learning capabilities can be used to learn these fuzzy decision rules automatically, thus creating a hybrid system which overcomes the limitations of fuzzy systems.

Table 1.2 provides an assessment of the four intelligent techniques (neural networks, genetic algorithms, fuzzy systems and expert systems) with respect to the five desired properties (learning, adaptation, flexibility, explanation, discovery) discussed earlier in the chapter. As can be seen from the table, a fuzzy-neural hybrid can be viewed as combining a particular technique (fuzzy systems) that scores low in a particular property (learning capability) with a technique that scores high in that property (neural networks). Such hybrid systems can be referred to as *function-replacing hybrids* (Goonatilake & Khebbal, 1995). Other examples of similar hybrid systems are the use of genetic algorithms to find fuzzy membership functions (Karr, 1995), using neural networks as pattern matchers in expert systems (Tirri, 1995) and the use of genetic algorithms to find weights in neural networks (Montana, 1995).

Hybrid systems are also important when considering the varied nature of business applications. Most complex domains have many different component problems, each of which may require different types of processing. For example, if a complex business problem (e.g. corporate budgeting and planning) has three component problems — a forecasting task, an optimization task and a serial reasoning task — then a neural network, a genetic algorithm and an expert system can be used to solve the respective component problems. The different component intelligent systems communicate their results among themselves to produce the final result(s). Hybrid systems of this type are referred to as *intercommunicating hybrids* (Goonatilake & Khebbal, 1995); examples of this type include fuzzy preprocessing for neural networks (Klimasauskas, 1995), the use of expert system rules as 'seeds' for genetic algorithms (Powell et al., 1995) and multiple cooperating neural networks (Scherer & Schlageter, 1995).

Table 1.2 Comparison of intelligent techniques

Technologies	Learning	Flexibility	Adaptation	Explanation	Discovery
Neural networks	✓✓✓✓✓	✓✓✓✓✓	✓✓✓✓✓	✓	✓✓
Genetic algorithms	✓✓✓✓✓	✓✓✓✓	✓✓✓✓	✓✓✓	✓✓✓✓✓
Fuzzy systems	✓	✓✓✓✓✓	✓	✓✓✓	✓
Expert systems	✓	✓	✓	✓✓✓✓✓	✓

Intelligent hybrid systems cover not only the combination of different intelligent techniques but also the integration of intelligent techniques with conventional computing systems such as spreadsheets and databases (Khebbal & Shamhong, 1995). For intelligent systems to add value to organizational decisions they must be able to extract and use information from a wide variety of sources. In addition, the decisions or results produced by the intelligent systems should be disseminated to existing applications or other systems for further processing. For these reasons it is vital that there are methods and protocols for integrating intelligent systems with other conventional computing systems. One such method is object-oriented programming (Wiener & Pinson, 1988) which is a software engineering methodology that can provide the 'glue' to join together different processing techniques. This forms a natural model for intelligent hybrid systems because individual techniques can be defined as objects which interact by sending a common set of messages (Khebbal & Shamhong, 1995).

Strengths and Limitations

Intelligent hybrid systems are a very powerful class of computational methods that can provide solutions to problems that are not solvable by an individual intelligent technique alone. As for their limitations, because the development and application of hybrid systems is still relatively new, there is not the same availability of tools and development environments compared with more established techniques such as expert systems or neural networks.

The other problem associated with the development of intelligent hybrid systems is an 'educational' one. To develop successful systems, one needs to be aware of the detailed workings of several intelligent techniques as opposed to just knowing a single method. This can pose problems as there are currently only relatively few personnel who have a sufficient training and experience in the development and application of more than one intelligent technique. In fact, most specialized intelligent systems companies are currently geared towards only providing uni-technology solutions. To get the full benefits of hybrid systems one cannot be religiously devoted to a single technique — one has to take a pragmatic view and mix and match techniques as the business problems dictate.

Business Applications of Intelligent Hybrid Systems

Intelligent hybrid systems have recently been applied in the area of insider dealing detection. The London Stock Exchange has completed the first phase of an automated system to combat this type of fraud which is extremely difficult to detect using manual methods. The system, called *MonITARS* (Monitoring Insider Trading and Regulatory Surveillance) and developed by SearchSpace, uses a combination of genetic algorithms, fuzzy logic and neural networks to detect suspicious trades (Economist Publications, 1994; Holder, 1994). The detection of suspicious trades is difficult because it is very easy to camouflage a fraudulent trade in the masses of trading data — there are 100 000 transactions each day, hundreds of brokers and millions of investors participating in trading.

MonITARS uses a combination of statistics and neural networks to identify market conduct which is significantly different from *usual* behavioural 'profiles' of individuals and firms that trade in the market. A genetic-fuzzy hybrid system is used to search for particular patterns, or combinations of patterns, within the vast amount of data that passes through the exchange each day. The system can even detect *dealing rings* where several individuals (or one individual with several accounts) trade across all their accounts for the purpose of insider dealing or market manipulation.

Goonatilake (1995) describes the application of a genetic algorithm–fuzzy logic hybrid system for foreign exchange trading. Here the genetic algorithm attempts to find optimal fuzzy rule-bases for making two weeks-ahead predictions using technical trading data. The data consists of price, volume, and open interest levels and transformations of these such as moving averages and oscillators (Kaufman, 1987). These indicators which are in a numeric format (e.g. volume 8989, open interest 23672) are first converted into fuzzy values (e.g. volume *low*, open interest *high*) through the use of a clustering algorithm (Goonatilake, 1995). Then the genetic algorithm is used to find good fuzzy rules by assigning fitness according to how well they perform on historical data. Fuzzy rules found by the genetic algorithm are of the form 'if the price is *increasing* and the open interest is *high* and the volume is *low* then the market is likely to go up'. New rule-bases are learnt continuously by the genetic algorithm so as to adapt to changes in the market.

Because of the use of common linguistic categories to describe market behaviour, traders that use the system find the trading models easy to understand and validate. Further, the traders also find it easy to make revisions to the conditions contained in the rules if they feel it is necessary.

4   FUTURE DIRECTIONS

In the next few years intelligent systems will undoubtedly play an increasingly important role in many areas of business and financial analysis. These techniques provide an alternative to currently established data analysis methods such as linear regression and operations research methods such as linear programming. Apart from their benefits in increased accuracy, some intelligent systems have the capability to produce decision models that are easily understood by technical personnel and high-level strategic decision makers alike. This contrasts with the current practice of someone having to 'translate' the results of quantitative decision models into language that decision makers can understand.

An emerging trend is the embedding of intelligent techniques in other business applications software. Neural networks are now being incorporated into forecasting tools on financial data feeds and fuzzy systems in database retrieval products. As the use of intelligent techniques becomes more common, it is likely that applications that contain them will cease to mention them explicitly unless as part of a marketing strategy.

A significant area of likely growth is the use of intelligent hybrid systems. Most currently seemingly intractable business problems will benefit from the use of multiple intelligent techniques. Further, the quality of integration of intelligent systems with other corporate software systems is likely to improve with the use of object-oriented programming and object-oriented databases. This is important because in most corporate intelligent systems a large proportion of the effort is spent on either developing or integrating with software that deals with data retrieval, data preprocessing and user interfaces.

In terms of applications, there is likely to be considerable growth in the retail sector. As we enter a world of remote retailing through the Internet and other on-line services, software systems known as agents (Maes, 1994) are likely to play a very important role. Agents have the ability to negotiate on behalf of their owners and navigate through on-line sources to retrieve information or services. When used for shopping for an air ticket, for example, a shopping agent should be able to check prices, available dates, and packaged deals at hundreds of 'virtual' travel bureaus and find the best ticket that matches the owner's needs. If there are neural networks or genetic algorithms built into such agents then they will be able to learn from their shopping experiences. They might learn that a specific travel agency consistently provides cheaper flights to the Far East and that they normally have a larger range of connecting flights to Australia. The agents might also learn that the owner has a favourite airline (probably because of frequent-flyer benefits) and that the owner does not usually like late-evening flights. Using this information the agent can decide on which travel bureaus to approach first when a new request is made, and to prioritize the wishes of the owner in purchase negotiations.

Agents are also likely to feature in the financial markets of the future. They will have the capacity to traverse the financial information networks and negotiate deals with other agents residing at different brokers and exchanges around the world. The agents may lower their offer prices if the volume sought after is large, or conversely raise them if they know there is a strong demand for the commodity being sold. Apart from agents that carry out specific tasks upon receiving instructions from their owners (traders), there is also the possibility of trading agents that are more autonomous. There might be 'arbitrage agents' that base their trading strategies on exploiting temporary price differences between financial instruments. In this scenario, these agents will lie 'dormant' in financial networks around the world until they spot, and within seconds trade, profitable trading opportunities. The effects, if any, of large numbers of such autonomous trading devices in the financial markets are a complete unknown at present.

5   ORGANIZATION OF THE BOOK

The book is organized into six parts according to different business areas. Each part contains a representative selection of applications of intelligent systems in these domains. Parts I to V are concerned with Credit Services, Direct Marketing, Fraud Detection and Insurance, Securities Trading and Portfolio Management, and Economic Modelling. The final part deals with the implementation of intelligent systems.

Chapter 2 by Robert Didner describes the pioneering work at American Express in using expert systems for credit authorization. The Authorizers Assistant system is detailed and the financial savings and productivity improvements are discussed. An overview of current neural network projects at American Express is also presented in this chapter.

Chapter 3 by R. Walker et al. describe a genetic algorithm approach for credit evaluation. The genetic algorithm is used to induce formulae that describe relationships among credit variables. Comparisons are also made with competing rule induction and neural network approaches.

Chapter 4 by David Leigh discusses a project on the use of neural networks for credit scoring. He examines issues raised in the construction and training of neural networks and their advantages over conventional credit scoring methods.

Chapter 5 by Peter Furness presents a review of the use of neural networks in direct marketing covering, database enhancement, customer segmentation, retail modelling and sales analysis. The pitfalls and advantages of using neural networks are described and critical comparisons with other data-modelling techniques are made.

Chapter 6 by Richard Webber examines the use of clustering methods for segmenting marketing databases. The applications of this approach for locational modelling and advertising analysis are discussed.

Chapter 7 by Earl Cox presents the advantages of fuzzy modelling and describes a fuzzy system for fraud and abuse detection for managed healthcare. This system which is being used in companies such as Blue Cross and Blue Shield is claimed to detect fraud equal to, or better than, the best fraud-detection departments.

Chapter 8 by Steve Mott explains how Case-Based Reasoning is being used at the Toronto Stock Exchange for detecting insider dealing. The chapter details the complexity of the problem and describes the methods used for knowledge engineering, alert generation and alert explanation.

Chapter 9 by John Major and Dan Riedinger on EFD (Electronic Fraud Detection) describe how The Travelers Insurance Companies are using an intelligent hybrid system to detect fraud in health-insurance claims. The system which uses a combination of expert rules, statistical techniques and machine learning is detailed and its performance and business benefits are evaluated.

Chapter 10 by Colin Talbot reviews the use of expert systems at Lloyd's of London. He describes the implementation and operation of the 'Slipstream' system which is used for the automated checking of insurance contract details. The financial savings of this system are presented, and proposals for a generalized system for understanding insurance contracts are also discussed.

Chapter 11 by A.N. Refenes et al. explores the relationship between neural networks and regression techniques and its relevance to financial modelling. The example of tactical asset allocation is used to compare neural network performance with multiple linear regression on the basis of forecasted returns between equities and cash.

Chapter 12 by Shun'ichi Tano presents a fuzzy system for foreign exchange trading that was developed at the Laboratory for International Fuzzy Engineering in Japan. The fuzzy trading system has the capability to handle 'news' reports as well as numeric information when making foreign exchange predictions.

Chapter 13 by Jae Kyu Lee and Hyun Soo Kim describes the use of an inductive learning approach to predicting stock market behaviour. Price chart patterns are first described by a particular syntactic grammar and then the learning algorithm uses these pattern descriptions to generate trading rules.

Chapter 14 by John Koza, the architect of the 'genetic programming' (GP) paradigm, describes how to use GP for economic modelling. In this chapter, he shows how genetic programming rediscovered the well-known non-linear 'exchange equation' relating the money supply, price level, gross national product and velocity of money in an economy.

Chapter 15 by Paul Tayler presents work he conducted at the Santa Fe Institute on the use of genetic algorithms to create an 'artificial stock market'. Here the artificial traders, represented as genetic algorithm rules, compete with one another to buy and sell a stock for profit. Over time, they evolved better trading rule sets, and displayed market behaviour with many of the complex features found in real stock markets.

Chapter 16 by Peter Allen introduces a class of evolutionary models that derive their inspiration from self-organizing systems observed in nature. The application of these models in urban modelling and futures markets prediction is detailed.

Chapter 17 by Philip Treleaven reviews the types of software available for implementing intelligent systems in finance and business. Three categories of software systems are introduced and example packages for neural networks, genetic algorithms, fuzzy systems and hybrid systems are evaluated.

ACKNOWLEDGEMENTS

I would like to thank Konrad Feldman and John Campbell of University College London and Mike Luck of Warwick University for constructive comments on earlier drafts of this chapter.

ENDNOTES

1. Because of space limitations we have not discussed other approaches such as Case Based Reasoning (CBR) systems and Tree Induction systems. The reader is referred to Kolodner (1993) for an introduction to CBR and to Weiss & Kulikowski (1991) for an introduction to tree induction systems.

2. A more complex fitness assessment would be used in a real application with penalty functions to minimize the finding of statistically insignificant relationships (Goonatilake & Feldman, 1994; Packard, 1990).

REFERENCES

Aleksander, I. & Morton, H. (1990) *Introduction to Neural Computing*, North Oxford Press.

Beale, R. & Jackson, T. (1990) *Neural Computing — an Introduction*, Adam Hilger, Bristol.

Bunn, D. & Wright, G. (1991) Interaction of judgmental and statistical forecasting methods: Issues and analysis, *Management Science*, **37**(5).

Cox, E. (1994) *The Handbook of Fuzzy Systems*, Academic Press, New York.

Davis, L. (1991) *Handbook of Genetic Algorithms*, Van Nostrand Reinhold, New York.

Deboeck, G. (ed) (1994) *Trading on the Edge: Neural, Genetic, Fuzzy Systems for Chaotic Financial Markets*, John Wiley, Chichester.

Dutta, S. & Shekhar, S. (1988) 'Bond rating: A non-conservative application of neural networks', *Proceedings of IEEE International Conference on Neural Networks*, San Diego.

Economist Publications (1994) *A Neural Network is Watching You, the Year in '95.*

Evans, J. St B. T. (1988) 'The knowledge elicitation problem: a psychological perspective', *Behaviour and Information Technology*, **7**, 2, 111–130.

Feigenbaum, E. McCorduck, P. & Nii, H. (1988) *The Rise of the Expert Company*, Macmillan, London.

Fraudwatch (1994) Third Quarter.

Goldberg, D.E. (1989) *Genetic Algorithms In Search, Optimization and Machine Learning*, Addison-Wesley, Reading, MA.

Goonatilake, S. (1995) 'Intelligent hybrid systems for financial decision making', in the Proceedings of the 1995 ACM Symposium on Applied Computing, pp. 471–476, ACM Press, New York.

Goonatilake, S. & Feldman, K. (1994) 'Genetic rule induction for financial decision making', in J. Stender et al. (eds), *Genetic Algorithms in Optimization, Simulation and Modelling*, IOS Press, Amsterdam.

Goonatilake, S. & Khebbal, S. (eds) (1995) *Intelligent Hybrid Systems*, John Wiley, Chichester.

Harmon, P. & King, D. (1985) *Expert Systems: Artificial Intelligence in Business*, John Wiley, Chichester.

Holland, J.H. (1987) 'Genetic algorithms and classifier systems: foundations and future directions', *Genetic Algorithms and their Applications: Proceedings of the 2nd International Conference on Genetic Algorithms.*

Holder, V. (1994) 'Tackling insider dealing with fuzzy logic', *Financial Times*, 29 September.

Holder, V. (1995) 'War on suspicious payments', *Financial Times*, 7 February.

IEEE Expert (1987) Special Issue, 'Financial applications', **2**, No. 3.

Intertek Group (1994) *Adaptive Computational Methods in Retail Banking and Finance*, Paris.

Jackson, P. (1986) *Introduction to Expert Systems*, Addison-Wesley, Reading, MA.

Karr, C. (1995) 'Genetic algorithms and fuzzy logic for adaptive process control' in Goonatilake S. and Khebbal S. (eds), *Intelligent Hybrid Systems*, John Wiley, Chichester.

Kaufman, P.J. (1987) *The New Commodity Trading Systems and Methods*, John Wiley, Chichester.

Kingdon, J. & Feldman, K. (1995) *Genetic Algorithms for Bankruptcy Prediction*, SearchSpace Research Report No. 01–95, SearchSpace Ltd, London.

Khebbal, S. & Shamhong, D. (1995) 'Tools and environments for hybrid systems', in Goonatilake, S. and Khebbal, S. (eds), *Intelligent Hybrid Systems*, John Wiley, Chichester.

Klimasauskas, C. (1995) 'Using fuzzy pre-processing with neural networks for chemical process diagnostic problems', in Goonatilake, S. and Khebbal, S. (eds), *Intelligent Hybrid Systems*, John Wiley, Chichester.

Kolodner, J. (1993) *Case-Based Reasoning*, Morgan Kaufmann, San Mateo, CA.

Kosko, B. (1992) *Neural Networks and Fuzzy Systems*, Prentice Hall, Englewood Cliffs, NJ.

Leinweber, D. (1988) 'Knowledge-based systems for financial applications', *IEEE Expert*, **3**, No. 3, 18–31.

Maes, P. (1994) 'Agents that reduce work and information overload', *Communications of the ACM*, July.

McNiel, D. & Freiberger, P. (1993) *Fuzzy Logic*, Simon & Schuster, New York.

Montana, D. (1995) 'Neural network weight selection using genetic algorithms', in Goonatilake, S. and Khebbal, S. (eds), *Intelligent Hybrid Systems*, John Wiley, Chichester.

Ormerod, P., Taylor, J.C. & Walker, T. (1991) 'Neural networks in economics', in Taylor, M.P. (ed.), *Money and Financial Markets*, Blackwell, Oxford.

Packard, N.H. (1990) 'A genetic learning algorithm for the analysis of complex data', *Complex Systems*, **4**, 543–572.

Partridge, D. (1986) 'Is intuitive expertise rule-based?' University of Exeter.

Piatetsky-Shapiro, G. & Frawley, W. (eds) (1991) *Knowledge Discovery in Databases*, AAAI Press/MIT Press, Menlo Park, CA, Cambridge, MA.

Pilote, M. & Fillion, M. (1991) 'Automated underwriting at Continental Canada: results and major obstacles', *Proc. First AI Conference on Wall St*, IEEE Computer Press, New York.

Powell, D., Skolnick, M. & Tong, S. (1995) 'A unified approach for engineering design', in Goonatilake, S. and Khebbal, S. (eds), *Intelligent Hybrid Systems*, John Wiley, Chichester.

Scherer, A. & Schlageter, G. (1995) 'A multi-agent approach for the integration of neural networks and expert systems', in Goonatilake, S. and Khebbal, S. (eds), *Intelligent Hybrid Systems*, John Wiley, Chichester.

Tirri, H. (1995) 'Replacing the pattern matcher of an expert system with a neural network', in Goonatilake, S. and Khebbal, S. (eds), *Intelligent Hybrid Systems*, John Wiley, Chichester.

Wasserman, P.D. (1989) *Neural Computing: Theory & Practice*, Van Nostrand Reinhold, New York.

Waterman, D.A. (1985) *A Guide to Expert Systems*, Addison-Wesley, Reading, MA.

Weiss, S.M. & Kulikowski, C.A. (1991) *Computer Systems that Learn: Classification and Prediction Methods from Statistics, Neural Nets, Machine Learning and Expert Systems*, Morgan Kaufmann, San Mateo, CA.

Wiener, R.S. & Pinson, J. (1988) *An Introduction to Object-Oriented Programming and C++*, Addison-Wesley, Reading, MA.

Zadeh, L. (1984) 'Making computers think like people', *IEEE Spectrum*, August, 26–32.

Part I
Credit Services

2
Intelligent Systems
at American Express

ROBERT S. DIDNER

1 INTRODUCTION

American Express deployed one of the first commercial expert systems to handle large volumes of transactions (Klahr et al., 1987; Dzierzanowski et al., 1989). That early success, the Authorizer's Assistant (AA), continues to authorize millions of dollars' worth of credit on the American Express Personal and Gold cards. Beyond its own success, AA has made Amex management amenable to supporting R&D efforts aimed at improving decision making based on new technologies, particularly those related to intelligent systems applied to risk analysis. Key to the sustained support is the demonstration of tangible business benefit from initial 'Proof-of-concept' projects before deployment is recommended. These projects can clearly articulate the benefits of intelligent systems with respect to either cost avoidance or the generation of new revenue. Further, they have been very useful in estimating how much time is required to develop a fully operational system and in deciding on the various costs (both apparent and hidden) associated with the project.

In this chapter we will describe the operation of the Authorizer's Assistant, discuss its business benefits, and provide an overview of the use of neural networks at American Express.

Intelligent Systems for Finance and Business. Edited by S. Goonatilake and P. Treleaven
© 1995 John Wiley & Sons Ltd

2 THE AUTHORIZER'S ASSISTANT

Unlike competing payment products, most American Express accounts do not have revolving debt balances, and a fixed ceiling that those balances may not exceed (e.g. $5000). Therefore, we have long had a policy of authorizing each charge as it occurs. In doing so, we provide greater flexibility to customers in terms of their spending requirements, and have a greater probability of spotting fraudulent or risky charges sooner than if we waited for a fixed balance to be exceeded.

The credit authorization process is, however, a very careful balancing act. If credit is extended too freely, customers may not be able to pay off their accounts. Similarly, if credit is denied too often, the company will lose business, and has the potential of damaging relationships with profitable customers.

In the first stage of the authorization process, all requests from merchants (American Express refers to them as Service Establishments) are sent to a system called the Credit Authorization System (CAS) which resides on an IBM mainframe. CAS then applies a very simple, rather rigid set of rules to determine whether a transaction should be authorized. If, for example, a card member has reported his or her card lost or stolen, or if there are abnormally frequent charge requests, then a flag is raised. If the transaction passes these initial tests then the transaction is approved, otherwise it is forwarded to a human authorizer for approval.

Prior to the use of the Authorizer's Assistant a very large number of transaction were subjected to manual authorization. The authorizers can access numerous screens from databases holding information about the cardmember, and can conduct interviews with the people presenting the cards. The data includes previous uses of the card, payments made, the status of bad checks, address and phone numbers and other credit bureau information. The authorizers have to quickly scan this data, mentally transform the data into meaningful information, and apply credit policies to determine if the card and card member were legitimate and that the transaction represented reasonable credit risk.

We at American Express found that human authorizers had varying degrees of skill and were usually inconsistent. Their decisions varied from instance to instance and from authorizer to authorizer. Furthermore, they could introduce excessive delays while they went about gathering and analyzing additional information. The cost associated with human authorizers was also high, with an average cost of $15.

The AA project addressed these issues by speeding up the data collection and analysis process, and automatically approving some of the cases that would have been referred to a human authorizer. While AA can approve some cases that used to be considered marginal, it cannot disapprove a case by itself; it can only refer these to a human. Cases referred to human authorizers come complete with AA's recommendations and reasoning with all the available information appropriately formatted. The authorizer can then accept the recommendation, talk to the card holder, or take other appropriate action to render a decision (see Figure 2.1).

The credit authorization knowledge contained in the Authorizer's Assistant is based on senior authorizers, whose judgments tend to have better than average

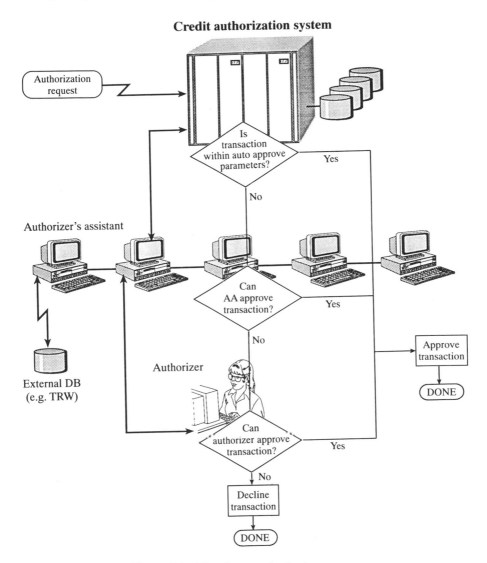

Figure 2.1 The charge authorization process

outcomes. The knowledge-elicitation process involved approximately 4 knowledge engineers over a 13-month period. After a pilot development of the core expert system, it was subjected to an extensive validation and performance evaluation process. The validation involved running thousands of actual cases that were captured from on-line transactions for this sole purpose. In addition to the experts used for initial knowledge specification, several other expert authorizers assisted in the process of reviewing cases either on development machines or on paper copies of the AA results. The system went live in November 1988, three years after the beginning of the initial pilot project.

The Authorizer's Assistant has reduced the cost of a transaction referred to a human authorizer from $15.00 to $1.40, and fewer transactions are referred to a human authorizer. More importantly, the consistency and the overall quality of decisions made by the combination of human authorizers with the AA are superior to those made by the human authorizers alone, and the time to make a decision (including those still referred to human authorizers) has been significantly reduced.

On the implementation side, the decision to deploy the expert system on a Local Area Network (LAN) of workstations was key to the success of the project. Inference engines executing expert system rules tend to make very heavy use of processing resources as they explore the myriad possible implications from a given set of data. In the cost analyses it was concluded that although mainframe computers have the capability to manage and move extremely large amounts of data, their costs were high given the level of processing power that was required. A LAN of workstations, optimized for such a task, proved to be a much better choice.

While the AA has been extremely successful, there is always room for improvement. One of the potential areas of improvement is that of automated rule generation and refinement. Currently the rules contained in the AA are manually changed by experts in responses to changes in the economy or business strategy. Once a new rule is devised either as a response to a management directive or end-users, it is tested against off-line data and on-line within a test environment before it is incorporated into the on-line system. There are several opportunities here for a machine-learning method that learns new rules based on past authorization data and system performance data. Such an approach may potentially further enhance the overall AA performance.

3 NEURAL NETWORKS AT AMERICAN EXPRESS

With the success of Authorizer's Assistant, Amex began to explore other forms of intelligent systems to assist in decision-making tasks. A current area of active development at American Express is the use of neural networks for prospect modeling and fraud detection.

While an expert system executes decision rules specified by existing experts, neural nets can discern these relationships from the experiential data itself. There is now considerable evidence to suggest that neural networks have advantages in terms of accuracy over other pattern-detection techniques used in business (e.g. multiple regression, logistic regression, or discriminant analysis). They can detect complex non-linear relationships which other linear techniques fail to detect. For example, any credit expert knows that length of time at a current address is a positive indicator of creditworthiness. What a credit expert may not convey and a simple regression technique will not detect (but a neural network will) is an exception to this relationship when occupation = military.

However, in applications where the underlying data does not contain complex non-linear relationships neural networks will yield results that are only comparable to (or in some cases worse than) regression techniques. There are other reasons why in our experience neural networks can sometimes fail to produce superior results. A main reason is that given the very large number of parameters (e.g. number of hidden layers, nodes in hidden layers, momentum values, etc.) it is very easy to overfit the model to the training data. Therefore one has to conduct disciplined and methodical experiments and have a good mathematical understanding of the principles of neural networks to achieve robust results that will translate into tangible business benefits.

As with expert systems, it is critical to evaluate the performance of a neural network against the process that was used before. Alternate approaches (e.g. expert systems, regression analysis and experience) should be compared with neural network performance. It is conceivable that these other approaches can sometimes outperform neural nets for a variety of reasons: the learning and test data sets may have sampling errors or sampling anomalies, or may violate statistical assumptions about stationarity (such anomalies could tend to favor an expert system).

From an organizational point of view, the introduction of neural networks has additional challenges. A primary concern is that the decision-making model derived from the data may not be readily comprehensible to managers, experts, or even the modelers themselves. The model may have captured complex non-linear interactions between variables which solves a very difficult problem, but sometimes performance itself is not sufficient to convince management. The use of techniques that identify variables that contribute the most to a given neural network model can significantly help in these situations.

4 CURRENT PROJECTS

Research in using neural networks at American Express started in 1988. Today there are three projects in full operational use. Each American Express business unit has at least one project in an active R&D phase with a total of 13 projects.

The three deployed projects include an intelligent character-recognition system to read the handwritten amounts off charge slips, a direct mail prospect modeling system, and a portfolio management and trading support system developed by a recently divested investment banking division. The last system assesses several types of risk associated with a mixed portfolio of fixed rate and derivative instruments. It is deployed in conjunction with a virtual reality system.

For most large organizations direct mail advertising is very costly given the volumes of pieces mailed and the extremely low response rates (often in the order of 1–2%). Any tool that can increase the response rate by even a small fraction of a percent can therefore be extremely valuable. Epsilon Inc. is a unit of American

Express that specializes in the optimizing of direct marketing mailing lists for other Amex units and external customers. Lately Epsilon has been using neural nets running on a massively parallel computer.

Neural nets and parallel processors are a natural combination as each node in a given layer of a neural net model is inherently parallel to the other nodes of that layer. Traditionally, internodal weights are calculated in a serial fashion by computers that can only emulate parallel processes by dealing with one node at a time. Neural networks executing on a massively parallel processor, however, can take advantage of the simultaneous processing facilities and be trained much faster than on serial processors. This is particularly important for the problems Epsilon addresses, viz. databases are extremely large, there are many variables, and subtle relationships are being sought. Currently Epsilon's neural networks can evaluate up to 500 variables in a single application and is soon expected to be able to handle 2500 variables. Because neural nets can yield superior marketing models, and the parallel processor can train these models in a relatively short time, Epsilon can charge its customers a premium price for response modeling, and still provide a greater level of satisfaction and cost-effectiveness compared to its competition.

Neural networks have also been used at Amex for detecting fraud. Among the discernible patterns related to credit-card fraud are those related to merchants (Service Establishments or SEs). Some perpetrators prefer certain types of SEs for committing their crimes. Sometimes the SEs may know the accomplices, or be the perpetrators themselves. Neural networks have been quite successful at finding the underlying patterns that identify SEs most likely to commit fraud. These models are now being extended to evaluate prospective SEs before fraudulent transactions are encountered and to identify cardmember applicants who are most likely to have fraudulent intent. In a pilot study, the neural network fraud detection model trained on a large database provided a 3% improvement over the previously used logistic regression model.

5 CONCLUSIONS

American Express through its Authorizer's Assistant project has demonstrated the use of intelligent systems to automate critical core business functions. The quality of the credit and fraud expertise in the system met and has exceeded management expectations. By having authorization expertise in a computer program, it has also given management more insight and control over the credit authorization process. Following the lead of expert systems technology, American Express is now researching, prototyping and deploying neural networks in important business areas. Prospect modeling and fraud detection are two of the main areas where neural networks are showing significant commercial promise.

REFERENCES

Dzierzanowski, J., Chrisman, K., MacKinnon, G. & Klahr, P. (1989) 'The Authorizer's Assistant: A knowledge-based credit authorization system for American Express', *Proceedings of the Conference on Innovative Applications of Artificial Intelligence*, pp. 168–172, Stanford, CA.

Epsilon High Performance Computing Newsletter, 1993.

Klahr, P., Bakin, J., Dashiell, Fl., Dzierzanowski, J., Goklman, B., Hudkins, G., Koff, L., Mela, J., Nishiyama, C., Piketty, L., Rmesh, B. & Miller, L. (1987) 'The Authorizer's Assistant, A large financial expert system application' Invited Keynote Paper, *Proceedings of the Third Australian Conference on Applications of Expert Systems*, pp. 11–32. Sidney, Australia.

3

Credit Evaluation Using a Genetic Algorithm

R. F. WALKER, E. W. HAASDIJK and M. C. GERRETS

1 INTRODUCTION

Generating predictive models from historic data is a general problem encountered in a wide variety of financial domains. Predictive models, for instance, can help to:

- Select clients for a direct mail campaign
- Screen applicants to identify those likely to repay the loan they applied for
- Assess accounts to identify further business opportunities.

Predictive models are often developed using statistical methods. Now, neural networks and machine learning techniques are increasingly used for these tasks. Although these techniques perform reasonably well, the demand for better-performing, reliable, comprehensible and easily implemented models is still growing.

In this chapter a new forecasting system based on a genetic algorithm is described. This tool, called OMEGA,[1] aims:

- To be more predictive than conventional and alternative techniques used for evaluating credit and insurance risks
- To rapidly produce decision models that can be easily implemented
- To be operable by non-technical users (e.g. financial managers).

Intelligent Systems for Finance and Business. Edited by S. Goonatilake and P. Treleaven
© 1995 John Wiley & Sons Ltd

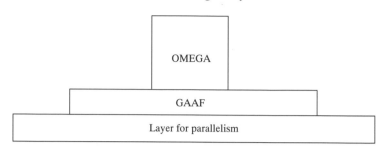

Figure 3.1

OMEGA consists of several modules that together are able to process databases; analyse and prepare the data; induce intelligible, robust models that capture the implicit relationships in the data; exercise and validate the models; generate source-code for embedding the models in an administrative system; and generate high-level reports targeted at financial management. OMEGA is built on top of generic components (Figure 3.1).

GAAF, a Genetic Algorithm for the Approximation of Formulae, is a genetic algorithm that searches for the *algebraic* specification of a model (i.e. a formula) that will accurately predict a set of values in a so-called *training-set*.[2] GAAF is a generic tool and as such not dedicated to financial applications. It takes on arbitrary data-sets and generates formulas that map observed values to known outcomes. For future performance enhancement, GAAF optionally employs a parallel layer as developed within the PAPAGENA project (Kingdon, Ribeiro & Treleaven, 1993).[3] GAAF and OMEGA will be discussed in Sections 5 to 7.

2 APPLICATION DOMAINS

2.1 Common Problems

Financial databases have specific properties not always found in otherwise comparable domains. They often are:

- *Big* Insurance or mortgage databases often contain over 100 000 cases. In addition, the number of variables (*predictors*) can easily grow beyond 60.

- *Inconsistent* This can be caused by erroneous data-entry, poor database management, and either incorrect or incomplete information.

- *Incomplete* On most occasions, information that would allow truly accurate decisions is simply not available (someone's honesty, for instance, can only be judged from indirect evidence). In addition, banks, to give just one example, may not keep records for rejected loan applications. Even if they do, there is no telling whether the cases were rightfully rejected (which, of course, is useful information for predictive modelling purposes).

- *Expensive* Some data, such as a potential customer's debt history, may have to be purchased. For this and other reasons, modelling is usually multi-staged. That is, models are developed over a progressively increasing number of predictors but over a diminishing set of cases.

- *Dynamic* Not only can the data be very sensitive to external factors (such as economic growth), it is also likely to be frequently updated (consider credit card purchases). Therefore, model development time should preferably be short.

It should also be appreciated that decisions based on this data usually involve large amounts of money. Consequently, a manager has to (be able to) justify the choice for a particular model. For this reason, financial models, in addition to being highly predictive, have to be robust and, if at all possible, *comprehensible*.[4]

2.2 Introduction to Credit Scoring

The idea behind credit scoring is to assign a score to an existing or prospective loan based on characteristics of the applicant (e.g. salary, age, marital status) and decide on the basis of that score whether to grant (or pursue) the loan or not. Typically, a highly scored case represents a good prospect: the credit will be repaid; low scores forewarn of more risky engagements.

Historically, credit scoring has been based on simple methods: 'points' were awarded per parameter (or *predictor*) and the scores for the various predictors were added together to get the score for the case. As a method of classification (into 'good' or 'bad' loans), these linear score-cards are very limited. They will not, for instance, be able to capture a set of rules as simple as:

(1) Grant loan to applicants with very high incomes (because they have the money to repay and, apparently, are quite successful individuals from a lender's perspective).

(2) Grant loan to young applicants (because they do not dare to fool around with a bank they will continue to depend upon).

(3) Do not grant loan to young applicants with very high incomes (because they form a risk category for various, undisclosed, reasons).

Even so, score-cards tend, on average, to produce better and more consistent scores than credit-managers do. Score-cards are less subjective, not easily distracted by charm or beauty (unless the score-card includes these parameters), and will not become ill or agitated when important decisions have to be made.

Barrow (1992) mentions some of the problems associated with conventional scoring of consumer credits:

- Weak score-cards, unable to discriminate due to the complexity of the data

- Score-cards that do not work in practice (although they do correctly classify the cases on which they were developed)

- Tired score-cards, overtaken by change
- Excessive costs for score-card development
- Conflicting objectives between score-card developers and credit or marketing management.

Some of the above problems can be addressed by more complex models; others can only be tackled by a radical new way of constructing these models. Before presenting a new approach to credit scoring it is useful to agree on a measure that will give an indication of the quality of a (two-valued classifier) model.

2.3 The Coefficient of Concordance and Accuracy Measures

Given a set of cases C and a model M the Coefficient of Concordance (CoC) measure indicates how well the model distinguishes between *good* and *bad* cases. More accurately, the measure calculates how well the scores as produced by the model can be used to sort the cases in C in such a way that good cases get high scores and bad cases get low ones. The worst case, involving a random scoring procedure, corresponds to a CoC of 50%. Anything less than 50% means that the model M has the goods and bads reversed. That is, good cases are assigned low scores and bad cases are assigned high ones. Since this is apparent from the CoC value (being below 50%), it is possible to reverse the scores and calculate a new CoC' as 100% − CoC. Such models are called *crosswired*, but, once reinterpreted, can be used as effectively. Consequently, a CoC score cannot sensibly get below 50%. Quite different is the *accuracy* measure. Although a 100% accuracy implies a 100% CoC and vice versa, accuracy is more concerned with reducing misclassifications. It is defined as the percentage of correct classifications over the total number of cases.

In a perfect world — where the attributes of any case $c \in C$ are the only ones relevant to c's good or bad status and C is consistent — the CoC and accuracy of a given model M could get as high as 100%. In that case, M assigns scores to the cases in C such that the cases are ordered as follows:

Status: ...B B B B B B B B B B B B B B B | G G G G G G G G G G G G G...
Scores: 0.0   1.0

In the above example the scores are in the range [0.0, 1.0]; since the scores are only used to sort the cases, the actual range is irrelevant.

The vertical bar separating the bad from the good cases determines the *cutoff* value, the score above which a case is considered good. Consider a close examination of the cutoff area in this situation (Table 3.1). It follows that any cutoff value in between 0.41 and 0.45 will be equally good in separating the goods from the bads over C and reaching a 100% CoC or accuracy.

Table 3.1

B	B	B	G	G	G
0.32	0.35	0.41	0.45	0.49	0.51

Table 3.2

G	B	G	B	B	G	G	G	B
0.46	0.48	0.49	0.52	0.53	0.54	0.59	0.60	0.61

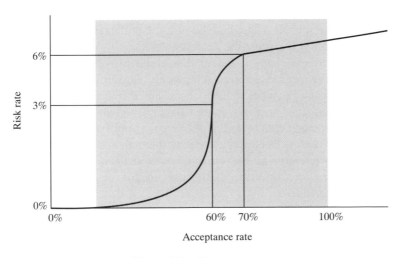

Figure 3.2 Strategy curve

In practice, however, the following situation is far more likely to occur:

Status: ...B B B B B B B | G B G B B G G G B | G G G G G G G...
Scores: 0.0   1.0

or, in close-up as shown in Table 3.2.

Now there is no single cutoff value to tell the goods from the bads and both the CoC and accuracy measure will be less than 100%. In situations like the above, several strategies are conceivable. The cutoff can be set somewhere above 0.61, for instance. The accept rate (the percentage of cases deemed good with respect to M) becomes small, but this cutoff avoids any risk of misclassifying bad cases as good. If one is prepared to accept a higher risk, the cutoff value can be decreased to below 0.45. This leads to the so-called *strategy curve* shown in Figure 3.2.

It can be seen from the figure that raising the acceptance percentage from 60% to 70% will increase the risk from 3% to 6%. Depending on other factors, the cutoff can sensibly be set anywhere within the shaded area. Note that accuracy merely counts the number of misclassifications (and thus depends on a single cutoff) where the CoC measures the separation between good and bad cases (and thus represents a measure of predictive power independent of a cutoff). As a consequence, accuracy does not realistically reveal M's capacity within the shaded area. For models with a high CoC score, it makes sense to exercise the cutoff to meet different business objectives like risk or bad rate (percentage of bad cases accepted by M), accept rate (percentage of accepted cases), maximum response (for direct marketing purposes), profit (summed gain per accepted minus the summed loss per reject), etc.[5] In contrast, for models with a high accuracy, cutoff exercising makes no sense (changing the cutoff will change the accuracy itself).

Obviously, cutoff exercising is essential to credit managers. Some banks may favour volume over quality, whereas others only engage in low-risk loans. The latter type of company has more reliable clients and therefore needs to reserve less money for bad debts. It is, however, more vulnerable to fluctuations in its customer base. Or consider a credit card issuer: to preserve a 'members are privileged' image, the company may wish to minimize erroneous fraud alarms during the verification procedure and thus tolerate a higher risk (but it is more likely to maintain a skeptical scoring policy for new members). Both cases require cutoff exercising *given a highly predictive model*.

Given a cutoff score, it is possible to define a so-called *confusion* matrix. An example of such a matrix is given in Table 3.3. Here, 1000 good cases have been correctly identified by M. Also, 800 bad cases have been accurately labeled as such. However, 250 bad cases have erroneously been identified as goods by M and 100 good cases were considered bads. Obviously, this matrix is helpful if the costs of wrongly labeling bad cases as good are different from identifying good cases as bad. The percentage of good predictions over total predictions — (1000 + 800)/2150 = 83.7% — constitutes the accuracy. Note, however, that the accuracy does not differentiate between the costs of M's wrongly assigning goods versus wrongly assigning bads.

A model's accuracy is often used as a quality measure (Graf & Nakhaeizadeh, 1993), but given the low predictive power of real-life financial predictors it is not as useful in practice as the CoC method. Consider a data-set containing 95% good

Table 3.3

	Actual good	Actual bad	
Predicted good	1000	250	1250
Predicted bad	100	800	900
Totals	1100	1050	

cases, as often occurs in financial practice since outcomes (good or bad) are usually only available for credits applications that *have already been accepted*.[6] Such a data-set would have a *default accuracy* of 95% because the simple default model M — 'always accept' — will yield this accuracy. Unfortunately, this percentage is hardly informative of M's capacity to distinguish good from bad cases. In contrast, the CoC measures the distribution of the 5% bad cases with respect to the scores assigned by M. If M were to assign scores such that the bad cases were distributed evenly, the CoC could get as low as 50% whereas the accuracy would still be 95%.

An analysis as outlined above requires a model that captures client behaviour; that is, is able to translate specific client information, such as salary, age, etc. into a score that represents the propensity of the client repaying his or her loan. Consequently, a model *generator* is needed, an engine that builds models that assign scores to cases. On many occasions, this 'engine' is human; an expert applying his or her 'gut feeling' (whatever that is) to available case descriptions.

The same kind of models and analyses of models are applicable in a variety of domains that involve binary classifications (for instance, to determine whether a credit card purchase is suspect or not; or to decide if a tax form is questionable). With only a slight modification, the models can be used in direct marketing applications to point out likely responders or someone's propensity to buy a product.

3 SURVEY OF CURRENT TECHNIQUES AND APPLICATIONS

In credit scoring problems, human intuition is frequently challenged and often surpassed by mathematical models. These models can be built using statistical methods like regression analysis, artificial neural networks, or machine-learning systems (Graf & Nakhaeizadeh, 1993). These so-called bottom-up approaches have in common that they construct models on the basis of examples. Alternatively, human expertise itself can be modelled in a knowledge-based system. This top-down approach, as opposed to the methods mentioned above, obviously relies on accurate 'mental models' and faces severe problems in the area of knowledge elicitation (Evans, 1988).[7] In Sections 5 to 7 a new bottom-up method to induce mathematical models from sets of historical examples will be presented.

Three bottom-up approaches to credit scoring are readily available: statistical techniques, neural networks and machine learning (Graf & Nakhaeizadeh, 1993; Statlog, 1993). The most common approach, statistics, has the advantage of a strong theoretical basis. As a method of model development, the statistical approach can be divided into two subclasses: linear and non-linear. Linear methods include a variety of regression techniques. All require the underlying *density* function of the variables to be known. In most real-world problems, however, this assumption does not hold. Non-linear methods like, for instance, *k*-nearest neighbour, are used in these cases where the densities are unknown. A drawback of statistical methods is that *a priori* knowledge is required to select data, transform variables and structure the problem. Moreover, statistical methods presuppose a fixed (for instance, polynomial) relationship between the data. Additionally, they are rather data hungry and have serious problems in handling incomplete cases (missing values).

The neural network approach is inspired by the mechanics of the human brain. The basic elements of neural networks are called *neurons*. Each neuron receives a number of weighted signals that are either external (input) or arrive from other neurons. The information in the network is represented by the weights on the links (*axons*) between neurons. A neuron processes the incoming signals and, when they are strong enough, transfers a new signal to the outside world (output) or other neurons. A neuron is characterized by its internal response threshold and (non)linear transfer-function. Learning takes place by adjusting the weights and thresholds in response to observed discrepancies between actual and expected output (Rumelhart et al., 1986).

Because neural networks tend to produce more predictive credit scoring models than statistical methods do, their popularity has grown substantially over the last couple of years. In addition, they require less (but, for optimal results, still significant) knowledge to be used effectively. However, an important drawback of neural networks is their non-transparency: it is difficult to explain what model a neural network actually constitutes. Furthermore, neural networks show a tendency to overfit: they predict very accurately on the example data-set, but perform badly on new data.

Machine-learning approaches are based on the principle of automatic rule induction from examples. They became popular because of the knowledge acquisition bottleneck encountered in expert system technology (Evans, 1988). Machine learning, widely applied to classification problems, comes in two flavours: the specific-to-general and the general-to-specific method. The former starts with a model consisting of the most specific set of hypotheses that explain a single positive example. The latter will initialize its model to contain the most general hypotheses that reject a single negative example. Both subsequently modify their set of hypotheses to accept positive and reject negative examples as they are presented (Carbonell & Langley, 1990). One of the best-known machine learning techniques are decision tree algorithms, as incorporated in NewId and AC^2 (Statlog, 1993; pp. 61–8).

Machine-learning techniques are intuitively easier to understand than statistical methods. Also, they do not require a high level of expertise in order to be used effectively. However, an easy-to-understand algorithm does not automatically lead to comprehensible models. In fact, for real-life data, machine learning often suffers from a combinatorial explosion and the resulting decision trees are too complex to be understood. More importantly, the essence of this induction technique is trying to explain every single example. Consequently, it shows a strong tendency to overfit. In fact, to generate robust models consistently care must be taken in selecting and ordering the examples. Insofar as the ordering is concerned, some implementations use heuristics to identify the optimal sequence of examples to present to the algorithm (Quinlan, 1986).

Although all the techniques mentioned in this section are already being exploited, the pressure of a growing and more critical market prompts the need for even better predictive systems. Genetic algorithms offer a completely new approach to bottom-up modelling.

4 BACKGROUND AND INTRODUCTION TO GAAF

4.1 Genetic Algorithms

Genetic algorithms (GAs) are based on elementary genetics. They emulate biological evolutionary theories to solve optimization problems. In this section a brief introduction to the GA paradigm will be given. For a detailed discussion on the basics of GAs, see Goldberg (1989) and Davis (1991).

A basic GA represents candidate solutions to a problem (known as *individuals*) as strings of *genes*, called a *chromosome*. If, for instance, the solution consists of a number, genes could be envisaged as bits and a chromosome would then be the binary representation of the candidate number. The genetic representation (i.e. the chromosome) is known as the *genotype* and the real-world meaning (in this case, a number) is known as the *phenotype* of an individual.

Basically, GAs operate in four steps:

- Creation of a set of initial individuals[8]
- Evaluation of individuals
- Selection of 'good' individuals
- Manipulation to create a new set of individuals

The GA loops over the last three of these four steps until an optimal (or adequate) solution to the problem at hand has been found.

Normally, the creation phase simply builds a set of random individuals. If, however, *a priori* knowledge about a solution to the problem at hand is available there is no reason to withhold it from the GA. It can be useful in building more successful initial candidates, thus closing off particularly unprofitable avenues of exploration.

The evaluation phase determines the 'meaning' or phenotype of each individual and uses this as a basis to determine how well an individual solves the problem at hand (its *fitness*). If, for instance, a GA were to be used to locate the optimum of some mathematical function f, an individual's phenotype would be a set of arguments for f; its fitness would be the result of applying f to its phenotype.

The selection phase selects individuals that will mate to produce a member of a new generation. The higher an individual's fitness, the higher its chances of being selected for reproduction. This is achieved by using *roulette wheel* parent selection: each individual is assigned an area of an imaginary wheel of fortune which is proportional to its contribution to the total fitness of the population. The wheel is then spun and when it stops, an imaginary needle points at the area owned by an individual. This individual is thus selected as one of the parents from which to breed a member of the next generation. It is obvious that individuals with a relatively high fitness stand a better chance of being selected. The rationale behind this scheme is that the combination of two fit solutions is more likely to yield an even fitter solution to the problem at hand. 'Bad' individuals, however, are not entirely ruled out for reproduction because they may contain some valuable genetic material.

A possible drawback of standard roulette wheel selection is the proliferation of *studs*. Studs are individuals that have much higher fitness than the rest of the population and thus get to mate more often. Especially if *elitism* is used (when a specified number of top individuals is guaranteed to make it into the next generation unmodified)[9] a stud's genes may 'infest' a population. This is fine if they are part of an optimal solution but possibly detrimental otherwise. Alternative schemes seek to overcome the ensuing premature convergence in various ways. Most common are methods to normalize the fitnesses before these are used as the basis for parent selection. Linear normalization, for instance, will keep individuals in the original order but assign new fitnesses in a linear way (i.e. the best individual gets a fitness of N, the second best of $N - \delta$, the third best of $N - 2\delta$, etc.). Less sentimental schemes may use truncation (killing off the worst $N\%$ of a population) and randomly select from the rest of the population. Popular normalization methods are discussed by Davis (1991, pp. 31–4) and Mühlenbein, Schomish & Born (1991).

Another method to maintain genetic diversity is the *parallel genetic algorithm* or PGA (Mühlenbein, Schomish & Born, 1991). A PGA maintains multiple pools that are bred concurrently and in isolation and among which migration occasionally takes place. With the advance of parallel hardware PGAs become increasingly feasible and are used, if not to prevent sub-optimal convergence then to simply increase the evolutionary pace.

As for actually building the new generation, the newly made individuals are usually simply inserted into the new population and the process is repeated until the new population is of the desired size. More elaborate strategies have been devised in which, for instance, the child is inserted into the new population only if it is fitter than its parents or if it is sufficiently different from the rest of the population (*anticrowding*). Several replacement strategies have been proposed to maintain genetic diversity in order to prevent the GA from converging prematurely[10] (Eshelman & Schaffer, 1991). Most of these methods depend on a similarity measure between individuals. For complex representations this may be computationally prohibitive.

The manipulation phase normally uses two kinds of operators: *crossover* operators to combine two chromosomes and *mutation* operators to introduce new genetic material (Figure 3.3). To not stretch the biological metaphor unduly, the two operations are perhaps better labeled *combination* and *modification*, respectively. Both of these operators are associated with a probability. In the case of, for instance,

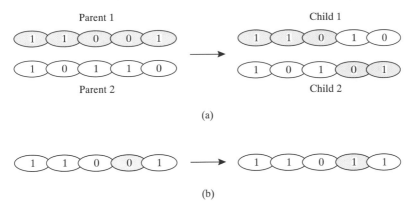

Figure 3.3   (a) The crossover operator; (b) The mutation operator

crossover this means that the two candidates will be combined only with a certain probability. If an individual has been selected for mating and crossover does not take place, it is copied as is into the new population.

In a GA that represents chromosomes as strings of bits (or reals, or integers) a crossover operator would combine two chromosomes by randomly choosing a crossover from the first chromosome and the rest from the second chromosome. More complicated crossover implementations involve multiple crossover points, intelligent selection of crossover points or more than two parents (Eiben, 1991).

The mutation operator in a GA which uses strings of bits simply logically inverts a gene's value. Another way of mutating a gene is assigning a value to it that was randomly chosen from the set of possible values. In either case, the mutation operator introduces random genetic material that may prove useful.

4.2   Advanced Techniques

The basic bitstring GA, although very suitable for experimental purposes and research on theoretical frameworks, is often not particularly well adapted to practical problems. Section 5 will introduce GAAF, a much more elaborate PGA. Apart from multiple pools, discussed earlier, GAAF uses a complex representation and matching operators. In addition, it is able to alternate between several fitness normalization methods, fitness calculation methods, and optimization methods (besides a GA, GAAF supports simulated annealing (Press et al., 1992, pp. 444–55) and conventional hill-climbing techniques). On some occasions GAAF employs a competing GA that breeds so-called 'parasites' to optimize the models bred by the primary GA (Hillis, 1992).

It is an ongoing debate whether GAs must be kept simple to facilitate analysis and reusability (Goldberg, 1989) or that they must be hybridized (combined with proven technologies) and optimized where possible (Davis, 1991). However, advanced techniques are becoming increasingly more common in real-life GA applications.

Now that GAs are being applied more often to practical problems (such as economic or financial forecasting, missile-evasion strategies, image recognition, etc.) it is likely that useful modifications to the basic GA paradigm will propagate because of the simple, perhaps even ironic, observation that, when results are all that counts, the best solutions survive.

5 INPUT DATA AND OPERATION

Compared to the basic genetic algorithm GAAF has adopted a tree-structured representation similar to the one proposed by Koza (1992).[11] Although the definition of a GA does not preclude this particular representation, it is common to refer to this technique as *genetic programming* (GP). The tree format can be used to represent mathematical formulas since the normal infix notation can be translated into a tree structured prefix notation in a straightforward manner. The tree on the left in Figure 3.4(a), for instance, represents $(x + y) * 3$. The tree representation is most advantageous, however, when it comes to mutation (modification) and crossover (combination), since these tree operations can be implemented efficiently.

How does a GA that uses these tree structures to represent formulas operate? In essence, not very differently from a standard GA where flipping a bit constitutes a bitstring mutation. Here the mutation operation consists of a node within a tree being replaced by another (e.g. changing the $*$ to $+$ in one of the trees in Figure 3.4(a) or changing the constant 2.0 to 2.1). Likewise, swapping bitstrings between individuals (crossover) is analogous to exchanging subtrees. It is easy to see that such operations preserve syntactic validity (i.e. yield well-formed trees). As an example, consider the two trees in Figure 3.4(a) that have their crossover points marked. Figure 3.4(b) shows the two children that result from crossing the trees in Figure 3.4(a) at the marked nodes.

Since an individual now represents a mathematical formula (or model) various ways are conceivable to assess its fitness. The main consideration in choosing among the alternatives is, of course, the task of the model. Will it be used to assign a score to a particular case? Should it predict a future exchange rate? To tackle the latter problem, for instance, Koza (1992, pp. 237–88) proposes a least residuals fitness calculation: let the fitness depend on the (summed, squared, weighted)

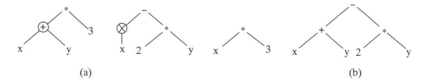

(a)   (b)

Figure 3.4

Table 3.4 Kepler's Third Law in tree format

Radius	Diameter	Period
0.387	0.384	0.24
0.723	0.972	0.62
1.000	1.000	1.00
1.524	0.533	1.88
5.203	9.775	11.86
9.569	9.469	29.46
19.309	3.692	84.01
30.284	3.492	164.79
39.781	0.447	247.69

$$\sqrt{}$$
$$|$$
$$*$$
$$\diagup \quad \diagdown$$
$$\text{radius} \quad \wedge$$
$$\diagup \quad \diagdown$$
$$\text{radius} \quad 2$$

differences between predictions and observed outcomes. Consider Table 3.4 that lists, for each planet in the solar system, its distance to the sun (radius), its diameter, and the time needed for a single orbit (period).

Assume that the task of the GA is to find the relationship between the two variables (*radius* and *diameter*) and the outcome (*period*). The answer, Kepler's Third Law, states that the period is equal to the square root of the radius cubed.[12] Note that the diameter has no bearing on the time it takes a planet to orbit the sun. An error-driven GA that minimizes the residual will apply the model as carried by an individual to each planet and calculate the error in its prediction of the period. The smaller the overall error, the higher the fitness.

Initially, models may arise that attempt to predict the period using some function of the diameter, but they will eventually become extinct in favour of models that link radius to period (as such models have a higher fitness potential). Having established this link, the GA will evolve increasingly accurate models in its everlasting quest for the optimal fitness (corresponding, in this case, to zero error). Eventually, GAAF will breed a model like the one shown in Table 3.4. Figure 3.5 illustrates the evolutionary path to this solution. Note that the process shows the stepwise improvements characteristic of an evolutionary process rather than the gradually decreasing error (up to a certain point) witnessed in, for instance, neural networks or regression analysis.

Besides least residuals,[13] GAAF supports other fitness calculation methods. For credit-scoring purposes, or indeed any classification task, it can use both the coefficient of concordance and accuracy measures (see Section 2.3).

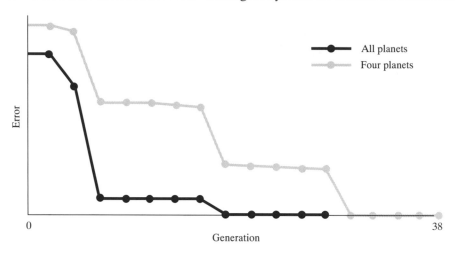

Figure 3.5

6 STRENGTHS AND WEAKNESSES

In discussing the strengths and weaknesses of GAAF, it is useful to distinguish between aspects of genetic algorithms in particular and those specific to financial modelling. The weaknesses of a GA in general are:

- No thorough theoretical framework for the evolutionary process exists (as compared to, for instance, statistical algorithms).
- There are no guarantees that a solution will be found, not even a mediocre one (as compared to exhaustive search methods).
- As in natural evolution, progress is intermittent, not gradual (as compared to iterative statistical methods or neural networks). As a result, the type of solution for serious problems and the time it takes to find it (possibly infinite) are hard to predict.

Their strengths can be summarized as follows:

- The algorithm is less vulnerable to local optima than traditional optimization methods (Goldberg, 1989, pp. 2–10).
- Search is opportunistic: although results are difficult to predict (a weakness: see above), the ultimate solutions are quite often pleasantly surprising.

In generating mathematical models in a tree format (Section 5), a drawback of GAAF is the single outcome its models can produce (value at the root of the tree). Neural networks, for instance, can accommodate multiple outcomes since they allow more than one output node. To simultaneously predict n outcomes, GAAF must be run n times, each run generating a model dedicated to a particular outcome.

Although single valued, GAAF models can predict multi-class outcomes by defining appropriate score ranges (see Section 2.3 about cutoff scores). For added flexibility, future versions of GAAF will support individuals that carry multiple models.

In searching for a model in an algebraic form, GAAF offers additional advantages over a standard GA:

- In all trials conducted to date it outperformed any other known method for credit scoring (see Section 7.3).

- The models it generates are algebraically specified mathematical functions that can be interpreted and analysed using conventional means.

- If so desired, it can be a hands-off tool: no interaction is required from database specification to model implementation (see Section 7.2).

- It supports incremental development: more up-to-date cases can be incorporated into the learning process at any time.

7   A GENETIC ALGORITHM FOR CREDIT SCORING

7.1   Introduction

OMEGA, shown in Figure 3.6, is a full-fledged model development tool that takes industry standard databases, generates predictive models from them, and allows the user to analyse and validate the resulting models statistically. It encompasses GAAF, a Genetic Algorithm for the Approximation of Formulae. GAAF's genetic engine supports multiple pools of arbitrary size, hybrid model-generation methods, multiple-fitness calculation methods, multiple-fitness normalization methods, application-specific operators, and much more. It solves toy problems like Kepler's Third Law (see Section 5) in about 45 seconds on a standard 486-based PC. In practice it is applied to databases containing over 30 000 examples with 60 variables each.

OMEGA is intended primarily as a business tool. Although a user can influence virtually every aspect of the evolutionary process, he or she does not need to know about the GA at all. Also, OMEGA's modelling engine, GAAF (third button), is not dedicated to GAs. It automatically switches to alternative breeding strategies, like *simulated annealing* (Press et al., 1992, pp. 444–55) and standard hill-climbing techniques (Mühlenbein, Schomish & Born, 1991) when the need arises (e.g. when genetic diversity deteriorates).[14] The various buttons on the toolbar in Figure 3.6

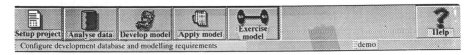

Figure 3.6   The OMEGA button bar

depict the possibilities for the user to define the database layout, specify business and modelling parameters, develop, analyse and exercise the models. A case study may clarify the process of developing a financial model for credit scoring.

7.2 A Sample Session: Developing a Credit-scoring Model

Suppose a credit manager, Julia, wants to apply OMEGA to derive a forecasting model for loan applicants. Assume that data is available in the format shown in Table 3.5.

In the table the first column simply numbers the attribute. The second column lists the role. From the various available roles, shown here are *predictor* (allow attribute as variable in the model), *benchmark* (identifies a benchmark score), *weight* (the number of actual cases represented by the record), *outcome* (the value to be predicted by the model) and *ignore* (refrain from using attribute in the modelling process, at least in the current stage). Both type and role have to be specified by Julia. She can define the above record layout by pressing the first button on the OMEGA button bar (see Section 7.1).

Note that some of the entries are probably correlated like, for instance, 'residence' and 'zip-code'. Also, the data needs preprocessing to map symbolic entries onto numeric values. The first step is to define the record layout in order for OMEGA to interpret the data. The record layout depicted in the table may serve as an example. Worth mentioning are the first field that stores Julia's (or somebody else's) personal judgement. In this case she chooses for her own assessment to be ignored, but it is perfectly feasible to have it taken into account by OMEGA. The sixth field represents a benchmark score generated by an alternative model (e.g. the model Julia is currently using). The seventh field assigns a weight to the record. Sometimes the database itself is the result of some statistical analysis and a set of actual cases may have been sampled from a larger database. The weight then reflects the relative importance of the record. The next field stores the outcome to be predicted. More than one field can be marked as outcome, although OMEGA must generate multiple models to cope (see Section 6).

Table 3.5

	Role	Type	Description	Example
1	ignore	numeric ordinal	subjective score	15
2	predictor	numeric ordinal	age of applicant	34
3	predictor	numeric categorical	zip code	101
4	predictor	symbolic ordinal	residence	{London, ...}
5	predictor	numeric ordinal	maximum quarterly balance	6000
6	benchmark	numeric ordinal	benchmark score	18
7	weight	numeric ordinal	weight	80
8	outcome	symbolic categorical	loan repaid?	yes
...	...	...	...	...
20	predictor	numeric ordinal	time at address	10

The next step involves the setting of various parameters. For instance, the business objective must be stated. Is it a direct mail application (maximum response models) or credit scoring? On a more trivial level, an identifier for an accepted case may be chosen (e.g. 'good') or the gain per good and loss per bad case can be specified to allow the system to generate profit graphs. It is also specified at this stage what, to Julia's taste, would constitute an acceptable model in terms of performance, robustness, accept rate, etc.

In addition to the above business parameters, modelling parameters can be set (the number of pools, their size, the mutation and crossover rates, model constraints, etc.). All modelling parameters take default values that work well in most cases, thus allowing Julia to disregard the intricacies of the actual modelling stage.

Once the database layout and business objectives have been defined, the data analysis module can be invoked (by pressing the second button on the OMEGA button bar). The data analysis module performs several tasks using a variety of statistical methods. It will transform symbolic to numerical data (assigning, for instance, neighbourhood codes to neighbourhood names); assess predictor interactions; do spatial analysis, calculate the univariate performance for each of the predictors, etc.

After data analysis, the prepared data can be fed into the modelling engine (GAAF). OMEGA then initializes its first generation of models, either randomly or based on the statistical information provided by data analysis. From this point onwards, OMEGA essentially generates models as outlined above with respect to the Kepler example. Julia can choose to monitor the genetic process and interact with it. She can change any of over a hundred parameters, ranging from the mutation rate for operator modifications to the fitness bonus for comprehensible models. Being a credit-manager, it could make more sense to stay with OMEGA's default parameters. These will typically beat other modelling techniques by 2–4%, especially if the problem is very hard (see Section 7.3). A knowledgeable operator may squeeze an additional percent out of OMEGA by closely monitoring the GA.

Eventually, OMEGA will propose a set of promising models like the one depicted in Figure 3.7. Note that the generic mathematical operators like $*$ and $+$, as used in representing Kepler's Law, are replaced by custom operators like 'concave' and 'convex'. OMEGA supports any mix of generic and custom operators, but custom operators often help to make the models more comprehensible (if the behaviour of the operators is well understood). Also, when carefully designed, such operators can aid in preventing overfitting. The model in the figure tells Julia that a convex shape over the applicant's residence and age, combined, in a concave fashion, with the maximum quarterly balance, succeeds (under predefined criteria) in predicting whether the loan will be repaid or not. OMEGA will annotate model performance by various tables (e.g. score distribution) and graphs (e.g. bad rate, profit rate, accept rate). Optionally, the model can be applied to other databases, separately kept for *a posteriori* validation.

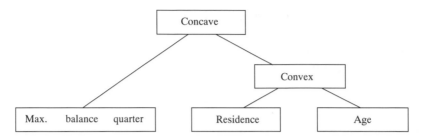

Figure 3.7 A financial model

As a next step Julia may choose to analyse the model in more detail. She may, for instance, exercise the cutoff and study the effect on the accept rate (see Section 2.3). If she is satisfied she may either set up the next stage or implement the model within her organization.

7.3 Results

Experiments on financial databases obtained from banks that are using OMEGA show that OMEGA beat the benchmark model (the scoring system, either human or artificial, that used to rate loan applications) by at first glance a meager 2.31%. It goes without saying, however, that a marginal improvement in this area translates to an impressive reduction in costs and profit gain.

The results in Table 3.6 were obtained over a (confidential) data-set from a British bank. It comprised 5640 cases with 17 predictors each. The benchmark model was generated by an artificial neural network.

Graf and Nakhaeizadeh (1993) compare several methods with respect to their ability to generate predictive models for a real-life credit-scoring data-set. Both neural networks and machine learning techniques were investigated in addition to statistical techniques. OMEGA was tested on one of their data-sets[15] that contained 1000 cases (700 good and 300 bad). Each case was represented by 20 predictors, seven of them continuous (like age), the others categorical (like current account status). Graf and Nakhaeizadeh did a fivefold cross-validation on all methods. That is, they took five disjunct test-sets of 200 cases and, in each case, applied

Table 3.6

	Benchmark	OMEGA	Improvement
Coefficient of concordance	63.68%	65.15%	2.31%
Robustness[a]	2.54	2.41	5.12%

[a] A model's robustness is assessed by first applying the model to numerous (1000, say) random samples from the data. This procedure generates 1000 outcomes. Second, the standard deviation σ of the outcome distribution is calculated. The robustness of the model is now equal to σ. For robust models, the outcomes over disparate randomly selected samples should not differ too much and σ should therefore be small.

Table 3.7

Algorithm	Method	Accuracy (default 70%)
OMEGA	Genetic algorithm	77.4%
CN2	Rule induction (Clark & Niblett, 1991)	72.0%
NEWID	Rule induction (Statlog, 1993, pp. 61–3)	65.1%
C4.5	Rule induction (Quinlan, 1986)	72.7%
AD	Neural network	72.7%
MAD	Neural network	70.9%
COUNTER PROPAGATION	Neural network	68.7%

the methods to the remaining 800 examples. The average accuracy over the five *test*-sets was then taken as a performance measure.

To judge the performance of OMEGA on the same data-set, the average accuracy was also calculated over five test-sets of 200 examples. Rather than being disjunct, however, the five test-sets were taken from a data-set that was fully randomized before each run (cf. Statlog, 1993, p. 9). The results are listed in Table 3.7 and correspond to those of the best OMEGA model over the *training*-set. Thus, the learning process was not aborted at a convenient time, i.e. when an otherwise average model happens to generalize properly.

Over the actual training-set, OMEGA achieved an accuracy of 82.5%. Although the results are encouraging, it should be noted that the accuracy measure is misleading here. Since the data-set contains 700 good cases on a total of 1000, the default accuracy is as high as 70%. More importantly, highly accurate models may not be useful at all in practice where misclassification does not tell the whole story (see Section 2.3). OMEGA reached the more useful coefficient of concordance score of 84.4% on the same test-set, but no such scores are available for any of the other methods.

ACKNOWLEDGEMENTS

The authors wish to express their gratitude to David Barrow of KiQ Business Solutions Ltd for teaching us about credit scoring. The OMEGA system is a joint development of KiQ and Cap Volmac. The OMEGA and GAAF systems have largely been developed in the course of the ESPRIT III project PAPAGENA (6857), which was sponsored by the European Union.

ENDNOTES

1. OMEGA's functionality is based on the system as described in Barrow (1992) and has been implemented in collaboration with its authors.
2. As opposed to a *test-* or *validation-set* which is kept apart and later used to assess a model's generalization capability. This is one of the more popular methods to gauge a

model's *robustness*. In some financial domains, where robustness may even be more important than sheer predictive power, other methods (e.g. *bootstrapping* (Press et al., 1992)) are used in combination.

3. PAPAGENA is an ESPRIT III project (6857) sponsored by the European Union.
4. Nervous or conservative managers may even favour models they can explain to their organization over more predictive alternatives.
5. In fact, it is even possible to find the cutoff that maximizes the accuracy.
6. For this reason OMEGA (Sections 1, 5 and 7) supports *reject inferencing*, the deduction of outcomes for cases that were not accepted. Reject inferencing, although essential to practical credit scoring systems, is beyond the scope of this chapter.
7. In light of this observation it makes sense, if useful expertise is available, to consider hybrid architectures that combine the strong points of bottom-up and top-down approaches (Walker, 1992).
8. In the standard GA, each individual is associated with a single chromosome. Individuals that carry multiple chromosomes are called *polyploid*. In biology, polyploidy is used in combination with *dominance*: gene expression at one chromosome is affected by gene expression at other chromosomes (Gardner, Simmons & Snustad, 1991, pp. 33–6). In GA practice the same technique is also occasionally used (Goldberg, 1989, pp. 148–65).
9. The idea behind elitism is to prevent valuable genetic material from accidentally getting lost. Roulette wheel selection, by its very nature, occasionally causes this to happen. Although elitism encourages (possibly premature) convergence, it is useful in maintaining a monotonically increasing fitness across generations.
10. i.e. losing population diversity before satisfactory results have been found.
11. This follows from his objective to 'breed' programs in the LISP prefix notation.
12. Deriving Kepler's Third Law from astronomical data is a popular test-case for symbolic machine learning techniques (Langley, Simon & Bradshaw, 1990).
13. GAAF uses several ways to map an error onto a fitness. Obvious candidates are subtracting the (summed, weighted, average) error from some large value or taking its reciprocal.
14. GAAF is set up to accommodate alternative optimization methods that compensate for a GA's possible weaknesses (e.g. premature convergence). In practice, however, the GA need rarely be suspended in favour of simulated annealing or hill-climbing techniques.
15. Only one data-set was available, since the others are confidential.

REFERENCES

Barrow, D. (1992) 'Making money with genetic algorithms', in *Proc. of the Fifth European Seminar on Neural Networks and Genetic Algorithms*, IBC International Services, London.

Carbonell, J.G. & Langley, P. (1990) 'Machine learning', in Shapiro, S.C. (ed.), *Encyclopedia of Artificial Intelligence*, Vol. I, John Wiley, New York, pp. 464–88.

Clark, P. & Niblett, T. (1989) 'The CN2 induction algorithm', *Machine Learning*, **3**, 261–83.

Davis, L. (1991) *Handbook of Genetic Algorithms*, Van Nostrand Reinhold, New York.

Eiben, G. (1991) *A Method for Designing Decision Support Systems for Operational Planning*, thesis, Technische Universiteit Eindhoven.

Eshelman, L.J. & Schaffer, J.D. (1991) 'Preventing premature convergence by preventing incest', in *Proc. of the Fourth International Conference on Genetic Algorithms*, Morgan Kaufmann, San Mateo, CA, pp. 53–60.

Evans, J. St, B.T. (1988) 'The knowledge elicitation problem: a psychological perspective', *Behaviour and Information Technology*, **7**, 2, 111–30.

Gardner, E.J., Simmons, M.J. & Snustad, D.P. (1991) *Principles of Genetics*, 8th edition, John Wiley, New York.

Goldberg, D.E. (1989) *Genetic Algorithms in Search, Optimization & Machine Learning*, Addison-Wesley, Reading, MA.

Graf, J. & Nakhaeizadeh, G. (1993) 'Recent developments in solving the credit-scoring problem', Plantamura V.L., Soucek B. & Vissagio, G. (eds), *Logistic and Learning for Quality Software, Management and Manufacturing*, John Wiley, New York.

Haasdijk, E.W. (1993) *Sex Between Models: On Using Genetic Algorithms for Inductive Modelling*, Master's thesis, Dept. of Computer Science, University of Amsterdam.

Hillis, W.D. (1992) 'Co-evolving parasites improve simulated evolution as an optimization procedure', Langton, C.G., Taylor C., Farmer, J.D. & Rasmussen S. (eds), in *Artificial Life II: Proceedings of the workshop on artificial life 1990*, Addison-Wesley, Redwood City, CA, pp. 313-24.

Kingdon, J., Ribeiro Filho, J., & Treleaven, P. (1993) 'The GAME programming environment architecture', in Stender, J. (ed.), *Parallel Genetic Algorithms: Theory and Applications*, IOS Press, Amsterdam, pp. 85-92.

Koza, J.R. (1992) *Genetic Programming: On the Programming of Computers by Means of Natural Selection*, MIT Press, Cambridge, MA.

Langley, P., Simon, H.A. & Bradshaw, G.L. (1990) 'Heuristics for empirical discovery', in *Readings in Machine Learning*, Morgan Kaufmann, San Mateo, CA, pp. 356-72.

Mühlenbein, H., Schomisch, M. & Born, J. (1991) 'The parallel genetic algorithm as function optimizer', in *Proc. of the Fourth International Conference on Genetic Algorithms*, Morgan Kaufmann, San Mateo, CA, pp. 53-60.

Press, W.H., Teukolsky, S.A., Vetterling, W.T. & Flannery, B.P. (1992) *Numerical Recipes in C: The Art of Scientific Computing*, 2nd edition, Cambridge University Press, New York.

Quinlan, J.R. (1986) 'Induction of decision trees', *Machine Learning*, 1, 81-106.

Rumelhart, D.E., McClelland, J.L. & the PDP Research Group (1986) *Parallel Distributed Processing: Explorations in the Microstructure of Cognition*, Vol. I, MIT Press, Cambridge, MA.

Statlog (1993) *Machine Learning, Neural and Statistical Classification*, Deliverable 4.1 ESPRIT project 5170.

Walker, R.F. (1992) *An Expert System Architecture for Heterogeneous Domains*, thesis, Free University Amsterdam.

4

Neural Networks for Credit Scoring

DAVID LEIGH

1 INTRODUCTION

Recently, our Advanced Technology Group made a commitment to the deployment of emerging technologies that have the potential to provide a significant return on investment, reduce costs and support business objectives. Neural Networks (NN), in our opinion, is a good example of one of the more promising technologies with the potential to support applications in the domains of business and finance. This chapter reviews the application of neural network technology in the evaluation of installment loan applications.

Artificial neural network models have been studied for many years in the hope of achieving human-like performance in a variety of fields including speech and image recognition (Hecht-Nielsen, 1990; Wasserman, 1989; Rumelhart, 1986). These models are composed of many non-linear computational elements operating in parallel and arranged in patterns reminiscent of biological neural nets. Instead of executing a program of instructions sequentially as in a Von Neumann computer, neural net models explore many competing hypotheses simultaneously using many parallel computational elements.

Also, unlike classical artificial intelligence approaches that depend on rule-based algorithms, non-algorithmic neural networks are governed by systems of coupled differential equations. The equations governing neural network behavior can be modified by learning and accordingly modifying the response of the system. As a

Intelligent Systems for Finance and Business. Edited by S. Goonatilake and P. Treleaven
© 1995 John Wiley & Sons Ltd

result, neural networks can take in new data and 'learn' new relationships without using traditional programming techniques.

Neural networks are applicable in the general areas of sensor processing, knowledge processing, and more recently in the support of both business and financial applications — specifically, credit scoring, behavior scoring, stock market predictions, bankruptcy prediction and financial forecasting. One of the more successful financial applications of neural network technology to date is in providing effective credit evaluation for supporting the granting of loans.

2 NEURAL NETWORKS AND CREDIT SCORING

It is difficult to compile a comprehensive survey of neural network applications as applied to credit scoring in the financial services industry. There is no question that many financial services organizations have investigated neural network technology, developed prototypes and have deployed operational neural network-based credit systems. However, it is difficult to put an exact figure on the number of neural network credit applications that are in operational use. Some have not progressed beyond the prototype stage because of political reasons, issues regarding providing sufficient explanations regarding the rejection of an applicant due to a neural network decision, or concern with risk. We are aware of an instance of a neural network application that was deployed and later withdrawn due to a change in management. As with most cutting-edge technologies, some companies are reluctant to publicize their deployed models. If a company experiences a major failure, they are reluctant to speak about it, so as to avoid embarrassment. Similarly, if they produce a major success and experience significant cost savings or improvement in market share, they might prefer to keep the information confidential.

One bank that has publicly announced its neural network operations is Security Pacific Bank (SPB) which uses a neural network-based on-line financial scoring model (PCAI 1991). The commercial loan group is currently using it to analyze the risk factor associated with small business loans. SPB has a portfolio of thousands of small business loans, and this system periodically reassesses each of these loans, assigning it a risk code. It is regarded as being quite successful and has thought to have captured the expertise of their human loan-analysts through the neural network training procedures.

Apart from credit scoring, there are many other opportunities to apply neural network technology in the financial services industry. For example, a similar application would involve developing a neural network scorecard for mortgage underwriting. Other categories of neural network applications are found in the areas of behavior scoring, e.g. using an NN to determine the size of an increase to be applied to a credit line. Other areas that could also exploit the pattern recognition and predictive powers of neural network models include product cross-selling, bankruptcy forecasting, optimizing a collections strategy and fraud detection, e.g.

detecting the fraudulent use of a credit card. Another potential application is to automate signature verification for checks.

We now turn to an application of neural networks at Citibank.

3 CASE STUDY

This section describes how neural networks were applied to the development of a scorecard to evaluate installment loan applications. Due to space limitations we do not detail the basics of neural networks, and we encourage the reader to refer to Eberhart & Dobbins (1990) or Beale & Jackson (1990) for excellent introductions to neural networks.

There were several credit products that were initially considered in the application domain. They included credit cards, mortgages, secured loans and installment loans. We finally selected installment loans, primarily due to the availability of sufficient data. An installment loan is a loan for a predefined amount of money for a fixed period of time. The customer completes payment of the loan by making regular fixed payments (installments) comprising both principal and interest during the period of the loan.

Traditionally, installment loans have been evaluated using discriminant analysis, a traditional linear statistical approach. A scorecard is produced for the installment loan product and each selected credit variable is assigned a specific value according to the occurring category or value. For example, owning a home will receive a higher score than renting a home. The employed status will certainly be assigned a higher value than unemployed, a poor credit record might be assigned a negative value. A cutoff score is established and in order to receive a loan, a customer has to attain an accumulative score in excess of the assigned cutoff score. Borderline cases are reviewed very carefully and evaluated according to specific rules. In general, the creation of a scorecard by traditional approaches is very time consuming, requires a large amount of detailed analysis and is expensive when subcontracted to external vendors.

Neural network technology can offer several advantages over conventional credit scoring approaches. The primary advantage is the potential to provide an improved function fitting capability due to the intrinsic non-linear pattern recognition capabilities of neural networks.

Many financial institutions have their credit-scoring software developed by consulting companies specialized in this field. In this instance, we developed the neural network model in-house. The challenge was to achieve sufficient reliability in the predictive capability of the developed model where even a small improvement can translate into large savings. For example, just a 1% improvement in reducing losses in a large loan portfolio translates into a $1 million savings for every $100 million of losses.

We established the project in partnership with a credit policy group within the Bank. The overall objective of the initial phase of the project was to develop a neural network software application that would function as a prototype for install-ment loan credit scoring. A second phase was planned to further optimize the performance of the initial prototype and a third phase was designed to deploy the prototype. This chapter describes the initial project phase.

4 PROTOTYPE DEVELOPMENT APPROACH

The credit department stipulated that the target should be to attempt to outperform an existing scorecard for installment loans. This scorecard was initially devel-oped by the Fair Isssacs Corporation (FICO), a company based in San Francisco that specializes in developing scorecards. The FICO scorecard assigns a certain number of points to the attribute of each variable. We were constrained to using the same variables for our initial prototype. There were no constraints on the variables selected for our second prototype. Accordingly, the initial development sample used to produce the FICO scorecard was used to train and develop the installment loan neural network model. By using the same variables, we were able to compare the results of the two models for identical development data. In addition, the use of identical variables would facilitate operational development.

The neural network scoring model was developed using the back-propagation paradigm on a HNC neurocomputer. The HNC neurocomputing workstation is based on a 386 PC and includes the HNC ANZA neurocomputing coprocessor and the HNC Neurosoft software package. The coprocessor provided a processing speed of nearly 2 million interconnections during training.

4.1 Input Data and Operations

Figure 4.1 provides an overview of the tasks required to prepare the 'raw data' and transform it into the required training data-set and the validation data-set. The diagram illustrates the initial segmenting of the raw data into rejects, good records and bad records. The good and bad records are then randomized to improve the training process. The records are then selected and separate training and validation files are created.

It was important that sufficient data was available to provide both an adequate training data set and an adequate validation data-set. We selected close to 3000 records that were subdivided into 2000 for the training set and 1000 for the vali-dation set. The training set was further subdivided into 1000 good records, i.e. customers with a good payment history and 1000 bad records, i.e. customers who had made late payments several times in a predefined period or completely defaulted on the loan. We also ensured that the selected data reflected payment experience that was accumulated over a sufficient period of time.

Data analysis was performed using conventional statistics to determine the predic-tive ability of the attributes of the variables selected for the model. An example

65

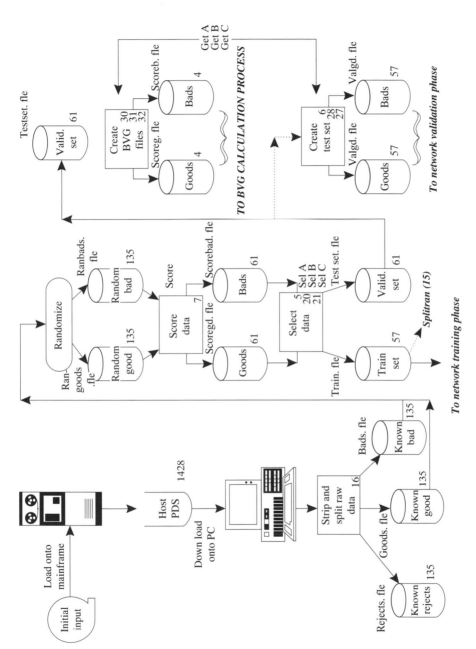

Figure 4.1

of the input data used in the credit-scoring model included the following types of variables:

- Employment data
- Income data
- Credit bureau data
- Banking account information

Each financial institution will select variables based on their own specific requirements. In general, the variables are selected based on previous experience in the specific credit domain under consideration. In this instance, the variables were selected based on a statistical analysis that identifies the variables that have the optimal predictive ability.

The selected input variables are subdivided into symbolic and continuous variables. For example, a discrete variable might be Occupation with multiple categories or Residence with one category for renting and another for ownership. Examples of continuous variables are Salary or Age (if legally permitted). There are several approaches to optimally segmenting a continuous variable. Whatever approach is selected, the objective is to provide a mapping from the continuous variable into a number of discrete and well-defined segmentations of the continuous variable. The segments may or may not overlap.

Also, the inputs require encoding so as to normalize the raw input data and map it into a form suitable for the neural network. Accordingly, both the symbolic and the continuous credit variables are mapped into the input vector of the network. The occurrence of a particular value or symbol in the original credit application is correspondingly presented to the network at the input layer. Specific software was developed to read the selected file, subdivide the data into the training set and the validation set and also create the required input vector.

5 TRAINING APPROACH

A key consideration in neural network modeling is the selection of an appropriate topology. The size of the input vector had now been determined as a result of the initial data analysis. The output layer consisted of one neuron and provided a measure of the projected performance of the loan under evaluation. A range of 0.1–0.9 was selected and an appropriate cutoff was determined to decide if a loan should be accepted or rejected. The key issue is determining the size of the hidden layer(s). We invested a large amount of time in testing various topologies. The published information in the field indicates that 90% of applications using backpropagation can be solved using one hidden layer and that, as a guide, the size of the hidden layer should not exceed 30% of the size of the input layer. Our experience was in accordance with these guidelines. Other key considerations are the selection of a learning approach, for example batching, momentum, delta bar delta, etc., selection of initial weight sizes and hidden and output layer training rates. Extensive time was invested in experimenting with various combinations of parameters.

The overall objective is to train the neural network on the training data to produce a network that can potentially perform well on out-of-sample data. The procedure was as follows:

(1)   Set initial weights to small random numbers
(2)   Select number of passes of input vector for training
(3)   Continue training until Mean Square Error (MSE) stabilizes on the validation sample
(4)   As appropriate, train the NN using alternative topologies, training rates, training methods to see if the MSE can be further minimized for the validation set
(5)   Apply trained NN on out-of-sample data

The approach we took was to train for 100 passes of the training data and then quantify the performance of the validation data set by measuring the Mean Square Error (MSE). Training is resumed for another 100 passes of the training file and the MSE is measured again on the validation set. This process was repeated until the MSE stabilized.

The above training approach was repeated for different topologies and training parameters until the minimum MSE was determined. The neural net topology and related values of the other parameters provides the optimally trained net. A key point is that the optimal neural net was determined based on the performance of the validation test set and not on the performance of the training data.

6   PERFORMANCE EVALUATION AND RESULTS

The performance of the neural net software was compared to the conventional credit scorecard by quantifying the ability of each scoring approach to discriminate between bad and good records. In addition, small adjustments were made to the final results to account for 'reject inferencing' considerations or how to allocate the rejected records according to our 'good' and 'bad' criteria for model development purposes. Other minor adjustments were made for the bias given to the FICO model as FICO were able to select the original variables and test data.

The approach used to calibrate performance was to calculate the proportion of bad records accepted compared to the proportion of good records accepted. This was determined by finding the percentile score for the good ones and calculating the fraction of bad scores scoring above each of the 100 good percentile scores. The overall measure of performance is the sum of the 100 bad fractions calculated above. The performances of the two scoring approaches were then compared. In addition to the above approach, a more conventional statistical test, the Kolmogrov–Smirnoff (K/S) test was also used to compare the results. The K/S test also provides a measure of the capability of a scorecard to separate between the good and bad loan applicants. Both of the above tests indicated that the neural network scoring approach was superior to the conventional scoring approach.

7 ASSESSMENT

The major strengths of the application of neural networks to the credit domain are summarized as follows:

- Formulation of a specific algorithm is not required — learns from the data itself.
- Provides an improved accuracy, due to the intrinsic non-linear learning capabilities of NN technology.
- The NN can easily be retrained to remain adaptive to changing economic, demographic, regulatory or business conditions.
- Improved discrimination may reduce loan losses.
- Potential to increase market share by offering competitive interest rates and lower fees.
- Less expensive to develop NN scorecards in-house compared to paying for outside services to develop conventional scorecards.

Overall, NN technology provides the potential to produce increased profitability by reducing loan losses, increasing market share and reducing costs. The major weaknesses of the application of neural networks to credit applications are summarized as follows:

- Requires supporting explanation capability as to why an applicant is rejected.
- Need to ensure that the training set provides maximum generalization (also true for conventional statistical techniques).
- Difficulties in selecting training approach and key parameters, e.g. rate of change parameters for each weight, initial weights, size of hidden layer, etc.
- Requires availability of sufficiently large amount of data for both training and validation purposes.

Regarding the above weaknesses, there is no simple solution for solving any of these concerns. Sufficient data should be provided to be fully representative of the total population and tests should be performed to try to ensure that the data provides optimal generalization. The selection of appropriate values for the key parameters is important as, for example, if the rate of weight change is too high, it could degrade the optimal solution, alternatively, if the rate of weight change is too slow, then the duration of training will be very long. A hidden layer that is too large will result in overfitting, while a hidden layer that is too small will not generalize sufficiently and produce a suboptimal model.

Concerning the need for providing an explanation, it is good customer service and often a legal requirement to provide to the customer the specific variables that caused the loan application to be denied. If the loan is being judged solely by a credit expert, the specialist knows the variables that are causing concern. If an expert system is used, it is easy to identify the rules and associated values of variables that are causing the loan to be rejected. However, when a neural network is used, the learning and acquired knowledge is embedded in the internal weights and the variables causing the application to be denied are not explicitly provided. Usually additional tests need to be performed using the final model to determine which specific variables are responsible for the loan denial.

8 CONCLUSION

This chapter has described a proof of concept development effort that applied neural networks to credit scoring. There are several opportunities to improve the overall process and overcome some of the current weaknesses. First, irrespective of the technology used, the use of any credit-scoring technique needs to recognize not only the predictive parameters pertinent to the customer application but also the parameters relating to the overall trends in the economic environment. This would provide an effective management of economic risk. For example, historical experience indicates that there is an increase in the percentage of loans defaulting in a recession. Accordingly, any credit-evaluation technique needs to take into account the terms of the loan during the anticipated stage of the economic cycle. Specifically, additional input parameters need to be carefully selected that would provide a predictive capability regarding the health of the economy, i.e. interest rates, levels of unemployment and the stage of the economic cycle. Also, in general, the potential financial loss from a bad loan is far greater than the potential profit from a good loan. A future refinement of our neural network models for credit evaluation will be to develop models that map into profitability instead of a simple good/bad determinant. Finally, we believe that the use of *hybrid* approaches will also result in improved techniques in applying NN technology to the credit-evaluation process. In particular, the use of genetic algorithms for finding optimal neural networks may potentially improve the accuracy of neural credit scoring systems.

REFERENCES

Beale, R. & Jackson, T. (1990) *Neural Computing — an Introduction*, Adam Hilger, Bristol.
Eberhart, R.C. & Dobbins, R.W. (1990) *Neural Network PC Tools — a Practical Guide*, Academic Press, San Diego, CA.
Hecht-Nielsen, R. (1990) *Neurocomputing*, Addison-Wesley, Reading MA.
PC AI (1991) May/June.
Rumelhart, D., McClelland, J. & the PDP Research Group (1986). *Parallel Distributed Processing*, MIT Press, Cambridge, MA.
Wasserman, P. (1989) *Neural Computing*, Van Nostrand Rheinhold, New York.

Part II
Direct Marketing

5
Neural Networks for Data-driven Marketing

PETER FURNESS

1 INTRODUCTION

Data-driven marketing is becoming increasingly sophisticated through the use of advanced targeting and segmentation methods. The richness of the available customer and other marketing data puts a premium on methods which can model the often subtle relationships in the data in a way that can be turned to profitable advantage.

The market analyst has a range of statistical and graphical tools which can be brought to bear. This includes the traditional methods of cross-tabulation and correlation analysis as well as more sophisticated multivariate techniques such as regression, cluster analysis, log-linear methods and CHAID (Kass, 1980; David Shepard Associates, 1990). Techniques for data visualization, including spatial mapping, are becoming widespread stimulated by the advances in computer graphics (Brodlie et al., 1992; Furness, 1992a). Linked to a geographical information system (GIS) the marketing database can be used for retail modelling and other forms of spatial analysis such as sales territory planning (Sleight, 1993).

Neural network computing is an empirical modelling technique which is being increasingly used in data-driven marketing to complement, and in some cases supplant, more traditional statistical methods (Hruschka & Natter, 1992; Furness, 1992b). Although the technique has been around since the 1940s it has only relatively recently begun to make an impact in commercial applications, fuelled by

Intelligent Systems for Finance and Business. Edited by S. Goonatilake and P. Treleaven
© 1995 John Wiley & Sons Ltd

the reducing costs of computing power and advances in the underlying theory of neural networks (Dayhoff, 1990; Wasserman, 1989).

Unlike conventional computing, where a computer relies on instructions written by a programmer, a neural computer is 'trained by example', rather as a dog would be trained to sniff out drugs or explosives, or a child taught to recognize letters and words. Neural network architecture is loosely based on an analogy with biological brains and, not surprisingly, it is in areas related to machine perception and robotics that neural networks were first used.

Given a suitable data environment, neural networks can offer a more powerful and straightforward way of modelling complicated non-linear relationships than conventional modelling tools (Rumelhart & McClelland, 1986). They are being used very successfully in areas as diverse as medical diagnosis (Bounds et al., 1988) and financial forecasting (Refenes et al., 1993).

In this chapter the range of applications of neural networks in data-driven marketing is surveyed. The technical aspects of neural networks are introduced through an illustrative example from direct marketing; examining the way neural networks function and looking at the overlap with other statistical methods. The common pitfalls encountered with neural networks are highlighted and guidelines are given for their practical application. Finally, there is a brief discussion of possible future developments of neural networks for data-driven marketing.

2 DATA-DRIVEN MARKETING

Information technology is revolutionizing marketing by mobilizing corporate data assets and making them available for analysis and targeting. Marketers now have access to rich sources of customer and other marketing data and seek ways to use the data to help improve the efficiency and the effectiveness of the marketing process.

Over the past few years there has been a rapid growth in the availability and use of analysis tools for data-driven marketing. The considerable reductions in the costs of computing have meant that these tools are now readily accessible on the desktop. The availability of user-friendly graphical interfaces and presentation software has given further impetus to this trend.

In parallel with the invasion of the desktop, a number of new computing-intensive analysis methods have appeared on the scene which, only five years ago, would have been impractical. These methods, which include neural networks, push the current generation of computers to the limits, but appear to offer advantages over more conventional statistical methods in many situations.

It should be emphasized at the outset that although these methods are often claimed to be 'new' there is a great deal of overlap with more traditional methods such as cluster analysis and regression modelling. In some cases the methods have been pioneered by computer scientists and engineers rather than statisticians. In the study of neural networks, for example, this has led to many situations where the 'wheel has been reinvented' and apparently new techniques have turned out to be well known within the statistical community. However, this intermixing of cultures (and sometimes clash of cultures!) makes the subject particularly stimulating and exciting.

There are a great many potential applications of neural networks in data-driven marketing. The main ones are as follows.

2.1 Modelling Customer Behaviour

Here one uses neural networks to analyse historical patterns of customer behaviour. The resultant model is then applied to a marketing database to help predict (at least in probability terms) future behaviour. Examples include:

- Prospect scoring (as in the illustrative example described later in this chapter)
- Retention and loyalty studies
- Profitability analysis
- Credit scoring
- Delinquency and 'behavioural scoring'

Conventional statistical methods have been applied very successfully in this area (David Shepard Associates, 1990). However, neural networks are beginning to be used as an alternative method and are achieving better results in some cases. Recent examples include:

- Customer analysis and holiday package targeting in the travel sector (Ryman-Tubb, 1993)
- Targeting cross-selling in the financial services sector (Coyne, 1993)
- Predicting computer software purchasers and insurance buyers (Murray, 1993)

2.2 Database Enhancement

A marketing database of customers and prospects has usually been trawled from a number of sources, many of which cover only a part of the base. The marketer is thus faced with a patchwork of data where information vital for marketing is missing for many customers and prospects.

Neural networks can be used to model (as far as the data permit) one set of variables from another. If a particular variable is 'patchy' then it may be possible to model it with a neural network using those parts of the base where the variable is present for training and testing. The network can then be applied to the rest of the base to 'fill in the gaps'.

This approach works particularly well where one is trying to interpolate from a market research survey of customers to the whole customer base, using globally available transactional, account and geodemographic data as the inputs to the neural network (Furness & Gregory, 1993; Gregory & Nellis, 1994).

Some sources of marketing data may not be very up to date or there may be other reasons to doubt the quality of the data. A neural network trained on data certified as high quality can then be used to comb a database looking for data quality problems.

2.3 Customer Segmentation

Certain types of neural network (the 'unsupervised' networks which are described briefly later in this chapter) can be used to develop segmentation systems. Here the networks are used to find patterns in the data rather than being taught to recognize known patterns. They are proving to be more effective than the conventional cluster-based methods in many cases (Hruschka & Natter,1992; Openshaw & Wymer, 1990).

Another commonly occurring situation is where a segmentation system has been developed using a rich source of data, taken from a market research survey, for example. A problem is then encountered when the segmentation has to be applied to a customer database where the data used to build the segmentation is available only for a tiny minority of customers. This is a special case of the database-enhancement application of neural networks discussed above.

2.4 Retail Modelling

In retailing and other activities involving the distribution of goods and services to consumers located over a geographical area it is often necessary to build models of local market potential. This is usually done by combining market research or customer data, which are available at a national or regional level, with census or other data available for much smaller areas. Geodemographic classifications such as ACORN or MOSAIC are often used in this process (Sleight, 1993). Neural networks offer a potentially more effective way of doing this type of small-area modelling by being able to make more effective use of the available data (Openshaw, 1992b)

2.5 Sales Analysis

Often in marketing one is faced with data in the form of time series. Product sales together with data on advertising and promotions, competitor activity and external economic factors are available, perhaps by day or week going back over a long period. The market analyst has to build models which will help disentangle these variables, perhaps to determine the effect of pricing or promotions on sales.

Neural networks can be of great help here. To forecast sales, for example, a network is first trained to model sales across historic time periods. The output from the model might be sales one day ahead; the inputs might be sales on the previous day, together with sales on a number of preceding days, plus the values of other variables on those days (Hoptroff, 1993).

In this context, the neural network can be seen as an alternative to the more conventional autoregressive forecasting models. In situations where the underlying dynamics are non-linear and even chaotic, neural networks are known to be more effective than the conventional methods (Furness, 1994a).

2.6 Data Visualization

In market analysis one is usually faced by large, noisy data-sets; perhaps containing thousands or millions of records, with each record containing a large number of variables. Neural networks provide a means of representing noisy data-sets analytically in a highly distilled form. Computer graphics can then be used to visualize the data and bring it to life (Furness, 1992a). In effect, we can 'play back' a trained network to picture the relationships between the variables in the problem.

3 NEURAL NETWORKS — AN INTRODUCTION

We shall work through a simple example to show how neural networks can be used in data-driven marketing. This will illustrate the main steps in building a neural network model and, at the same time, allow us to compare the approach with conventional statistical methods.

3.1 Illustrative Example

The example is entirely fictitious but it does contain a number of features encountered by the author in real applications. A great deal of complicating detail has been ignored so as not to obscure the underlying principles.

Consider the case of a building society which has about 5 million customers and is using direct mail to promote a new investment product to existing savers. An initial test mailing has been done to 50 000 customers selected at random and a total response of 1000 (2%) achieved in terms of product take-up. The objective is to analyze the response from this test campaign and find a way of targeting the roll-out campaign so as to double response rates to 4% and bring in at least 40 000 new investment product holders.

We will assume that the building society has an account-based system and that the only information available for targeting is:

TIMEAC: time the account has been open (in years)
AVEBAL: the average account balance taken over the last three months (in £)

In reality, of course, there would be many more account variables available for analysis, as well as demographic and geodemographic data. Neural networks will work just as well in these more complex situations, but we have chosen to consider just two variables so that we can picture what is going on.

Figure 5.1(a) shows a plot of the TIMEAC and AVEBAL values of each of the 1000 respondents from the test campaign. For comparison, Figure 5.1(b) shows the corresponding plot for a sample of 1000 savers from the 50 000 that were mailed who did not respond. It is clear that the 'pattern' of the respondents is markedly different from that of the non-respondents. For example, the respondents appear to be more concentrated around a diagonal line running from the bottom-left to the top-right of the figure.

There could be a number of reasons for these differences. Although it is hardly surprising that the likelihood of a given customer responding will vary with TIMEAC and AVEBAL, the nature of the variation will be complicated by factors such as joint/solus accounts and secondary holdings (where a customer holds most of his or her savings in another institution).

As we shall see, neural networks provide a way of modelling the patterns in the data without having to make any assumptions about the underlying reasons for the patterns.

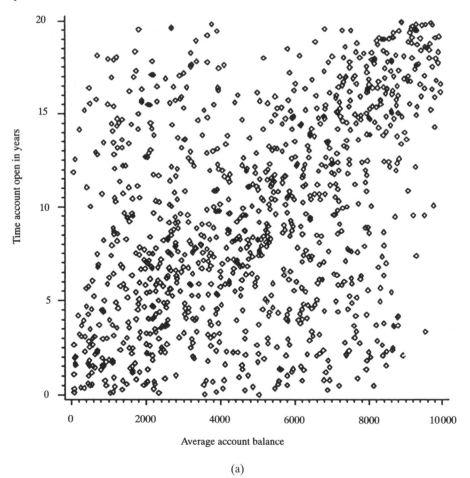

(a)

Figure 5.1 (a) Test mailing responders; (b) test mailing non-responders

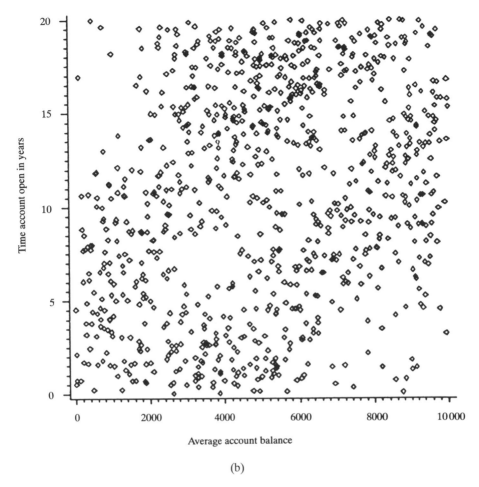

(b)

Figure 5.1 (*continued*)

3.2 Neural Network Model

For the moment we shall think of a neural network as a black box with a set of inputs and a set of outputs. In the example (Figure 5.2) there are two inputs (the variables TIMEAC and AVEBAL) and a single output (labelled SCORE).

Ideally, we would like the black box to output a value for SCORE of 1 whenever we put in the TIMEAC and AVEBAL values of a responding customer, and to give us an output of 0 for a non-responding customer. However, we can see from Figures 5.1(a) and 5.1(b) that there is a great deal of overlap between the responding and non-responding groups and the best we can expect is that savers with higher scores are more likely to respond than those with lower scores.

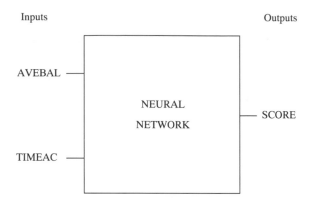

Figure 5.2 The neural network as a black box

To build the model we split the 1000 respondents randomly into two groups of 500 each. We also do the same with the sample of 1000 non-respondents. We combine one of the groups of respondents with one of the groups of non-respondents to create a 'training set' of 1000 cases; the remaining groups are combined to create a 'test set', also of 1000 cases.

The idea is that we 'train' the black box on the training set and then confirm that it is able to 'generalize' and give valid results by running it against the test set. In very simplified terms the training consists of:

- Presenting each saver in the training set to the black box. The values of TIMEAC and AVEBAL are input and a number, SCORE is output.
- If the black box gets the 'right' answer (i.e. the output is 1 if the saver is a respondent or 0 if the saver is a non-respondent) then nothing happens and we move on to the next saver in the training set.
- If the black box gets the answer wrong (the output is 0 for a respondent or 1 for a non-respondent, or an intermediate value between 0 and 1 is output) then an adjustment is made inside the black box so that when presented with the same saver again its output will be closer to the correct answer (an 'error' value is calculated as the difference between the black box output and the target value of 0 or 1; and the training is designed to reduce this error).

Each time we make a complete pass through the training set we can calculate an average error (in fact a mean square error) and this error will reduce on each pass. The training set is processed repeatedly, perhaps hundreds of times, until the average error has dropped to an acceptable level and the network gives satisfactory results when run against the test set.

The black box will now have 'learnt' the patterns in the data and Figure 5.3 shows the output of the black box plotted in three dimensions as a function of the two input variables. When you compare this with Figure 5.1(a) you can see that

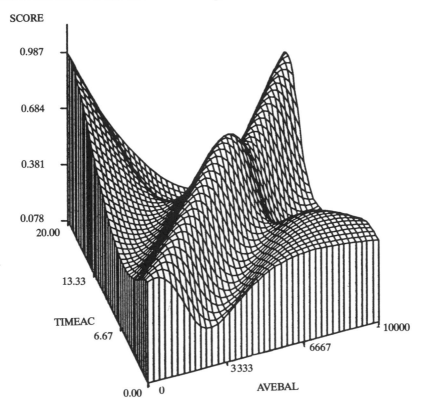

Figure 5.3   Neural network model output as a function of the inputs

the 'high' regions of the graph follow the concentrations of respondents relative to non-respondents; the ridge-like diagonal feature is particularly evident, thus showing that the black box has modelled the pattern we had already detected by eye.

Figure 5.4 shows the result of applying the black box model to the test set and presenting the results as a gains chart. The model has been used to calculate a SCORE value for each saver in the test set; the set has then been ranked in descending order of SCORE. The horizontal axis value (cumulative non-response) and vertical axis value (cumulative response) represent the result of working down the test set on this ranking and adding up the number of respondents and non-respondents found. The 45° line is there to show the result one would get with a random ranking; the extent to which the graph bends up and away from the 45° line gives a measure of the model's power in discriminating between respondents and non-respondents. One can see from the gains chart that there is a SCORE value for which, if we were to pick all savers with SCORES above this value, would yield 50% of all respondents but only 20% of non-respondents.

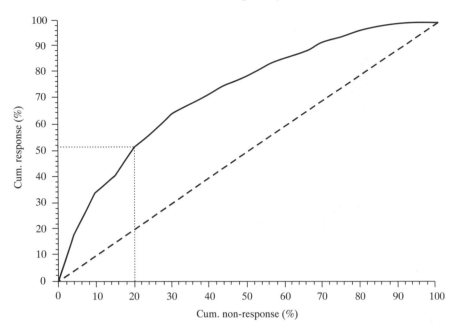

Figure 5.4   Neural network model gains chart

Some simple arithmetic shows that if we extrapolate this to our roll-out mailing we can expect to double the response rate from 2% to at least 4% if we pick from among the top 20% of the customer base on the model's output. By mailing the top 1 million savers out of the total base of 5 million we should be able to generate 40 000 new investment product holders, which was our objective. This very precise targeting would probably save more than £300 000 in mailing costs!

3.3   Inside the Black Box

The type of network used in the example is a Multi-Layer Perceptron (MLP) as shown schematically in Figure 5.5. This is probably the most popular type of neural network in commercial applications (Hart, 1992). In this example there are just three layers of processing units (often referred to as neurons from the analogy with biological brains) connected up in such a way that the units in one layer are connected to every unit in the next layer.

For an MLP network the processing carried out by each unit is very simple. The unit takes the sum of its inputs and applies a function to this sum, either a linear function or a simple non-linear 'squashing function', as we shall see later.

A pair of input values (AVEBAL, TIMEAC) are presented to the input layer units; after processing by the input layer the values pass along the connections to the hidden layer and are modified by applying weights (w1, w2, ...) as they go. The values of the weights are decided during training, as described below.

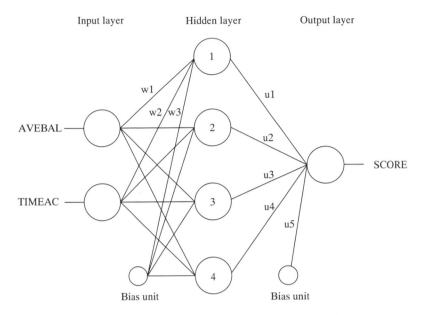

Figure 5.5 Multilayer perception: example with three layers

The hidden layer units then process these weighted values, and the processed values are passed along the final set of connections and modified by another set of weights (u1, u2, ...) before reaching the output unit. The output unit applies a further process to compute the value of SCORE, the network output.

Note also the presence of 'bias units'. These output a fixed unit value and can be thought of as constant terms in the equations defining the processes carried out by the network.

Network training involves adjusting the connection weights to try to make the network reproduce the known output values in the training set. If we consider the average (mean square) error of the network taken over the training set to be a function of the weights, then the training process amounts to finding the minimum of this function. In the simplest training algorithms this is analogous to rolling a ball down the slope as in Figure 5.6. Algorithms have also been developed (Wasserman, 1989) to locate the global minimum and to avoid getting trapped in local minima.

The training process can be slow, especially with large networks because of the considerable amount of computation required (the illustrative example took a few minutes on a 386 PC). Once trained, however, the weights in the network are fixed. It is then a very simple and fast process to calculate the output value corresponding to any pair of inputs.

In a MLP the input and output layer units are usually linear units (that is, they process values by applying a linear transformation) and the hidden layer units apply a 'squashing function' F(.) defined as follows:

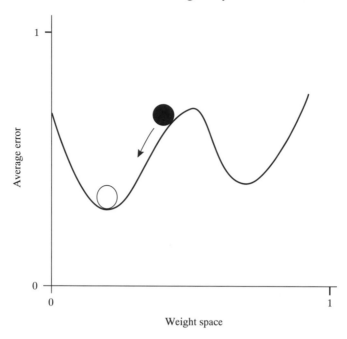

Figure 5.6 Error function

- Add together all the incoming weighted values to the unit, call this S.
- Transform S into the number $1/(1 + \exp(-S))$ where $\exp(.)$ is the exponential function. This has the effect of 'squashing' the output into the range 0 to 1.

This is shown diagrammatically in Figure 5.7. Squashing functions are used because they provide a smooth approximation to the sort of 'threshold' behaviour observed in biological neurons, where a neuron 'fires' if its total input is above some threshold but does not fire if its input is below the threshold.

In the illustrative example (Figure 5.5) the units in the input layer apply a linear transformation which 'normalizes' the input data values (this has the effect of scaling the values of AVEBAL and TIMEAC so that they both have zero mean and unit variance). The output unit is also linear, in this case just adding together the values which feed into it.

For the mathematically inclined reader, the equations defining the network in Figure 5.5 are:

$$\text{SCORE} = u1 \cdot H1 + u2 \cdot H2 + u3 \cdot H3 + u4 \cdot H4 + u5$$

where H1, H2, ... are the outputs from the hidden layer units. Thus:

$$H1 = F(w1 \cdot \text{AVEBAL}^* + w2 \cdot \text{TIMEAC}^* + w3), \text{ etc.}$$

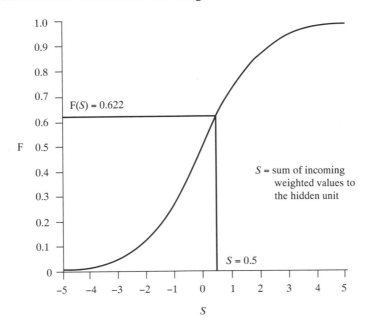

Figure 5.7 Squashing function

and AVEBAL* and TIMEAC* represent the normalized values of the inputs AVEBAL and TIMEAC, and F(.) is the squashing function defined above.

It is the non-linear hidden layer units which give MLPs their power in modelling data patterns (Rumelhart & McClelland, 1986). If we focus on the hidden layer units 1 and 3 in our network and look at their outputs separately we get the functions as shown in Figures 5.8(a) and 5.8(b). When combined together using the weights (u1, u3) (Figure 5.8(c)) they give the central ridge-like feature which can be seen in the raw data (Figure 5.1(a)) and in the output from the complete model (Figure 5.3).

The hidden layer units are often called 'feature detectors' insofar as they decompose the data patterns into simpler features. This is quite a helpful idea for understanding simple networks such as the one above. However, for more complicated networks the precise role of particular hidden units is usually very difficult to disentangle from the other units in the network.

This internal complexity gives rise to a common criticism of neural networks, namely that it is difficult for the user to understand how the neural network model arrives at a particular output from a given set of inputs. No explicit set of rules is generated which the user can interpret to see how the model represents relationships in the data. If the user does not understand the 'reasoning' that is going on inside the network, so the argument goes, he or she may have less confidence in its predictive capabilities.

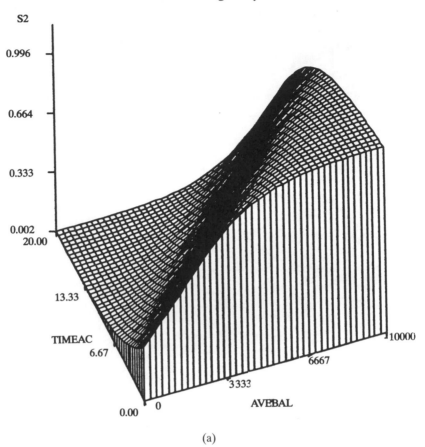

(a)

Figure 5.8 Neural network model: (a) output of hidden unit 2, (b) output of hidden unit 3 and (c) combined outputs of units 2 and 3

This is a serious criticism, which can be countered to some extent by the following arguments:

- Neural network models must be rigorously validated against test data; success in these tests will help convince the user of the usefulness of the model, even if its internal workings are obscure.

- Techniques exist to 'visualize' the data relationships captured by a neural network (Furness, 1992a) rather as we did with Figures 5.3 and 5.8. This may help the user to gain some insights into what is going on in the black box even though this falls short of delivering a complete understanding.

- The same criticism can be levelled at many other empirical modelling techniques used in data-driven marketing, including regression analysis.

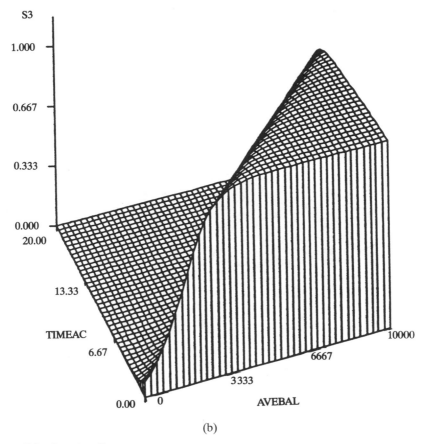

(b)

Figure 5.8 (*continued*)

- In some cases the underlying relationships may be too complex to model in an explicit manner. No amount of rule induction or reductionist analysis will reveal an 'understandable' set of linkages between the outputs being modelled and the inputs.

4 TYPES OF NEURAL NETWORK

There is a bewildering variety of neural networks. Different application areas often create their own specialized types of network, characterized by different network connection structures, the types of 'squashing function' used and the training algorithms (Dayhoff, 1990).

In this chapter we shall look only at so-called 'supervised networks'; that is, where there is a training set for which target output values are known in advance

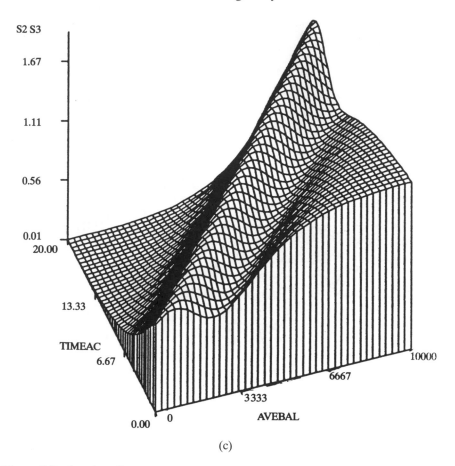

(c)

Figure 5.8 (*continued*)

(the response/no-response of our example) and where the 'supervisor' can apply corrections to the network so that the average error between target and actual output reduces.

There is another class, the 'unsupervised' networks, which function without the need for known target outputs. In effect, they find patterns in the data, rather than being trained to recognize known patterns. They fulfil a role similar to that of cluster analysis. Their use in data-driven marketing is still at an early stage (Openshaw & Wymer, 1990; Gregory & Nellis, 1994) and so we shall not consider them here.

So far we have looked at a simple network with two inputs and one output. Networks can be built with any number of inputs and outputs. For these more general input/output problems there have been some important theoretical developments in recent years (Rumelhart & McClelland, 1986; Funahashi, 1989) which demonstrate the power of MLP networks. These show, for example, that any continuous function from an n-dimensional space to an m-dimensional space can be modelled (to any specified accuracy) by a three-layer MLP, providing one has enough hidden units and sufficient data.

Another important class is the Radial Basis Function (RBF) networks (Broomhead & Lowe, 1988). In their simplest form these are three-layer networks with linear input and output layers. The only adjustable weights are between the hidden and output layer and this reduces the network training to a linear optimization process, with ensuing benefits in terms of speed of training. The middle-layer units are determined by a sample of input data points and each unit defines a 'radial' function (typically a Gaussian or Thin Plate Spline) around one of the data points.

Some applications may benefit from hybrid networks which combine different types of network together in a single model. In data-driven marketing, for example, it may sometimes be advantageous to use an unsupervised network to help reduce the number of input variables before applying an MLP model to produce a prospect score.

Also, separate networks can be built to solve different parts of a problem; these network submodels can then be combined to create a complete solution.

In our illustrative example, we could have combined our response scoring model with a separate model to predict the investment value taken on for each respondent. The combined model could then be used to target savers who are most likely to invest large amounts.

5 OVERLAP WITH OTHER STATISTICAL METHODS

There is a great deal of overlap between neural networks and conventional statistical methods. This is an area in which a great deal of research is currently taking place (White, 1989; Ripley, 1993, 1994).

Three of the most popular techniques used in data-driven marketing are linear regression, logistic regression and CHAID (David Shepard Associates, 1990; Kass, 1980). It turns out that linear regression and logistic regression can both be formulated as very simple types of neural network (Ryman-Tubb, 1993).

In particular, any linear regression model can be specified as a two-layer network with a single output unit and where all units are linear; logistic regression can be specified as an MLP with three layers and one unit in the hidden layer. Neural networks with more than one hidden unit thus offer greater generality than either linear or logistic regression. It is also the case that neural networks do not depend on assumptions about the independence and distribution of residuals or the collinearity of input variables. Such assumptions are usually required with conventional regression methods.

CHAID (Kass, 1980) is a decision tree induction method for modelling the interactions between categorical variables and is often used to break a problem down and remove troublesome interactions before applying linear or logistic regression. Neural networks offer two advantages over CHAID:

- They can handle continuous variables directly (there is no need to band a continuous variable in order to make it categorical, and lose valuable information in the process).
- Since networks are modelling the underlying relationships in the data (Funahashi, 1989) they will automatically model the non-linearities which give rise to interaction effects, thereby removing the need for a separate 'interaction detection' exercise.

Thus, neural networks can reduce the amount of effort required to build models as well as offering greater discriminatory power in many cases.

We can illustrate this point by reference back to our example. Figure 5.9 shows the result of banding the variables AVEBAL and TIMEAC into 10 bands and applying CHAID to the problem; presenting the result as a gains chart. The discrimination of the neural network model can be seen to be significantly better than the CHAID model.

Some academic studies have been undertaken to compare the performance of neural networks with more conventional methods, albeit in non-marketing domains. For example, a comparison has been done against linear discriminant analysis and decision tree induction using data from a variety of business and medical sources as well as artificially constructed datasets (Curran & Mingers, 1994). It was found that neural networks consistently outperformed the other methods when there was a significant amount of non-linearity present in the data.

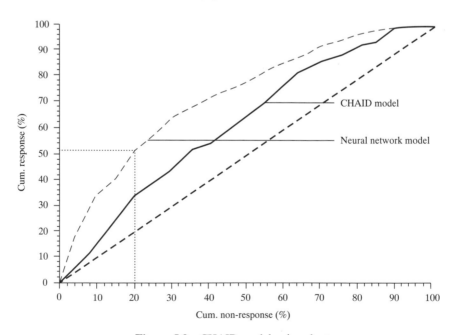

Figure 5.9 CHAID model gains chart

Notwithstanding the above remarks, neural networks should not be seen as substitutes for conventional statistics; rather, they are complementary. Methods such as principal components analysis (Mardia, Kent & Bibby, 1989) (which is used to reduce the number of variables needed to describe the data) have a vital role to play in transforming data prior to input to a neural network. Some practitioners are finding that decision tree induction methods such as CHAID can be used to preprocess categorical variables to create an input coding for a neural network. Combining techniques in this way sometimes seems to yield better results than using neural networks in isolation (Murray, 1993). On the other hand, neural networks can augment the power of linear regression models by 'removing the non-linearity' in a problem. The network outputs are used as the inputs to a conventional regression model, with the latter being used to analyze residual errors.

6 COMMON PITFALLS

As with more conventional modelling techniques, neural networks carry all the attendant risks associated with poor model specification and data preparation. As these are shared by all the analytical techniques used in data-driven marketing we will not go into them here. Worthy of comment, however, are two serious traps which can be encountered with any empirical method including neural networks.

The first is 'overfitting'. Neural networks can have a large number of 'degrees of freedom'. Each adjustable connection weight represents a degree of freedom and in our illustrative example there were seventeen such weights (twelve between the input and hidden layer and five between the hidden and output layer — see Figure 5.5). In networks in which there are tens or hundreds of inputs, and perhaps tens of hidden units, the number of degrees of freedom will run into thousands. This great 'flexibility' of neural networks is a major strength, but if the number of cases available for training is too small then the large number of degrees of freedom can quickly lead to problems.

In simple terms, if there is insufficient data, the network can 'learn' the training data but have no power of generalization, giving poor results when run against the test set. Effectively the network becomes a look-up table. Figure 5.10 shows such a situation. The ten data points sampled from the straight line have been used to train a network with twenty hidden units. The network model (curved line) goes through all the data points and is thus a perfect fit with the training set. Unfortunately, when presented with new input values it will almost always give a very inaccurate answer.

There are some rules of thumb for deciding how much data is needed to train a neural network and quite a lot of progress on the theoretical front (Shawe-Taylor & Anthony, 1991). As an absolute minimum it is advisable to have as the number of cases in the training set at least ten times the number of weights in the network; and a corresponding number in the test set. Some commercial neural network software

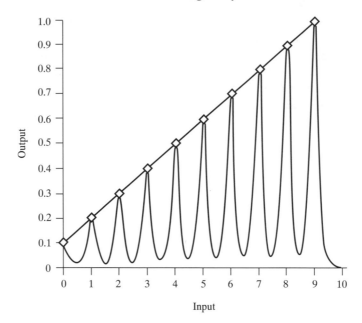

Figure 5.10 Overfitted neural network

has features to prevent overfitting by constantly 'cross-validating' the network against a reserved set of test data as it is trained, to detect when overfitting occurs.

If there appears to be insufficient data to train a network it may be worth while to try to reduce the size of the network by, for example, reducing the number of input variables. Conventional methods such as principal components analysis can help here and some neural network software has this type of functionality built in.

The second major potential pitfall is 'overextrapolation'. Put simply, this is trying to use a neural network on data outside the domain on which the network has been trained; i.e. on data which is very different from that in the training set. The more degrees of freedom in the network, the greater the potential for problems. Provided the user is careful to restrict the neural network application to a domain which falls within, or close to, the training domain then the problem will not arise.

This pitfall is most commonly encountered when 'time' plays a role in the problem and users have been careless about building time into the model; perhaps by training and testing the network using historical data from the same time period and neglecting to have any explicit time dependent factors in their model. Then they attempt to use the model for forecasting ahead. As time moves on, so will the data domain and consequently the forecasts may be poor. Special care is needed in data-driven marketing when extrapolating from a test to a roll-out campaign. Often, as in the illustrative example, one implicitly assumes that factors affecting response do not vary much over time (Furness, 1994b).

7 USING NEURAL NETWORKS

Neural networks will almost certainly be worth using if the following conditions apply:

- Variables in the problem interact strongly, or the problem exhibits other forms of non-linearity.
- There are sufficiently large volumes of data with which to train and test a model.

The former will imply that conventional statistical methods may be inappropriate or cumbersome to use. The latter relates to the problem of overfitting discussed earlier.

Other factors which would point toward a neural network solution include:

- The presence of 'missing values' (networks can be adapted relatively easily to cope with missing values or other data quality problems)
- The model has to be implemented in an application where computational efficiency and ease of maintenance are important (updating a neural network just involves some extra training).

There is some excellent neural network software on the market with which to build and implement neural network solutions (Gregory, 1990). However, as with any sophisticated methodology, the potential user would be well advised to get some expert advice before tackling a problem of any substantial size.

As we have already seen, neural networks can be viewed as black boxes which are trained to convert a set of inputs into a set of outputs. As such, they can obviously be used in applications where one is attempting to model one set of variables from another set.

Although apparently built from a number of separate processing units, neural networks can be simulated on a conventional serial computer. Software can be purchased for a variety of common computing platforms from powerful PCs (with 386 or 486 processors) to Unix workstations and mainframes. Often the neural network software will need to be used in conjunction with a more conventional statistical package to handle basic data manipulation, transformation of inputs, analysis of residuals and presentation graphics.

A review of available software is not possible here but the following is a list of important features which should be considered when choosing software for use in data-driven marketing:

- Data input and output compatibility with other software which the analyst may use (statistical packages, spreadsheets, GIS, etc.)
- The ability to apply a variety of transformations to input variables and to handle the problems associated with missing values and other data quality problems
- Cross-validation during training (to prevent overfitting)

- Training speed (there can be enormous differences in speed between software packages because of the different training algorithms used)
- Variety of neural network types available (MLP and RBF networks are the most powerful for data-driven marketing, and 'unsupervised' models such as Kohonen networks for mapping data patterns may increase in importance)
- The ability to create composite models by bolting together separate neural network models and conventional statistical models (this is especially important when there are very large numbers of input variables and it becomes necessary to build separate models for groups of inputs, perhaps combining this with principal components analysis to reduce the number of variables)
- An export facility to take a trained network and produce program code which can be used to implement the neural network model on the marketing database.

8   FUTURE DIRECTIONS

Looking to the future, the inherent 'parallelism' of neural networks, where a number of simple processing units are functioning 'in parallel', will enable software vendors to take advantage of parallel computer architectures as these become more widely available. Specialized parallel 'neural chips', such as the Ni1000 from Intel, are coming onto the market and these will make it possible to build even more powerful models.

The amount of data available to marketers is growing rapidly as operational systems widen in scope and sophistication, making it possible to track the purchasing behaviour of customers in ever-increasing detail. A good example is in retailing where loyalty cards linked to EPOS systems make it possible to record complete details of all transactions made by customers. Market analysts will demand integrated analysis capabilities which allow neural networks and other new techniques as well as conventional statistical methods to be used singly or in combination to suit the particular characteristics of the data being used in each application.

9   CONCLUSION

Neural networks have an important role to play in data-driven marketing. An illustrative example has been used to show that the application of the technique is conceptually very simple; one trains a black box to predict one or more output variables from a set of input variables.

There is an overlap with conventional statistical methods such as regression and CHAID, but, in situations where there are large quantities of data available for network training, neural networks often appear to be more powerful for model building. Furthermore, commercial software is readily available which the market analyst can use for building and implementing neural network models on marketing databases.

The range of applications and potential applications of neural networks in data-driven marketing is considerable with areas such as behavioural modelling, database enhancement and data visualization well established.

ACKNOWLEDGEMENTS

This chapter is based on two papers by the author:

- Furness, P. (1992c) 'Applying neural networks in database marketing — an overview', *Journal of Targeting, Measurement and Analysis For Marketing*, **1**, No. 2, 152-69.
- Furness, P. (1994) 'New pattern analysis methods for database marketing' (Parts 1 and 2), *The Journal of Database Marketing*, **1**, No. 3, 220-32; **1**, No. 4, 297-306.

and is reproduced by permission of Henry Stewart Publications, London, UK.

REFERENCES

Bounds, D. et al. (1988) 'An MLP network for the diagnosis of low back pain', *Proc. IEEE Second Int. Conference on Neural Networks*, San Diego, **2**, 481-8.

Brodlie, K.W. et al. (eds) (1992) *Scientific Visualisation*, Springer-Verlag, New York.

Broomhead, D.S. & Lowe, D. (1988) 'Multivariable functional interpolation and adaptive networks', *Complex Systems*, **2**, 321-55.

Coyne, A. (1993) 'The application of a neural network as a tool to drive targeted cross-selling activities in financial services', *Journal of Targeting, Measurement and Analysis For Marketing*, **2**, No. 1, 9-22.

Curran, S.P. & Mingers, J. (1994) 'Neural networks, decision tree induction and discriminant analysis: an empirical comparison', *J. Opl. Res. Soc.*, **45**, No. 4, 440-50.

David Shepard Associates (1990) *The New Direct Marketing*, Business One Irwin, Homewood, IL (available in the UK from Raymead Consulting).

Dayhoff, J. (1990) *'Neural Network Architectures — An Introduction'*, Van Nostrand Reinhold, New York.

Funahashi, K. (1989) 'On the approximate realisation of continuous mappings by neural networks', *Neural Networks*, **2**, 183-92.

Furness, P. (1992a) 'Data visualisation in marketing', Data Mining in Finance and Marketing Conference, IBC Technical Services Ltd.

Furness, P. (1992b) 'Neural network applications in marketing', TIMS Marketing Science Conference.

Furness, P. (1992c) 'Applying neural networks in database marketing — an overview', *Journal of Targeting, Measurement and Analysis For Marketing*, **1**, No. 2, 152-69.

Furness, P. (1994a) 'New pattern analysis methods for database marketing', *The Journal of Database Marketing*, **1**, No. 3, 220-32; **1**, No. 4, 297-313.

Furness, P. (1994b) 'Predicting the effects of marketing — the importance of market dynamics', Advances in Targeting, Measurement and Analysis for Marketing Conference, Henry Stewart Conference Studies.

Furness, P. & Gregory, P. (1993) 'Neural computing — will it revolutionise database marketing'. The Market Research Society Annual Conference.

Gregory, P. (1990) 'Neural networks: developing an effective strategy', Conference — Neural Networks '90, Blenheim Online.

Gregory, P. (1993) 'The role of neural networks in database marketing', *J. Database Marketing*, **1**, No. 1, 11-23.

Gregory, P. & Nellis, J. (1994) 'The use of supervised neural networks for customer response analysis and data imputation', Advances in Targeting, Measurement and Analysis for Marketing Conference, Henry Stewart Conference Studies.

Hart, A. (1992) 'Using neural networks for classification tasks — some experiments on datasets and practical advice', *J. Opl. Res. Soc.*, **43**, No. 3, 215-26.

Hoptroff, R.G. (1993) 'The principles and practice of time series forecasting and business modelling using neural nets', *Neural Comput & Applic.*, **1**, 59-66, Springer-Verlag London Limited.

Hruschka H. & Natter, M. (1992) 'Using neural networks for clustering based market segmentation', Research Memorandum No. 307, Institute for Advanced Studies, Vienna.

Kass, G.V. (1980) 'An exploratory technique for investigating large quantities of categorical data', *Appl. Statistics*, **29**, No. 2, 119-27.

Mardia, K.V., Kent, J.T. & Bibby, J.M. (1989) *Multivariate Analysis*, Academic Press, New York.

Murray, J. (1993) 'Experiences of using neural networks in practice', *Journal of Targeting, Measurement and Analysis for Marketing*, **2**, No. 1, 23-9.

Openshaw, S. (1992a) 'A review of the opportunities and problems in applying neuro-computing methods to marketing applications', *Journal of Targeting, Measurement and Analysis For Marketing*, **1**, No. 2, 170-86.

Openshaw, S. (1992b) 'Some suggestions concerning the development of AI tools for spatial modelling and analysis in GIS', *Annals of Regional Science*, **26**, 35-51.

Openshaw, S. & Wymer, C. (1990) 'A neural net classifier for handling census data', in Murtagh F. (ed.), *Neural Networks for Statistical and Economic Data*, Munotec Systems, Dublin.

Refenes, A.N., Azema-Barac, M., Chen, L. & Karoussos, S.A. (1993) 'Currency exchange rate prediction and neural network design strategies', *Neural Comput & Applic.*, **1**, 46-58, Springer-Verlag London Limited.

Ripley, B.D. (1993) 'Statistical aspects of neural networks', SemStat (Denmark, April 1992) Proceedings, Chapman & Hall, London.

Ripley, B.D. (1994) 'Neural networks and related methods for classification', *J. R. Statist. Soc. B*, **56**, No. 3, 409-56.

Rumelhart, D.E. & McClelland, J.L. (1986) *Parallel Distributed Processing*, MIT Press, Cambridge, MA.

Ryman-Tubb, N. (1993) 'The use of neural networks to identify the characteristics of holiday-makers', *The Journal of Database Marketing*, **1**, No. 2, 140-49.

Shawe-Taylor, J. & Anthony, M. (1991) 'Sample sizes for multiple-output threshold networks', *Network*, **2**, 107-17.

Sleight, P. (1993) *Targeting Customers; How to Use Geodemographic and Lifestyle Data in Your Business*, NTC Publications Ltd.

Wasserman, P.D. (1989) *Neural Computing — Theory and Practice*, Van Nostrand Reinhold, New York.

White, H. (1989) 'Learning in artificial neural networks: a statistical perspective', *Neural Computation*, **1**, 425-64.

6
Intelligent Systems for Market Segmentation and Local Market Planning

RICHARD WEBBER

Market segmentation is becoming recognized by an increasing number of organizations as a key strategy for achieving long-term corporate success. This trend, evident throughout the advanced industrial world, involves the definition of discrete subpopulations within the consuming public for whom specialized variants of mass products need to be developed on account of their differences in personal circumstances, values and lifestyles.

In the early post-war years, economies of scale enabled manufacturers to prosper by bringing new products within the reach of mass markets, promoting them to an undifferentiated mass audience using mass communication channels such as television and national press. Today's marketers, in contrast, operate in an environment in which the overriding commercial imperative is the development of unique product features which will build brand identities and maintain operating margins by increasing their appeal to specialist markets.

The shift away from mass to micro marketing is fuelled by four social and technological trends. Perhaps the most important of these is the growing automation of the production process. Whereas volume producers in the early post-war period were typically constrained by the inflexibility of assembly-line operations and their time-consuming logistic planning, automated production planning systems offer opportunities for the customization of the base product without the loss of the

Intelligent Systems for Finance and Business. Edited by S. Goonatilake and P. Treleaven
© 1995 John Wiley & Sons Ltd

economies of scale inherent in volume production. This greater versatility from computerization affords benefits not only to manufacturers but also to retailers and financial service organizations.

A second trend is the increasingly atomized nature of modern society. In earlier generations, when leisure activities were undertaken in a social setting, when communities exerted greater control over the behaviour of their members, when people used buses rather than cars and worked in recognizable occupations, consumer behaviour was largely driven by class membership and occupational status. Today, with family, class and community exerting less influence on a person's identity, consumer choice becomes a far more powerful means of defining and expressing one's personal values.

Where once branded products would sell because of their ability to provide basic needs at an affordable price, now it is necessary that they offer lifestyle and image connotations and embody the values cultivated by the target audience for which they have been developed.

The fragmentation of media is a third key factor contributing towards market segmentation. As existing media channels proliferate and new ones, such as cable and satellite TV, emerge, once-dominant channels increasingly fail to deliver the mass audiences required by mass marketing. It becomes increasingly cost effective to limit media advertising to minority channels that are more cost efficient in reaching the target audience for the product.

The fourth contributing trend to micromarketing is the growing capacity, speed and ease of access of modern computers. Now it is practical to capture, store, retrieve and analyse data on the behaviour of millions of customers. Using statistical analysis software that non-technical people themselves can operate, marketers can for the first time directly explore the patterns of demand within their markets. Strategies for pattern recognition, segmentation and optimization are clearly necessary if the full benefit of this opportunity is to be realized.

Until 1980, the principal means by which consumer markets were segmented in the UK were through the use of age, family status and occupational grade (A, B, C1, C2, D, E). The information used to profile consumer markets was collected in the form of market research surveys. In some instances these would take the form of quantitative research commissioned by a single sponsor. In others the data would be collected through syndicated research studies such as the Target Group Index or surveys commissioned by joint industry committees of media owners such as the National Readership Survey or the Broadcast Advertising Research Board.

Although these databases provided advertisers with useful insight into the profile of their products' users, and, in particular, could be used to identify the national media that they were most likely to read or watch, these surveys were less effective when it came to micromarketing. For example, they were unable to help qualify which names and addresses on a mailing list would most likely belong to a desired target audience, they were unable to help with the selection of door-to-door distribution areas for selective leafleting, they could not reveal the quality of local newspaper circulation areas or help retailers select the shopping centres which attract the highest proportions of specific target audiences. They could not help with the analysis or segmentation of existing customer files. All these limitations were a consequence of the restricted sample size of national surveys. At levels of geography below the TV region, most national surveys cease to remain statistically reliable.

A further limitation of traditional market research surveys, it was felt at that time, lay in the weakness of occupation as an effective measure of status. With the decline of class behaviour, the growth of multi-earner households, the appearance of affluent manual workers and the growing number of pensioners on occupational benefits, the conventional AB, C1, C2, D and E classification was increasingly felt to be inadequate as a basis for market segmentation. The need had come for a more flexible classification system which could offer a common basis for segmentation across all the different aspects of segmentation and targeting.

Cluster analysis has proved to be both an effective and an enduring solution to this requirement. In all the major European countries, in the USA, Canada and Australia, cluster-based classifications of residential neighbourhoods are now regularly used by marketers across most market sectors as a basis for market segmentation. Table 6.1 lists the principal suppliers of these services, gives the names of the geodemographic systems that they operate and provides an approximate estimate of their turnover. In addition to these separate national systems, EuroMOSAIC offers users access to a single consistent neighbourhood classification system covering most of the major European markets.

Using units of geography ranging from 17 households on average (in Britain) to 2500 (in Sweden), these neighbourhood classifications, or geodemographic systems as they are popularly referred to, typically classify each national market into between 30 and 60 discrete types of residential neighbourhood on the basis of fine area statistics derived from a variety of sources. Table 6.2 uses the GB MOSAIC classification to illustrate the types of neighbourhood that are typically created in such an exercise.

Using a correspondence table that links consumer addresses to the units of geography used to build the classifications it becomes possible to add the resulting classification codes to a number of different sorts of file. For example, by adding classification codes to market research surveys it is instantly possible to evaluate the clusters most likely to purchase, read or use any of the many thousands of products covered by the surveys. Likewise, appended to the customer databases that companies use to drive their customer communications, the cluster codes are used to identify the neighbourhood types which feature disproportionately among the customer database and to show the differences that exist between purchasers of different products or between heavy and irregular users of each product.

Having established the neighbourhood segments which generate highest sales, response or profits, whether using market research surveys or customer addresses, organizations can then apply the cluster typology to the targeting of advertising and

Table 6.1 Major geodemographic segmentation systems

	Vendor	Turnover band[a]	Data sources
Belgium			
MOSAIC	Sopres	1	Various
Canada			
Cluster	Compusearch	3	Census
Finland			
Acorn	Gallup/Post Office	1	Census
France			
Ilot-type	Coref	3	Census
Germany			
Regio	Bertlesmann	1	Customer files
MOSAIC	CCN	1	Street surveys
Pan Address	Pan Address	1	Customer files, Models
Ireland			
MOSAIC	CCN	1	Census
Italy			
Cluster	Sarin	3	Census
Netherlands			
MOSAIC	CCN	2	PTT, CARS, Surveys, children and mail order
GEO	Geomarktprofiel	2	Various
Spain			
Regio	Bertlesmann	1	Various
MOSAIC	CCN/PDM	1	Various
Sweden			
MOSAIC	MarknadsAnalys	1	Personal registers
UK			
MOSAIC	CCN	3	Census and others
Acorn	CACI	3	Census
Super-profiles	CDMS	1	Census
Define	Infolink	1	Census and others
Neighbours & Prospects	EuroDirect	1	Census
USA			
Prizm	Claritas	3	Census
Microvision	Equifax	3	Census
Acorn	CACI	1	Census

a. Turnover band
   1 < £1 million p.a.
   2 £1 million–£5 million p.a.
   3 > £5 million p.a.

Table 6.2

Group	Type	Descriptor	%
L1 High Income Families (9.9%)	M1	Clever Capitalists	1.5
	M2	Rising Materialists	1.5
	M3	Corporate Careerists	2.4
	M4	Ageing Professionals	1.7
	M5	Small Time Business	2.7
L2 Suburban Semis (11.0%)	M6	Green Belt Expansion	3.4
	M7	Suburban Mock Tudor	3.2
	M8	Pebble Dash Subtopia	4.4
L3 Blue Collar Owners (13.0%)	M9	Affluent Blue Collar	2.9
	M10	30s Industrial Spec	3.8
	M11	Lo-Rise Right to Buy	3.3
	M12	Smokestack Shiftwork	3.1
L4 Low Rise Council (14.4%)	M13	Coop Club & Colliery	3.4
	M14	Better Off Council	2.1
	M15	Low Rise Pensioners	3.2
	M16	Low Rise Subsistence	3.5
	M17	Problem Families	2.2
L5 Council Flats (6.8%)	M18	Families In The Sky	1.3
	M19	Graffitied Ghettos	0.3
	M20	Small Town Industry	1.4
	M21	Mid Rise Overspill	0.7
	M22	Flats For The Aged	1.4
	M23	Inner City Towers	1.8
L6 Victorian Low Status (9.4%)	M24	Bohemian Melting Pot	2.3
	M25	Victorian Tenements	0.1
	M26	Rootless Renters	1.5
	M27	Sweatshop Sharers	1.1
	M28	Depopulated Terraces	0.8
	M29	Rejuvenated Terraces	3.5
L7 Town Houses and Flats (9.4%)	M30	Bijou Homemakers	3.5
	M31	Market Town Mixture	3.8
	M32	Town Centre Singles	2.1
L8 Stylish Singles (5.2%)	M33	Bedsits & Shop Flats	1.2
	M34	Studio Singles	1.7
	M35	College & Communal	0.5
	M36	Chattering Classes	1.9
L9 Independent Elders (7.4%)	M37	Solo Pensioners	1.9
	M38	High Spending Greys	1.3
	M39	Aged Owner-Occupiers	2.7
	M40	Elderly in Own Flats	1.5
L10 Mortgaged Families (6.2%)	M41	Brand New Areas	1.0
	M42	Pre Nuptial Owners	0.8
	M43	Nestmaking Families	1.7
	M44	Maturing Mortgagees	2.7

(*continued overleaf*)

Table 6.2 (*continued*)

Group	Type	Descriptor	%
L11 Country Dwellers	M45	Gentrified Villages	1.5
(7.0%)	M46	Rural Retirement Mix	0.6
	M47	Lowland Agribusiness	1.8
	M48	Rural Disadvantage	1.2
	M49	Tied/Tenant Farmers	0.6
	M50	Upland & Small Farms	1.3
L12 Institutional Areas	M51	Military Bases	0.3
(0.3%)	M52	Non-Private Housing	0.1

promotional activities. Cluster profiles are used to evaluate advertising opportunities across many different media — TV stations, regional and local press circulation areas, radio coverage areas, poster sites, door-to-door distribution sectors — and individual clusters can be used to select the names and addresses that should be selected for direct communications whether via the phone, the mail or cable. Each of these media offer their own unique 'profile', this term being used to describe the respects in which the mix of cluster types they reach differs from the national average (see Table 6.2). Clearly these profiles can be compared for goodness of fit with the corresponding profile created from the analysis of customer address files or market research surveys. Similarly, profiles are used by marketers to qualify the character of any local area, thereby enabling marketers to determine whether the level of demand is sufficient to support a local outlet of a given size or to establish which retail concept or product mix is most likely to meet the specific requirements of the local population.

The assumptions underlying this approach to modelling are that if a set of areas are broadly similar across a wide range of demographic indicators then they are also likely to share similarities in terms of disposable income, consumer preferences, media usage and social values. For this reason, each of the national classification systems is built using a wide variety of variables collectively covering as many different topics as possible. The cluster programs attempt to create an optimal set of clusters using an iterative relocation algorithm and 'minimum sum of squares' as a method of measuring similarities across the input variables. In some systems principal component analysis has been used to identify and then represent the dominant dimensions of demographic differentiation within that market. Other systems, including all the MOSAIC classifications, use a minimum spanning tree algorithm (or single linkage analysis) (Hartigan, 1975) to identify occasions where candidate input variables display excessive levels of auto-correlation.

The levels of geography at which these various sources of information are available will usually vary within as well as between countries. For example, in the United Kingdom data from sources such as the electoral register, the Postal Address File and from credit databases can be accessed at full postcode level whereas data relating to age, car ownership and house tenure is available at the level of the census enumeration district. In such circumstances it makes sense to classify the finest level of geography — in this case the postcode — but to assign to each postcode census statistics pertaining to the census enumeration district into which the postcode falls.

However, there are often variables which, as a result of their thin or uneven distribution, or by virtue of the small size of the geographical units being clustered, are of uneven statistical reliability at the finest level of detail for which they can be calculated. In such situations it has often proved effective to combine the values for these variables at both the finest level of detail at which they can be calculated and the higher-level zones within which these areas fall. Using the Shaw Test (Evans & Webber, 1994), the values can be combined in proportions that intelligently change according to the populations of the finest area level, the population of the high-level zone in which it falls and the national penetration of that particular variable. In this way the value of each data item is calculated at the level at which its reliability can be statistically validated.

Whichever technical method is used, it is important that the different demographic dimensions are appropriately represented and balanced among the input variables. As a general rule, there are three domains, each of which need to be represented by the input variables if the classification is to operate effectively across all markets: these are age and household characteristics, housing and measures of income, status and employment.

Age and household composition are fundamental drivers of market segmentation in most consumer markets. In addition to these basic variables it is also helpful to have access to data on the ethnic origin of the local population, the level of residential mobility and the proportions of households of various sizes.

Housing variables that add predictiveness to the results include measures of house type (detached, semis, terraces, flats), the size of the housing and the level of overcrowding, the levels of different forms of house tenure (owned, rented) and the availability of amenities such as central heating.

Status measures often are related to employment–unemployment, distribution of workers by occupational status and by the type of industry in which they work. Car ownership is a commonly available and effective surrogate for household income, a variable which is seldom otherwise available at a local level. Other useful indicators of disposable income are the level of educational qualifications and the proportion of women who are economically active.

Once an appropriate selection has been made from these variables and principal components or individual weightings have been decided for each of them, it is necessary to decide the number of clusters that should be contained by the classification system. In making this decision it is necessary to strike a fine balance between the need for a fine level of discrimination and the need to be able to recognize intuitively the key distinguishing feature of each cluster. The number of clusters must not be so small that they become too heterogeneous, nor so large that the differences between them are not recognizable to the average user.

The most commonly used methodology for building geodemographic classifications is a form of cluster analysis known as iterative relocation. This operates according to the following sequence. The first step involves the calculation of means and standard deviations for all the input variables and the representation of the input database in the form of standard deviations from the national average in place of raw percentage scores. Given the uneven population size of geographic units and the tendency for size to be correlated with input variables, all computations, including the calculation of means and standard deviations, are weighted by the population or number households in the input areas.

On the basis of the number of clusters specified for analysis, a sample of input areas is selected on a population-weighted basis to act as seeds for the formation of the clusters. The algorithm then measures the similarity of each input area to each seed and assigns the input area to the cluster code of the seed to which its similarity is greatest. Similarity is measured in terms of the squares of the differences in the standard deviation of the input area and the seed, summed across all input variables and, where appropriate, weighted by the weight assigned to each input variable. The assignment is based on the seed for which this weighted sum of squares has the lowest value.

At the end of this process, the algorithm computes, for each of the seed clusters, a vector containing the average score of each of the input zones assigned to that cluster on each of the input variables. This set of vector scores typically will be fairly close to the original vector of scores for the seed input area around which the cluster was formed.

Second and subsequent passes of the file are made to establish whether, as a result of the recalculation of the vector averages for each cluster, any individual input zone now finds itself closer in terms of similarity to a cluster different from the one to which it was originally assigned. Such reallocations themselves cause further changes to the vector averages so that it may be necessary to conduct as many as a dozen further iterations before the solution stabilizes itself at an optimum solution. Clearly, the more representative the input seeds reflect the variations in the input database, the fewer the iterations needed to reach an optimal solution.

Once the iterative relocation process is complete, the system adopts a second clustering algorithm, known as stepwise fusion, to arrange the n clusters into higher-order groupings. This process searches for the pair of clusters which can be fused for the least incremental loss of variance across the input variables. This loss of variance takes into account both the similarities of the fused clusters, measured in terms of minimum sum of squares, and the population sizes of each cluster. Thus the first clusters to be merged tend to be those which are both small in size and similar in character.

This fusion process is repeated for $n - 1$ steps until the entire universe has been recreated. On the basis of the fusion process the original clusters are intelligently renumbered so that similar clusters and similar cluster groups are denoted by consecutive codes. On the basis of the dendogram, the diagrammatic representation of the fusion process, the system will typically create a second higher-order grouping system, based on the number of higher-order groups required by the user. Each of these higher-order clusters will thereby consist of a consecutive set of the original clusters.

Some neighbourhood classifications are left to optimize themselves without user interference. This optimization represents the most efficient solution that an algorithm can find in terms of minimizing within-cluster heterogeneity and maximizing between-cluster variance. However, it is not uncommon for manual intervention to improve the value and power of the final solution since, as a result of random seeding of the cluster centroids, it is often possible to recognize that the algorithm has delivered a local rather than a global optimum.

Another common consequence of solutions wholly reliant on automatic optimization is that one or more clusters are exceptionally small. This may be as a result of input data being of uneven quality or statistical reliability. However, there will always be instances where very small categories represent genuinely distinct types of neighbourhood. As a rule, it is often more practical to merge these with other clusters and allow the cluster program to re-optimize. If this is not done, users soon encounter difficulties in generating adequate samples of survey respondents or of customer records in order to establish a statistically reliable measurement of their potential. Intervention may also be required where one category includes too large a share of a market's population, even if it displays a higher than average level of internal homogeneity.

In some solutions it has been recognized that it is inappropriate for the same balance of weights to be given to the input variables in every type of neighbourhood. In the UK version of MOSAIC, for example, the rural clusters created by the original classification were removed and subjected to a secondary clustering exercise in which the influence of specifically rural indicators was deliberately down-weighted. Whereas in the previous solution the rural types could be distinguished only on the basis of their relative rurality, the new solution created a set of clusters much more distinguishable from each other in terms of high/low status and owner farmer/tenant/prairie agribusiness.

Building an effective classification involves three resources, a plentiful array of statistically reliable data at a fine level of geographic detail, a sound understanding of cluster methodologies and the judgement that comes from the experience in knowing where and how best to intervene manually in the solution generated by the computer. If effectiveness of a geodemographic classification as a discriminator depends on these resources, its use within an organization depends on how effectively the statistics showing the variance of each cluster from the national average have been used to build meaningful descriptive profiles. Although each system is constructed from a limited and restricted set of data, the statistical profiles and the maps of cluster locations can often reveal the presence of characteristics far beyond those that were included in the original input data. In many respects the input data can usefully be seen as a series of indirect measures of a different type of community which can not themselves be measured by a single characteristic. Good examples of this from the UK MOSAIC are its ability to identify Military Bases (using proportions of young people, low levels of employment in manufacturing and high levels of rented accommodation) and former mining areas (large council houses, low proportions of women at work, few non-manual or professional workers).

For that reason it would be wrong to suppose that geodemographic systems are merely simplifications of the original data, data-reduction exercises that lose acceptable proportions of the predictive power of the input variables. On the contrary, many of the input variables represent populations that have been classed in arbitrary and not entirely appropriate ways. Examples are the pre-classification of stockbrokers and vicars into the same social grade and the lumping together of the city and the military as instances of service employment. A well-designed cluster typology will, in such circumstances, effectively delineate the quite different sorts of areas which score high on the same variable and thereby separate the differently behaving populations assigned to the same categorical class. As a modelling tool the classification systems also have the advantage that they overcome the problem caused by the non-linear relationship between the input variables and the behaviours with which each one is correlated.

The most serious issues surrounding the reliability of cluster-based classification systems for market modelling lie in problems of regionality, whether of the distribution of certain types, of consumer behaviour or of the physical distribution of particular products. A nice illustration of this is the modelling of demand for golf. For various reasons, Scotland is distinctive for its high proportions of middle-income households living in council housing and for its very much smaller size of dwellings as measured by the numbers of rooms they contain. Both MOSAIC and ACORN have, as a consequence, a number of types whose locations are principally north of the border.

Whether on account of their overcrowded accommodation or the plethora of available golf courses, the Scots are disproportionately more likely than the English people to play golf. As a consequence, on a national basis the highest-performing MOSAIC cluster for playing golf is a mid-market Scottish council estate cluster. But within Scotland the penetration of golfers is even higher among Scottish 'Clever Capitalists' while in southern England the penetration of golf players within the predominantly Scottish clusters is very much lower than a simple analysis of the results would indicate. Accurate market modelling in this case needs to incorporate a regional adjustment factor on top of the classifications scores.

Another important issue is whether the patterns that surveys are picking up measure supply or demand. For example, we would be making a big mistake if we used a national survey to examine the profile of Sainsbury's shoppers (a large UK supermarket chain) by MOSAIC and then used this data to model Sainsbury's market share in a local area. On a local level it is accessibility and competition rather than geodemographics that determines grocery retailers' market share. The factor we would have modelled would be the level of demand for Sainsbury's rather than its penetration or market share. However, if Sainsbury's outlets are highly over-represented in a few untypical regions of the country then the profile will be a reflection of the regional distribution of the product and relevant only to the selection of merchandise that should be sold in the stores.

A not dissimilar issue is whether the apparent profile of existing customers of a product is relevant to the effective targeting of new ones. If we consider people who travel abroad on holiday, the profile of last year's travellers is normally a reliable guide to the profile of prospective travellers this year. But if we used the profile of existing holders of a cheque account as the basis for targeting our promotional expenditure, we would be channelling our resources into precisely the least appropriate of areas. In the case of a product which already is close to market saturation and where users remain loyal to existing brands, it is the areas where people do not yet have a cheque account that offer the greatest opportunity.

REFERENCES

Evans, N. & Webber, R. (1994) 'Advances in geodemographic classification techniques for target marketing', *Journal of Targeting, Measurement and Analysis for Marketing*, **2**, 4, February.
Hartigan, J. (1975) *Clustering Algorithms*, John Wiley, New York.

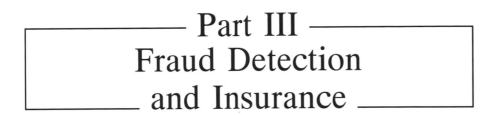

Part III
Fraud Detection
and Insurance

A Fuzzy System for Detecting Anomalous Behaviors in Healthcare Provider Claims

EARL COX

1 FUZZY LOGIC AND THE PROBLEM OF FRAUD AND ABUSE

Estimates of provider fraud — fraud committed by doctors and other care givers — range between 10% and 12% of the $650 billion spent annually on healthcare in the United States. Given the enormous amounts of money involved in the American healthcare industry, the shallowness of regulatory and business oversight, the complexity of today's medical services protocols, and the relative ease with which abusive behaviors can be disguised or buried in the high transaction volumes processed by most insurers, it is easy to understand how abusive and ultimately fraudulent behavior can arise. Fraud detection is further complicated by the dispersal of claims across many insurance companies so that no single insurer has a complete picture of a provider's activities. Conventional analytical approaches to finding fraudulent providers are based on statistical and mathematical models, rule-base expert systems, and, more recently on the use of neural network technologies to 'discover' patterns of abuse in the data. Yet no system today appears to address satisfactorily the enormous complexities of finding partial behavior patterns and correlating these into a cohesive picture of the provider's overall claim profile.

Intelligent Systems for Finance and Business. Edited by S. Goonatilake and P. Treleaven
© 1995 John Wiley & Sons Ltd

1.1 Why Fuzzy Logic?

The use of fuzzy logic or approximate reasoning to address the issues associated with abusive behavior detection is a natural outgrowth of the need to pry more deeply into the nature of the information underlying the detection process. Much of the data as well as the relationships in the real world of managed healthcare are imprecise, that is, they are amenable to multiple interpretations, have varying degrees of ambiguity, and have characteristics that are not easily partitioned into discrete, well-defined categories. Fuzzy systems are designed to address these kinds of problems. In addition, fuzzy models have other properties that significantly facilitate the exploration of complex, poorly understood dynamics found in such areas such as fraud detection, risk assessment, and asset (or resource) allocation. A few of the more important properties include:

- *Fuzzy rules are suggestive, not definitive.* Fuzzy rules accumulate evidence for or against the ultimate value of a solution variable. The degree to which the predicate of a rule is true (or false) indicates the degree to which the solution variable takes the shape of another fuzzy region. Consider a rule such as,

> if NumEveningOffVists are HIGH
> then FraudLikelihood is INCREASED

This rule says 'To the degree that the Number of Evening Office Visits are representative of the concept *HIGH*, make the fuzzy solution region for *Fraud-Likelihood* look more like the shape of the fuzzy set *INCREASED*'. This relationship need not be linear. As an example, Figure 7.1 shows how the metric fuzzy set that represents INCREASED appears.

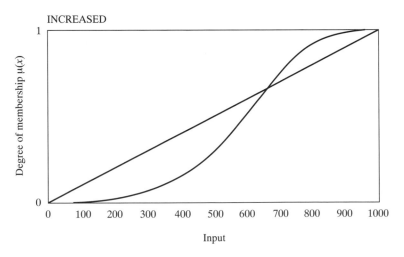

Figure 7.1 The INCREASED anomaly metric fuzzy set

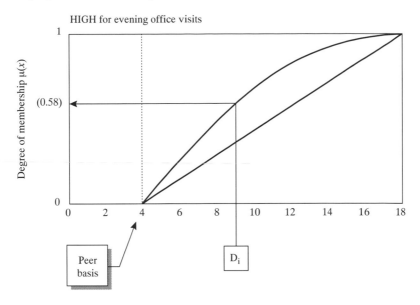

Figure 7.2 A data point in the HIGH Office Visits fuzzy set

The set is scaled across an arbitrary domain measuring the concept of *INCREASED* from zero through 1000. The sigmoid curves models the perceived behavior of how increased should be related to the underlying concept of fraud likelihood. In Figure 7.2 a data point representing a number of Evening Office Visits is mapped against the concept for *HIGH* for this behavior pattern. The concept of *HIGH* is biased from the general peer population value of 4.2. We find that this provider has a moderately elevated membership in the *HIGH* fuzzy set.

This membership value of $\mu[0.58]$ is the compatibility between the data value and the concept associated with the *HIGH* fuzzy set. As Figure 7.3 now shows, we can take this value and use it to correlate the value of *INCREASE* and update the *FraudLikelihood* solution variable.

In an actual model, of course, many rules would fire simultaneously, each adding to the shape of *FraudLikelihood*.[1] In the end, when all the rules have fired, the shape of the *FraudLikelihood* fuzzy set indicates the preponderance of evidence for a value for this solution variable.

- *Fuzzy models can directly represent superpositional states.* A fuzzy set represents the gradual shift in membership or representation from a point that is completely unrepresentative of the set concept to a point that is completely representative of the set concept. Because points in between can have partial degrees of membership, a fuzzy set can overlap other fuzzy sets that have complementary or even contradictory meanings.

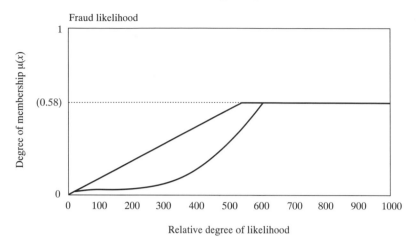

Figure 7.3 Evidence for likelihood of fraud after firing one rule

PATIENT WORKLOAD

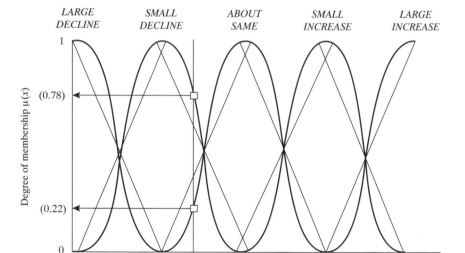

Figure 7.4 Overlapping (superpositional) fuzzy states

Figure 7.4 illustrates this concept. In considering the provider's current change in patient workload, we can decompose this change into several fuzzy regions. These regions overlap since there is no absolute point where, say, a decline in patients is about the same from week to week, and then suddenly represents a consistent small decline. As the number of patients per week decreases, the concept of 'about the same' slowly changes to 'a small decline'. Obviously some patient per week values have some degree of representation in both fuzzy sets. Patients-per-week value P_1 is only marginally representative of the fuzzy set (concept) *ABOUT SAME*, but has a significant representation in the fuzzy concept *SMALL DECLINE*. The model exists in both of these states simultaneously. Which state we wish to examine depends on the current state of the model. This ability to explore multiple interpretations of a variable's value is very powerful, since this is exactly the kind of imprecision and ambiguity that exists in the real world.

- *Fuzzy models can incorporate multiple conflicting experts*. An underlying, if often unstated, assumption of nearly all conventional expert and decision support systems is that a single domain expert exists (or for many experts, that they are, for all practical purposes, in agreement with each other.) With the exception of toy problems, problems appearing in academic journals, and problems that remain forever in the limbo of the 'prototype' (having lost any usefulness for the end user), this is seldom ever the case for real-world systems. In these cases we often find that experts are in serious disagreement about how to interpret important model variables, how to assess the objective or utility function of the model, how to assess the meaning of model transition states, and how to make decisions on sets of input data. Fuzzy models are able to directly incorporate multiple conflicting experts and blend their knowledge into a meaningful system. As a brief example, consider the following four rules from a product pricing model developed in the early 1980s for a leading British retailer,

> our price must be high
> our price must be low
> our price should be around 2*MfgCosts
> if the competition price is not very high
>   then our price
>   should be near the competition price

Notice that these rules directly incorporate contradictory viewpoints from the finance, sales, inventory, and regional marketing managers. Fuzzy systems can tolerate contradictory evidence and conflicting rules. This kind of tolerance provides an important interpretation and evidential reasoning capability in the fraud-detection model.

- *Fuzzy systems are universal approximators*. Important work by Bart Kosko, Fred Watkins, and Jim Buckley on the representational power of fuzzy systems has yielded a surprising array of solid theorems about the mapping capabilities of these systems. In particular, Bart Kosko has shown in his Fuzzy Approximation Theory that a fuzzy system is capable of representing any function. Figure 7.5 illustrates the basic premise of this approach. For any arbitrary function $g = f(X, Y)$ we can partition X and Y into any number of fuzzy sets.[2] We can then

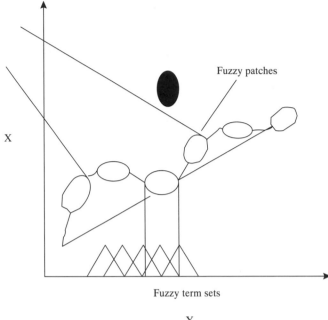

Figure 7.5 Approximating an arbitrary function

describe the system behavior within arbitrarily small regions along the function through rules and the fuzzy sets — creating little fuzzy patches along the curve. The more patches, the closer the approximation becomes to representation. A fuzzy system is a universal approximator. We can approximate any function to any degree of granularity.

- *Fuzzy models reduce cognitive dissonance.* Fuzzy systems are built using the concept of a *linguistic variable*. A linguistic variable is a fuzzy set, but it can also contain qualifiers, called hedges. These hedges change the meaning of a fuzzy set. As an example, the bold terms in the following rules are linguistic variables,

> if margins are **low** then profits are **reduced**
> if margins are **very low** then profits are **positively reduced**
> if margins are **not very low** then profits are **quite high**
> if margins are **generally not very low**
>   then profits are **not usually very reduced**

Along with the fact that a single fuzzy rule can perform the same amount of work as many conventional rules, the modelling of complex problems using fuzzy logic generally means that we can describe the problem space in terms that are very much closer to the way the expert describes the problems. We seldom need to decompose a concept into a set of rules that must deal with the rigid dichotomy of Boolean logic. A fuzzy model is smaller, externally simpler, and closer to the way the expert (or experts) actually think about the problem.

- *Fuzzy systems provide semantic-based explanatory facilities.* Finally, the explanatory facility in a fuzzy model must, of necessity, depend on a higher level of semantic understanding. Since all the rules are run in parallel we cannot simply wind back the rule execution tree to produce a explanation of how we arrived at a particular answer. Also, since fuzzy models deal with overlapping concepts and degrees of membership, the explanatory facility must describe the underlying decision process that leads to a particular solution rather than just the chain of instantiated values. Thus, fuzzy models provide the end user with a more robust and rigorous understanding of how a decision was reached and highlights the subtleties of reasoning that often escapes the end user in traditional expert and decision support systems.

2 DETECTING AND ANALYZING BEHAVIOR PATTERNS

The fuzzy systems approach to isolating abusive and fraudulent healthcare providers is based on the concept of non-parametric anomaly detection within a population whose behavior characteristics are governed (we suppose) by the Law of Large Numbers and the Central Limit Theorem. In particular, the weak Law of Large Numbers says that for a sufficiently large population, the measurement of behavior characteristics will approach the mean for the population. Thus we can 'look into the data itself' to find providers that have behaviors which are significantly at variance from their peers.

2.1 Identifying the Proper Peer Population

However, we cannot simply compare one provider against another or one provider against an arbitrary collection of providers. We must place the provider among the proper set of practitioners that comprise a *peer* group. Unusual behaviors are identified by comparing the behavior of an individual provider of a specific type, geographic region, and organization size against the behavior of the provider's peers of the same type and within the same geography and organization size. Figure 7.6 shows how the providers are arrayed in such a three-dimensional space.[3]

Organizations can be individuals, small, medium, and large clinics, or hospitals. Provider types are based on the practice: osteopaths, neurosurgeons, podiatrists, forensic pathologists, and so forth. Demographics isolate providers that live in roughly the same cultural, social, economic, and business-practice community. Figure 7.7 shows how a set of providers is chosen for analysis based on the total population.

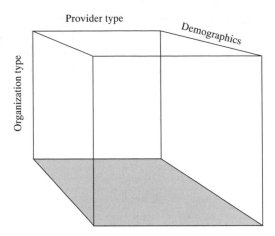

Figure 7.6   Partitioning of providers for analysis

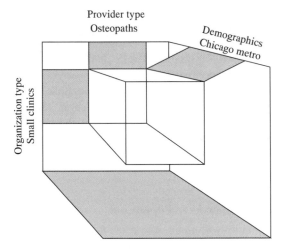

Figure 7.7   Choosing a set of providers

From this perspective we can see that the model depends on properly identifying the correct organizational and demographic characteristics. (In fact, the
model behavior is more dependent on proper isolation of population demographics
than the organizational type. In areas such as the American midwest and southwest
where major metropolitan areas tend to rapidly diffuse into rural and farm populations, the providers on the demographic cross-over edge tend to appear frequently
on the anomalous behavior curves. This factor must be incorporated into the model
analysis.)

2.2 The Focus on Behavior Patterns

The model depends on the identification of behavior patterns for each type of provider. A behavior pattern corresponds to some statistical measure in the underlying data associated with how a particular provider provides service. Such patterns include the type and degree of service provided, the frequency of service and billings, the cost of the service, the frequency and type of follow-up activities, the day and time of services, and the logical necessity of the service. In order to understand how the behavior patterns relate to the detection of anomalous behavior, we group them into Financial, Maintenance, Suitability, Utilization, Operational, and Type. For each Cartesian product of provider type, organization, and demographic profile a measure of the peer population's value for each behavior pattern is found. We then compare each provider with the behavior of the peer group. The greater the distance from the center of normal behavior, the higher the possibility that the provider is engaging in some form of anomalous behavior.

2.3 Identifying Behavior Patterns

How do we find behavior patterns for the model? Most behaviors are identified by the model user's fraud-detection department from their experience investigating suspect providers. Generally, this forms the nucleus of the anomaly detection process. We have also investigated two methods of automatically discovering behavior patterns to supplement the core patterns. Both are forms of knowledge mining that attempt to identify relationships in the data. These relationships form operational behavior patterns defining the way the provider peer population provides service, files claims, and handles patients.

The first method involves the use of an unsupervised neural network to 'learn' the relationships inherent in the claim data. Using the *DataSculpture* data transformation facility and *NeuralWorks Professional* package from NeuralWare, we broke claim data down into its basic properties (approximately 84 data elements) and used both a probabilistic neural network and a modification of the Fuzzy ARTMAP Classification (which is a generalization of the ART1 processor.) The results of the Fuzzy ARTMAP processing produced some encouraging results, identifying nine additional patterns. (These showed, for osteopaths as an example, a marked relationship between certain disease combinations and high treatment frequencies that might otherwise be considered abusive, and a relationship between billing decomposition and certain treatments that might be considered either abusive or a result of 'unbundling'.)

The second method, while not strictly a discovery technique, is used to automatically generate a fuzzy model from a knowledge of the decision variables. Employing the Wang–Mendel algorithm, the input and output states of the model are used to discover the relationships between claim data elements and acceptable, marginal, abusive, and fraudulent behaviors. This approach requires a training data-set containing providers with their patterns that fall into these classifications. The Wang–Mendel algorithm obeys the general mapping function:

$$v_i^1, v_i^2, v_i^3, \ldots, v_i^n, v_0$$

where the input and output variables are supplied to the algorithm and the corresponding fuzzy representations for each variable are produced as well as the rules that describe the behavior of the system. The algorithm also provides parameters that allow for both the incorporation of time series variables as well as an adjustment for data that is uncertain or 'dirty'. We have found that the Wang–Mendel algorithm produces a good 'core' model for new provider types, allows the exploration of system performance variables, and provides a good validation and verification technique. We were initially drawn to the Wang–Mendel rule synthesis process by its ability accurately to model and predict a chaotic time series. A chaotic time series is produced from deterministic non-linear systems of sufficient complexity to appear random, but, because of their underlying deterministic nature, they are, in fact, not random at all. The complexity and dimensionality of the anomaly-detection process appeared to possess this property (and was subsequently confirmed during the generation of the initial fuzzy models).

2.4 Analyzing Behavior Pattern Properties

For each of the behavior patterns we need to compute the normal value for the peer population. There are several methods of doing this, and the one used in this fuzzy system model relies on measuring three fundamental statistical quantities: the mean, variance, and the standard deviation. In the statistical analysis we also consider the distribution kurtosis, and the distribution skew. We make the assumption that the peer population statistics are close to being normally distributed around a central value (thus, the Law of Large Numbers.) The first statistic, the mean (equation (7.1)), estimates the central value for a population of N observations (x_1 through x_n):

$$\bar{x} = \frac{1}{N} \sum_{i=1}^{N} x_i \tag{7.1}$$

We next want to determine the diffusion or variability around this central value. This is done by calculating the variance of the distribution

$$v = \frac{1}{N-1} \sum_{i=1}^{N} (x_i - \bar{x})^2 \tag{7.2}$$

and then taking the square root of the variance to find the standard deviation as shown in equation (7.3). The standard deviation allows us to determine how widely the behavior values in a population vary and thus restricts how we view the idea of anomalous behaviors:

$$\sigma = \sqrt{\frac{1}{N-1} \sum_{i=1}^{N} (x_i - \bar{x})^2} \equiv \sqrt{v} \qquad (7.3)$$

We should note, however, that the statistical evaluation that precedes the fuzzy systems analysis often deals with population distributions that may not have a second moment (in other words, it may approach infinity). In such a case the predictability power of the standard deviation is useless nor will the population distributions converge as points are added to the equation. To compensate for this possibility we have adopted a more robust width estimation, the mean absolute deviation:

$$\bar{D} = \frac{1}{N} \sum_{i=1}^{N} |x_i - \bar{x}| \qquad (7.4)$$

In deciding whether or not the provider behavior pattern characteristics match that of the peer population at large we are actually asking the question *Are the two population distributions the same?* There are two general methods of approaching this task: through the use of the Chi-square test for non-continuous data and the Kolmogorov–Smirnov (KS) test for continuous data. Although any continuous function can be turned into a non-continuous function by separating the spectrum of values into ranges or bins, we have chosen the Kolmogorov–Smirnov test since the distributions in our model are basically continuous and the KS metric is both straightforward and simple. The KS statistics, D, is the maximum value of the absolute difference between two cumulative distribution functions and is defined by

$$D = \max_{-\infty < x < \infty} |S_1(x) - S_2(x)| \qquad (7.5)$$

Figure 7.8 shows how this metric is used to find the values in the distributions that have the maximum absolute distance. (Absolute is important since either positive or negative displacement is important.)

A full exploration of the methods associated with generating the KS statistic are beyond this chapter, although a complete discussion can be found in most statistics and probability texts. In the context of the anomaly detection model, the KS statistic, the degree to which the distributions are different, is used as a measure of the compatibility between the peer and provider populations for each behavior pattern.

There are two other important statistical properties used by the anomaly detection process involving the third and forth statistical moments. These are the *skew* and *kurtosis* of the peer and provider populations. The skew measures the property of *asymmetry* in the population. A population skew can be either positive (the tail of the distribution extends toward more positive values of x_i) or negative (the tail of the distribution extends toward negative value of x_i). Figure 7.9 shows both

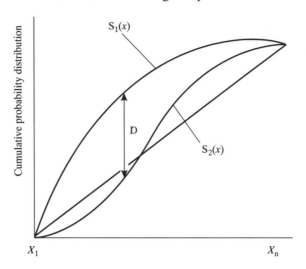

Figure 7.8 The Kolmogorov–Smirnov distance metric on series S_1 and S_2

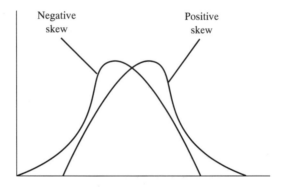

Figure 7.9 Skew in population distributions

positive and negative skew. The following equation shows how skew is calculated given the mean and standard deviation of the population:

$$\text{Skew} = \frac{1}{N} \sum_{i=1}^{N} \left[\frac{x_i - \bar{x}}{\sigma} \right]^3 \tag{7.6}$$

The fourth parameter we use in the analysis of population characteristics is the kurtosis of the population distribution. The kurtosis measures, relative to a normal distribution, the sharpness or flatness of the curve. Kurtosis, like skew, can be both positive and negative. A positive or leptokurtic kurtosis indicates a sharply pointed distribution. A negative or platykurtic distribution indicates a flat, wide distribution. A normal distribution has zero kurtosis and is a mesokurtic curve.

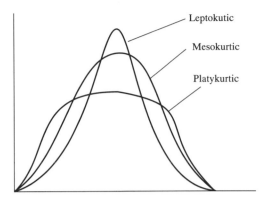

Figure 7.10 Kurtosis in population distributions

Figure 7.10 illustrates the three kinds of curves. The following equation shows how kurtosis is calculated from the mean and standard deviation. Note that the -3 makes the value zero for normal distributions:

$$\text{Kurtosis} = \left\{ \frac{1}{N} \sum_{i=1}^{N} \left[\frac{x_i - \bar{x}}{\sigma} \right]^4 \right\} - 3 \qquad (7.7)$$

Having calculated the mean and standard deviation for the two populations we also calculate their skew and kurtosis. If the populations have significantly different values (and this a fuzzy quantity measurement) we increase or decrease the overall compatibility parameter by the absolute difference between the populations. Since the degree of difference in the Kolmogorov–Smirnov analysis is indifferent to the x-axis (it has the same significance for x and $\ln x$), this adjustment for curve topology (or morphology) insures that population shifts are isolated and identified.[4]

3 THE FUZZY MODEL DISCOVERY PROPERTIES

Thus we can compute for all the providers of a similar type a similar organization size, and within the same geographic area a set of statistics that define how, for each identified behavior pattern, their service is distributed. We can also look at any individual provider within this population and compute a distribution of data points for his or her behavior patterns. As Figure 7.11 illustrates, when these distributions have significant variations, then the behavior can be, to some degree, anomalous.

The discovery model rests on three major static criteria metrics and one time-varying metric in the population space. Roughly these correspond to the insurer's exposure to fraudulent behavior (the total claims dollars paid to the provider), the degree of variance from the center of the peer population (the population compatibility number) for each behavior pattern, and the number of behaviors that are significantly at variance. The time-varying metric is the change in the behavior

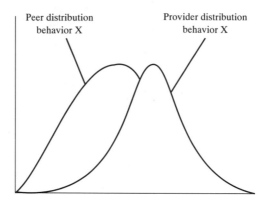

Figure 7.11   Behavior pattern variations for peer and provider

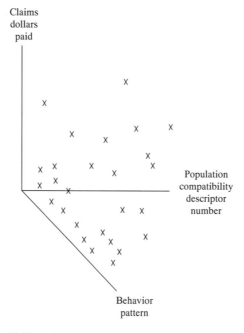

Figure 7.12   Distribution of providers in the analysis space

population dynamics over time and is discussed later. Figure 7.12 shows how a number of behavior patterns are distributed across the analysis space.

Within the distribution analysis space the model can detect anomalous behaviors of several degrees. The first-degree variances correspond to major variations in the peer. Figure 7.13 illustrates the outliers that would be found by the gross model sieve. These are also the abusive or fraudulent providers that we would expect the insurer's manual fraud investigators to uncover.

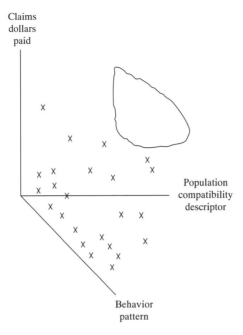

Figure 7.13   First-degree anomalies in the peer population

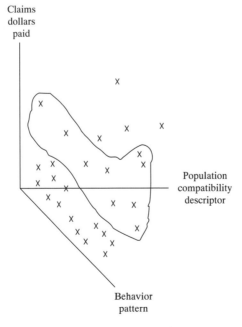

Figure 7.14   Second-degree anomalies in the peer population

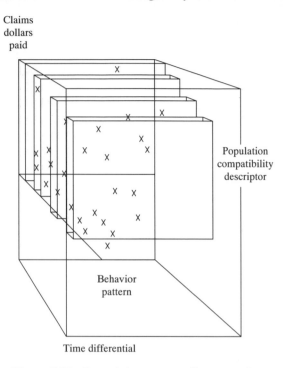

Figure 7.15   Second-degree anomalies across time

The fuzzy anomaly-detection model, on the other hand, is designed to detect the second level of outliers, those that are not easily recognized by conventional abuse and fraud techniques. Figure 7.14 shows that these providers lie close to the edge of the acceptable domain. The fuzzy model isolates these behaviors by recognizing the degree to which they are at variance from the peer behaviors.

As Figure 7.15 illustrates, the fuzzy model provides a differential analysis of the provider behavior across time. This accomplishes two objectives. First, it readjusts the system parameters to account for changes in regulatory requirements, economic, as well as social and cultural expectations. Second, it identifies anomalous behaviors early in the detection phase so that the behavior can be interdicted. Economically and socially it is usually better to correct a behavior rather than prosecute a provider. This has been general overview of the design philosophy behind the provider fraud detection system. We now turn to the actual model organization itself in terms of example fuzzy sets and typical analysis rules.

4   THE FUZZY SYSTEM APPROACH

The fuzzy model consists of rules that examine the incoming data elements and adjusts the composite degree of abuse likelihood. There are two kinds of fuzzy sets in the systems: descriptive and metric. The descriptive fuzzy sets describe the underlying semantics of each system variable and parameter. The metric fuzzy sets are used on the right-hand side of the rule consequent expressions. These metrics establish the degree of fraud or abuse likelihood for each of the behavior patterns. An example of the *INCREASED* metric fuzzy set has been encountered previously (see Figure 7.1).

4.1 The Basic Fuzzy Set Vocabularies

The descriptive fuzzy sets provide for the semantic decomposition of the major model variables into terms that reflect how the fraud-detection experts think about each parameter. As an example, Figure 7.16 shows the fuzzy set that represents the idea of High for the amount of money paid to a particular provider. It is a logistic or S-curve whose inflexion point represents the median amount paid to the peer set.

Descriptive fuzzy sets rarely appear alone. They are usually associated with collections of sets describing the underlying domain of each model variable. As we can see in Figure 7.17, the *HIGH* for dollars fuzzy set is one component of the ProviderPayments model variable. In this case, the variable is decomposed into three fuzzy terms.

Decomposition of model variables into component fuzzy sets is very important. Each fuzzy set is a base linguistic variable. These fuzzy sets map the semantics of the model back to the concepts used by the experts to state conditions and actions in the model. Other fuzzy sets measure model performance properties and are not directly tied to the data characteristics of the claim data. One example is the fuzzy set that measures the number of behavior patterns for a provider that are significantly at variance. Figure 7.18 shows this slightly convex fuzzy set.

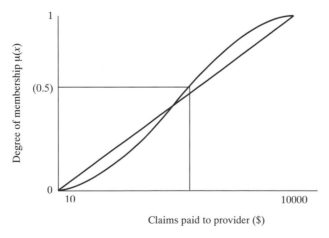

Figure 7.16 High claim dollars paid to provider

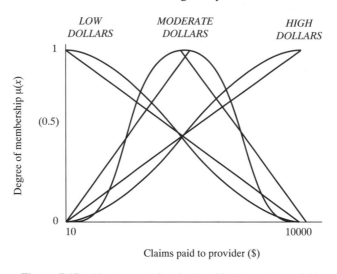

Figure 7.17 The term set for the ProviderPayments variable

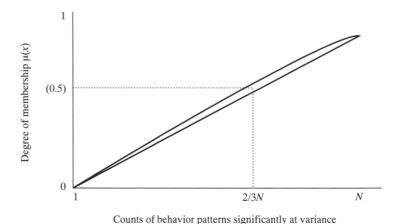

Figure 7.18 Number of highly significant behavior patterns

This fuzzy set acts to adjust the system so that a provider with one or two behavior patterns that are anomalous will not unduly bias the model. This means that a few spikes in the manifold will not promote a provider to the first frontier of the anomaly curve. On the other hand, if the spikes are consistent across time, then the cumulative variance (this is an additive fuzzy model) will exceed the damping effect of the significant count fuzzy set. Conversely, it is possible that several behavior patterns were at variance, but not sufficiently to promote the provider to the anomaly curve. This count is also used to check for a provider that has many variances but none of them with a high profile.

A behavior pattern fuzzy set is modeled after the statistical first and second moments of the behavior distribution in the peer population. This is generally a PI or Beta distribution centered around the mean of the distribution. The width of the PI curve is based on the standard deviation as well as the distribution kurtosis. Figure 7.19 shows how such a prototypical fuzzy set appears.

In the model itself we measure whether or not the behavior of the provider is significantly at variance with the behavior of the peer population. Often this measurement is direction biased, that is, we want to know whether or not the

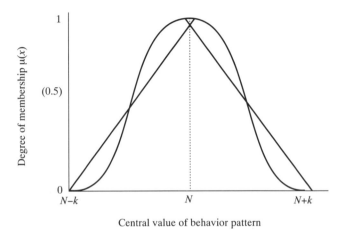

Figure 7.19 The fuzzy representation of a behavior pattern central value

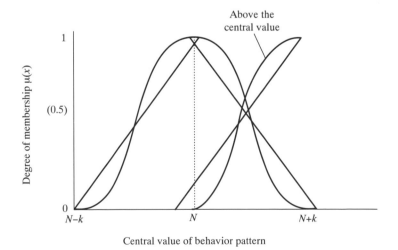

Figure 7.20 The fuzzy region above the central value

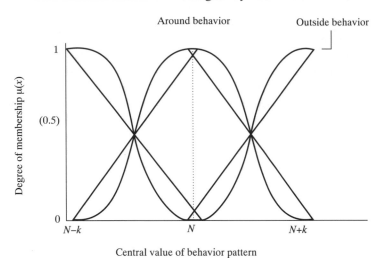

Figure 7.21   The fuzzy region outside the central value

provider value is greater than or less than the central measure of the peer population. This is also done through fuzzy analysis by constructing a fuzzy region that approximates a space above or below the fuzzy distribution space associated with the peer. Figure 7.20 illustrates how such a fuzzy region is constructed.

For non-directional behavior patterns, that is, patterns which are significant when they are highly above or highly below the central behavior fuzzy region, we use the complement of the central value behavior pattern fuzzy set to bracket the fuzzy region. Figure 7.21 shows how this complementary fuzzy region appears.

In earlier versions of the anomaly model only non-directional fuzzy metrics were used. This approach proved to be insensitive to certain kinds of behavior patterns where the direction of variance is important (as an example, the dollars paid to the provider is seldom of interest when it is less than the peer population central value.)

4.2   The Basic Analysis Rule Protocol

This is the nucleus of the anomaly-detection model. Using the set of descriptive and metric fuzzy sets, the rule base reads statistically processed claims data. Listing 1 shows (in a somewhat simplified manner with commentary) the top-level rule that accesses the underlying transaction database and runs the anomaly-detection model. The first part of the rule opens and activates the anomaly knowledge base, reads the specified dimensionality data and finds all records that meet this criterion. The selected records are then sorted. We set a cursor (i) to a built-in control, the record cursor, which will retrieve each record in turn from the file.

```
open 'anomaly.kbs'
in TransactionFile
    find provider=&PID and providerSize=&Size and providerArea=&Area;
    into TheseProviders;
    order TransactionFile.provider TransactionFile.bp Variance
    reccursor i;
```

Before starting the analysis, we indicate that the current provider's fraud likelihood is *NONE* (a narrow bell-shaped fuzzy set in the knowledge base.) The *for i* statement loops through the transaction file. Each transaction represents a behavior pattern associated with the provider. Once a behavior pattern instance is active, the select statement chooses which rule should execute. The rules increase the likelihood of fraud (or abuse) based on the degree to which the behavior pattern variance is true:

```
solution FraudLikelihood is NONE;
for i;
select(DirectionalType[i])
    case ABOVESENSITIVE
        if bpVariance[i] is ABOVE PEERNorm[i]
        then FraudLikelihood is INCREASED;
    case BELOWSENSITIVE
        if bpVariance[i] is BELOW PEERNorm[i]
        then FraudLikelihood is INCREASED;
    otherwise
        if bpVariance[i] is OUTSIDE PEERNorm[i]
        then FraudLikelihood is INCREASED;
    end select;
end i
```

It is possible that many behavior patterns are at variance from the peer or that only a few patterns had any significance. In the case where the count of behavior patterns at variance is well below a significance threshold we want to decrease the possibility that the provider is anomalous. On the other hand, when many behavior patterns are significant we want to indicate that the possibility of abuse is definitely increased:

```
if cnt(any(bbVariance[*] is well below SignificantLevel) is HIGH
    then FraudLikelihood is POSITIVELY DECREASED;
if cnt(any(bbVariance[*] is above SignificantLevel) is HIGH
    then FraudLikelihood is POSITIVELY INCREASED;
```

Listing 1   The main driver rule

The result of executing this rule for the set of providers is an order list of providers that have significant anomalous behavior profiles. The ranking is in the distribution metric [0,1000] where zero indicates a provider that is exactly compatible with the peer population central measure for each behavior pattern and one thousand [1000] indicates a provider that has significant variance from the peer population across a broad spectrum of behavior patterns.

5 CONCLUSION

A fuzzy system-based fraud and abuse detection system for managed healthcare has proven itself a powerful and response weapon in the search for providers that are abusing the healthcare system. Its primary audience has been the general insurance companies, casualty companies, and Blue Cross and Blue Shield organizations. Since the system adapts to the professional behavior patterns in target demographic regions for providers of specific organizational types it can be used across a broad spectrum of insurance industry locations without extensive recalibration of the internal statistics. The system has shown itself capable of detecting anomalous behaviors equal to or better than the best fraud-detection departments. Its ability to mimic the approximate (commonsense) reasoning of fraud experts, to explain its reasoning, evaluate large quantities of data, and adapt to changes in performance makes it an economically viable option for any insurance organization.

ENDNOTES

1. For those not accustomed to fuzzy models, a brief explanation is in order. The variable *FraudLikelihood* is, itself, not a fuzzy set. But, the fuzzy modelling system creates a temporary fuzzy set that represents the current evidential state for *FraudLikelihood* as the model is executing. When all the rules have contributed to the evidence for or against the likelihood of fraud, a value for the scalar variable *FraudLikelihood* is found through a process called *Defuzzification*. This method of handling solution variables is a consequence of a basic property of fuzzy models: they are parallel processing systems. All the rules are, in effect, run in parallel to produce a final result.
2. This is only an example. The function is not restricted to two variables.
3. As a reminder, of course, this is really a four-dimensional space since the anomaly-detection model looks for changes in the provider behavior across time. The time axis has been generally omitted for clarity but should not be forgotten.
4. This process of scaling the KS metric by the variances in skew and kurtosis may not seem to obey any well-known statistical methods but we have found that it works well within the preprocessing requirements of the anomaly-detection model. In this respect it is a heuristic or 'rule of thumb' for intensifying any differences in the population dynamics.

FURTHER READING

Cox, E.D. (1991a) 'Approximate reasoning: the use of fuzzy logic in expert systems and decision support', *Proceedings of the Conf. on Expert Systems in the Insurance Industry*, 24–25 April, Institute for International Research, New York.

Cox, E.D. (1991b) 'Company acquisition analysis: formulating queries with imprecise domains', *Proceedings of the First Intl. Conf. on Artificial Intelligence Applications on Wall Street*, 9-11 October, IEEE Computer Society Press, Los Alamitos, CA. 194-9.

Cox, E.D. (1992a) 'The great myths of fuzzy logic', *AI Expert*, January, 40-5.

Cox, E.D. (1992b) 'Solving problems with fuzzy logic', *AI Expert*, March, 28-37.

Cox, E.D. (1992c) 'Integrating fuzzy logic into neural nets', *AI Expert*, June, 43-7.

Cox, E.D. (1992d) 'Fuzzy fundamentals', *IEEE Spectrum*, October, 58-61.

Cox, E.D. (1992e) 'Effectively using fuzzy logic and fuzzy expert system modeling — in theory and practice', *Proceedings of the Conf. on Advanced Technologies to Re-Engineer the Insurance Process*, 17-18 September, Institute for International Research, New York.

Cox, E.D. (1992f) 'Fuzzy logic and fuzzy system modeling', *Proceedings of the Fourth Annual IBC Conf. on Expert Systems in Insurance*, 28-29 October, IBC USA Conferences, Southborough, MA.

Cox, E.D. (1992g) 'Applications of fuzzy system models', *AI Expert*, October, 34-9.

Cox, E.D. (1992h) 'A close shave with Occam's razor: fuzzy-neural hetero-genetic object-oriented knowledge-based nano-synthetic reasoning models: throwing the kitchen sink at problem solving', A Workshop in the Industrial Applications of Philosophy and Epistemology to AI, *Proceedings of the Third Annual Symposium of the International Association of Knowledge Engineers*, 16-19 November, Software Engineering Press, Kensington, MD.

Cox, E.D. (1993a) 'Adaptive fuzzy systems', *IEEE Spectrum*, February, 67-70.

Cox, E.D. (1993b) 'A fuzzy systems approach to detecting anomalous risk behaviors in portfolio management strategies', *Proceedings of the Second Intl. Conf. on Artificial Intelligence Applications on Wall Street*, 19-22 April, Software Engineering Press, Gaithersburg, MD, 144-8.

Cox, E.D. (1993c) 'Fuzzy information systems with multiple conflicting experts', *Proceedings of the Computer Design Magazine's Fuzzy Logic '93 Conference*, March, M223-1-13.

Cox, E.D. (1993d) 'A model-free trainable fuzzy system for the analysis of financial time-series data', *Proceedings of the Computer Design Magazine's Fuzzy Logic '93 Conference*, March, A124-1-7.

Cox, E.D. (1994) *The Fuzzy Systems Handbook*, Academic Press Professional, Cambridge, MA.

Dubois, D. & Prade, H. (1980) *Fuzzy Sets and Systems: Theory and Applications. Mathematics in Science and Engineering*, Vol. 144. Academic Press, San Diego, CA.

Dubois, D. & Prade, H. (1988) *Possibility Theory, An Approach to Computerized Processing of Uncertainty.* Plenum Press, New York.

Jamshidi, M., Vadiee, N. & Ross, T.J. (eds) (1993) *Fuzzy Logic and Control*, Prentice Hall, Englewood Cliffs, NJ.

Jones, P.L. & Graham, I. (1988) *Expert Systems: Knowledge, Uncertainty and Decision*, Chapman & Hall, London.

Klir, G.J. & Folger, T.A. (1988) *Fuzzy Sets, Uncertainty, and Information*, Prentice Hall, Englewood Cliffs, NJ.

Kosko, B. (1992) *Neural Networks and Fuzzy Systems, A Dynamical Systems Approach to Machine Intelligence*, Prentice Hall, Englewood Cliffs, NJ.

Kosko, B. & Isaka, S. (1993) 'Fuzzy logic', *Scientific American*, July, 76-81.

Masters, T. (1993) *Practical Neural Network Recipes in C++*, Academic Press, San Diego, CA.

Pedrycz, W. (1993) *Fuzzy Control and Fuzzy Systems*, 2nd edition, John Wiley, New York.

Schmucker, K.J. (1984) *Fuzzy Sets, Natural Language Computations, and Risk Analysis*, Computer Science Press, Rockville, MD.

Smets, P., Mamdani, E.H., Dubois, D. & Prade, H. (1988) *Non-Standard Logics for Automated Reasoning*, Academic Press, London.

Smithson, M. (1987) *Fuzzy Set Analysis for Behavioral and Social Sciences*, Springer-Verlag, New York.

Terano, T., Asai, K. & Sugeno, M. (1991) *Fuzzy Systems Theory and Its Applications*, Academic Press, San Diego, CA.

Wang, L.-X. & Mendel, J.M. (1991) 'Generating fuzzy rules from numerical data, with applications', *USC-SIPI Report No. 169*, Signal and Image Processing Institute, University of Southern California, Los Angeles, CA.

Wang, Z. and Klir, G.J. (1992) *Fuzzy Measure Theory*, Plenum Press, New York.

White, D.A. & Sofge, D.A. (1992) *Handbook of Intelligent Control, Neural, Fuzzy, and Adaptive Approaches*, Van Nostrand Reinhold, New York.

Yager, R.E. & Zadeh, L.A. (eds) (1992) *An Introduction to Fuzzy Logic Applications in Intelligent Systems*, Kluwer Academic Publishers, Norwell, MA.

Yager, R.R., Ovchinnikov, S., Tong, R.M. & Nguyen, H.T. (1987) *Fuzzy Sets and Applications: Selected Papers by L.A. Zadeh*, John Wiley, New York.

Zadeh, L.A. & Kacprzyk, J. (eds) (1992) *Fuzzy Logic for the Management of Uncertainty*, John Wiley, New York.

Zimmerman, H.J. (1985) *Fuzzy Set Theory — and Its Applications*, Kluwer Academic Publishers, Norwell, MA.

Zimmerman, H.J. (1987) *Fuzzy Sets, Decision Making, and Expert Systems*, Kluwer Academic Publishers, Norwell, MA.

Zurek, W.H. (ed.) (1990) *Complexity, Entropy and the Physics of Information*, Vol. VIII, Santa Fé Institute, Studies in the Sciences of Complexity. Addison-Wesley, Redwood City, CA.

8

Insider Dealing Detection at the Toronto Stock Exchange

STEVE MOTT

1 INTRODUCTION

Stock market trading surveillance suffers from all the information-processing problems inherent in any job function where the volume, accuracy, timeliness, density and complexity of data overwhelm the humans charged with fusing, synthesizing and making sensitive decisions from it. Several stock exchanges, who are charged with ensuring that the markets are open, fair and equitable to all investors, have attempted to cope with information-processing problems through the use of various knowledge-based systems (KBS). Increasingly, these exchanges are also turning to KBS to meet expanding regulatory compliance provisions not only to avoid such unfair trading phenomena as price-fixing, insider trading and front-running but also to detect more heinous activities such as money laundering. In many respects, the processing-automation task for identifying insider dealing is the reverse of financial forecasting: Instead of trying to predict the anomaly in the future (i.e. an attractive investment scenario), stock market surveillance analysts must look backwards to detect a pattern, anomaly or relationship that could have been generated by information not available to the general market.

As in many information synthesis and retrieval tasks, the automated system must balance two conflicting goals: how to give analysts everything they need that represent target suspicious activities while avoiding inundating them with superfluous alerts or warnings. In most respects, determining suspiciousness of a transaction or set of transactions is very difficult to establish empirically or to quantify.

Intelligent Systems for Finance and Business. Edited by S. Goonatilake and P. Treleaven
© 1995 John Wiley & Sons Ltd

Investigative experience or judgment is called for, and that expertise is very difficult to model with conventional rule-based or hard-coded approaches. Nevertheless, exchanges such as the National Association of Securities Dealers (NASDAQ) and the New York Stock Exchange (NYSE) have attempted at least to partition some of the masses of information needed through extensive use of rules. The inherent difficulty of modeling dynamic behavior with rules and adjusting them to changing patterns of activity, however, disinclined the Toronto Stock Exchange (TSE) to rely on rules alone. TSE, a rather small exchange, was not certain it had the manpower and expertise to model the behavior well, and needed another technique that was more flexible, dynamic and capable of learning. That technique was Case-Based Reasoning, or CBR.

2   CBR VERSUS OTHER KNOWLEDGE-BASED APPROACHES TO THE PROBLEM

2.1   Hard-coded Edits

The ever-present but conflicting goals of catching all the truly anomalous events without inundating the analysts with excessive numbers of alerts clearly defies conventional 'hard-coding' solutions. Typically, the primary task is to sort through the unusual variances between price and volume changes for particular securities as the day's trading progresses. Prior to application of technology at the TSE, the mainframe-based trading system merely channeled 'alerts' to market surveillance analysts based on primitive 'hard-coded' strings such as:

'Flag every price or volume movement in excess of 2%.'

The result was literally thousands of alerts — few of which were relevant or interesting. Analysts would occasionally scan the heaps of printouts, using only the sporadic anomaly caught coincidentally by visually scanning the printouts.

Over time, the seasoned analyst would learn to spot true anomalies with higher rates of accuracy by applying their prior experience against the more or less randomly filtered alerts. For example, they might know that a significant movement in a particular stock (say, IBM) was unusual, particularly when it appeared to be moving out of sync with the rest of the market. Perhaps, as quarterly earnings announcements came out, the analyst knew that it was rare to see the stock move more than 4% in volume or 2% in price — as a heuristic not proven by empirical data — unless it was moving with broad market aggregates.

At such times, the analyst could begin to assemble a case to see if, indeed, the quarterly earnings announcement, or any other news event, could explain the unusual movement. In rare circumstances, the analyst could call a trading halt in a stock until it could force the company to make information generally available to the public as to why the movement might be occurring. In even rarer circumstances, if the movements occurred prior to public dissemination of the news/explanation, and the company's officers or connected individuals profited by trades in the stock prior to public revelation, an insider trading case would be proffered by the surveillance department. Many other sources of information would then be collected to mount a case for prosecution.

Fine-tuning these edits on the mainframe trading program turns out to be only a remote alternative, as the resources required and costs of implementing filtering mechanisms in that environment are often prohibitive. Thus TSE opted for a workstation-based system that produced the filters on data imported from the mainframe program.

2.2 Rule-based Systems

At this same primary task level, rule-based expert systems have been tried in at least three other exchanges: NYSE, AMEX and NASDAQ. The simple notion is to spot deviances in trading events that might indicate unusual or illicit activity — especially insider trading — but at a higher level of abstraction. Thus, chains of linked rules are developed to encode existing knowledge about individual stock movements for better alert filtering:

'Rule:
IF:
    (1) IBM trading volume exceeds 10 million shares for any three-hour market interval;
and   (2) price changes by more than 2% in that interval;
THEN: (1) the activity is out of normal ranges.
    (2) Generate Alert.
    (3) Assign Priority X.'

That sort of logic can be applied stock by stock and adjusted over time as experts fine-tune the efficacy of the alerts based on statistical or heuristic measures of alert relevance versus trading history. From these alerts, more formal rule-based mechanisms can be applied to determine investigatability. For example, at the American Stock Exchange, there is a rule that triggers investigations for selling of a security:

'Rule:
IF:
    (1) The investigation is for insider trading;
and   (2) [EXPECTEDMOVEMENT] is greater than 0;
and   (3)
[LARGESELL]+[SECONDSELL]+[THIRDSELL]/[VOLUMEPERIOD]
    is greater than.X

THEN:

> Open an Investigation.-Confidence $= Y/100$

NOTE: If the investigation is for insider trading and the expected movement is less than 0 and the three largest sellers account for $X\%$ or more of the volume, then investigate $p = Y.$'

Further, and in line with the ultimate TSE implementation, additional rules attempt to correlate investigations with corroborating information to determine likely malfeasance to pursue:

'Rule:

IF:

        (1) The investigation is for insider trading;

and   (2) The news is that there will be a takeover or merger;

and   (3) For the merger or takeover, the AMEX company is being acquired

and   (4) ([TAKEOVERPRICE]-[LOWGAIN])/[LOWGAIN] is less than X

THEN:

        (1) Open an investigation.-Confidence $= Y/100$'

In a turbulent market, however, such static and therefore rigid approaches — even when extended to complex chains of qualifying rules — can inundate analysts with unnecessary and/or irrelevant alerts. The important issue is what is suspicious? Often, suspicious activity can be easily disguised in the normal course of trading activity. For example, insiders anticipating an equity's decline (due to poor earnings or growth or other unfavorable announcements as yet to be made) in market price can 'short' the stock as well as selling it outright. The analyst would have to determine related activity in options and futures markets in conjunction with the normal market activity — and associate it with a single entity or related entities in order to suggest insider trading. Moreover, a looming event (e.g. earnings announcements, management changes, mergers/acquisition bids, etc.) may legitimately be known by some, while the general market still has not become aware of the underlying (and, normally legitimate) cause for the movement.

Thus, the difficulties of creating, refining and changing a rule-based approach to this problem present several problems for developers:

(1) Extensive time and resources are spent trying to develop the rules from experts during the knowledge engineering process.

(2) Despite this investment, important components of the domain are frequently not covered by the rules, and involve hard-to-codify experience, intelligent guesswork, judgment and intuition.

(3) Structuring the rules is very time-consuming and 'dicey', given the inherent ambiguities and contradictions in this domain.

(4) Adding new rules or knowledge is typically difficult and expensive, and requires extensive testing.

(5) Only one finite version of 'expertise' winds up in the system, perhaps at the exclusion of other 'experience' in the analytical function, and perhaps alienating other productive users of the application.

2.3 Neural Networks/statistical Pattern Recognition

This ambiguity makes market integrity and surveillance difficult for applications of neural networks as well. Neural nets first must rely on extensive training on actually suspicious activity. Insider trading cases are rare — at least at the level of prosecution — so training data is hard to come by. Effects by exogenous events (natural disasters, weather, macro-economic shifts, political turbulence, etc.) are difficult to sort through, and are extremely difficult to ferret out of an explanation-poor neural network.

Statistical pattern recognition represents another, common approach to this task, and to market monitoring in general. Most systems attempt to observe patterns in stock price and volume measurements, and lack any fundamental view of the companies involved. In fact, statistical approaches are inherently limited in their ability to evaluate non-numeric data. Yet the stock market is frequently influenced by factors that cannot be easily represented by equations — news stories being the most prominent example (Klein & Prestbo, 1974).

So the solution attempted by TSE was a more 'fuzzy' reasoning mechanism that resembled the somewhat unstructured process that analysts themselves employed: Case-based Reasoning (CBR), or reasoning from prior experience. CBR is a close approximation technology that induces the 'outcome' (here, a suspicious event) from the data that is fed to it. Items of data used in explaining or predicting an outcome become features of a 'case'. Numbers of cases are composed (from real events) sufficient to constitute a library that covers most of the 'domain' at hand. Cases and their features (and the range of values within those features) 'train' the inductive engine to predict or explain the outcome. As new data (features of a new 'case') arise, the induction finds (retrieves) the best matching case from the library to inform the user of the likely outcome based on past experience. (A comprehensive description of the original underlying precepts of CBR can be found in Reisbeck & Schank, 1981.)

For example, the characteristics of trading from the illustration above become features of a case in a CBR application:

'Case Name: IBM — 2/2/94
Field Name: 21 — Trading Activity
Field Type: Integer
Field Role: Match field
Field Value: Trading Volume (Field 14)/Time Interval=3 (Field 5)

Field Name: 28 — Trading Volume Variance
Field Type: Boolean
Field Role: Outcome field
Field Value: Trading Activity/Industry Aggregate Activity (Field 17) greater
than 1.25=True — (Alert generated)
Trading Activity/Industry Aggregate Activity (Field 17) less
than or equal to 1.25=False (No Alert)'

There may perhaps be 20–40 information fields (or case features) that can be numerical calculations, boolean statements, text descriptors, etc. — the CBR application will make use of some or all of them in making its calculations whichever are most important to explaining or predicting the targeted outcome. The outcome field, or any field derived from relationships of raw data fields, may be expressed as an IF:THEN:ELSE rule, as appropriate to the design. If there is missing data, the application will go ahead and retrieve a matching outcome.

CBR does not require extreme precision; nor does it have to have complete data. Qualitative text field descriptors can be processed as easily as equations. Induction does have to have enough data to make sensible inductions, however, and for targeted tasks such as monitoring insider trading it needs actual suspicious data. Besides its flexibility in acquiring and using data, the explanation-rich capabilities of induction provide an extremely useful instructional guide for users to assess how the data they use tumble to the solution. And CBR provides live examples of what was done in the past to instruct analysts what to do today.

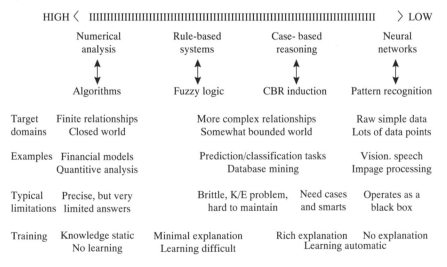

Figure 8.1

Thus, CBR as a close approximation technology is now being intensely scrutinized for similar 'detection' tasks, such as monitoring for money-laundering payments in the banking system, picking tax returns that qualify for audits, determining risk levels of financing activities, and even picking investments. The trade-offs of using CBR *vis-à-vis* other knowledge-based systems in this type of domain are summarized in Figure 8.1, where each KBS is measured along the continuum of domain knowledge on parameters important to any application developer.

3 INTELLIGENT MARKET MONITOR (IMM)

3.1 Background Operating Environment

The application itself was built by Cognitive Systems, Inc. with the help of an internal TSE team. The transaction processing system of IMM is written in C and runs on a Data General AV4020 machine under Unix. It is interfaced directly to TSE's transaction feed and surveillance workstations. The knowledge base has been developed with ReMind® on an Apple Macintosh computer. A translation program converts the case library into a decision tree that can be used by the C runtime environment.

The IMM application will eventually be ported to other machines running Unix, and integration with another ReMind® CBR application reading news stories to categorize them into appropriate explanation classifications (Newswatcher_) to help analysts sort out IMM alerts is planned in the near future.

3.2 Runtime Environment

As Figure 8.2 describes, the runtime application works in two distinct phases. In the first phase the system filters the large, continuous flow of data that enters the surveillance room at the TSE to find the small percentage of transaction (trades)

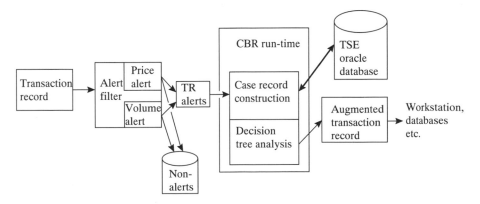

Figure 8.2

that require explanation. This filter identifies alert conditions based on unusually high price or volume changes evaluated by a mathematical formula. Usually, fewer than 10% of the transactions on the exchange signal an alert by these filters.

In the second phase, any transactions that pass through the alert filter are then sent to an explanation module that augments the basic transaction data with other data from TSE databases and passes the resulting augmented data through the decision tree to produce an explanation (or possibly that there is no explanation) for the alerted transaction. The augmented data structure and explanation are then passed to the surveillance analyst's workstation. This two-step process of filtration and explanation enables the analysts to focus their monitoring efforts on truly suspicious activities that warrant further investigation.

In addition to the transaction identified by the alert filter, other information from the exchange's databases is included in the 'case' that describes the current situation. Some of the information used in constructing cases and explanation include:

- Detailed data on recent trades of that particular stock
- Price trends within the stock's industry
- Other exchanges the stock trades on
- Recent economic data, including changes in interest rates and commodity prices
- Ex-dividend date
- Information about recent news stories. The information on news stories is classified and extracted with CBR/Text_, another tool using case-based reasoning. The technology in CBR/Text_ was originally described by Goodman, 1990
- Identity of the buyer and seller.

The 15 possible explanations generated by the CBR runtime module may include, for example, observations that the stock is simply moving with its industry trend, or that a recent news release has justified that price change. Unusual transactions that have no explanation based on the available information are, of course, considered essential for surveillance analysts to investigate. Furthermore, the IMM-generated explanation may also guide analysts in their evaluation of transactions with complete explanations.

Knowledge engineering for the IMM was straightforward. First, the relevant factors in explaining unusual transactions were identified by a surveillance expert (factors like those listed above). These factors may include additional computations or, when required, specialized database queries. Next, the data for approximately 2000 transaction cases was assembled. For each case, the expert provided an evaluation of the situation. The cases and the expert's decision for each were entered into a ReMind® case library. ReMind® induced that relevant factors leading to the specified outcomes (a process called 'clustering'), producing a binary decision tree that can be used for case retrieval. The importance of each feature in the tree is determined by the correlation between the feature and the variance in case outcome. This decision tree is then transferred to the C program for installation in the runtime environment. In the final runtime system, the cases themselves are not included in the decision tree, only their associated outcomes. As a result, the decision tree addition to the C program is quite small (less than 100K).

The case-based reasoning paradigm encourages incremental development. The knowledge engineer can enter new cases for classification, examine the criterion used by the system for classification, and automatically test its accuracy. Debugging the knowledge base consists of adding cases and correct outcomes for transactions that do not classify properly. Reclustering will integrate the additional discriminating information provided by these cases, usually improving the overall results. If conflicting outcomes are described to the system, as is frequently the case if more than one knowledge engineer or expert works on the project, the result is a "mixed cluster", a leaf in the decision tree with mixed outcomes. These conflicting cases can then be re-examined and changed if necessary.

The demands of the surveillance environment require that the runtime system be accurate as well as very fast. The alert filter can process at least twenty transactions per second, and the CBR explanation module can evaluate up to six transactions per second, depending on the number of database queries made in the explanation process. While the C program that traverses the decision tree for explanation is very fast, some of the case features require relatively complicated SQL queries to the exchange database. However, in times of peak market activity, the explanation mechanism may be configured to reason with less information. The system has a target accuracy rate of 80–90% for alert explanations.

4 CONCLUSIONS

The ultimate implementation at TSE will involve application integration with another CBR module that seeks to categorize news stories in a manner that permits the investigative analysts to attempt to explain the IMM alert. This 'explanation' can be complex, in that there may be several items in a given news story that might be pertinent to explaining the stock's movements. A merger/acquisition categorization, for example, may have been routine in the 1980s, but the fact that it was financed with junk bonds from Drexel, Burnham was the salient tip-off to inside traders, and that might have been buried deep in the story.

Our experience developing a surveillance application for the Toronto Stock Exchange has verified that case-based reasoning provides a valuable technological approach for developing knowledge-based systems in financial domains. CBR's ability to automatically induce important features from cases simplifies the task of structuring a knowledge base. This not only improves the knowledge engineering process but clearly provides a more maintainable architecture than conventional rule-based systems, and the learning features inherent in CBR are a major win for sustaining the effectiveness of the application.

This level of knowledge-based system deployment, however, is more a filtering activity than it is an intelligent processing task. The application, after all, is not attempting to identify insider trading behavior *per se* but orchestrate the data needed to surveil potential insider trading situations. In other applications being designed by us, including regulatory compliance and surveillance for the much more complicated derivative products (index options, futures, currencies, etc.), and money-laundering payment detection, the intelligence to understand the intricacies of these financial mechanisms must be built into the application. Combined with advanced quantitative filtering techniques and CBR-based pattern identification, this level of intelligence can ultimately do much of the 'data-crunching' work done by human analysts, while dramatically extending coverage of the domains they are monitoring. TSE represents a modest start down this road, but an important step that was absolutely vital to making progress on more sophisticated applications.

REFERENCES

Buta, P. & Barletta, R. (1992) 'Case-based Reasoning for market surveillance', *Proceedings of First World Congress on Expert Systems.*

Goodman, M. (1990) 'Prism: A Case-based index classifier', *Proceedings of IAAI-90*, AAAI Press, New York.

Klein, F. & Prestbo, J.A. (1974) *News and the Market*, Henry Regnery, Chicago, IL.

Lucas, H.C.J. (1993) 'Market expert surveillance systems', *Communications of the ACM*, **36** December, No. 12.

Reisbeck, C. & Schank, R.C. (1981) *Inside Case-Based Reasoning*, Lawrence Erlbaum Associates, Hillsdale, NJ.

9

EFD: Heuristic Statistics for Insurance Fraud Detection

JOHN A. MAJOR and DAN R. RIEDINGER

1 INTRODUCTION

Insurance fraud perpetrated by healthcare providers has come under increasing scrutiny over the past few years. Insurers have found that fraud control activities can more than repay their costs. The National Healthcare Anti-fraud Association (NHCAA) estimates that 10% of all healthcare claims contain some element of fraud (Frieden, 1991; Guzzi, 1989).

Typically, detection of potential fraud has depended on claim personnel to notice abnormalities in the documents submitted. Fraud 'warning signs' include cross-outs and erasures, photocopied bills instead of originals, similar handwriting of doctor and patient, etc. Not only is manual document examination costly, it is not readily automated. Moreover, there is increasing use of electronic transmission where claims go from the healthcare provider's computer to the insurer's computer with no paper documents at all. These issues motivated our research into the possibility of using the claim data itself to identify potential fraud. A number of difficulties emerged.

First, the task had never been done before. No one had ever systematically examined a large number of claims to identify potential frauds. The company has experts on claim processing, and experts on the investigation of fraud, but no experts on the detection of fraud in this sense. Bits of knowledge were available (Table 9.1), but there was no problem-solving repertoire that put them all together.

Intelligent Systems for Finance and Business. Edited by S. Goonatilake and P. Treleaven
© 1995 John Wiley & Sons Ltd

Table 9.1   Examples of knowledge-engineering results

- Some frauds are more likely to have insurance company payments assigned directly to them rather than bill through the patient.
- Some frauds may attempt to avoid Internal Revenue Service reporting, in which case they will be more likely to refuse assigned benefits.

Second, there was a relative dearth of positive examples. The known fraud cases were judged inadequate for a statistical or neural network approach.

What was needed, first, was a way to combine the available knowledge about fraud in a robust manner to identify potential cases of fraud. Second, the identified potentials had to be delivered in an environment that would allow the Investigative Consultants to examine case details and decide efficiently whether to refer the cases to the Regional Investigators. Third, the architecture should avoid *ad-hoc* approaches and support extension as our understanding of how to perform the task improved.

The basic strategy that emerged is as follows:

Operations cycle

Step 1.   Measure each provider's behavior.

Step 2.   Compare his behavior to that of his peers (providers with the same organizational structure and specialty, practicing in the same geographical area).

Step 3.   IF: The provider stands out from the mainstream
THEN: bring him to the attention of the Security Unit.

Development cycle

Step 1.   Induce rules that emulate the Investigative Consultants' selection of providers for referral to Investigators. Validate these rules on the set of known fraud cases.

Step 2.   Determine the relative contribution of the various heuristics to the induced rules. Delete unsuccessful heuristics. 'Clone and mutate' successful heuristics.

Step 3.   Enhance the system accordingly.

2   EFD'S TASK DOMAIN

Every day, millions of dollars are paid out to families and medical providers under the terms of The Travelers Managed Care and Employee Benefits contracts. Naturally, this large flow of money is under considerable scrutiny and control. One form of scrutiny is provided by the Security Unit. Activity in the Security Unit starts with some sort of tip-off. Inside tips are usually a matter of the claim processor detecting something abnormal about the claim. Also, there can be tips from other internal units, law enforcement sources, and a fraud Hotline (800 number).

After the tip-off, there is an investigation and, potentially, legal action. Investigations are sometimes initiated by the home office Investigative Consultants and carried out by the Regional Investigators in the field. The groundbreaking or early phase of investigation often starts in the home office.

EFD aids this process in two ways. First, EFD is another source of tips, operating in parallel with the other channels. Second, EFD helps in the groundbreaking. The old way of using the claim system to look for fraud was very cumbersome, because the claim payment system is designed to pay claims, not to be an investigative tool. EFD is specifically designed to assist the early phases of investigation.

3   EFD ARCHITECTURE

We can consider EFD to consist of a number of layers:

Layer 1: Behavioral heuristic measurements
Layer 2: Statistical information assessment, frontier identification, and rules
Layer 3: Natural language query/data exploration environment
Layer 4: Decision making and action
Layer 5: Validation, learning, and enhancement

3.1   Layer 1: Behavioral Heuristic Measurements

The source of the data is our claim payment system. Due to data volume constraints, the system examines one business segment, usually a geographic area.

Examination consists first of measuring the behavior of the providers. Today, we have 33 heuristics in five categories: FINANCIAL, MEDICAL LOGIC, ABUSE, LOGISTICS, and IDENTIFICATION (Table 9.2). A specific example is shown in Table 9.3. Heuristics are discussed in more detail below.

3.2   Layer 2: Information, Frontier, and Rules

The next step is to compare measurements among the providers and flag those providers who are out of line relative to their peer group. These providers are on the 'frontier' of abnormal behavior. To put the highly varied measurements on a comparable footing, EFD uses information numbers. Information numbers do two things for us. First, they reflect an adjustment for credibility. Second, they enable us to compare the results of different heuristics.

Table 9.2   Categories of behavioral heuristics

FINANCIAL.   The flow of dollars.
MEDICAL LOGIC.   Whether a medical situation would normally happen.
ABUSE.   Frequency of treatments.
LOGISTICS.   The place, time, and sequence of activities.
IDENTIFICATION.   How providers present themselves to the insurer

Table 9.3   Example of a behavioral heuristic

FINANCIAL: ASSIGNMENTS/NUMBER

RATIONALE: Frauds where the patient is not seen must of necessity use assigned payment (i.e. the payment goes directly to the provider rather than to the insured). Alternatively, a provider may wish to avoid scrutiny by the IRS. In that case, he must avoid direct payment from the insurer, because the insurer reports direct payments.

DESCRIPTION: Measure {0, 1} whether each bill is assigned.

SENSE: Both positive and negative deviations are significant.

Each provider's set of information numbers represents how 'out of line' from his peers he is with respect to each of the behavioral heuristics. We apply a multivariate maximum-identification procedure to pick out a small number of providers on the 'frontiers'. Rules then select which providers are brought to the attention of the Investigative Consultants. The details of Layer 2 are discussed in Major and Riedinger (1992).

3.3   Layer 3: Data Exploration

The EFD database contains the extracted claim records (for a large metropolitan area there might be a million or so), some basic patient and provider data, the behavioral measurements, and extensive cross-reference information.

Reporting consists first of the frontier identification. This list of 100 or so providers is the electronic 'hot tip' that EFD gives to the Security Unit. Other reports that the Investigative Consultants can call up are specific to providers, patients, or policyholders.

Finally, the natural-language query capability gives the Investigative Consultants *ad hoc* access to the database. No practicable set of standard reports is going to be able to answer all the questions an investigator might ask. The *ad hoc* query capability gives us the flexibility to approach the data in arbitrary ways. The query process is discussed in detail below.

3.4   Layer 4: Decision and Action

The decision to initiate an investigation is in the hands of the home office Investigative Consultants. Their findings from EFD, plus other information systems, go into the decision process.

The output of this process consists of a short memo (from one to three pages) on each of the studied providers. If the decision is to initiate an investigation, this memo goes to the appropriate Regional Investigator. The memo describes the basic characteristics of the provider as measured by EFD and the Investigative Consultant's findings and recommendations.

The kernel of this memo is a translation of the Frontier Summary Report into more business-oriented terms. An English text-writing back-end produces a word processing document with the basic financial data and findings. The Investigative Consultants edit this and add their specific comments.

3.5 Layer 5: Enhancement

EFD is a system that is helping to perform a task, a mass review of claim data for potential fraud, that has never been done. Therefore, early user training focused primarily on the tactical, low-level use of the system and very little on the strategic, high-level use of the system. Now, learning occurs at many levels among various parties.

First, the developers conduct validation studies, using the available data on fraud suspects to examine the performance of the processes in layers 1 and 2. Beyond global measures of performance, we are using machine-learning techniques to improve performance. This is discussed in more detail below.

Second, the Investigative Consultants develop tactics for using the system. Any *ad-hoc* query they formulate in layer 3 can be turned, overnight, into a standard report, and many have since the introduction of the system.

4 THE ROLE OF HEURISTICS IN LAYERS 1 AND 2

Heuristics are at the core of Artificial Intelligence. Most textbook definitions of 'heuristic' resemble 'a procedure to make a choice that is likely, but not guaranteed, to be correct'. In Lenat (1983) heuristics are rule-like structures specifying tests of applicability and actions to consider in exploring a space of concepts. In Pearl (1984) heuristics are numerical functions that evaluate the relative worth of alternative steps in a search path. In EFD, a behavioral heuristic is 'a dimension of observable behavior'. This means, in particular:

(1) It is computable from the claim data (observable).
(2) It is a numerical measurement in some scale of units (dimension).
(3) It reflects aspects of the data that are more or less under the control (behavior) of the healthcare provider.

These three criteria affect our implementation of behavioral heuristics. The full characterization of a behavioral heuristic consists of three parts:

(1) A method of partitioning the data into entities that are associated with each provider. Entities are usually data partitions that correspond to natural entities, for example a patient, a bill, a payment record, or a day. Entities may be further 'qualified' by admitting only those that meet certain criteria, for example a female patient, an assigned bill, a payment record for a surgery, or a day with at least five patients. Quite complex entities are possible, however, such as the 'patient–month diagnosis profile' where data is aggregated to patient, month of payment, and the occurrence bit pattern of certain classes of diagnoses.

(2)   A measurement function applicable to each of those entities. Each heuristic makes not one measurement on the provider but rather many measurements (one on each entity associated with the provider). We will see below why having multiple entities associated with the provider brings added power to the heuristics.

Measures must be real-valued, although integer counts and binary (0,1) values are considered proper subsets of reals. Continuous measures can be dimensionless (proportions) or can have natural units such as dollars. Boolean tests, for example predicates on the entities, are conventionally scored 0 for false and 1 for true.

In constructing measures on entities, the key concern is that moment statistics (mean, variance) must have a meaningful interpretation. This rules out some alternative approaches to measuring behavior. For example, categorical measures might be coded with arbitrary numerical scores. A classification of type of service into {office visit, surgery, diagnostic, other} might yield measures of {1, 2, 3, 4}, respectively, on service entities. In such a case, however, the average score among a set of entities is uninterpretable. Therefore this approach is unacceptable as an EFD heuristic. Since the mean of an indicator (binary) variable equals the frequency of 'true', boolean tests are interpretable, therefore admissible. Multi-valued categorical measures must be implemented as N-1 boolean measures. Similarly, a measure such as automorphic numerical signatures (Sparrow, 1993) cannot be made directly into an EFD heuristic.

(3)   An interpretation of algebraic 'sense'. Each heuristic must somehow suggest the possibility of fraud or conditions related to fraud. Is a higher value of the measure suspicious and a lower value negligible? Or is it vice versa? Or is any sufficiently deviant value suspicious, positive or negative?

For example, in the FINANCIAL:ASSIGNMENTS/NUMBER heuristic, the entity is a bill. This is defined as all payment records sharing the same patient, provider, dates of service and assignment. The measure on this entity is the binary indicator of the bill's assignment to the provider (1) or not (0). The sense interpretation is two-tailed: deviations in either direction are noteworthy.

The use of entities and distributional summary statistics adds an extra dimension of power to EFD's ability to detect unusual situations. Consider, for example, the LOGISTICS:TOO FAR heuristic. This heuristic's entity is the patient's address. The measure is the distance, in miles, between the patient's address and the provider's address. The sense is two-tailed.

Figure 9.1 displays two distributions from this heuristic: the foreground distribution represents the provider, the background his or her peer group.

A typical approach would focus on a single measure such as the average distance or the proportion of distances that are greater than a particular value. This approach

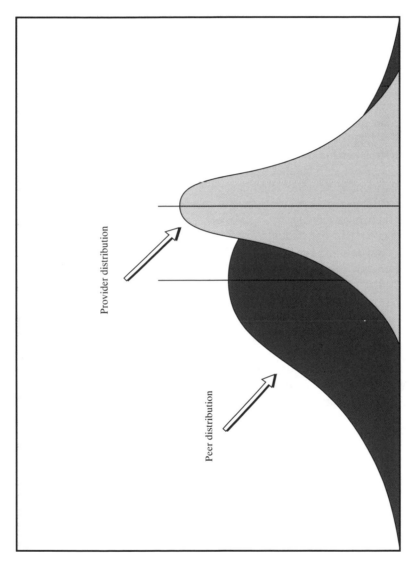

Figure 9.1 Provider–patient distance distribution

provides only one dimension of discrimination: whether the provider's measures tend to be greater than or less than those of the peer group. However, EFD's distributional comparisons (through the mechanism of the information number) can also detect whether the provider's measures tend to be more spread out or less spread out than those of the peers.

Consider the following extreme example. The average provider–patient distance is twenty miles, plus or minus a standard deviation of ten miles. One provider, however, has all his patients come from the same block of apartments twenty miles away. Without distributional information, this highly unusual situation could go undetected.

After constructing a 33-dimensional vector of $\{0, 1\}$ flags for each provider, indicating the provider's extremity with respect to each behavioral heuristic, EFD must now synthesize these findings into a decision: which providers should be brought to the attention of the Investigative Consultants?

Ideally, conjunctive rules that referred to the co-occurrence of particular frontier flags would identify the most important providers. However, there is no expertise to support the knowledge engineering of such rules, nor is the extant data sufficient to induce such rules reliably.

An alternative is to use 'fuzzy' rules (Goodman and Nguyen, 1985) in an attempt to 'soften the edges' and create more robust rules. Experiments with a fuzzy logic approach are equivocal.

To date, the method EFD uses is based on *polymorphous (M-of-N) logic*. A polymorphous category (set, concept) is defined by a predicate of the following form:

'$P(x)$ iff at least M of $\{P_1(x), P_2(x), \ldots, P_N(x)\}$ are true.'

This is also known as 'majority logic' or 'M out of N logic' (Hanson & Bauer, 1989). We call M the *rule parameter*, and the set of P_i the *base predicates*.

In the first pilot version of EFD, a single M-of-N rule decided the issue:

'If the provider is on the frontier of 4 or more behavioral heuristics, then report the provider to the Security Unit.'

By varying the rule parameter in an M-of-N predicate, we create a graded family of predicates, analogous to a fuzzy predicate. The original cutoff of $M = 4$ flags was chosen because it generated a volume of referrals the Investigative Consultants could reasonably handle. In later sections we discuss changes in both the rule parameter and the set of base predicates.

5 EFD'S PERFORMANCE

To date, EFD has been used on twelve metropolitan areas, covering nearly 43 000 providers. A study, conducted in 1991, analyzed EFD's performance on the first six metropolitan areas. There, 898 (about 4%) of 21 786 EFD-examined providers had been brought to the attention of the Security Unit through the electronic 'hot tip'.

To validate EFD (that is, layers 1 and 2; validation of layers 3 and 4 will have to wait for the results of legal action), we use the existing files of suspected frauds as a reference standard. We refer to providers who appear both in the files and among the 21 786 examined providers as 'candidates'.

The first step in validation is the analysis of confusion matrices (Indurkhya & Weiss, 1989). These are two-way candidate-by-multiple (4+) frontier contingency tables. There are six such tables, one for each metro area. We also pool the data and study a seventh, aggregate table.

The results are set out in Table 9.4. The column labeled 'Concentration ratio' is the ratio of the frequency of candidates among multiple frontiers to the frequency of candidates among non-multiple frontiers. It is a measure of EFD's effectiveness in concentrating the known suspects among the subset of providers reported to the Investigative Consultants.

Chi-square statistics were analyzed by Fisher's Exact Test. EFD is undoubtedly selecting candidates in a better-than-random fashion. All but site 5 were confirmed significant. The concentration ratios indicate that the multiple frontiers are at least five times as likely to appear in the suspect files as non-multiple frontiers.

Does EFD provide a benefit to the business? There are several difficult-to-quantify benefits, including its deterrent and competitive marketing value. Highly publicized cases give us visibility in the healthcare provider community that may make a provider think twice before committing fraud against a Travelers policy-holder. Also, our existing and potential customers like knowing that The Travelers is active in fighting healthcare fraud.

But does EFD produce a measurable benefit to the business? In the first five sites alone, Security Unit management estimates that EFD-detected cases have resulted in at least $3.5 million in savings. Because the investigation and prosecution of healthcare fraud cases can extend well beyond their date of detection, the Security

Table 9.4 EFD (layers 1 and 2) performance statistics

Site	Providers examined	Candidates examined	Multiple frontier points	Multiple frontier candidates	Concentration ratio
1	4 795	22	203	3	3.574[a]
2	2 267	6	149	2	7.111[a]
3	7 539	39	156	4	5.411[b]
4	2 555	10	130	4	12.444[b]
5	3 419	6	157	1	4.160 n/s
6	1 211	8	103	5	17.934[b]
Total	21 786	91	898	19	6.144[b]

n/s: not significant
[a]Significant at 5%.
[b]Significant at 1%.

Unit has yet to see complete results from more recently run EFD sites. They do expect continued positive benefits.

6 CHANGING THE RULE PARAMETER

The above analysis measures the diagnostic performance of layers 1 and 2 with the rule parameter set at four frontier flags. A more general approach to the assessment of diagnostic systems is provided by A_z, the area under the Relative Operating Characteristic (ROC) curve (Swets, 1988). Table 9.5 details the computation of the ROC curve for the family of M-of-N predicates based on the 33 behavioral heuristics.

We start with the same set of providers and candidates as before. Let the 'hypothesis' event H+ mean that a provider is a candidate, H− that he is not. Then there are 91 providers for which H+ holds and $21\,786 - 91 = 21\,695$ for which H− holds.

At any particular setting of the rule parameter, a certain number of providers have at least that many flags, and would be labeled 'multiple frontiers'. Denote this 'test' event T+, with the complementary event being T−. At a setting of four, we saw above that T+ holds for 898 providers and T− holds for $21\,786 - 898 = 20\,888$ providers. At different threshold settings, these numbers will vary. There are two natural extremes. With a threshold of zero, all providers are T+. With a threshold of infinity, all providers are T−.

The ROC curve is determined by two rates: False Positives and True Positives. The False Positive rate is defined as the probability of T+ given H−. The True Positive rate is defined as the probability of T+ given H+. This curve reflects the trade-off in sensitivity (ability to obtain T+ when H+ holds) versus specificity (ability to obtain T− when H− holds) at various settings of the diagnostic threshold (Indurkhya & Weiss, 1989).

Based on the data in Table 9.5, a decision was made to shift the rule parameter from four flags to five flags. This provided a significant enhancement in specificity with little loss of sensitivity.

Table 9.5 EFD (layers 1 and 2) relative operating characteristic

#{T+} Rule parameter	#{T + &H+} Multiple frontiers	p{T + |H−} Frontier candidates	p{T + |H+} False positives (%)	p{T + |H+} True positives (%)
0	21 786	91	100.0	100.0
1	3 507	43	16.0	47.3
2	2 034	30	9.2	33.0
3	1 310	24	5.9	26.4
4	898	19	4.1	20.9
5	564	18	2.9	19.8
6	470	11	2.1	12.1
7	326	11	1.5	12.1
	0	0	0.0	0.0

The preferred measure of diagnostic power is A_z, the area under a curve fit to the locus of (False Positive Rate, True Positive Rate) points. If the diagnostic system is performing perfectly, A_z will be 1. If it is performing randomly, A_z is expected to be one-half.

A_z is 0.734 for the ROC in Table 9.5. This level of performance is comparable to that measured in studies of severe storm weather forecasting and some polygraph lie-detection studies (Swets, 1988).

7 DISCOVERING BETTER RULES

To date, the use of automated discovery techniques in EFD has focused on choosing a subset of the base predicates in the M-of-N rule. A hill-climbing search through the power set of the 33 behavioral heuristics was used to maximize A_z *with respect to fraud referrals that the consultants made in the first three sites.* The database of candidates was used to evaluate the final result of the search procedure.

The search was initialized as follows. Twenty-seven confusion matrices were computed, sorting providers by each behavioral heuristic flag (T) versus their occurrence on a list of referrals made by the Investigative Consultants to the Regional Investigators (H). The three heuristics whose matrices had the highest value of the chi-square statistic were used to initialize the list of base predicates. The ROC for the three initial predicates, and the associated A_z, were computed.

The search iterated by appending each unused heuristic, in turn, to the current set of base predicates, and computing A_z. The heuristic which yielded the greatest improvement in A_z was retained and the cycle repeated. If no heuristic's inclusion was able to increase A_z, the search stopped with the current set as the solution.

From the ROC of the final set of 11 base predicates, we chose an appropriate rule parameter by hand. This rule was able to reduce the size of the Multiple Frontier Summary list by 45% *with no loss of candidates.*

8 THE QUERY SYSTEM

The EFD query system is the user's view of the results from the behavioral heuristic measurement process as described in Section 4. The user's initial contact with the query system is through a menu of available sites. Multiple EFD sites may be studied concurrently by the Security Unit, depending on their current 'hot spots' of activity.

From site selection, the system routes requests to an individual knowledge base of studied providers and their respective behavior. Typically, an EFD site has included:

- 5000–10 000 studied providers of medical services
- 50 000–100 000 patients that allegedly have visited the studied providers
- 1–3 million medical services being claimed by patients of studied providers

Site definition and boundaries are determined by the user (prior to the measurement process). Many sites in the past have focused on major metropolitan areas of the United States, but we have had sites such as *'providers of medical services in rural areas east of the Mississippi River'*. Better peer comparisons result from sites that encompass more demographically and culturally homogeneous groups of patients and providers.

The query system for each site has three basic components that make up the user interface. First, there is the set of data and its associated definitions and lexicon of terms by which the users can reference the data. This comprises a set of 23 relational tables including providers, patients, behavioral heuristic measurements, medical service records, and various cross-reference tables. The Investigative Consultants have access to the lexicon whenever they have questions about how a concept is defined or used. There is a built-in look-up facility that makes finding lexicon concepts easy. We continue to expand the lexicon as user needs dictate.

Second, a group of menus and reports form the standard investigation mechanism used to peel back the layers of a provider's behavior. These menus and reports allow the user to jump easily from point to point, following the trail of a particular provider's activity. Many of the reports are actually in fact, hypertext-like menus that make the drill-down effect possible. (See Figure 9.3 for an example of such a report.) The **bold-italic** text in Figure 9.3 is a set of tab-stopped fields that allow the user to select a particular patient and go directly to another report for details on that patient. There are a number of places within the menu system where we have provided this drill-down ability.

The third component of the EFD query system is a link into Trinzic's INTELLECT™ natural language query system that allows the information to be queried in English. This *ad-hoc* mechanism allows arbitrary questions to be asked of the data that may not have been formulated previously into standard report request. *Ad-hoc* queries can be transformed from English-like questions to standard report(s) that are either added to a menu or simply named and made available to the user as short form requests. This has occurred regularly during the first years of operation.

The usual work flow of the Investigative Consultant interacting with the EFD query system starts with the main menu of standard reports. The primary entry point in examining a site is the Multiple Frontier Summary Report. This is the list of unusual providers identified in layer 2.

The task of the EFD user, the Investigative Consultant, is to review the list of identified providers and determine which, if any, should be referred to a Regional Investigator.

For illustrative purposes, we will follow the user's interaction with the EFD query system through a series of figures similar to what the user might see. Although this is an illustration, the basis for it was derived from a real fraud case. All names, identities, places, and dates have been altered to ensure anonymity.

For this example, we will select 'Dr B', an individual osteopath that ranked number one on the Multiple Frontier Summary Report. For this provider, the

```
Copyright 1989-1994, TheTravelers          EFD          FEBRUARY 9, 1994

           F R O N T I E R   S U M M A R Y   R E P O R T

----- Provider Identification Section ----------------------------------
Name: BXXXXXX DO/RXXXXXXX
TIN: 2-123456789-001        Type: OSTEOPATH        Org: INDIVIDUAL
Address: 999 XXXXXXX Avenue, Anytown, USA 12345
Total Paid: $60,683.60        Amount Assigned: $60,683.60
Span of Services:  06/01/92 -  02/16/93        12 Times Flagged

----- Behavioral Heuristic Section -------------------------------------
                            ----- Mean -----    Num
Group:   Heuristic          Subject  Peers    Entity   Flag
ABUSE:   XXXXXXXXXXXXXXXXXXXX  49.00    6.32      16    1ST ORDER
ABUSE:   XXXXXXXXXXXXXXXXXXXX   4.25    2.56      16    1ST ORDER
FINANCIAL:XXXXXXXXXXXXXXXXXXX  23.93   21.20    1041    1ST ORDER
FINANCIAL:XXXXXXXXXXXXXXXXXXX 577.65  188.93     159    1ST ORDER
FINANCIAL:ASSIGNMENTS/NUMBER 100.00   74.12     159    1ST ORDER
LOGISTICS:XXXXXXXXX            3.61    5.31      16    1ST ORDER
LOGISTICS:XXXXXXXXXXXXXXXXXXX 23.46   11.21      35    1ST ORDER
LOGISTICS:WRONG DAY           6.56    0.92    1052    1ST ORDER

4B-□
```

Figure 9.2 Frontier summary report

Investigative Consultant calls up a Frontier Summary Report (Figure 9.2). The top panel lists basic information about the provider, in our case, Dr B. The bottom panel details the behavioral heuristics for which this provider is a frontier. 'Mean' are average measurements, with 'Subject' referring to this provider and 'Peers' his peer group. 'Num Entity' is the number of entities (patients, claims, etc.) in the distribution for that provider with respect to that measurement.

Two behavioral heuristics were left uncensored on this figure: FINANCIAL: ASSIGNMENTS/NUMBER and LOGISTICS: WRONG DAY. (The Travelers regards most of the behavioral heuristics as proprietary and confidential.)

The average of ASSIGNMENTS/NUMBER is the proportion of claims assigned to the provider. Dr B had 100% of his 159 claims assigned versus an average of 74% among the peers.

More significant is WRONG DAY, which measures whether a non-emergency service was rendered on a Sunday or a holiday. Of 1052 services rendered, over 6.6% were on a Sunday or a holiday. This occurs less than 1% of the time in the peer group.

Next, the Investigative Consultant would follow the trail toward the patients, seeing which patients saw the selected provider on wrong days. To do this, the Investigative Consultant selects the Provider/Patient Report (Figure 9.3), which lists those patients of the selected provider that participated in out-of-line behavior. In this case, we see that the first patient (SMITH) contributed 30 times to this provider's WRONG DAY behavioral heuristic measurement. Once this report is on the screen, the Investigative Consultant can simply tab to any patient identifier and go directly to the Detail Patient History Report. This report allows the Investigative Consultant to examine the patient's medical service interaction with providers. It lists the chronology of events as they have been claimed and answers the following questions:

'Who provided the service, who received the service, and who received the payment, if any?'
'What was the diagnosis, service(s), the amount charged, and the amount paid?'
'When did the service occur?'
'Where was the service rendered?'
'Why was the service either paid, adjusted, or not paid?'

Following the paths from provider to patients, the Investigative Consultant now begins to formulate questions for which we have no pre-built reports. Here the natural language query capability of INTELLECT™ is used to explore arbitrary connections in the data.

In our example, the Investigative Consultant would want to know what the provider was doing on Sundays and holidays. The answers are in the Detail Patient History Reports, but it may be laborious to find them among the normal claim transactions. Therefore, the Investigative Consultant enters the *ad hoc* query screen. This is an input area where the user can enter queries in English-like form, such as:

```
Copyright 1989-1994, TheTravelers          EFD          FEBRUARY 9, 1994

------ P R O V I D E R  /  P A T I E N T   R E P O R T  ------

--- Provider Identification Section ------------------------------
Name: BXXXXXX DO/RXXXXXXX
TIN: 2-123456789-001          Type: OSTEOPATH        Org: INDIVIDUAL
Address: 999 XXXXXXX Avenue, Anytown, USA  12345
Total Paid: $60,683.60        Amount Assigned: $60,683.60
Span of Services:  06/01/92 -  02/16/93        12 Times Flagged

------ Patient Identification Section ----------------------------
Patient: 111111S13456789000: SMITH  $5,419.75  07/06/92 08/24/92
    MEDICAL:   XXXXXXXXXXXXXXXXXXXXXXXXX    3
    LOGISTICS: WRONG DAY                    30
Patient: 222222S567234400102: JONES  $4,510.32  04/16/93 06/18/93
    MEDICAL:   XXXXXXXXXXXXXXXXXXXXXXXXX    10
Patient: 333333S223344455600: YOUNG  $4,180.80  06/30/92 11/11/92
    LOGISTICS: WRONG DAY                    6
    MEDICAL:   XXXXXXXXXXXXXXXXXXXXXXXXX    5
Patient: 444444S987654321000: HANSON $3,771.38  12/16/92 01/15/93
    LOGISTICS: WRONG DAY                    4
    MEDICAL:   XXXXXXXXXXXXXXXXXXXXXXXXX    2

4B-□
```

Figure 9.3 Provider–patient report

```
Copyright 1989-1994, TheTravelers          EFD          FEBRUARY 9, 1994

Next Request: REPORT PATIENT, FIRST DATE, WRONG DAY TYPE, AND
SERVICE CODE FOR SELECTED POLICY AND SELECTED PROVIDER


EMPLOYEE         PATIENT      FIRST       WRONG
LAST             FIRST        DATE OF     DAY         SERVICE
NAME             NAME         SERVICE     TYPE        CODE

SMITH            OSCAR        02/07/93    SUNDAY      89998
SMITH            OSCAR        07/21/93    SUNDAY      89998
YOUNG            CLARE        04/11/93    HOLIDAY     90060
YOUNG            CLARE        04/25/93    SUNDAY      90060
YOUNG            CLARE        12/19/93    SUNDAY      90040
HANSON           ESTER        05/16/93    SUNDAY      90060
HANSON           JAMES        01/15/93    SUNDAY      90060
```

4B-▢

Figure 9.4 Example of an *ad hoc* query

'REPORT PATIENT, FIRST DATE, WRONG DAY TYPE, AND SERVICE CODE FOR SELECTED POLICY AND SELECTED PROVIDER.'

Such a request is then interpreted by INTELLECT™ and the results are shown in a custom report (Figure 9.4). In this example, the Investigative Consultant sees that Dr B claims to have rendered office visit services (service codes 90040 and 90060) on several Sundays and, notably, Easter Sunday, in 1993. This information is added to the Investigative Consultant's file for referral to the Regional Investigator.

After selecting providers for referral, the Investigative Consultants write up their findings in memo form. An English text-writing back-end, written in PROLOG, produces a non-technical description of the information on Figure 9.2 as a word-processing document. Much of it is essentially form-filling, but part of the translation, the choice of phrase fragments, is rule-based. The Investigative Consultants edit this and add their specific findings and recommendations.

9 FUTURE DIRECTIONS

With the current set of heuristics, true positive rates over 50% appear unattainable. Over half the candidates are not frontiers for *any* behavioral heuristic. There are several possibilities for this. They may, in fact, not be perpetrating fraud. (Candidates are *suspects*.) They may be misbehaving in ways that escape our measurements. Or their measurements may be 'masked' by more extreme behavior in their peer group. Only further research can determine which is the case.

As different behavioral heuristics are defined, they will be tested in the same way as the current ones. Survivors, i.e. those that are retained among the base predicates of induced M-of-N rules, will suggest variants to try in later sites. In effect, they will spawn mutations. In addition, knowledge engineering sessions with the Investigative Consultants will suggest more specific target groups for modeling. This way, we can develop multiple rules, operating in parallel, not only to identify providers for the Multiple Frontier list but also to begin to characterize them at a high level.

Another issue is change over time. As we continue operations, we must consider whether behaviors will change and how perishable our behavioral heuristics might be. To begin addressing this question, we are maintaining a longitudinal database in one metropolitan area and are testing our most significant heuristics for occurrence trends over time.

A third issue is geographic constraint. EFD deals with transactional claim data, of which our company has many gigabytes. It is impractical to use EFD to examine all areas of the country on an annual basis. To escape this constraint, we are examining the feasibility of an EFD-like system that works on higher-level summary data. We hope to take behavioral measurements of *all* our providers in one 'universal review'.

10 CONCLUSION

EFD is an expert system performing a task for which there is no expert and to which statistical techniques are inapplicable. No one had ever reviewed large populations of claims for potential fraud, and not enough positive cases are (yet) available for statistical or neural network learning methods.

Design goals were, first, to combine available knowledge in a robust manner to perform the task, second, to deliver identified potential cases in an environment that would allow the Investigative Consultants to examine details efficiently, and third, to avoid *ad-hoc* approaches and support extension as understanding of the task improved.

The architecture that ultimately emerged is an opportunistic use of available micro-knowledge (the 33 behavioral heuristics) coupled, in a modular fashion, with information-theoretic outlier detection and selection rules, delivered in a flexible data-exploration environment.

Knowledge discovery is used on two levels. At the performance level, EFD integrates expert knowledge with statistical information assessment to identify providers whose behavior does not 'fit the pattern' of their peers. At the development level, we use a search in the power set of our heuristics to find better identification rules. EFD's performance is statistically significant and valued in millions of dollars.

EFD addresses a class of identification problems that are more likely to be encountered in business than in science or engineering. This class is characterized by fragmentary, theory-less micro-level knowledge and voluminous, yet sparse, data. If a hybrid approach combining knowledge-based systems, statistics, and machine learning proves to be a successful 'bridge' to the acquisition of more complete theories and data, while at the same time yielding value in the performance of the task, it will enable knowledge-based systems techniques to be applied to a much wider class of task domains.

ACKNOWLEDGEMENTS

The development of EFD was sponsored by The Travelers Insurance Companies, Hartford, Connecticut. The views and conclusions contained in this chapter are those of the authors and do not represent official Travelers policy. Many people helped with the development of EFD. The authors would like especially to thank R. James Guzzi, G. David Cooper, John Visnauskas, MD, Mark Gosselin, Ken Rains, and James Cross, MD. The authors would also like to thank the reviewers for their helpful comments.

REFERENCES

Frieden, J. (1991) 'Fraud squads target suspect claims', *Business & Health*, **9**(4), 21–33.
Goodman, I. & Nguyen, H. (1985) *Uncertainty Models for Knowledge-Based Systems*, North-Holland, Amsterdam.

Guzzi, R. (1989) 'Furious about fraud', *Best's Review — Life/Health Insurance Edition*, **89**(12), 66–8.

Hanson, S. & Bauer, M. (1989) 'Conceptual clustering, categorization, and polymorphy', *Machine Learning*, **3**, 343–72.

Indurkhya, N. & Weiss, S. (1989) 'Models for measuring performance of medical expert systems', *Artificial Intelligence in Medicine*, **1**, 61–70.

Lenat, D.B. (1983) 'The role of heuristics in learning by discovery: three case studies', in Michalski, R., Carbonell, J. & Mitchell T. (eds), *Machine Learning: An Artificial Intelligence Approach*. Tioga, Palo Alto, CA.

Major, J. & Riedinger D. (1992) 'EFD: A hybrid knowledge/statistical-based system for the detection of fraud', *International Journal of Intelligent Systems*, **7**, 687–703.

Pearl, J. (1984) *Heuristics: Intelligent Search Strategies for Computer Problem Solving*, Addison-Wesley, Reading, MA.

Sparrow, M. (1993) 'A linear algorithm for computing automorphic equivalence classes: the numerical signatures approach', *Social Networks*, **15**, 151–70.

Swets, J. (1988) 'Measuring the accuracy of diagnostic systems', *Science* **240**, 1285–93.

10
Expert Systems at Lloyd's of London

COLIN TALBOT

1 BACKGROUND

Expert systems are being used at Lloyd's of London to support the process of placing insurance risks and issuing evidence of cover documentation to the assured. This chapter explains the nature of the business problem, the background to the development work, the position today and the plans for more ambitious developments.

Traditionally, insurance risks are placed at Lloyd's by a Lloyd's broker acting as the agent of the client requiring cover. The process is founded on the principle of face-to-face negotiation between the broker and underwriters working on the floor of the Underwriting Room. There follows a description of the process as traditionally carried out.

The broker prepares details of the risk to be covered on a paper document called a 'slip'. This document is used for placing business in the London insurance market (which includes Lloyd's). Initially, the broker uses it as the basis for discussions with an underwriter specializing in the type of business involved. The terms and conditions of the insurance cover, including the premium to be charged, are negotiated and agreed. The underwriter then writes his 'line' on the slip, specifying the proportion of the risk he is accepting. That underwriter thus becomes the leading underwriter on the risk.

Intelligent Systems for Finance and Business. Edited by S. Goonatilake and P. Treleaven
© 1995 John Wiley & Sons Ltd

Using the same slip, the broker then visits other underwriters in Lloyd's and elsewhere in the London insurance market to obtain further cover. Normally, each following underwriter accepts the terms and conditions already negotiated by the leading underwriter and adds his own line to the slip.

Once all the Lloyd's cover has been obtained, the broker prepares a single Lloyd's policy document to be signed on behalf of all the subscribing Lloyd's underwriters. The policy constitutes the formal evidence of cover and must show the precise details of the insurance contract between the assured and the insurer(s).

The slip and the policy are both sent to the Lloyd's Policy Signing Office where the details are sight-checked by an expert insurance technician specializing in the type of business concerned. For each business type, a large number of checks are performed. Any errors, omissions or discrepancies in the information must be referred back to the broker for resolution. Once the policy is correct, it goes through a formal signing and sealing process and is then returned to the broker to be forwarded to the assured (or retained in safe keeping for the assured).

Once a risk has been placed, changes to the client's requirements may result in the risk information being amended in various ways during the period of the insurance. Such changes are effected by an endorsement procedure. The broker prepares a slip endorsement document (known colloquially as a 'honeycomb') and then follows a procedure similar to the placing procedure to gain under-writers' agreement to the change. He then produces a formal policy endorsement document to be checked and returns it to the broker for attachment to the orig-inal policy.

Several variations in these basic processes have evolved to streamline the more standardized types of business. One of these is the use of 'Binding Authority' arrangements. For many types of business written in Lloyd's, the business volumes are high but the individual risks can be described in a relatively uniform manner. To place each risk in the traditional way would therefore be very inefficient. A Binding Authority is an agreement between a set of subscribing underwriters and one or more 'coverholders' (insurance brokers but not necessarily Lloyd's brokers) whereby each coverholder is authorized by the underwriters to accept appropriate risks on their behalf and to issue 'certificates' constituting the evidence of cover. The certificate is issued instead of a policy, and may either explicitly show the full wording or simply refer to an equivalent Policy form.

Apart from such business-driven innovations, the basic placing processes are also undergoing various technology-driven changes due to the increasing use of elec-tronic records in place of hardcopy slips and the use of networking facilities. This provides opportunities for dispensing with face-to-face negotiation for relatively standard business types, low-value risks and simple endorsements. However, the traditional paper-based placing process with face-to-face negotiation is still used, particularly for the most complex risks. The process to produce evidence of cover documentation is also undergoing changes to be described later.

TYPE:	HOUSEHOLDERS INSURANCE		
FORM:	ABC01		

ASSURED: Mr J B Smith, 35 Acacia Avenue, Newtown, Oldcounty, ENGLAND, AA1 9ZZ

PERIOD: 1 January 1994 to 31 December 1994 (inclusive)

INTEREST:	Section 1:	Buildings	£ 80,000.00
		Accidental Damage Extension	Not Included
	Section 2:	General Contents	£ 15,000.00
		Accidental Damage Extension	Not Included
	Section 3:	Accidents to Domestic Staff	As Per Form
	Section 4:	Liability to the Public	As Per Form
	Section 5:	Valuables and Personal Effects	
		I. Gold, Silver As per Spec A	£ 700.00
		II. Pictures	Not Included
		III. Jewellery As per Spec B	£ 5,000.00
		IV. Furs	Not Included
		V. Personal Effects	Not Included
	Section 6:	Domestic Deep Freeze	Not Included
	Section 7:	Pedal Cycles	Not Included
	Section 8:	Personal Money and Credit Cards	Not Included

SITUATE:	Sections 1, 2, 5 I, 5 II, 6	35 Acacia Avenue, Newtown, Oldcounty, ENGLAND, AA1 9ZZ
	Sections 5 III, 5 IV, 5 V, 8	United Kingdom, Europe; and elsewhere in the World for up to 30 days in all.
	Sections 7	United Kingdom

CONDITIONS:	1.	Index Linking Clause (Endorsement No. 14)
	2.	Safe Clause (Endorsement No. 3)
	3.	Dangerous Dogs Act Exclusion Clause (CLS2001)

RATES:	Section 1	£ 80,000.00	@	2.000% =	£ 1,600.00
	Section 2	£ 15,000.00	@	1.250% =	£ 187.50
	Section 5 I	£ 700.00	@	2.000% =	£ 14.00
	Section 5 III	£ 5,000.00	@	2.500% =	£ 125.00

PREMIUM:					£ 1,926.50

INFORMATION: Jewellery kept at 10 Normanton Street, Newtown, Oldcounty, ENGLAND. Stratford 1711 Safe installed.

Figure 10.1 Example of part of a slip for a Householder's risk

2 THE BUSINESS PROBLEM

High rejection rates have always been experienced at the Lloyd's Policy Signing Office (LPSO) in the policy-checking process. For most business types, between 20% and 60% of first-time submissions are rejected. For a few particularly complex business types, the rejection rate may even approach 100%. There are several explanations for these high rates, but one key point is that many brokers have never considered that policy production should be a broking function, since it offers no business benefit for them. They have argued that Lloyd's, like the insurance companies, should produce policy documentation centrally.

The risk information on a slip is a mixture of formatted data (e.g. dates, codes, references and amounts) and free text. An illustration of a typical (fictitious) slip is shown in Figure 10.1. The slip quotes a Form Identifier ('ABC01' in the example shown) specifying the standard form on which the policy is to be based. The example refers to Specifications A and B which would be attached to show detailed descriptions and valuations for individual items.

A number of policy forms are used for each main type of business. Each form constitutes a pre-printed set of 'wordings' describing the basic terms and conditions of the insurance, and also incorporates a 'schedule' in which the risk-specific information is shown. For a particular risk, further wordings (usually referred to as 'clauses') may be added to specify extensions, exclusions, conditions, etc.

The fact that much of the risk information on a slip is free text presents fundamental difficulties in automating the process. The information needs to be captured in a manner that enables an intelligent system to interpret its insurance meaning. The necessary checks could then be performed using a knowledge base expressing rules for the relevant business type. From this, the slip and the evidence of cover documentation could be produced automatically.

This approach also offers significant opportunities to introduce a degree of automation into the process of notifying losses and claims, and determining whether a claim is valid under the terms of the insurance contract. Again, much of the information captured is free text and is currently assessed by specialist claim technicians. Automation could be achieved if the information were captured in a manner enabling an intelligent system to match it against the risk information and make a decision accordingly.

3 RELATED APPLICATIONS

To meet the immediate requirement to produce high-quality policy documentation centrally, Lloyd's has developed a set of systems known collectively as the Policy Preparation System (PPS). PPS consists of a core function supplemented by further functions specifically developed for each business type. It has been developed using Microsoft VisualBasic and Word for Windows is deployed on PCs running Windows. A number of business types have been implemented and more are scheduled, leading to all standard Lloyd's policies being implemented by the end of 1995.

PPS assumes the existence of the slip and provides for LPSO staff to enter the risk information from it in a particular manner to facilitate the production of the policy. Despite its advantages in terms of policy production, it does not support an ideal long-term business scenario, as the risk information is being entered first by the broker to produce the slip then subsequently by LPSO staff in a different manner to produce the policy.

PPS uses a wordings database from which required standard wordings can be requested for inclusion in the policy. It performs a number of basic checks on the formatted data and checks involving the presence or absence of wordings. However, wordings are treated as indivisible entities and the system has no understanding of their insurance content. In insurance terms, the checking rules implemented in PPS are limited and the more technical insurance checking must still be done manually. Moreover, the rules are implemented procedurally rather than being incorporated into a knowledge base.

4   BACKGROUND AND INTRODUCTION TO THE 'SLIPSTREAM' SYSTEM

To streamline the business process further, Lloyd's investigated the feasibility of developing a system to capture risk information at source in a manner which would enable automatic checking of the insurance contract details and production of the evidence of cover documentation (policy or certificate). Such a system could then be deployed in brokers' offices and coverholders' offices where risk information could be initially captured and transmitted to Lloyd's over a network.

It was concluded that it should be feasible to automate the process to a significant extent by using an expert system approach. Such a system would have to understand the insurance meanings of wordings and apply a deep level of checking based on this understanding. It was envisaged that the approach would have to cater for the majority of risks within each business type, and risks would be referred for manual resolution only if unusual features were present which could not be interpreted by the system.

After a prototyping exercise to prove feasibility and gain support from the Lloyd's market, it was decided to develop a pilot system which would cater for the majority of risks within the Householders business type. This is a relatively straightforward type of high-volume business written by Lloyd's underwriters on a Binding Authority basis.

A Lloyd's broker acting as a coverholder for Householders business agreed to assist in the building of the knowledge base and in using the resulting pilot system. The 'SlipStream' system was designed and developed during 1992, using IntelliCorp's KAPPA-PC product, an Object Oriented development environment incorporating a 'production rule' language. The system uses a Microsoft Visual-Basic front-end to capture the risk information and perform basic data validation. It then invokes the expert system to apply the detailed insurance checking rules.

The system was installed in early 1993 on a PC running Windows, and has proved highly successful. Prior to the system being implemented, the coverholder had been using an external bureau to produce certificates, and the resulting savings are estimated at around £40 000 per year.

5 INPUT DATA AND OPERATION

The SlipStream input data consists of the information about a risk, and is entered by the accepting broker or coverholder. In summary, the data describes the assured and the premises to be covered, the period of cover, details of the contents and values and any particular conditions relating to the cover. A given risk can include more than one premise, and the overall cover required for each premise can include cover given under eight possible sections. The data also specifies additional clauses to be included either within a specific section or for the overall insurance.

A number of windowed forms are used, and basic validation is performed during data entry (e.g. to check that the expiry date is later than the inception date). The data is stored and the user can elect to either have the insurance checking carried out immediately or wait until a later time (e.g. if a number of risks are to be entered).

The knowledge base contains 80 rules covering the insurance checks needed on the Householders form. The system has been designed to operate in a goal-driven mode using backward chaining. The structure of the knowledge base is relatively simple. The rule-tree is flat and there is only one goal, i.e. to establish that there is an error condition on the risk being checked. The antecedent for each rule is a sequence of conjuncts (i.e. conditions, each of which must hold).

When using backward chaining in KAPPA-PC, the inferencing process would normally terminate as soon as the goal had been established. In this case, only one error (the first to be found) would be identified, whereas the business requirement is to report *all* detectable errors for a risk being checked. To ensure exhaustive checking, the final conjunct in each rule is a call to a procedure which adds the error details to a growing report list and then returns 'false', thus forcing the inferencing process to continue until all rules have been evaluated. (A rule antecedent therefore consists of at least two conjuncts.)

The following is an example of a rule in the knowledge base, as coded in KAPPA-PC:

```
MakeRule (chk2, [prem|Premises],
    Section6Covered(prem:premisesNo)
  And Not(Section2Covered(prem:premisesNo))
  And Not(IsThereAny?([cls|AC.DDD3057],
        Member?(cls:premisesApplyingTo,
            prem:premisesNo)))
```

```
And    Error(FormatValue ("Section 6 is covered for Premises No. %s
without Section 2 being covered or the \"Section Six Amendment
(DDD3057)\" being used.", prem:premisesNo)),
errorReport:found = TRUE);
```

This rule checks to establish that if Section 6 of the Householders coverage applies to a particular premises, then either Section 2 must also apply to that premises or the 'Section 6 Amendment' clause must be included and must apply to that premises.

6 CURRENT DEVELOPMENTS

The SlipStream project has proved that it is possible to build a knowledge-based system for a particular type of business which can dispense with the requirement for manual insurance checking. However, as this was a pilot system intended for rapid implementation, the design was strongly biased toward the particular business type. To pursue a similar approach for other business types would require a significant amount of further development effort for each type, of which there are approximately 200.

Lloyd's is now considering the feasibility of developing a generalized knowledge base which can contain insurance rules related to any business type, and a generic inference engine to evaluate such rules. Adding a new business type will then become a matter only of populating the knowledge base with the rules applying to that business type. The inference engine will need to be extended only in the event of a new type of construct being needed to represent certain rules.

The inference engine and its knowledge base can then be embedded into systems used by Lloyd's brokers and coverholders, so that risk details can be fully checked at source and are known to be correct when they are passed to Lloyd's.

Hitherto, the interpretation of insurance wordings does not appear to have benefited from any significant work in expert systems development. This would require the development of a formalized language to represent the content of wordings in a knowledge base environment.

Such a language will incorporate a lexicon with entries representing basic 'vocabulary items' quoted in wordings, e.g. 'fire', 'uk', 'europe', 'generalContents', 'carpets', 'fixedGlass', 'standardGlass', 'toughenedGlass', etc. Lexicon entries will be defined in grammatical categories such as Causes, Locations, Physical Items, Financial Items, etc.

Most lexicon entries will be independent atomic items, used simply for the purposes of identifying connections between wordings. The system will not necessarily need to understand anything about 'fire' except that it is a Cause, but it would need to identify any inconsistencies in the conditions relating to coverage against fire. For example, a clause specifically excluding fire may be requested when the insurance does not specify coverage for fire in any case.

On the other hand, some lexicon entries may have particular relationships to other entries. For example, the system might need to know that 'uk' is contained within 'europe' and that 'carpets' and 'fixedGlass' would both be regarded as contained within 'generalContents'. It may also need to know that 'toughenedGlass' and 'standardGlass' are both types of 'fixedGlass', and that one is less likely to break than the other. For a risk involving cover against breakage of fixed glass of both types with separate excesses quoted, it would then be able to verify that the excess for breakage of toughened glass is not higher than that for breakage of standard glass.

The language will also need the concept of 'constructors' to define the syntactic roles of lexicon entries within wordings. A constructor is applied to an 'argument' which may be a single entry or a list of several entries. As an example, the wording:

loss or damage to buildings caused by
(1) fire, lightning, explosion or earthquake
(2) storm, tempest or flood, excluding loss or damage caused by subsidence, landslip or heave

might be represented as follows:

```
PhysicalCover:lossOrDamage
To:buildings
CausedBy:@[
    [fire lightning explosion earthquake]
    [storm tempest flood]
    ButExcluding:
        PhysicalCover:lossOrDamage
        CausedBy:[subsidence landslip heave]
]
```

In this example, lexicon entries start with a lower-case letter (e.g. `buildings`) and constructors start with an upper-case letter and end with a colon (e.g. `PhysicalCover:`). The constructors `PhysicalCover:`, `To:`, `CausedBy:` are used in combination, each having its own argument. Lists of entries are enclosed in square brackets, and, depending on the context, the entries in a list may be either conjuncted or disjuncted. The use of the @ character indicates that a list is segmented into a number of sub-lists, each of which is treated differently. The result of applying a constructor to an argument can represent an argument to which a further constructor can then be applied. Thus, in the example, the constructor group {`PhysicalCover:`, `CausedBy:`} and the constructor `ButExcluding` are applied successively.

In order to populate the knowledge base, the system will need a front-end to capture the content of a wording by requesting information via selection from lists of options. The interface will have to be user-friendly while still enabling a formalized representation to be built from the responses provided.

When details of a risk are entered, the information provided will identify the form to be used and the risk-specific data which will be defined as variable 'slots' in particular wordings. It will specify any additional standard clauses to be used, and may also provide non-standard (i.e. bespoke) wordings to be used. The latter will be entered in the same way as described above for populating the knowledge base.

The basic object class structure representing the knowledge base will consist of classes representing forms, sections within forms, coverages within sections and associated clauses (i.e. extensions, exclusions, conditions and definitions). Each clause may relate either to a particular section or to the overall form. Each form, section, coverage and clause will be formally represented as a wording by means of further classes representing the formalized language components described above.

The inference engine will first resolve each wording into a number of 'atomic' elements, each specifying one type of cover (e.g. 'lossOrDamage', 'staining', etc.), one interest (e.g. 'buildings', 'generalContents', 'carpets', etc.), one cause (e.g. 'fire', 'leakingOfOil', etc.), one location (e.g. 'saidPremises', 'uk', 'europe', etc.) and one sum insured or limit. This resolution will take account of all relevant clauses both for the overall form and for the relevant section.

The elements will then be checked to detect any inconsistencies. These might arise due to duplicated or overlapping cover, exclusions to non-existent cover, contradictory limits, etc. These checks will make use of relationships between vocabulary items defined in the lexicon, for example, the fact that 'carpets' would be regarded as a part of 'generalContents'.

Provided that such a generic inference engine proves practicable, it will need to be steadily refined so that its business range is extended as far as possible. Lloyd's will maintain a Class Library and will establish procedures for making classes available on a commercial basis for embedding in third-party systems in the immediate Lloyd's community and possibly beyond.

Lloyd's views this generic approach to knowledge engineering in the field of insurance wordings as a considerable challenge which can potentially result in considerable savings within the insurance industry.

Part IV
Securities Trading and
Portfolio Management

11

Neural Networks in Investment Management

A. N. REFENES, A. D. ZAPRANIS,
J. T. CONNOR and D. W. BUNN

1   INTRODUCTION

Neural networks is a field of research which has enjoyed a rapid expansion and increasing popularity in both the academic and industrial research communities and are essentially statistical devices for performing inductive inference. From the statistician's point of view they are analogous to non-parametric, non-linear regression models. The novelty about neural networks lies in their ability to model non-linear processes with few (if any) *a priori* assumptions about the nature of the generating process. This is particularly useful in investment management where much is assumed and little is known about the nature of the processes determining asset prices.

The prevailing wisdom among financial economists is that price fluctuations not due to external influences are dominated by noise and can be modelled by *stochastic* processes. Consequently we try to understand the nature of noise and develop tools for predicting its effects on asset prices. It is, however, possible that these remaining price fluctuations, to a large extent, are due to *non-linear* processes at work in the marketplace. Therefore, given appropriate tools, it is possible to represent (and possibly understand) more of the market's price structure on the basis of completely or partially *deterministic* but *non-linear* dynamics.

Intelligent Systems for Finance and Business. Edited by S. Goonatilake and P. Treleaven
© 1995 John Wiley & Sons Ltd

Non-linear modelling techniques are the subject of increasing interest from practitioners in quantitative asset management with neural networks assuming a prominent role. Neural networks are being applied to a number of 'live' systems in financial engineering and have shown promising results. Various performance figures are being quoted to support these claims but there is rarely a comprehensive investigation of the nature of the relationship that has been captured between asset prices and their determinants. The absence of explicit models makes it difficult to assess the significance of the estimated model and the possibility that any short-term success is due to 'data mining'.

In Section 2 of this chapter we review the basics of neural networks. We show that neural learning can be described in terms of established additive non-linear regression. This provides an explicit representation of the estimated models and enables modellers to use a rich collection of analytic and statistical tools to test the significance of the various parameters in the estimated neural models. The methodology can be applied to modelling asset returns in various markets and uses modern financial economics theory on market dynamics to investigate the plausibility of the estimated models and to analyse them in order to separate the non-linear components of the models which are invariant through time from those that reflect temporary (and probably unrepeatable) market imperfections.

In Section 3 we review the process of quantitative investment management and explain how and where neural networks can be applied to enhance the process. The key idea here is that a particular portfolio will depend on the universe of assets under consideration and the properties of those assets at that time. The main proposition of the theory (e.g. Arbitrage Pricing Theory, APT) is that the return of each asset can be explained by a set of (economic and other) factors and can be computed as a *linear* function of each asset's exposure to these factors. In later sections of this chapter we challenge this hypothesis and provide experimental evidence to show that a *non-linear* estimate based on a simple back-propagation network is more accurate.

In Section 4 we introduce the topic of tactical asset allocation which will serve as our benchmark for evaluating linear against non-linear modelling methodologies and describe the data and set-up for our experimental analysis. In Sections 5 and 6 we evaluate linear regression against neural modelling in this context of estimating differential returns between asset classes, on the basis of a universe of economic and financial factors. Much of the work in neural networks has been compared to statistical estimation theory. However, it is very rare that researchers in the machine-learning community actually practise the principles of statistical estimation theory and model construction. Section 5 concentrates on factor analysis using regression and demonstrates the methodological considerations which are an integral part of the model-construction process. Having concluded the phase of variable selection for predicting differential returns between asset classes, Section 6 uses those variables to evaluate the performance of neural networks against a linear approach using real-world data.

2 NEURAL NETWORKS AND NON-PARAMETRIC REGRESSION

The basic computing element in a neural network is a *neuron*. Its operation is directly analogous to the operation of the neuron in the human brain. We model this operation in terms of the neuron's electrical activity: the neuron receives electrical stimuli (signals) from other neurons in the brain; it adds up all these signals to compute the total energy received; some of this energy is expanded to overcome the neuron's natural resistance, and the remaining energy is propagated to neighbouring neurons.

In Figure 11.1 these signals are denoted by v_i. Depending on its point of origin each signal has a different importance. For example, a neuron which is physically in the visual cortex area may assign more weight to a signal coming from neighbouring cells than to one coming from a long-range connection. To account for these differences in importance, the incoming signal is adjusted (i.e. multiplied) by a corresponding weight w_i. Once all the incoming signals are thus adjusted, the neuron sums them up to calculate the total energy. Each neuron induces a local energy loss, say c, which is subtracted from the total energy. Therefore the output (say y') of a neuron is given by:

$$y' = \sum_{i=0}^{n} w_i v_i - c \tag{11.1}$$

So, given this rather simple energy transfer function, how can we build complex computational systems? The answer is twofold. First, the neuron is capable of *learning*. This means that the weights, w_i, for each incoming signal v_i are not fixed but the neuron is capable of adjusting them. For example, if a neuron is told by other neurons that its output signal y' is too weak (or too strong) the neuron is capable of adjusting its weights w_i to increase the strength of its output (or the reverse). Second, neurons can be *interconnected* to form complex structures in a way which mimics the structure of the human brain. Simple structures can solve simple problems; as the complexity of the structure increases so do the computational capabilities of the system. This will become apparent in later sections, but

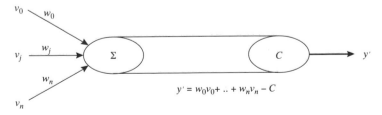

Figure 11.1   The basic operation of neurons. Inputs v_j are weighted by a corresponding amount w_j to form the total energy which is produced as an output y' after adjusting for a local energy loss c

for the time being let us start with a simple structure to demonstrate its resemblance to traditional statistical modelling tools.

2.1 Neural Networks as Linear Regression Estimators

Suppose that we have a simple neural network as shown in Figure 11.2. It consists of three so-called *input units* (A, B and C) and an *output neuron* (y'). Connecting the input units to the output neuron are weighted connections denoted by α, β and γ. For arithmetic convenience we denote the internal resistance of the output neuron by a real number c and we shall represent it as an additional weight connecting the neuron to itself and always generating a signal equal to $1 \times c$. Input units A, B and C have no such constant connections (see Figure 11.2).

Thus given this connectivity, for any value of A, B and C the output of the neural network in Figure 11.2 will have the following parametric representation:

$$y' = \alpha A + \beta B + \gamma C - c \qquad (11.2)$$

The interesting property of neural networks is that they are capable of *learning (to adjust their internal weights) from experience*. A more conventional way of putting this is that neural networks are capable of *estimating parameters from data*. This means that given a set of observations for the variables A, B, C and y, it is possible to *train* the neural network to recognize y given A, B and C. Let us illustrate how this can be done by using a systematic but simple procedure.

Suppose we have a set of observations as shown in Table 11.1. We need to find the relationship between the dependent variable y and the independent variables A,

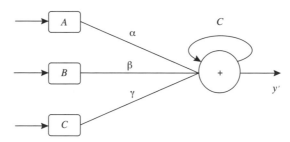

Figure 11.2 A simple neural network system with three input units and one output neuron using a linear energy transfer function

Table 11.1 Training a neural network to become a linear regression

A	B	C	y
−1.0	1.0	−1.5	1.0
0.7	−1.2	1.4	−0.8
...	...	...	...
0.3	0.1	−0.9	−0.3
1.2	−1.5	0.3	0.7

B and C. Initially, we start by assuming that the neural network has no knowledge of this relationship. Thus we initialize its starting weights α, β, γ and c to random numbers. Therefore if we now feed the network with values for A, B and C it will produce an *actual* (or estimated) output y' according to equation (11.2).

Clearly, y' is an inaccurate estimate of y (in fact it is just a set of random numbers). So for the current values of the parameters (i.e. the weights) the network is making an error which we can measure. A reasonable estimate of this error, E, is the difference between the observed (y) and the estimated (y') values averaged over all the observations. For this we can use the ordinary mean squared error, i.e.

$$E = \frac{1}{2N} \sum_{i=1}^{N} (y_i - y_i')^2 \tag{11.3}$$

(where the one half is a conventional scaling factor).

Now, what we need to do is to try to find values for α, β, γ and c which minimize this average squared error. There is a simple way to do so known as *gradient descent*, which iteratively adjusts the weights a, b, g and c in a way that is guaranteed to reduce the overall error E in each iteration. These iterations are performed as a series of steps in which the input data is represented to the network and a new value of the error computed. All we have to do is to estimate by how much we should adjust each weight at the current step. The question that gradient descent asks is: *if we have a unit change in one weight, say α, what is the effect on the average error?* (or conversely: *if we want to have a unit change in* E *what should be the change in, say,* a?). It can be shown easily that (if the initial weights are non-zero and unequal then) adjusting them in a way proportional to their contribution to the overall error will eventually lead to zero errors. This amount in each step for weight α, for example, is given by differentiating equations (11.3) and (11.2):

$$\Delta\alpha = -\lambda \frac{\partial E}{\partial \alpha} = -\lambda \left(\sum_{i=1}^{N} (y_i - y_i')A_i \right) \tag{11.4}$$

A similar expression is used for β, γ and c. The parameter λ is a user-controlled parameter known as the *learning rate* and controls the amount by which we adjust α during each step.

For the network structure shown in Figure 11.2, and particularly its closed-form representation in equation (11.2), statisticians and econometricians will recognize the problem as the (linear) regression of A, B and C on y. In fact, that is exactly what it is. There is indeed an alternative and more efficient way to estimate the weight values (α, β, γ and c) known as *maximum likelihood*. In fact under certain conditions (e.g. normality of the residuals, independence of the input variables) it can be shown that the gradient descent procedure is equivalent to the maximum likelihood procedure. However, we shall stay with the gradient descent procedure because of its generality and its usefulness in building more complex non-linear neural structures.

2.2 Neural Networks as Logistic Regression Estimators

So far, we have assumed that the basic transformation of the neuron's input to its output is simply the total sum minus the neuron's resistance. We have demonstrated that should this be the transfer function, neural networks are no more than linear regression estimators. Let us now consider a more biologically plausible transformation of the input. In fact it is widely believed that neurons do not simply produce an output which is a linear transformation of the input energy but they modulate their output to resemble a so-called sigmoid function, i.e. the larger the input, the larger the output, but there is a point at which the output simply decays exponentially with large increases in the input energy. This is shown diagramatically in Figure 11.3.

The mathematical expression for a typical non-linear energy transfer function such as the one in Figure 11.3 is given by the logistic equation:

$$y' = f(x) = \frac{1}{1 + e^{-x}} \tag{11.5}$$

Figure 11.4 shows a simple neural network with three input units A, B and C, and one output neuron which uses the sigmoid as its non-linear transfer function. The procedure for estimating α, β, γ and c (training procedure) is the same as before. Weights are initialized to (small but non-zero and unequal) random numbers and gradient descent is used to update these weights iteratively. The only difference now is the way in which we compute the partial derivative for equation (11.4). This is simple to do; $(\partial E / \partial \alpha)$ is computed by differentiating equations (11.3) and (11.5) with x being the total weighted input minus c:

$$\Delta \alpha = -\lambda \frac{\partial E}{\partial \alpha} = -\lambda (y_i - y_i') f'(y_i') A_i \tag{11.6}$$

where $f'()$ is the derivative of the sigmoid in equation (11.5).

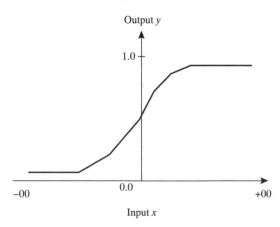

Figure 11.3 A non-linear energy transfer function from input (x) to output (y). The larger the input, the larger the output, but there is a point after which the output experiences exponential decay

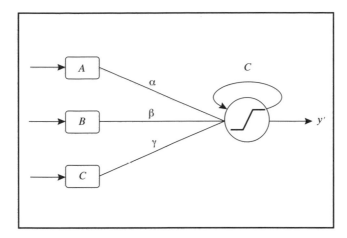

Figure 11.4 A simple neural network system with three input units and one output neuron using a non-linear transfer function

Once the neural network has been 'trained' (i.e. the parameters α, β, γ and c have been estimated) the neural network model has a familiar parametric representation:

$$y' = \frac{1}{1 + e^{-(\alpha A + \beta B + \gamma C - c)}} \tag{11.7}$$

Again statisticians and econometricians will recognize equation (11.7) as the logistic regression equation. If we assume that there exist no linear dependence among A, B and C and the residuals are normally distributed, the procedure is again equivalent to maximum likelihood.

2.3 Neural Networks as Non-linear Non-parametric Regression

So far, we have assumed that the structure of a neural network consists of a number of inputs (independent variables) directly connected to an output neuron. In fact there is no reason to restrict the connectivity of neurons in this way. Indeed, there are over 100 billion neurons in the human brain each of which typically has 100 000 connections. The majority of these connect adjacent neurons but there are also long-range connections. For the purposes of elucidating the capabilities of neural networks as non-linear non-parametric regression models, it suffices to consider a rather simplified form of connectivity whereby neurons are arranged in layers with each neuron in the layer connected to all neurons in the layer before and after.

Figure 11.5 shows one such network. It consists of two input units, a layer of two so-called *hidden* neurons and one output neuron. The non-linear transfer function is the sigmoid from equation (11.5), and we ignore the constant connections for clarity. Our purpose here is to demonstrate how complex non-linear relationships can be modelled.

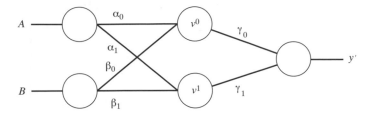

Figure 11.5 A feedforward network with one layer of hidden units

A and B denote input (independent) variables, y the output variable, α_0, α_1, β_0 and β_1 are the connection weights from the input units to the hidden layer and γ_0 and γ_1 are connections from the hidden units to the output unit.

The training procedure is the same as before except that for the connections in the first layer (i.e. α_i and β_i) we need to use the chain rule of derivatives. The task of the training procedure is to estimate a function between input and output which minimizes the ordinary least squares error. This function is parameterized by the network weights and the non-linear transfer function and takes the form:

$$y' = \frac{1}{1 + e^{-(\gamma_0 v^0 + \gamma_1 v^1)}} \tag{11.8}$$

where v^0 and v^1 are the outputs of the intermediate hidden units similarly parameterized by the weights between the input and hidden layer. Ignoring the constant components, we have:

$$v^0 = \frac{1}{1 + e^{-(\alpha_0 A + \beta_0 B)}} \quad \text{and} \quad v^1 = \frac{1}{1 + e^{-(\alpha_1 A + \beta_1 B)}} \tag{11.9}$$

Therefore, given this connectivity and (sigmoidal) energy transfer function the neural network has the following parametric representation:

$$y' = \frac{1}{1 + e^{-\left(\gamma_0 \frac{1}{1 + e^{-(\alpha_0 A + \beta_0 B)}} + \gamma_1 \frac{1}{1 + e^{-(\alpha_1 A + \beta_1 B)}}\right)}} \tag{11.10}$$

This representation is rather too complex to understand intuitively. Let us try to work out a simpler version that is easier to understand and to compare with traditional econometric approaches. To do so we make two rather weak simplifications. The first assumes that at the output level we use a linear energy transfer function. Thus,

$$y' = \gamma_0 v^0 + \gamma_1 v^1 = \gamma_0 \frac{1}{1 + e^{-(\alpha_0 A + \beta_0 B)}} + \gamma_1 \frac{1}{1 + e^{-(\alpha_1 A + \beta_1 B)}} \tag{11.11}$$

The second assumption is even weaker. In investment management applications, it is common to apply smoothing transformations to the input and output variables prior to training, in order for example to remove the effect of statistical outliers. A commonly used transformation is the logarithmic operation. Typically instead of estimating $y = f(A, B)$ one would use the reversible transformation $y = f(\ln(A), \ln(B))$. Using this transformation, the exponential term can be rewritten as:

$$e^{(\alpha_0 \ln(A) + \beta_0 \ln(B))} = e^{(\ln(A^{\alpha_0}) + \ln(B^{\beta_0}))}$$

$$= e^{\ln(A^{\alpha_0} B^{\beta_0})}$$

$$= A^{\alpha_0} B^{\beta_0} \tag{11.12}$$

Using equation (11.12) it is easy to show that equation (11.11) can be rewritten as the sum of two products:

$$y' = \gamma_0 \frac{A^{\alpha_0} B^{\beta_0}}{A^{\alpha_0} B^{\beta_0} + 1} + \gamma_1 \frac{A^{\alpha_1} B^{\beta_1}}{A^{\alpha_1} B^{\beta_1} + 1} \tag{11.13}$$

Overall we have six parameters $\{\alpha_0, \alpha_1, \beta_0, \beta_1$ and $\gamma_0, \gamma_1\}$ ignoring the constants. The task of the learning procedure is to estimate the parameters in a way that minimizes the residual least square error. In the general case for networks with n hidden neurons and m input variables equation (11.13) takes the form:

$$y' = \gamma_0 \frac{A^{\alpha_0} B^{\beta_0} \cdots M^{\mu_0}}{A^{\alpha_0} B^{\beta_0} \cdots M^{\mu_0} + 1} + \gamma_1 \frac{A^{\alpha_1} B^{\beta_1} \cdots M^{\mu_1}}{A^{\alpha_1} B^{\beta_1} \cdots M^{\mu_1} + 1} +, \cdots,$$

$$+ \gamma_n \frac{A^{\alpha_n} B^{\beta_n} \cdots M^{\mu_m}}{A^{\alpha_n} B^{\beta_n} \cdots M^{\mu_m} + 1} \tag{11.14}$$

Thus neural learning is analogous to searching the function space defined by the terms of equation (11.14) and the range of the permissible values for the parameters $(\alpha_0, \alpha_1, \beta_0, \beta_1$ and $\gamma_0, \gamma_1)$. This formulation is strikingly similar to the formulation of additive non-linear non-parametric regression (e.g. ACE and AVAS) (Hardle, 1989a; Breiman and Friedman, 1985) but it differs in many respects. Let us explore some of the implications of the estimation procedure and how they differ from traditional statistical models.

2.4 Universal Approximation and Data Mining

In theory, the parameters (α_i, β_i) can take any value which minimizes the residual error and they start from a random point. Since they raise the corresponding variable to a power we are effectively searching through function space to find the best combination of functions to fit the data. For example, suppose that the initial value of α_0 is equal to 0.5 (i.e. $A^{0.5} = \sqrt{A}$) and by gradient descent we end up with, say, $\alpha_0 = 2$ (i.e. A^2). In the process we have tried all intermediate functions (the learning rate λ controls the step size through this search). This has an important implication.

The procedure, under certain conditions, can be shown to produce a universal approximator (e.g. given enough parameters we will always find a composite function that minimizes the residual error). This is a very powerful property. Neural networks derive one of their main advantages from this property, but also one of their most important weaknesses.

Critics argue that this property makes neural networks perfect 'curve fitters' and epitomizes the 'data mining' syndrome. It may also produce relationships which are counter-intuitive and the whole process is competitive rather than synergetic with theory formulation. For the defence of neural networks, advocates will argue that this is definitely true but we can control the complexity of the search space in several ways. For example, we may introduce complexity penalty terms in the fitness function which penalizes overparameterized networks (models), constrains the search space, and drives redundant parameters to values near or at zero. Alternatively, we may introduce *a priori* constraints. For example, if financial economics theory suggests that there is a quadratic relationship between, say, changes in spot and changes in implied volatility (with spot being one of our independent variables) we may freeze that particular weight (or group of weights) to the value 2. In any case, by letting the data speak for itself not only about the coefficient of a parametric model but also about the nature of the relationship we have a much more powerful tool.

The use of the closed-form representation in equation (11.14) (or similar) makes neural networks synergetic to theory formulation. It enables us to examine the nature of the estimated relationship and conclude for ourselves as to whether it represents some temporary financial anomaly or it is invariant through time.

2.5 Variable Interactions and Non-linear Dependencies

Within typical statistical and econometric applications, the interactions between independent variables are often not systematically investigated. This is generally a crucial but common failing. Variables which are commonly used to explain asset returns (such as interest rates, unanticipated inflation, financial ratios, etc.) are hardly ever truly independent variables. Neural network modelling, as is evident from the closed form in equation (11.14), takes the exact opposite perspective. We start by assuming that all variables might interact with all others. If the data does not support this hypothesis, we expect that the gradient descent procedure will, at least in theory, produce estimates for the parameters α_i, β_i which are equal (or close) to zero. Similarly, if there are no strong direct non-linear relationships between independent and dependent variables the estimation procedure should produce estimates for α_i, β_i which are equal (or close) to one.

In general, non-linear dependencies in financial markets may arise partially because of interactions between independent variables and partially because of direct non-linearities between independent and dependent variables. Neural network models provide an elegant way to deal with both cases. Note that it is always possible (and in many cases desirable) to constrain the search space by using complexity penalty terms in the error function and/or incorporating sensible *a priori* knowledge into the model (for example, by freezing the α_i, β_i parameters to zero values between variables that are known to be truly independent).

2.6 Distribution Theory and Diagnostics

Perhaps the most important feature of linear statistical and econometric methods is that their sampling theory facilitates hypothesis testing on the parameter values (e.g. t-statistics). It is obvious from equation (11.14) that this is no longer possible with neural networks. This, together with the current shortage of general diagnostics, is still one of the largest disadvantages of neural networks.

The development of generalizable applications is therefore not straightforward and many problems remain unresolved. These include robustness to statistical outliers, structural changes, discontinuous and non-stationary data. These areas are currently the subject of intensive research in the statistical, mathematical and econometric sciences. Nevertheless, in its current state of development, neurotechnology has demonstrated that with careful use it is capable of outperforming traditional methods. In the next section we give some examples of successful application development at the NeuroForecasting Unit, London Business School, during the period 1993–5.

3 ACTIVE INVESTMENT MANAGEMENT AND NEURAL NETWORKS

The ultimate goal of any investment strategy is to maximize returns with the minimum risk. In the framework of modern portfolio management theory this is achieved by constructing a portfolio of investments which is weighted in a way that seeks to achieve the required balance of maximum return and minimum risk. The construction of such an optimal portfolio clearly requires *a priori* estimates of asset *returns* and *risk*. Traditionally, it used to be accepted that returns are random and that the best prediction for tomorrow's return is today's return. Over a longer period, expected returns were calculated by averaging historical returns. The prediction error was considered as unpredictable noise and so asset risks were estimated by the standard deviation of historical returns.

This traditional assumption was founded upon the theory of market efficiency, which, stated simply, implies that all public information on future price movement for a tradable asset has already been incorporated into its current price, and that therefore it is not possible to earn economic profits by trading on this information set. In statistical terms, this implies the so-called 'random walk' model above whereby the expectation for the next period is the current value. The empirical finance literature up to the 1970s universally reinforced this view for all actively traded capital markets by testing and failing to refute the random walk hypothesis on daily, weekly and monthly data. Yet this posed a serious dilemma, a gulf between theory and practice, as traders did continue to make profits in the short term. If they were merely lucky, their luck seemed to show no signs of running out.

By the end of the 1980s theory had matured to provide a more comfortable fit with trading realities. In the first place it was recognized that the conventional tests of the random walk hypothesis were very 'weak', in the sense that the evidence would have to be very strong to reject this null hypothesis. Typically, period-by-period changes were tested for zero mean and white noise. Minor departures from randomness would not be significant in these tests; yet it turns out that it only takes minor departures to offer real trading opportunities. From the perspective of scientific method, it is remarkable that the Efficient Market Theory should have gained such empirical support based upon a testing methodology that started by assuming it is true, and then adopted tests which would rarely have the power to refute it!

Econometric tests introduced during the 1980s specified a more general model for the time-series behaviour of asset returns, involving autoregressive and other terms, such that the random walk would be a special case if the first-order autoregressive coefficient were equal to 1 and all others were zero. Thus a more general structural model is proposed for which the random walk is a special case. It turned out that under this model-based estimation procedure it was possible to reject the random walk special-case hypothesis for almost all the major capital market series. Not only is this turnaround more satisfactory in providing results which close the gap between statistical conclusions and practical observation, it also demonstrated the methodological need to propose a general model first, before concluding that a time series has no structure. In terms of inviting the question of how general a model should be proposed in the first place, this focus on empirical model building allows us to consider the use of neural network technology as being a consistent, if extreme, example of this new approach. By proposing the most general of modelling frameworks, it is also providing a stronger 'test' for market efficiency conclusions, albeit with tests that are based not upon statistical hypothesis protocols but on accuracy and performance metrics.

Finally, finance theory has now matured to the position whereby markets can still be considered efficient in the more sophisticated way of representing the expectations, risk attitudes and economic actions of many agents, yet still have a deterministic component to their price movements relating to fundamental factors. Thus we now have the so-called 'multifactor' Capital Asset Pricing Model and Arbitrage Pricing Theory.

Hence the basic stages of analysis that we propose involve:

- *Factor analysis*: in this stage practitioners attempt to identify factors which have an influence on asset prices (and/or returns).
- *Estimating returns of the different assets*: in this stage practitioners attempt to estimate asset prices on the basis of the above factors.
- *Portfolio construction and optimization*: in this stage, given estimates of returns, the problem is to find portfolio weights which maximize the global return of the portfolio and minimize its risk.

We review these stages in more detail in order to describe the limitations of the classical approaches and to identify how and where neural networks can be used to enhance the process.

3.1 Factor Analysis

There are two principal ways to select factors that might have an influence on asset prices. The first is based on the experience, knowledge and judgement of financial economists. This is a perfectly acceptable approach but it suffers from the disadvantage of being subjective and informal. The second way is by statistical analysis. The main methodologies in this approach typically involve principal component analysis, stepwise regression or discriminant analysis. They are applied on the raw data and known factors and/or financial ratios. Both the regression and the PCA techniques are based on linear models. Unfortunately, this might bias the selection of the determinant factors by excluding those that have a non-linear influence on the return (e.g. threshold effect).

An alternative approach is to use neural networks to perform non-linear dimensionality reduction and sensitivity analysis. This might be useful when the influences of the individual factors on asset returns are not constant in time and depend on the value of the other factors. One of the ways in which neural networks can be used in non-linear factor analysis is by recoding multidimensional data in a representation of reduced dimensionality with minimal information loss. This can be achieved by training a neural network to learn the identity map through a so-called 'bottleneck' (see Figure 11.6).

The idea of using auto-associative networks for dimensionality reduction is quite straightforward. If we construct a network with n inputs, a single hidden layer of (say k) units and n outputs, the network computes a transformation from input to output. If the n inputs represent n lags of a time series and the n outputs are the same values we can compute weight values for (exactly) reproducing the input without loss of information. If the number of hidden units k *is less than n* and we are still able to reproduce the input without any loss of information then it can be shown that under appropriate conditions the activation values of the k units in the hidden layer will compute the first k principal components of the data. The obvious extension is to add additional hidden layers between input and earlier hidden layers

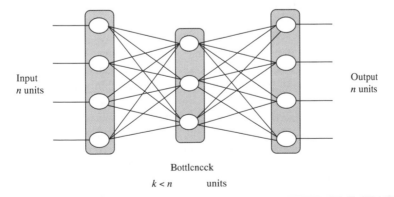

Input
n units

Output
n units

Bottleneck

$k < n$ units

Figure 11.6 General architecture of auto-associative networks for dimensionality reduction

for non-linear encoding. For a complete treatment see Carrol & Ruppert (1988) and Cleveland (1979). This is a simple way of non-linear factor analysis but, like all such models, it may suffer from *high variance* due to the changing dynamics of the data-generating process. An alternative to auto-associative back-propagation networks is the use of unsupervised learning algorithms such as self-organizing feature maps, etc. By constraining the dimensionality of the output grid a similar effect can be achieved.

3.2 Estimating Returns

With multiple-factor CAPM and APT, practitioners explain asset returns as a weighted combination of the different factors as shown in

$$R_i = a_i + b_{i1}f_1 + b_{i2}f_2 + \cdots + b_{in}f_n + \varepsilon_i \tag{11.15}$$

where R_i is the return of asset i, f_j the determinant factors, b_{ij} the exposure of asset i to factor j and ε_i the non-predictable part of the return, i.e. the error of the model. However, there is no reason to assume that the relationship between asset returns and their determinants is linear and independent. In other words, it is highly possible that these remaining price fluctuations ε are due to some extent to *non-linear and interrelated* processes at work in the marketplace. Therefore it might be possible with non-linear models such as neural networks to model more of the market's price structure on the basis of completely or partially *deterministic* but *non-linear* dynamics. The case for the existence of non-linear dependencies in the context of financial markets can be made by using a mix of observations on market microstructure, feedback effects in market prices, and empirical observations. Non-linear dependencies may be explained in terms of non-linear feedback mechanisms in price movements alone. When the price of an asset becomes too high, self-regulating forces usually drive the price down. If the feedback mechanism is non-linear then the correction will not always be proportional to the amount by which the price deviates from the asset's real value. It is not unreasonable to expect such non-linear corrections in the financial markets; they can be explained by the study of market psychology where it is understood that investors and markets overreact to bad news and underreact to good news. There are many participants in the financial markets with complex motivations, reactions and interrelationships. It would be a miracle if these complexities always average out to give an aggregate linear feedback. Once non-linear feedback mechanisms are introduced in the market description, many price fluctuations could be explained without reference to stochastic effects.

It is generally accepted that market imperfections, such as taxes, transaction costs and the timing of the information reaction, introduce non-linearities in the capital markets. Although information arrives randomly to the market, market participants respond to such information with lags due to transaction costs, for example. In other words, market participants do not trade every time news arrives at the market, rather they trade whenever it is economically possible, leading to clustering of price changes. Furthermore, non-linearities are observed when announcements of important factors are made less often than the sampling frequency. For example, weekly money supply announcements will cause non-linearities in daily but not in monthly data.

The prevailing capital market model is based on the rationality of individual investors. In other words, it is assumed that investors are risk-averse, unbiased when they set their subjective probabilities and they always react to information as it is received. The implication is that the data-generating process is linear. In practice, however, investors may well be risk-seeking instead of risk-averse when, for example, taking gambles to minimize their losses. Moreover, they may have excessive faith in their own forecasts thus introducing bias into their subjective probabilities and may not react to information instantaneously but delay their response until their peers reveal their preferences.

Non-linear model such as neural networks may provide a more reliable method of modelling asset returns, because they make no *a priori* assumption about the nature of the relationship between R_i and the selected factors F_j. The neural network approach is to model R_i as a non-linear combination of factor exposures (see, for example equation (11.7)). Having done so it is then possible to compute the expected returns (as a non-linear function of the different factors) and to estimate the risk of the asset as the prediction interval of the model.

3.3 Portfolio Optimization

It is possible to optimize a portfolio in a manner directly analogous to standard mean-variance optimization. The model prediction is used in place of the historical mean and the prediction interval replaces the historical variance. Correlations between asset prices are taken into account by calculating the correlation of the prediction errors of the model when applied to different stocks.

The expected return of the portfolio is the weighted-average of the predicted returns of individual securities in the portfolio. The expected risk σ_p of the portfolio is determined by three factors: the prediction standard error σ_i for each security in the portfolio, the correlation ρ_{ij} between the prediction errors for each pair of securities in the portfolio, and the proportion X_i of each security represented in the portfolio:

$$\sigma_p = \sqrt{\sum_{i=1}^{N} X_i^2 \sigma_i^2 + 2 \sum_{i=1}^{N-1} \sum_{j=i+1}^{N} X_i X_j \rho_{ij} \sigma_i \sigma_j} \qquad (11.16)$$

We can then construct a portfolio of assets that provides the highest return at a given level of risk, or, alternatively, the minimum risk at a given level of return.

Once the network has estimated the relationship between the stock returns and the different factors it is possible to use it to simulate the market for the different scenarios. Thus it is possible to compute the probability distribution for the return of each stock given the probability distribution of each scenario and also the prediction interval of the model. Because of the possible non-linearities of the modelled relationship the return probability distribution may not be normal. It is therefore dangerous to handle these returns in terms of historical expected return and standard deviation.

However, it is possible to construct portfolios on the basis of several criteria. For example, one might be interested in:

- Selecting stocks that have a probability of less than 10% of having a negative return over the next month.
- Constructing a portfolio with maximum expected return for minimum level of risk, or, alternatively, the minimum risk at a given level of return.
- Constructing a portfolio which is immune to interest and/or exchange rate risk; or, alternatively, making the portfolio sensitive to interest and/or exchange rate changes.

The advantage of dynamical systems such as neural networks rests in the ability of constructing a portfolio according to the current state of the market and economic variables rather than on the basis of past correlations and standard deviation of stock prices. Stocks move together because they are sensitive at a same level to certain factors. These sensitivities might not be constant in time. This is why a good diversification should take into account not the past correlation between stocks but the sensitivity of these stocks to certain factors and the probability that these factors will change.

4 TACTICAL ASSET ALLOCATION

Neural networks have been applied extensively to the three stages of investment management described in Section 3. Comprehensive reviews can be found in Demers (1992), Geman, Beienenstock & Doursat (1992) and Hardle (1989a). The research activity on neural networks in the Neuroforecasting Unit at the London Business School has looked at *Tactical asset allocation, Futures price sensitivity, Tactical intra-day currency trading, Factor models for equity investment, Modelling and trading concurrent futures indices*, and *Forecasting volatility for option pricing*. We now describe tactical asset allocation as an example of investment management based on neural networks. In this description we deal with the first two phases in the investment management process: factor analysis and the estimation of expected returns.

Tactical asset allocation refers to the task of allocating funds between different asset classes. The main asset classes considered here are equities, bonds and cash. This is done on the basis of forecasted (or expected) differences in returns between equities and cash versus (estimated) differences in returns between bonds and cash. Expected returns for $t + 1$ are computed on the basis of the values of several economic (and other) variables at time t. We use monthly data on economic variables to estimate differential returns between equities and cash one month ahead. These economic variables are to be selected from a universe of 17 variables and we use stepwise regression (as opposed to discriminant analysis,

Table 11.2 Universe of factors influencing differential returns

Variable	Type of indicator	Lag	Type
X1	Expected returns	0	Levels
X2	Financial	0	Levels
X3	Financial	0	Levels
X4	Financial	0	Levels
X5	Market valuation	0	Levels
X6	Business cycle	0	Level
X7	Investor risk	0	Levels
X8	Investor sentiment	0	Levels
X9	Market risk	1	Levels
X10	International	1	% Changes
X11	International	1	% Changes
X12	Economic conditions	1	% Change
X13	Inflation	2	% Changes
X14	Inflation	2	% Changes
X15	Economic conditions	2	% Changes
X16	Economic conditions	3	% Changes
X17	Economic conditions	3	% Changes

principal components analysis, auto-associative networks, or other methods) to reduce them to a manageable level. The factors selected through the stepwise regression are then used to estimate differential returns. For the estimation we compare the performance of linear regression against a feedforward OLS neural network. Clearly, this comparison is rather limiting to the network approach since the predictive variables have already been selected in a way that best suits the linear regression model. It is therefore probable that those factors explain only the linear part of the relationship. Nevertheless, our purpose is to see if even in these restrictive conditions a non-linear estimator can still provide some incremental value to the model. Furthermore, to the extent that one of the criticisms of neural network methods is their lack of statistical explainability, working from a platform of statistical understanding and looking for incremental value over a conventionally understood set of input variables, we can view this restriction as being the price for potentially improved credibility.

The data covers the period October 1982 to December 1992. The resolution is one month. The total number of independent variables is 17. Some of them must be used lagged due to availability constraints. All the relevant information is summarized in Table 11.2.

5 FACTOR ANALYSIS: STEPWISE VARIABLE SELECTION WITH BACKWARDS REGRESSION

In the factor analysis phase we use multiple linear regression to estimate the linear relationship between the independent variables (x_j^i) and the dependent variable (y).

The least-squares technique is used to estimate the coefficients (b_i) in an equation of the form

$$y_{t+1} = b_0 + b_1 x_{t-\tau_1}^1 + b_2 x_{t-\tau_2}^2 + \cdots + b_n x_{t-\tau_n}^n + \varepsilon_t \qquad (11.17)$$

where ε denotes a random disturbance term and τ a time lag. The regression coefficient b_i represents the expected change in y associated with a one-unit change in the ith independent variable.

Backwards stepwise variable selection was used to determine which of the 17 independent variables to include in the final regression equation which estimates expected returns. This procedure starts by including all the variables and then deleting variables one at a time. The criterion for deleting variables is to select the ones which reduce the sum of squared errors the most. One problem which can occur especially with financial data is multicollinearity — the situation where one or more independent variables are linear combinations of other independent variables. Among other implications (e.g. stability of estimates) it can result in making it difficult to obtain accurate estimates of the individual effects on variables. The t-values and significance levels are used to eliminate the low-sensitivity variables.

After repeated applications this stepwise procedure retains only three independent variables (X_1, X_7 and X_{14}), which account for the 3.13% of the variability in the dependent variable. Table 11.3 summarizes the most important performance metrics for the full regression and the reduced model.

Clearly, the percentage of explained variability is very low, although the estimates of the coefficients of the regression equation are statistically significant (the significance levels are ranging from 0 for the constant, to 0.1751 for X_{14}). This, however, is not unusual in financial engineering applications. The coefficients and other regression statistics are summarized at the end of this section. How poorly the regression equation fits the data is demonstrated in Figure 11.7.

Before proceeding further (or indeed giving up), it is desirable to test the assumption of regression to see if it is possible to make any improvements. This is a procedure which should be followed for all estimation methods including neural networks. The main areas of investigations include:

(1) Testing for serial correlation in the residuals (the presence of which may indicate that there is a systematic error component which could be modelled separately through an error-correction term).

Table 11.3 Regression statistics for the in-sample data-set

Number of independent variables	R-SQUARE	R-SQR (Adjusted)	SE	Durbin–Watson	F-Enter	F-Remove
16	0.10645	0.00000	0.180599	2.1895	na	na
3	0.06131	0.03135	0.171828	2.1330	2	1.5

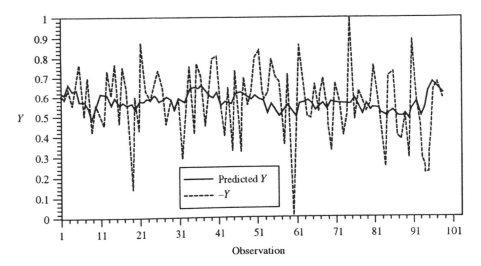

Figure 11.7 Predicted Y by multiple linear regression versus actual. Independent variables selected by a stepwise procedure (backwards elimination)

(2) Testing for possible non-linear transformations of the input variables (the presence of which may lead to an additive regression approach as shown in equation (11.1).

(3) Investigating the effect of influential observations in the data (the presence of which can be dealt with in various ways — e.g. robust regression methods or simple removal).

(4) Investigating the effects of possible non-stationarities in the data.

5.1 Testing the Assumptions of Regression Analysis

The assumptions of regression analysis are: linearity, constant variance, independence of the residuals and normality. It is always advisable to test all these assumptions. Many of these are also made by the Ordinary Least Squares Back-propagation procedure (e.g. constant variance, independence of residuals). The most basic type of residual plot is the one shown in Figure 11.8, the Studentized residuals versus the predicted values. As we can see, the residuals fall within a generally random pattern. Furthermore, because Y is a sequential variable we can use this plot to see if any pattern emerges. Clearly, this is not the case where the effect of carryover from one observation to the other makes the residuals not independent.

We assess the assumption of linearity through the analysis of the residuals and the partial regression plots. Figure 11.8 does not exhibit any non-linear pattern to the residuals, thus ensuring that the overall equation is linear. But we must also be certain that each predictor variable's relationship is also linear, to ensure its best representation in the equation. To do so, we use the partial regression plots for all

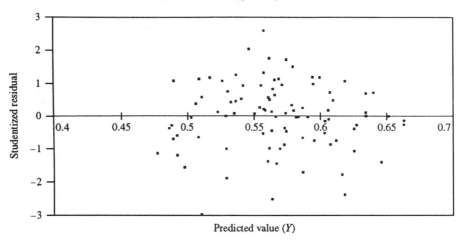

Figure 11.8 Analysis of Studentized residuals

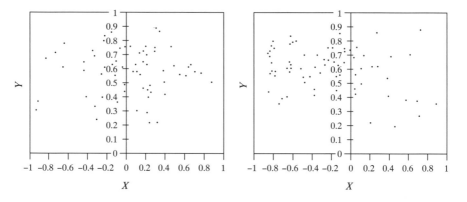

Figure 11.9 Partial regression plot (Y versus X_1) and (Y versus X_7)

predictor variables in the equation (see Figure 11.9 for sample scatter plots of Y against X_1 and Y against X_7).

As we can see from Figure 11.9 there is not a well-defined linear relationship between Y and any of the independent variables X_1, or X_7; thus the variables have not strong effects in the regression equation. Furthermore, these plots do not give any clear indication about any specific transformation that might be used to achieve linearity in the additive sense of equation (11.1) (e.g. Y^2, X^2, log Y, etc.).

From Figure 11.8 again, examination of the residuals shows no pattern of increasing or decreasing residuals. This finding indicates homoscedasticity in the multivariate case.

To test for normality of the residuals we construct the normal probability plot (see Figure 11.10). As we can see, the values do not fall exactly along the diagonal and

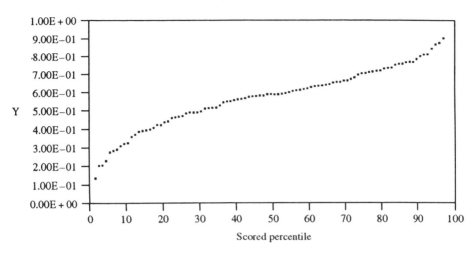

Figure 11.10 Normal probability plot, standardized residuals

there are systematic departures. This shape of the normal probability plot generally indicates a non-peaked distribution. In addition to examining the normal probability plot, a rule of thumb based on the skewness value can be used. The statistic value (z) is calculated as

$$z = \frac{\text{Skewness}}{\sqrt{(6/N)}} = \frac{-0.360956}{\sqrt{(6/98)}} = -1.45879 \tag{11.18}$$

The resultant z-value (-1.45879) is not in the range ± 1.44, and therefore the hypothesis about normality of the distribution can be rejected at the 0.15 significance level (± 2.58 at the 0.01 significance level).

In summary although the assumptions of homoscedasticity and independence hold, the linearity and normality assumptions do not.

5.2 The Effect of Influential Observations

Influential observations include all the observations that have a disproportionate effect on the regression results. Potentially, they include outliers and leverage points (but may also include other observations). Outliers are observations that have large residual values and can only be identified with respect to a specific regression model while leverage points are observations that are distinct from the remaining observations based on their independent variable values. It is always desirable to detect statistical outliers and leverage points which are then commonly removed from the data-set (although there are robust regression methods that can deal with their presence). Table 11.4 gives the outliers and leverage points which correspond to the regression equation discussed in the preceding sections and to the data-set used to derive that equation.

Table 11.4 Statistical outliers and leverage points

	Flagged observations for REG.var18			
Obs. number	Stnd. residual	Leverage	Mahalanobis Dist.	DFITS
19	−2.56937	0.01438	0.41113	−0.31037
60	−3.24460	0.07897	7.24090	−0.95004
75	2.67898	0.01396	0.36966	0.31879
91	2.13211	0.06761	5.97191	0.57415
93	−0.30837	0.12349	12.5355	−0.11575
95	−2.48968	0.03961	2.96981	−0.50563
97	0.11300	0.12546	12.7820	0.04280

Number of flagged observations (residual, leverage or DFITS) = 7.

Table 11.5 Comparative regression statistics for the full regression (REG0), stepwise variable selection (REG2), and stepwise variable selection after removing the influential observations (REG3)

Model	Variables in model	Inf. obs. removed	R-SQR	R-SQR (Adjusted)	SE	Durbin–Watson
REG0	All except X6	No	0.10645	0.00000	0.180599	2.1895
REG1	X1, X7, X14	No	0.06131	0.03135	0.171828	2.1330
REG2	X3, X7, X9, X14	Yes	0.15873	0.11960	0.139911	2.2140

These observations could be due to errors or they could be valid but exceptional observations. The recommended course of action is either to remove or transform them. We removed the seven observations listed in Table 11.3 and this resulted in a substantial improvement in the fit of the regression equation (see Table 11.5).

5.3 The Effect of Non-stationarities

In general, a time series is said to be *stationary* if there is no systematic change in mean (no trend), if there is no systematic change in variance, and if strictly periodic variations have been removed. In real-world applications non-stationary data is a common occurrence resulting in poor model fit and/or poor forecasting ability.

Another common source of concern in application development is what has become known as *model non-stationarity*. This refers to gradually or abruptly changing relationships between the explanatory variables and the dependent variable even in cases when we are dealing with relatively stationary time series.

So far, we have been using data from the period October 1982 to November 1990. The very modest figures for explained variability in the dependent variable (up to 11.96%) probably suggest some form of non-stationarity in our model or in our data. We decided to use another two periods consisting of 48 and 24 months,

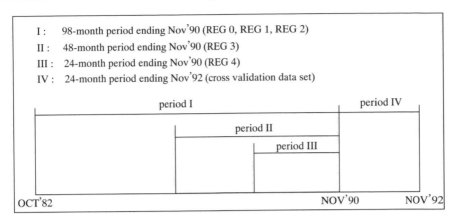

I : 98-month period ending Nov'90 (REG 0, REG 1, REG 2)
II : 48-month period ending Nov'90 (REG 3)
III : 24-month period ending Nov'90 (REG 4)
IV : 24-month period ending Nov'92 (cross validation data set)

Figure 11.11 Graphical representation of the periods used for the derivation of the regression models

ending also in November 1990. The period December 1990 to November 1992 was withheld for out-of-sample testing.

Table 11.6 summarizes for each of the periods depicted in Figure 11.8, (1) the variables selected by the stepwise procedure, (2) the explained variability of the dependent variable (in terms of R-squared and R-squared adjusted), (3) standard error and (4) the Durbin–Watson statistic. As we can see from the table, the Durbin–Watson is in the 'healthy' range for all regressions, suggesting that there are not spurious correlations in the residuals. The explained variability from a very modest 11.96% for the 48-month and 24-month periods becomes 18.46% and 25.59%, respectively. Clearly, these results suggest structural instabilities and short system memory. Consequently, non-robust techniques like MLR are inadequate when long periods are being used.

Table 11.6 Stability of the regression equation across different time periods

Model	Variables in model	Period	R-SQR	R-SQR (Adjusted)	SE	Durbin– Watson
REG0	All except X6	Oct. 1992– Nov. 1990	0.10645	0.00000	0.180599	2.1895
REG1	X1, X7, X14	Oct. 1992– Nov. 1990	0.06131	0.03135	0.171828	2.1330
REG2	X3, X7, X9, X14	Oct. 1992– Nov. 1990	0.15873	0.11960	0.139911	2.2140
REG3	X1, X3, X5, X8	48-Month Nov. 1990	0.25402	0.18462	0.180447	2.2540
REG4	X8	24-Month Nov. 1990	0.30741	0.25592	0.172228	2.4760

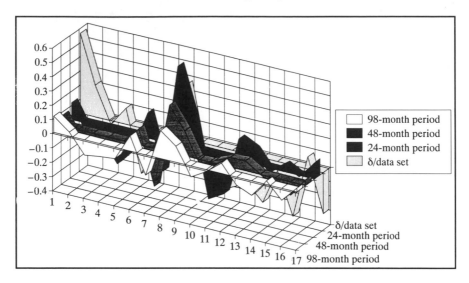

Figure 11.12 Cross-correlations (correlations between the independent variables and the dependent variable) for different periods (periods as in Figure 11.11). X-axis, independent variables; Y-axis, cross-correlations; Z-axis, period

To visualize the changes in the input–output relationships taking place in the period October 1982 to November 1992 we plotted the cross-correlations (correlations between the independent and the dependent variables — periods as described in Figure 11.8). The cross-correlations are shown in Figure 11.9. Observe the large changes in magnitude for some variables and the occasional sign inversions for others. Investor sentiment (X_8) is the single most important variable for all periods ending in November 1990. Since, in the last 24 months before November 1990, its correlation with the dependent variable becomes almost 0.5, it is not surprising that it is the only variable selected by the stepwise procedure in this period.

Having identified a reduced set of variables, we next proceed into the second phase of the process: estimating differential returns for $t + 1$ on the basis of factor exposures at time t (recall these are monthly observations). Since our primary purpose is to test the hypothesis of linearity, we compare Multiple Linear regression on the selected variables against a similar estimation with a simple backpropagation network.

6 ESTIMATING DIFFERENTIAL RETURNS: REGRESSION VERSUS NEURAL NETWORKS

6.1 Results with MLR Models

We mentioned earlier that the data for the period December 1990 to November 1992 was withheld for out-of-sample testing. For all five MLR models described in the previous sections (REG0 to REG4) we obtained forecasts for the dependent variable in that period. The correlation coefficients between the actual and the forecasted figures are reported in Table 11.7.

As expected, in terms of explained variability the full regression model (REG0) is disappointing (less than 1%). The REG1 model does better *out-of-sample* than *in-sample*, but this is spurious since, the cross-correlation for X_1 (expected returns) becomes almost 0.6 in the cross-validation period (see Figure 11.12). The removal of the influential observations (model REG2), although it improved the fit in-sample, out-of-sample it resulted in a negative correlation. Models REG3 and REG4 did much better, explaining what in financial engineering terms is a satisfactory 14.5–17.5% of the variability in Y. Figure 11.13 shows actual versus predicted figures out-of-sample for REG4.

Table 11.7 Correlation coefficients between predictions and targets for the regression models out-of-sample

Model	Correlation coefficient: actual versus predicted out-of-sample
REG0	0.09416
REG1	0.27579
REG2	−0.078701
REG3	0.42317
REG4	0.38074

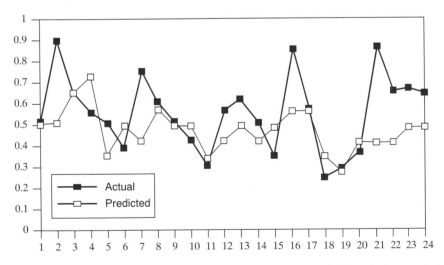

Figure 11.13 Actual versus predicted in the cross-correlation period. Predictions made by REG4

6.2 Results with a Simple Error Back-propagation Network

Modelling with Back-propagation

Neural networks are powerful model-free, universal estimators, which can represent any function. Back-propagation is one of possibly infinitely many algorithms for performing gradient descent in MSE-Weight space. It is a supervised learning algorithm used with multilayer, feedforward neural network architectures. As with any other gradient descent/ascent algorithm, it can potentially be trapped in local minima/maxima. Only extensive experimentation can reasonably safeguard against that event. The major parameters of the algorithm are (1) initial conditions, (2) training time, (3) transfer function, (4) gradient descent control terms, (5) cost function, and (6) topology.

We experimented extensively with training topology and training time, while the rest of the above parameters were fixed. Since our purpose is to provide a rather conservative comparison we deliberately choose a simple network with no error-correction terms, OLS cost function or robustification against influential observations. Some of these extensions to the OLS procedure are described in Refenes (1994). The transfer function was the asymmetric sigmoid with range (0,1). The cost function was the ordinary quadratic cost function. Learning rate was 0.1 and the momentum term also 0.1. The weights were updated after each presentation of a training pattern (continuous update as opposed to batch update).

Training time and topology are the two major parameters responsible for model performance. Normally, it is expected that for a given topology the MSE will tend asymptotically to a limit as training time tends to infinity. To the question of 'given the topology, when to stop training', unfortunately the answer is not 'when the MSE becomes reasonably small'. 'Overfitting' usually occurs well before that point, resulting in degenerate out-of-sample performance. A widely used method to overcome this problem is *training by cross-validation*. According to this technique, while we train the network, periodically we evaluate its generalization ability on the cross-validation data set. Training stops when the generalization MSE becomes minimum.

We trained networks for many different topologies, for periods I, II, III, cross-validating on period IV (periods as defined in Figure 11.11). Network performance was evaluated using the measures presented in the next section.

Measures of Prediction Accuracy

There is not a single measure of prediction accuracy which conveys all the available information to evaluate the quality of a model. Thus although, in our case RMSE is the most relevant, we use it in conjunction with a number of other measures:

- *RMSE*: The common root mean square error. It is an appropriate performance metric in this case since, we are using a quadratic cost function. Care must be taken in its interpretation when there are outliers since their presence has a strong effect on RMSE when the errors are squared.

- *POCID*: Percentage of change in direction correctly predicted. Although it is generally desirable to estimate the correct level in the response vector, in many financial data series it is equally important to predict directional changes. POCID should be used in conjunction with other metrics.

- *Correlation coefficient*: Pearson's correlation coefficient between actual and forecasted values. When equal to 1 the forecast is perfect.

- *T-coefficient*: Theil's coefficient of inequality. Compares the forecasting ability of the model with a trivial predictor (random walk). When 1, implies that the model has the same predictive power as the trivial predictor. When 0, the model does infinitely better.

6.3 Results of Neural Network Simulations

Tables 11.8 and 11.9 quote the values of several performance measures in- and out-of-sample for networks with topology 17-2-1, trained on data from October 1982 to November 1990 (Period I) and tested on data from December 1990 to November 1992 (period IV).The values of the performance measures are given as a function of training time. Observe how out-of-sample performance (Table 11.9) deteriorates as in-sample performance (Table 11.8) becomes better with training time. The need for cross-validation (see Section 4.1) is apparent. If cross-validation was used, normally, one would have stopped training after 500–1000 epochs. The resulting out-of-sample explained variability would be in the order of 15.5–17.5%; in-sample 15.5–32.5%. This, in comparison to a maximum of 7% out-of-sample with MLR (with optimum set of explanatory variables — REG1) seems very promising. Even

Table 11.8 Network in-sample performance. Period I. Topology 17-2-1. Learning rate: 0.1. Momentum term: 0.1

Training time	500	1000	1500	2000	2500	5000	10 000	15 000
POCID	0.78	0.78	0.80	0.84	0.82	0.80	0.80	0.82
RMSE	0.14	0.13	0.12	0.12	0.11	0.11	0.10	0.10
Correlation	0.42	0.57	0.65	0.67	0.68	0.71	0.73	0.75
T-coefficient	0.64	0.58	0.54	0.52	0.51	0.49	0.47	0.46

Table 11.9 Network (17-2-1) out-of-sample performance. Period IV. Learning rate: 0.1. Momentum term: 0.1

Training time	500	1000	1500	2000	2500	5000	10 000	15 000
POCID	0.69	0.78	0.69	0.60	0.60	0.60	0.56	0.52
RMSE	0.14	0.14	0.15	0.17	0.18	0.26	0.32	0.34
Correlation	0.42	0.39	0.36	0.37		0.28	0.26	0.29
T-coefficient	0.71	0.70	0.75	0.83	0.89	1.23	1.53	1.60

Table 11.10 Performance statistics for different networks in the cross-validation data set. Period IV

	Training period				Out-of-sample testing			
Model	Period used for training	Ind. var	Topol.	Epochs	RMSE	POCID	Theil's coeff.	Correl. coeff. O/S
NET0	98 months	all	17-2-1	1 000	0.14	0.69	0.71	0.42
NET1	24 months	X8	1-10-5-1	12 300	0.16	0.78	0.70	0.43
NET2	24 months	X1, X8 X10, X1 5	4-10-1	12 100	0.15	0.82	0.64	0.53
NET3	48 months	X1, X3 X5, X8	4-8-4-1	2 400	0.14	0.70	0.61	0.59
NET4	48 months	X1, X8 X10, X1 5 X10, X1 5	4-5-10-1	3 000	0.14	0.74	0.61	0.63

if we purposely 'overfit' the data for Period I, by training for as long as 15 000 epochs, the network still does better out-of-sample than the optimized MLR model (8.4% explained variability, i.e. correlation 0.29).

As we have seen in earlier sections, this is a problem characterized by structural instabilities and short system memory. Non-robust techniques are problematic when applied to long periods and clearly, ordinary back-propagation is no exception. This becomes apparent by looking at Table 11.10. In the table we see several measures for out-of-sample performance, for networks trained on Periods II and III (period II: 48-month period ending November 1990, Period III: 24-month period ending November 1990) and tested on Period IV (December 1990 to November 1992). As in the case of MLR, performance is clearly related to the period used for training.

Because of the small number of training patterns (either 24 or 48) the number of inputs is kept to a minimum. Although, the ratio patterns/connections is considered to be very low (0.4 to 0.7) this does not seem to be a problem. The inputs are either the ones selected by the stepwise variable elimination procedure or they were selected on the basis of their cross-correlations with the dependent variable.

In terms of explained variability (correlation squared), the networks trained on short periods do much better than NET0. In particular, the networks with four independent variables give correlations out-of-sample ranging from 0.53 to 0.63. *This is equivalent to explained variability in the range of 28–39.5%.*

Another very interesting feature emerging from the information in Table 11.10 is that there seems to be a consistency in the relation between training time and length of training period, i.e. 48-month periods correspond to training times in the range 2400–5000 epochs, 24-month periods correspond to training times in the range 12 100–12 300 epochs, irrespective of topology and number of independent

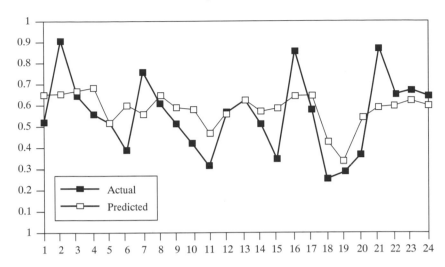

Figure 11.14 Actual versus predicted in the cross-correlation period. Predictions made by NET4

variables. This type of consistency can be very useful in a subsequent step of *confidence interval estimation*.

Figure 11.14 is equivalent to Figure 11.12. It depicts actual versus predicted values for the out-of-sample period. Predictions were made with NET4. For the characteristics of the network refer to Table 11.10.

Although the network fails to predict large deviations from the mean, it does predict directional changes much more accurately than the best regression and thus the higher correlation coefficient. It is more important to predict directional changes consistently than it is to predict a few large (and probably unrepeatable) deviations from the mean. The reason for this is that the estimated returns (together with estimates of risk) are subsequently fed into an optimizer (during the portfolio construction phase). Optimizers have a tendency to amplify these values.

To summarize, in this case study the neural network model outperformed multiple linear regression in- and out-of-sample with $R^2_{reg} \cong 0.17$ and $R^2_{net} \cong 0.35$. Even though this is out-of-sample, it should not be confused with unconditional predictability, as in an actual forecasting application the explanatory factors would need forecasting. However, for conditional forecasts based upon various assumptions for the explanatory factors, for example as one would undertake in a risk analysis, this extra fitting accuracy can be very valuable. Due to non-stationarities in the input–output relationships the appropriate period for model fitting for both techniques should be kept relatively short (not exceeding 48 months). This restricts the number of variables that can be used as inputs to the model to a possible maximum of five or six. However, neural networks do very well with as few as four inputs. Due to multicollinearities among the independent variables, potentially many sets of variables might be used interchangeably with similar results. Furthermore, neural network models exhibit a surprisingly consistent relationship between training time and length of training period, irrespective of topology and set of independent variables.

7 CONCLUSIONS AND CURRENTLY ACTIVE RESEARCH

Having discussed the ways in which previous views of market efficiency have now changed, we have identified persuasive reasons to believe that the relationships between asset prices and their determinants are complex non-linear processes. Neural networks provide a suitable methodology for modelling this type of relationship. However, the development of successful applications is not a straightforward task. It requires a synergetic combination of expertise in investment management, statistical analysis and neural network engineering. We have shown how standard investment management techniques of dividing up problems should be applied first, then a conventional statistical analysis to understand the structure of the data and identify a set of candidate explanatory factors, and only after this is completed should neural networks be applied to the identified subparts of the problem. Thus for the moment, we advocate the use of this conventional statistical modelling platform as a basis for seeking incremental value through neural network modelling in order to maintain a basic understanding of the proposed model.

Many problems of neural modelling remain unresolved. These include robustness to statistical outliers, robustness to discontinuous data and 'weak non-stationarity', dealing with serial correlation and multicollinearities in the independent variables, etc. These areas are currently the subject of intensive research in the statistical, mathematical and econometric sciences. Nevertheless, even in its current state of development, neurotechnology has demonstrated that, with careful use, it is capable of providing more accurate models.

We saw in the tactical asset allocation problem how non-stationarities are usually handled with 'brute-force' techniques which require large numbers of simulations. The major representative of this kind of approach is *windowing*, where models are fitted in rolling windows of fixed size. The window size is a parameter and the appropriate value is determined by extensive experimentation. Another approach is the class of *robust backpropagation* algorithms which can filter common non-stationarities such as level and trend shifts from the data and where neural networks can be applied to the resulting filtered data. *Time-sensitive* cost functions can also be used to assign more weight to the most recent observations, and retraining with the arrival of new data will allow the network to adapt (Hardle, 1989c).

We also demonstrated in the tactical asset allocation problem how in- and out-of-sample error measures differ and, indeed, are subject to such vagaries as the amount of training time. Assigning confidence intervals to forecasts is a problem very much related to the stability of the model performance in- and out-of-sample over different periods. *Jack-knifing or leave-one-out cross-validation* is a technique frequently used to determine the stability of a model. According to this technique, a model is fitted on the available data leaving out only one observation, which is subsequently used for *cross-validation*. The procedure is reiterated until all observations have been used as cross-validation points. The problem with this approach is that although it can be used for estimating confidence intervals for forecasts, if non-stationarities are present these intervals are probably going to be so wide that they will not be useful for any practical purposes. Other more sophisticated (but probably less practical approaches) include calculation of confidence intervals for the forecasts on the basis of several assumptions for the residuals and the data used to derive the model. The problem here is that very rarely are all these assumptions actually met.

We mentioned that factor analysis is an important problem of investment management. The most common technique for identifying factors or variables is a form of indirect sensitivity analysis, where a variable is substituted usually with its mean and its relevance to the dependent variable (and the model) is evaluated by the observed effect on the residuals. Other analysis decides the importance of independent variables by ranking them according to a sensitivity coefficient which is derived by a variety of methods (e.g. by perturbing the inputs and observing the effect on the output). We believe that the direct calculation of the partial derivatives of the outputs with respect to the inputs is a far superior technique which can be used to assess the importance of each individual variable and observe how it changes over time.

Clearly, all issues are interdependent. Handling the above problems and producing a reliable and practical model is neither a straightforward nor an easy procedure. Furthermore, these are not problems associated only with neural network techniques or particular algorithms for updating the synaptic strengths. In the future, estimation of error gradients may be replaced by more efficient algorithms. Instead, new algorithms may hop over, contract, vibrate or flatten the unknown weight-error surface, but the analyst will still have to tackle the problems mentioned above.

REFERENCES

Amari S. (1990) 'The mathematical foundations of neural computing', *IEEE Trans on Neural Networks*.

Breiman L. & Friedman J. (1985) 'Estimating optimal transformations for multiple regression and correlation', *Journal of the American Statistical Association*, **80**, 580–619.

Carrol R.J. and Ruppert, D. (1988) *Transformation and Weighting in Regression*, Chapman & Hall, New York.

Cleveland, W.S. (1979) 'Robust locally weighted regression and smoothing scatter plots', *Journal of the American Statistical Association*, **74**, 829–36.

DeMers, D. (1992) 'Dimensionality reduction for non-linear time series', *Proc. SPIE 1766 'Neural & Stochastic Methods for Image and Signal Processing'*, San Diego.

Geman S., Beienenstock E. & Doursat R. 'Neural networks and the bias/variance dilemma', *Neural Computation*, **4**, 1–58.

Hardle W. (1989a) 'Applied nonparametric regression', *Econometric Society Monographs*, Cambridge University Press, Cambridge.

Hardle, W. (1989b) 'Asymptotic maximal deviation of M-smoothers', *Journal of Multivariate Analysis*.

Huber, P. (1981) *Robust Statistics*, John Wiley, New York.

Leontief, W. (1947) 'Introduction to a theory of the internal structure of functional relationships', *Econometrica*, **15**, 361–73.

Leung, D. (1988) 'Some problems in robust nonparametric regression', unpublished manuscript.

Mallows, C.L. (1980) 'Some theory of nonlinear smoothers', *Annals of Statistics*, **8**, 695–715.

Oja, E. (1991) 'Data compression, feature extraction, and autoassociation in feedforward neural networks', in Kohonen T. *et al.* (eds), *'Artificial Neural Networks'*, Elsevier, New York, pp. 737–45.

Owen, A. (1987) 'Nonparametric conditional estimation', *Technical report 25*, Stanford University, Stanford, CA.

Refenes A.N. (ed.) (1993) 'Neural networks in the capital markets', NnCM'93, *Proc. First International Workshop, 'Neural Networks in the Capital Markets'*, London Business School, November.

Refenes A.N. (ed.) (1994) *Neural Networks in the Capital Markets*, John Wiley, Chichester.

Refenes A.N., Bentz Y. & Burgess N. (1994) 'Neural networks in investment management', *FICOM Journal of Finance & Communication*, to appear in Special Issue on New Investment Technology Issues.

Refenes A.N., Zapranis A.D. & Francis G. (1993) 'Neural network applications in financial asset management', *Journal of Neural Computing and Applications*, to appear.

Refenes A.N. & Mitrelias C. (1993) 'Network pruning by weight variance', *Proc. NIPS'93*, December.

Refenes, A.N., Bentz, Y., Burgess, A.N. & Zapranis, A.D. (1994a) 'Backpropagation with differential least squares and its application to financial time series modelling', *Proc. Snowbird'94*, April.

Refenes, A.N. (1994b) 'Measuring the performance of neural networks in modern portfolio management: testing strategies and metrics', *Proc. Unicom Workshop on Adaptive Computing and Information Processing*, London, January.

Stute, W. (1984) 'Asymptotic normality of nearest neighbor regression function estimates', *Annals of Statistics*, **12**, 917–26.

Tsybakov, A.B. (1982a) 'Nonparametric signal estimation when there is incomplete information on the noise distribution', (in Russian), *Problemy peredachi informatsii*, **18**, 44–60. English translation in *Problems of Information Transmission*, Plenum, New York, pp. 116–30.

Tsybakov, A.B. (1982b) 'Robust estimates of a function' (in Russian) *Problemy peredachi informatsii*, **18**, 39–52. English translation in: *Problems of Information Transmission*, Plenum, New York, pp. 190–201.

Tuckey, J.W. (1987) 'What is projection pursuit?' *Journal of The Royal Statistical Society*, Series A, **150**, 1–38.

Weigend, A.S., Rumelhart D. & Hulberman B. (1991) 'Generalisation by weight elimination applied to currency exchange rate prediction', *Proc. IJCNN'91*, IEEE Press, New York.

12

Fuzzy Logic
for Financial Trading

SHUN'ICHI TANO

1 INTRODUCTION

Fuzzy theory was first proposed by L. A. Zadeh in 1965 (Zadeh, 1965). This tends to be regarded as a mathematical theory because its basis is fuzzy set theory, which can be seen as an extension of the ordinal (non-fuzzy) set theory. However, it was originally proposed to deal with the fuzziness found in expert knowledge, represented in natural-language expressions such as 'smaller US inflation figures reduced the concern of overheating in the US economy'.

In this chapter we examine the challenges of applying fuzzy theory to foreign exchange trading. The chapter describes a fuzzy expert system called FOREX (Foreign Exchange Trade Support Expert System) and a fuzzy system development tool called FINEST (Fuzzy Inference Environment Software with Tuning). In fact, FOREX (Yuize et al., 1991) is one of the largest fuzzy expert systems, implemented with approximately 300 frames and 5000 fuzzy rules. FOREX was developed at LIFE (Laboratory for International Fuzzy Engineering Research, in Japan) as a case study to check the applicability of fuzzy theory to intelligent information systems. FINEST (Tano et al., 1993), on the other hand, is a knowledge-based system shell (not an expert system but an expert system shell), developed at the same laboratory, based on the experience of the development of FOREX.

In the following sections we first describe the characteristics of the application domain, i.e. foreign exchange trading. Next, we show the system architecture of

Intelligent Systems for Finance and Business. Edited by S. Goonatilake and P. Treleaven
© 1995 John Wiley & Sons Ltd

FOREX and evaluate its performance with actual data. Finally, we analyse the drawbacks of fuzzy theory applied to this domain and describe FINEST.

2 THE APPLICATION DOMAIN

Foreign exchange rates strongly depend not only on numerical data such as economic indices, stock prices and interest rates but also on information conveyed verbally (text data), such as comments from government officials, monetary agencies or news broadcasts about international politics. Thus, to forecast foreign exchange rates with a computer it is necessary (1) to devise a method to unify the information obtained from numerical data and text data as traders do in the foreign exchange market and (2) to develop a prediction method on the basis of such information.

Recently, several expert systems for the prediction of trends in foreign exchange and stock markets have been developed (Akiyama, 1990). Input are limited to numerical data and the systems are provided with nothing more than predictions based on expert knowledge concerned with technical analysis. However, other factors such as news regarding national policies or statements from trade officials also have a great effect on foreign exchange rates.

Moreover, as explained in the next section, numerical data as well as text data have inherent fuzziness, and the fuzziness plays an essential role in prediction.

3 FUZZINESS IN FOREIGN EXCHANGE TRADING

The features of foreign exchange trading with respect to fuzziness can be classified as follows.

3.1 Fuzziness of Information (Data)

The information obtained on political issues may be ambiguous. In addition, economic data have varying degrees of freshness. The latest data, of course, better represents the current status of the world. Some data, such as stock prices and foreign exchange rates, are released every day whereas others (commodity price indices, trade balance, etc.) are released semi-annually or quarterly.

For statistical data, moreover, it is very often the case that preliminary figures are released first and final (revised) figures are released at a later date. In many cases, however, there are large differences between preliminary and final figures. Therefore it is necessary to assess the reliability and importance of each figure.

It is important to interpret the meaning of each numerical value in the context of the market. For example, different people in the market will feel that the price of a commodity is high or low, depending on the situation of the market, even if the price is increasing at 4.5%.

3.2 Fuzziness in Knowledge (Rule)

Fuzziness is inherent in the economic knowledge (rules) used in the foreign exchange market. For instance, statements like 'If business activity is vigorous, the prices of the commodity will increase' contain fuzziness.

- *Fuzziness related to the reliability of rule*: With economic events it is sometimes difficult to understand and describe underlying conditions. For instance, the causes of an increase in a commodity price cannot be perfectly described in a rule. The result is that the conclusion of the rule is not always true, even if these conditions are satisfied. In such cases the reliability of the rule must be taken into consideration.

- *Fuzziness in the condition part of the rule*: The fact that economic activity is *vigorous* cannot be expressed with 'crisp' data. Although many indices can be used to describe an economic activity, it is more appropriate to express it with a fuzzy membership function, rather than simply say that it is vigorous.

3.3 Fuzziness in an Evaluation Structure

Suppose that the current economy is booming. One possible scenario is that the prices of commodities increase and interest rates may be increased to suppress these price rises. In this case, the foreign exchange rates will also usually rise. However, it is also possible to imagine a quite different scenario: the booming economic activity results in inflation, which in certain circumstances can reduce demand for the currency. In this case, the exchange rate will go down.

Therefore it is very important to evaluate the current status subjectively as well as objectively. The relative importance of indices such as the prices of commodities and unemployment rates reflects the subjective evaluations of each trader. These evaluations lead to the very different predictions mentioned above.

4   CASE STUDY: FOREX — FOREIGN EXCHANGE TRADE SUPPORT EXPERT SYSTEM

4.1   Basic Structure and Special Features

Figure 12.1 shows the basic structure of FOREX and its special features. FOREX consists of two parts, a state-recognition part and a scenario-evaluation part. First, numerical data and news data are input into the state-recognition part and each datum is transformed into one or a collection of qualitative linguistic values. Several important indices with significant influences on the foreign exchange market are deduced and used as inputs to the scenario-evaluation part. The indices are used to select the most suitable scenario, indicating possible future changes in the exchange rate.

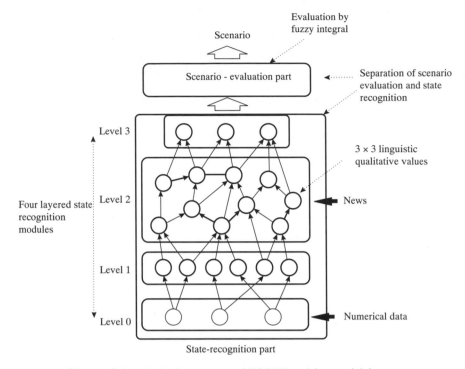

Figure 12.1 The basic structure of FOREX and its special features

The four special features of FOREX are summarized as follows:

- *Separation of the state-recognition part and the scenario-evaluation part*: In the state recognition part, numerical data and news information are analysed and transformed into abstract indicators of the foreign exchange market. These indicators are used in the scenario-evaluation part to choose the most possible scenario, stored in FOREX.

- *Four-layered state recognition*: The state recognition part is divided into four levels (0 to 3), the highest of which presents the highest degree of abstraction. The raw numerical data in level 0 is evaluated and translated into qualitative data, such as 'the Federal Funds (FF) rate of the US is very high', and stored in level 1. Level 2 represents the state transition network, where each state stands for an aspect of economic fundamentals. News data are directly input in level 2. The status of the network is summarized into a few dozen indicators in level 3, for use by the scenario-evaluation part.

- *State representation by* 3×3 *linguistic qualitative values*: Each state in levels 1, 2 and 3 is represented by 3×3 variables, expressing the combination of past/current/future and level/differential/quadratic differential values. The values of all the variables are linguistic qualitative not numerical data.

- *Scenario evaluation by fuzzy integral*: The condition of each scenario is given as a fuzzy measure on the state values used in level 3 of the state-recognition part. Each scenario is evaluated by fuzzy integrals and the results are sorted using fuzzy ranking.

4.2 State Recognition by Fuzzy State Description and Fuzzy Rules

The state-recognition part is divided into four levels, the highest of which represents the highest degree of abstraction. These levels correspond to the following three standpoints: 'Numerical data are converted into linguistic variables', 'Information is synthesized based on economic mechanisms' and 'States are integrated for evaluation as a whole'.

- *Level 0*: This level is used for time-dependent numerical data. Items handled here include stock prices, interest rates and various economic indicators from countries such as Japan, the United States and Germany.
- *Level 1*: This level is for maintaining the results of interpreted (standardized) numerical data. Items on level 1 generally correspond to those on level 0. However, there are more items in this level than in level 0 because some numerical data can be interpreted in different ways (e.g. price index in terms of either the annual or monthly rate of change).
- *Level 2*: This level is used for state recognition. It includes the identification of possible future trends for all items, based on the state values in levels 1 and 2 and on information extracted from news data.
- *Level 3*: In general, this level is used to represent abstract, macro items obtained from integrating two or more items from level 2. The scenario-evaluation function evaluates scenarios by referring to items from this level. Items in level 3 are prices, international expenditures, employment trends, productivity trends, personal consumption, stock market trends, long-term interest rates, short-term interest rates and official positions of trade ministries from countries such as Japan, the United States and Germany.

Figure 12.2 shows a small part of the state-recognition network. The network consists of blocks, representing state values, and arcs, and causal relations between these states. In FOREX each state is represented by 3 × 3 qualitative fuzzy variables and each causal relation is described by a fuzzy production rule as explained below.

3 × 3 *Qualitative Fuzzy Variable*

A state (corresponding to a block in Figure 12.2) is not a physical value but a psychological one and is represented by 3 × 3 fuzzy variables as shown in Figure 12.3. '3 × 3' is the combination of past/current/future and present/movement/pressure (or level/differential/quadratic differential). This representation was suggested by an expert psychological view of the market.

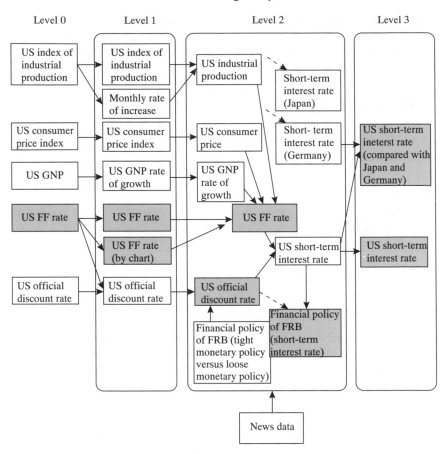

Figure 12.2 Example of a state recognition network

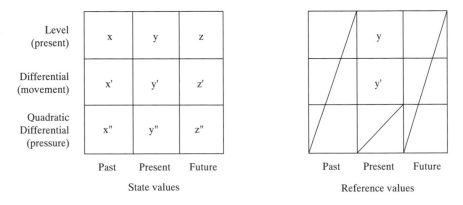

Figure 12.3 3 × 3 qualitative values

The numerical data in level 0 must be transformed into qualitative fuzzy values. A qualitative fuzzy value is a fuzzy set on an ordered set of seven distinct natural-language words. This also corresponds to the expert psychological view. For example, concerning the state, 'the financial policy of the Federal Reserve Board (FRB)', y is defined as a fuzzy set on the ordered set {very tight, tight, more or less tight, normal, somewhat loose, loose, very loose}. Similarly, y' is defined as a fuzzy set on {very strong pressure toward tight policy, strong pressure toward tight policy, some pressure toward tight policy, no pressure, some pressure toward loose policy, strong pressure toward loose policy, very strong pressure toward loose policy}.

All the state values, except the ones in level 0, are represented using a 3×3 relative representation. Reference values are therefore needed to transform numerical values into relative ones (qualitative fuzzy values). However, it is also difficult to represent a reference value as a numerical number. In FOREX, reference values are represented using fuzzy numbers, that is, fuzzy sets on real numbers. In Figure 12.3, the fuzzy numbers y and y' are used as reference values for the evaluation of the actual state values, y and y'.

Figure 12.4 shows how to transform a raw numerical value X (e.g. short-term interest rate 5.9%) into a fuzzy qualitative value Z. Note that the raw numerical value X is a crisp value (5.9%), whereas the reference value Y is a fuzzy number (about 6.5%). First, '$X - Y$' is calculated and the result is expressed as a distribution on the real number 'around zero'. Then the interpretation function, defining the meaning of natural language words, is used to define the qualitative value Z, in this case {0.1/low, 1/rather low, 0.5/normal}.

Handling News Data

At present, news information is processed manually by a domain expert. All the news is first converted into the following format:

(date of news, type of news, person who makes the statement, ...,
    state variable name = value, state variable name = value, ...)

The value of each state is represented using 3×3 qualitative fuzzy variables. State values and news are processed by a conjunctive combination. The actual example given below shows how news about the US short-term interest rates is converted. The date of the news as well as the person making the statement are omitted.

News example: "US Secretary of State, James Baker, announced in the afternoon of the 5th that economic growth, fueled by low inflation, is expected to continue and that there is a conservative attitude towards any increase in official interest rates."

Numerical data X to be interpreted
X : 5.9% (short-term interest rate)

Reference value Y (distribution)

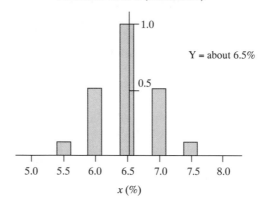

Interpreted value Z

Z={0.1/low, 1/rather low, 0.5/normal}

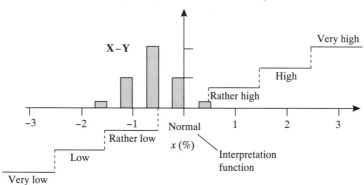

Figure 12.4 Interpretation of numerical data

The above news is transformed as follows:

y′ for *official discount rate* = {0.6/no pressure, 1.0/some pressure to increase}
y″ for *US price trend* = {0.3/rather low, 1.0/reasonable level}
y″ for *US price trend* = {0.3/no pressure, 1.0/some pressure to rise}

The policy for combating inflation is usually to increase the official discount rate. In this case, the degree of inflation is low, so that the pressure for a rise in the official discount rate is 'small'.

Production Rule

Causal relations between the states in Figure 12.2 are represented by fuzzy production rules. An example of a rule is as follows:

Rule 1

IF y'' for *US official discount rate* (*level 1*) has high pressure to increase, and
  y for *financial policy of FRB* (*level 2*) is tight,
THEN y'' for *US official discount rate* (*level 2*) has high pressure to increase.

Fuzzy propositions in the condition part and the consequent part of the rules are described using the 3×3 fuzzy qualitative variables (x, x', x'', y, y', y'', z, z' and z'') and fuzzy predicates (such as 'high pressure to increase' and 'tight').

Rules are usually interpreted using gradual equivalence (Dubois & Prade, 1992; Kato et al., 1992), where the value of a conclusion is determined by the antecedent input data. Another interpretation of the rules is the one based on the Generalized Modus Ponens.

4.3   Scenario Evaluation by Fuzzy Measure and Integral

The value of the macro states is obtained in the state-recognition part. In the scenario-evaluation part these values are used to generate the actual predictions. In FOREX it is necessary to provide the system with scenarios and to store several together with the conditions under which they are likely to occur. The most likely scenario is chosen by matching the conditions with the state values.

One feature of the scenario-evaluation part is that the likelihood of each scenario is evaluated using the fuzzy integral with respect to a fuzzy measure (Sugeno, 1987) defined on the set of conditions of the scenario. The integrated values are the results of the matching of each (usually fuzzy) condition with the value of the corresponding state.

The main reason for using fuzzy integral in the evaluation part is to obtain appropriate values for the overall condition part of each scenario (Grabisch, Yoneda & Fukami, 1991; Yoneda, Fukami & Grabisch, 1992). This cannot be accomplished by merely connecting the conditions using *t*-norm (logical 'and') and *t*-conorm (logical 'or') operations.

Data are collected on a 24-hour basis, from 9 a.m. one day to 9 a.m. the next day. They are processed and scenarios are evaluated using a fuzzy integral. Finally, the results of the evaluation are ordered using fuzzy ranking. The processing steps are described below and an example is shown in Figure 12.5.

- Step 1: Calculate the matching degree of each condition (for instance, calculate the matching degree between the value of the state (x for US business condition) and the fuzzy predicate (high)).
- Step 2: Perform the fuzzy integral, using the matching degrees of all the conditions and a fuzzy measure.

Scenario

A change in the upward trend of US output, a reduced feeling of overheating in the US business, less concern over US inflation, all lead to a decrease in pressure on US interest rates and depreciation of the dollar.

Conditions of scenario

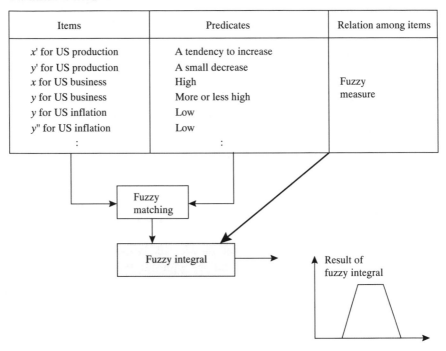

Items	Predicates	Relation among items
x' for US production	A tendency to increase	
y' for US production	A small decrease	
x for US business	High	Fuzzy
y for US business	More or less high	measure
y for US inflation	Low	
y'' for US inflation	Low	
:	:	

Figure 12.5 Example of a scenario and a processing flow

- Step 3: Perform Steps 1 and 2 for all the scenarios prepared by FOREX.
- Step 4: Order the scenarios according to the results of the fuzzy integral, by the fuzzy ranking method (Borotolan & Degani, 1985; Tseng & Klein, 1989).

4.4 Evaluation

To evaluate the performance of FOREX, we carried out a simulation for the period of June 1988. This period was chosen due to the three events which occurred at this time, as shown in Figure 12.6. These events were interpreted by experts (articles in newspapers) as follows:

- Point 1 (6th): An increase in the unemployment rate in the United States indicates the slowing of expansion in economic activity. It means that the

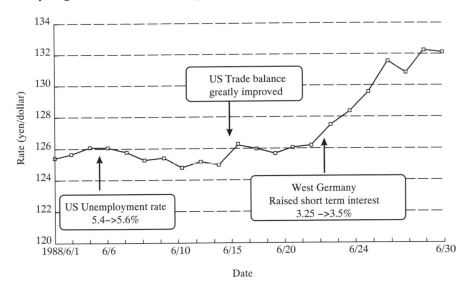

Figure 12.6 Foreign exchange rates in Tokyo in June 1988

government will not increase the official discount rate in the near future. Therefore the dollar will be sold and the exchange rate will fall.

- Point 2 (15th): The amount of the trade deficit is less than expected. It should lead to a rising dollar. However, the foreign exchange rate is stable because basic Japanese indices are still very good.

- Point 3 (22nd): The yen is constantly going down due to the following facts: (1) an improvement in the trade balance of the United States, (2) US monetary agencies seem to consider that a strong dollar is preferable, (3) high interest rates in Germany and (4) Japanese monetary agencies cannot manipulate the interest rate at this time.

FOREX succeeded in selecting the most suitable scenario which meets the analysis mentioned above. Not only were the predictions correct but the values of 3×3 qualitative fuzzy variables in the state recognition part were also adequate compared with those of experts.

5 PROBLEMS AND FURTHER RESEARCH: FINEST

5.1 Problems Found through Using FOREX

We implemented FOREX in order to verify the applicability of fuzzy theory not only to control systems but also to intelligent information systems. Experience proved that fuzzy methodology is feasible and quite effective. However, at the same time, we found several serious problems in fuzzy inference. We classified the problems and made up research themes to study at LIFE and we are now developing FINEST, which stands for Fuzzy Inference Environment Software with Tuning (Tano et al., 1993).

The two main problems we found through FOREX are (1) the insufficiencies of usual fuzzy inference methods and (2) the difficulty in selecting a suitable inference method from a large number of candidates.

5.2 Extended Fuzzy Inference and Tuning Function in FINEST

Concerning the first problem mentioned in Section 5.1, we improved the conventional inference methods in the following four ways:

- *Aggregation with synergy and cancellation*: Even though, in many cases, a rule is simply expressed in the form 'If X and Y Then Z', the 'and' operator has a vague meaning. It may have a strict 'and' meaning or a weak one. When we developed FOREX, we found that many 'and' operators have a synergistic nature.

  We defined a new aggregation operator '*and*' by adding a synergistic effect to an ordinary t-norm operator (Kato et al., 1993). This operator has four parameters expressing the strength of the synergistic effect and the area where this effect is required. When the user sets the value of the parameter controlling the strength of the synergistic effect to 0, our operator behaves like a standard t-norm. Otherwise the operator has a synergistic effect controlled by the value of the parameters. Furthermore, the cancellation property, which is of the same nature as the synergistic effect, can be expressed as a special kind of synergistic effect.

- *Parameterized implication method*: Although there are various implication functions in the field of fuzzy theory, it is difficult to select a suitable one for actual applications. However, if we can define the implication function as a parameterized function we can easily select a suitable inference method by changing the value of the parameters. For example, a parameterized implication function could be defined as a combination of some parameterized t-norm and t-conorm operators.

- *Fuzziness-reducing combination method*: A combination method indicates how to combine the results derived from different inference processes. Many systems use the max operator as a combination method, but this causes a constant increase in fuzziness. The more a particular inference process proceeds, the more the fuzziness of the result increases. Based on the concept of positive/negative belief and using stochastic rules representing dependency, we defined a parameterized combination function which can reduce fuzziness (Tano et al., 1993).

- *Fuzzy backward reasoning*: Although backward reasoning is an indispensable inference method for knowledge processing, its formulation has not yet been achieved. First, we regarded fuzzy backward reasoning as a problem of solving fuzzy relational equations. Two cases occurred: when a solution exists, it is not unique and, on the other hand, there are many cases where no solution exists. As a result, only a few rules can be used for fuzzy backward reasoning (Arnould et al., 1993). Therefore, we extended the goal representation to interval-valued fuzzy sets instead of ordinary fuzzy sets.

Concerning the second problem mentioned in Section 5.1 (i.e. the difficulty of selecting a suitable inference method), we reached the conclusion that automatic tuning of the inference method is indispensable. There have been many studies on the tuning of fuzzy predicates in the field of fuzzy inference. However, as mentioned earlier, the inference method also has many tuning factors. Until now, however, only fuzzy predicates were tuned, and tuning of the inference method has never been considered. We adopted a method similar to backpropagation, which tunes a network representing the calculation flow of the inference process.

5.3 Overview of FINEST

FINEST has an improved inference mechanism and tuning mechanism. In this section the definition and tuning mechanisms for unit-based fuzzy systems are described.

FINEST can be seen as a building tool for fuzzy knowledge-based systems. All the knowledge is represented by units and the final system is built as a collection of units. A unit is defined as an object which simply receives inputs through its input interface, processes them in a specified way and sends the results through its output interface. Thus each unit consists of three parts, i.e. the input interface, the data processing body, and the output interface. Figure 12.7 gives an abstract view of a unit.

A unit is regarded as a basic constituent of the target system. Usually, the target system is built as a combination of several blocks. FINEST can deal with a hierarchical structure of units as shown in Figure 12.8. At the top level of the figure, two units, unit 1 and unit 2, exist. Unit 1 itself is composed of three units, u11,

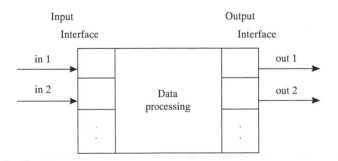

Figure 12.7   An abstract view of a unit

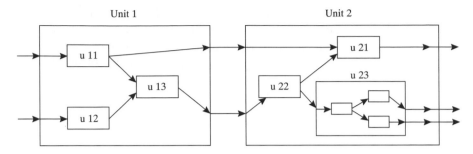

Figure 12.8   Example of a hierarchical definition

u12 and u13. Similarly, unit 2 consists of several units and one of them, u23, is again defined using other units.

FINEST has five types of units: rule units, function units, external units, memory units and composite units. The following is a brief description of each type of unit.

Rule Unit

A rule unit is composed of one or more rules. The rules inside a rule unit use input data for inference and the result is output through the rule unit's output interface. Rule-type knowledge is expressed in the form 'If x is A and/or y is B then z is C', where x, y and z are attribute names and A, B and C are attribute values. These attribute names and attribute values (linguistic label, etc.) are also defined in the rule unit. The inference method for each rule of the rule unit is also specified in the unit. Normally, the parameters of the aggregation operators, the implication function and the combination function can also be defined inside the unit.

Function Unit

A function unit is different from a rule unit insofar as calculations are done using LISP functions instead of rules. A function unit evaluates its input data from the input interface as arguments, and outputs the evaluated value through the output interface. A function unit can have some parameters inside, and the parameters can be tuned if the derivative functions are given. A function unit can be used to represent a defuzzification process or a process whose behavior is known algorithmically. That is, if the defuzzification function is represented using some parameters and the derivative functions with respect to the parameters are given, it can also be tuned.

External Unit

An external unit corresponds to an executable Unix file, and the calculation process of the external unit is executed as a Unix process. The external unit provides its input data to the process, receives the result from the process and then outputs the result through its output interface.

Memory Unit

A memory unit is an area to store information relative to the status of the system and the intermediate results of the inference. For example, rules in one rule unit refer to and update data in memory units. Similarly, functions in a function unit sometimes read from and write to a memory unit. Data in a memory unit are expressed in the form 'x is A'. 'x' represents an attribute name, and 'A' is its attribute value. The attribute value is a numerical value, character, fuzzy set or linguistic label. For example in the case of 'the temperature is 22.5' and 'the height is tall', 'temperature' and 'height' are the attribute names, and '22.5' and 'tall' are the attribute values.

Composite Unit

Units can be combined with each other. A combination of several units is called a composite unit. Using a composite unit, the user can build a system step by step and hierarchically.

Once units are implemented, they have to be tuned. FINEST supports the following two tuning methods:

- *Tuning Based on Input/output Data-set*: In this method, the user specifies the input variables and output variables of the target system to be tuned and provides with the tuning data set, that is, a set of desired input and output data pairs.
- *Tuning to Minimize the Summation of an Observed Variable*: When the user indicates some initial values, the time (or number of iterations) during which the system shall be observed, and a variable to be observed, the parameters of the system can be tuned in order to keep the summation of the value of the observed variable as close to zero as possible.

6 SUMMARY

FOREX is one of the largest fuzzy expert systems, implemented with approximately 300 frames and 5000 fuzzy rules, making full use of fuzzy theory. The experience of the development of FOREX convinced us that fuzzy theory can provide a set of methodologies to deal with the fuzziness found in foreign exchange trading.

Furthermore, we found several serious problems in fuzzy inference. To solve the problems, we are developing FINEST, which has an improved fuzzy inference and a powerful tuning mechanism. FINEST can be seen as a tool for quantifying the fuzzy meaning of natural language expressed in the form of rules.

We are convinced that the treatment of fuzziness is indispensable in building an intelligent system connected to human activities such as financial trading and believe that fuzzy theory is one of the most important technologies for tackling these complex tasks.

REFERENCES

Akiyama, T. (1990) 'New technologies related to AI that have started to be used for establishing a new financial DSS', *NIKKEI Computer*, 26 February.

Arnould, T., Tano, S., Kato, Y. & Miyoshi, T. (1993) 'Backward chaining with fuzzy "if ... then ..." rules', *FUZZ-IEEE'93*, pp. 548–53.

Borotolan, G. & Degani, R. (1985) 'A review of some methods for ranking fuzzy subsets', *Fuzzy Sets and Systems*, **15**, 1–19.

Dubois, D. & Prade, H. (1992) 'Gradual inference rules in approximate reasoning', *Information Sciences*, **61**, 103–22.

Grabisch, M., Yoneda, M. & Fukami, S. (1991) 'Subjective evaluation by fuzzy integral: crisp and possibility case', *Proceedings of IFES'91*.

Kato, Y., Yuize, H., Yoneda, M., Takahashi, K., Tano, S., Yagyu, T., Grabisch, M. & Fukami, S. (1992) 'Gradual rules in a decision support system for foreign exchange trading', *Proceedings of IIZUKA'92*, pp. 625–28.

Kato, Y., Arnould, T., Miyoshi, T. & Tano, S. (1993) 'Conjunction and disjunction with synergistic effect', *FUZZ-IEEE'93*, pp. 225–30.

Sugeno, M. (1987) 'Fuzzy measures and fuzzy integrals — a survey', in Gupta, M.M., Saridis, G.N. & Gains, B.R. (eds), *Fuzzy Automata and Decision Process*, North-Holland, Amsterdam.

Tano, S., Arnould, T., Kato, Y. & Miyoshi, T. (1993) 'Fuzziness reduction method for a combination function', *IFSA'93*, pp. 62–5.

Tano, S., Oyama, T., Kato, Y., Miyoshi, T., Arnould, T. & Bastian, A. (1993) 'Overview and special features of FINEST: fuzzy inference environment software with tuning', *First Asian Fuzzy Systems Symposium*, pp. 294–302.

Tseng, T.Y. & Klein, C.M. (1989) 'New algorithm for the ranking procedure in fuzzy decision making', *IEEE Trans. on SMC*, **19**, 1289–96.

Yoneda, M., Fukami, S. & Grabisch, M. (1992) 'Fuzzy evaluation and decision making in the decision making support system', *Collection of Monographs of Society of Measure Automatic Control*, **28**, No. 9, 1125–34.

Yuize, H., Yagyu, T., Yoneda, M., Katoh, Y., Tano, S., Grabisch, M. & Fukami, S. (1991) 'Decision support system for foreign exchange trading — practical implementation', *Proceedings of IFES'91*, pp. 971–82.

Zadeh, L.A. (1965) 'Fuzzy sets', *Information and Control*, **8**, 338–53.

13

Syntactic Pattern-based Inductive Learning for Chart Analysis

JAE KYU LEE and HYUN SOO KIM

1 INTRODUCTION

The application of intelligent techniques to aid investment decisions is currently a very active area of research. In this chapter, we focus on the support of financial chart analysis using indicators such as stock price trend lines, moving averages of stock prices, and trading volumes. A key assumption of technical analysis using charts is that at a given time the price will have some relationship with the symptomatic patterns that have occurred in previous price charts (Levy, 1966). We will not digress to the debate about the validity of technical analysis itself. However, if readers are interested in this discussion they should refer to Basu (1977), Chung (1987), De Bonnt & Thaler (1985), Joint Research (1988), Le Roy & Porter (1981) and Shiller (1981).

Most popular charts that we see in the daily newspapers display the daily stock price, trading volume, and their moving averages (see Figure 13.1). Typical issues that are raised while we use charts are what kind of patterns we should look for; how we can recognize the patterns; and how we should interpret the implications of the patterns. Most traders and fund managers have their own ways of interpreting these patterns based on their experiences. There are many hundreds of trading rules (Granville, 1976) that have been published using patterns such as moving

Intelligent Systems for Finance and Business. Edited by S. Goonatilake and P. Treleaven
© 1995 John Wiley & Sons Ltd

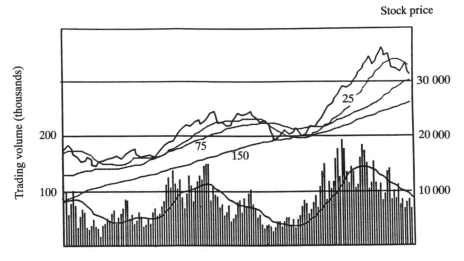

Figure 13.1   An illustrative chart

averages of stock prices as shown in Figure 13.2. However, our pattern definition, pattern recognition and rule generation capabilities are limited and tend to be *ad hoc* and error-prone. To overcome such limitations, we ideally need to automate the following aspects of chart analysis:

(1) Formalization of pattern definition
(2) Automatic recognition of patterns
(3) Rule generation based on the patterns
(4) Performance evaluation of the rules

In this chapter we propose a syntactic pattern-based inductive learning scheme which can support the above. However, we do not intend to claim that this approach can generate all necessary knowledge for investment, because some knowledge is by no means the extrapolation of past patterns. Such proactive knowledge should be obtained directly from 'news' information sources. Thus a mixed knowledge acquisition — a combination of an inductive learning from past patterns and a proactive human judgment from information sources — seems the best strategy. However, automated machine-learning capability alone can still be of great value, therefore we will explore how much machine learning alone can achieve.

2   BACKGROUND

Before we proceed with our approach, let us briefly review the literature about inductive learning, syntactic pattern recognition and their applications in the stock market.

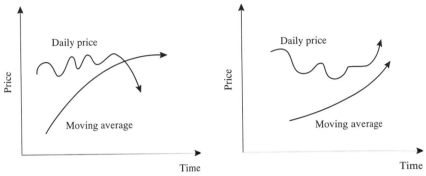

If the daily stock price curve has passed down through the increasing concave moving average curve, the price tends to go down.

If the daily price curve has gone down toward the moving average curve, but recently bounced upward without passing, the price tends to go up.

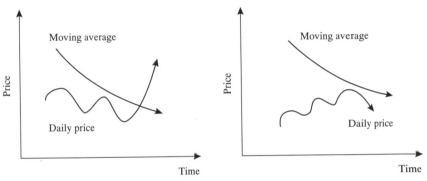

If the daily stock price curve has passed up through the moving average curve which has been non-increasing for a long time, the price tends to go up.

If the daily stock price curve has gone up toward the moving average curve, but recently bounced downward without passing, the price tends to go down.

Figure 13.2   Granville's patterns based on moving averages of stock price

2.1   Inductive Learning

According to Michalski (1983) inductive learning is a heuristic search through the symbolic description space via an inductive inference. The goal of inductive inference is to formulate more general and plausible assertions that can explain the known facts and predict the impact of new ones. Two main forms of inductive learning are learning from examples (concept acquisition) and learning from observation (descriptive generalization). Learning from examples induces the concept recognition rules based on characteristics of given preclassified objects. Learning from observation, on the other hand, constructs a more general description which can characterize a collection of observations.

One of the earliest works designed by Winston (1970) teaches toy block building; AM discovers new concepts in elementary mathematics (Lenat, 1976); BACON discovers classical scientific laws such as Ohm's law and Kepler's law (Langley, 1979); META-DENDRAL infers cleavage rules for mass-spectrometer simulation (Buchanan & Feigenbaum, 1978); ID3 derives discriminating decision trees from large collections of data (Quinlan, 1979); AQ11 induces rules and has been applied to the identification of soybean disease (Michalski & Chilausky, 1980). Recently these approaches have been commercialized and typical products include Expert-Ease, ACLS, Nextra, IXL, VP-Expert, Knowledge Shaper and SEED.

2.2 Inductive Learning Approaches in Stock Market Modelling

Braun & Chandler (1987) used rule induction methods to forecast movements of the Dow Jones industrial average. An enhanced version of the ID3 program was used to learn the weekly market movements using data from 20 technical analysis variables including the 10-day moving average of the Dow Jones, put–call ratios and the volume of transactions. The task was to classify the movements of the market in the following week — whether it would be higher, lower, or at the same level as the previous week.

The program induced rules from data over a period of 54 weeks, and the generated rules were tested on unseen data over a period of another 54 weeks. The decision trees which were generated had an average length of 22 nodes and were able to predict the market 64.4% of the time. The system performed slightly better than the human stock market expert (predictions were correct 60.2%) who had helped to identify the relevant variables to be used for the rule induction system.

2.3 Syntactic Pattern Recognition

A syntactic approach to pattern recognition is particularly useful for patterns which cannot be described with numerical measurements. This approach has been applied to a variety of domains such as fingerprint identification (Rao & Balck, 1980) and carotid pulse wave analysis (Stockman, Kanal & Kyle, 1976). However, there are few reported applications in financial data analysis. Kandt & Yuenger (1988) mention that their system has syntactic pattern-recognition features for technical analysis, but there is no detailed description of the mechanism and performance of the system.

Since our research adopts the syntactic pattern-recognition approach, we will briefly review the approach based on Fu's (1982) work. Syntactic pattern recognition views patterns as a complex of primitives and compositional operators. A pattern can be represented by the composition of simpler subpatterns, and the subpatterns can be described by even simpler subpatterns recursively. The terminals of subpatterns in the structure are the primitives. The structure of legitimate patterns are analogous to the syntactic grammar of languages. In this sense, a language that describes the structure of patterns in terms of a set of pattern primitives and their compositional grammar is called the pattern-description language. When the primitives and grammar of the patterns are defined, we can recognize specific patterns by identifying whether or not the pattern-derived sentence is syntactically legitimate.

3 DEFINITION OF ELEMENTS

In our syntactic pattern-recognition approach we used three popular types of charts: stock price trend lines (Figure 13.3), moving average curves of stock price

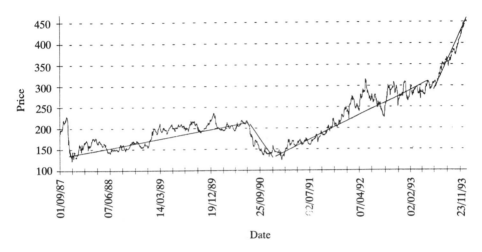

Figure 13.3 Illustrative stock price trend lines

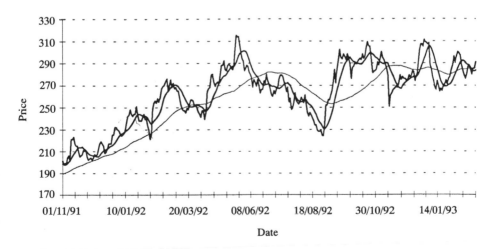

Figure 13.4 Illustrative moving average curves of stock price

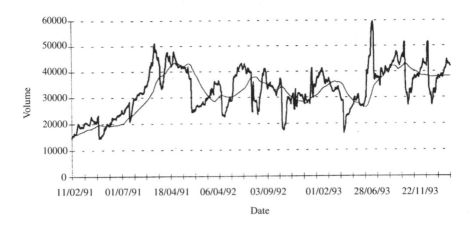

Figure 13.5   Illustrative moving average curves of trading volume

(Figure 13.4) and moving average curves of trading volumes (Figure 13.5). As a first step, let us define basic elements which are atoms of primitives in each of the charts.

3.1   Trend Line of Stock Prices (TLP)

Trend lines are piecewise fitted lines that indicate the local trends of stock prices. Three types of trend lines are central line, upper supporting line and lower supporting line. Figure 13.3 shows a central line which is the same as a simple linear regression line. However, if the mean square error exceeds the predefined tolerance, a new central line will be invoked. Thus the tolerance determines the degree of local fitness. Obviously, the larger the tolerance, the longer the central lines. On the other hand, the upper supporting line is drawn so as to minimize the mean distances between the line and stock price maintaining the stock price below the line. The lower supporting line is the opposite of the upper supporting line.

To define the trend lines formally, let us use the following notations:

t	time point in the time horizon
i	relative time point in a trend line, $i = 1, \ldots, l$
l	length of a trend line
s	starting time of the current line
$\underline{l}$	minimally required length to be a trend line
$P(t)$	stock price at time t
α, β	estimated parameters
$\hat{P}(t)$	stock price estimate at time t by the trend line $\alpha + \beta t$
$e(t) = P(t) - \hat{P}(t)$	estimation error at time t

Central Line

The central line is represented in a linear form $\hat{P}(t) = \alpha + \beta t$. Parameters α and β are estimated according to the following steps:

Step 1: Set the tolerance of the mean square error. Set $s = 1$ and $i = \underline{l}$.

Step 2: Solve model (13.1) which minimizes the mean square error to obtain α and β with the given s and i:

$$\text{Minimize} \sum_{t=s}^{s+i-1} ((P(t) - a - bt)^2/i) = \sum_{t=s}^{s+i-1} (e(t)^2/i) \qquad (13.1)$$

Step 3. If the mean square error is less than the tolerance, increment i by 1 and go to step 2. Otherwise, go to step 4.

Step 4. To trim the errors at the tail of the line, decrement i backwards up to the point whose mean square error is not increasing. Freeze $l = i$. Then a line is constructed.

Step 5. Reset $s = s + l$ and $i = \underline{l}$, and go to step 2 until all data points are exhausted.

Upper Supporting Line

The steps of drawing the upper supporting line is similar to those for the central line. The only difference is that the mean square error in model (13.1) is replaced by the term $\sum_{t=s}^{s+i-1}(-e(t)/i)$ in model (13.2). The model can be solved by a linear programming algorithm:

$$\text{Minimize} \sum_{t=s}^{s+i-1} ((a + bt - P(t))/i) = \sum_{t=s}^{s+i-1} (-e(t)/i) \qquad (13.2)$$

$$\text{subject to } a + bt \geq P(t)$$

Lower Supporting Line

In the same way, the lower supporting line can be defined by replacing model (13.1) by (13.3):

$$\text{Minimize} \sum_{t=s}^{s+i-1} ((P(t) - a - bt)/i) = \sum_{t=s}^{s+i-1} (e(t)/i) \qquad (13.3)$$

$$\text{subject to } P(t) \geq a + bt$$

Key elementary attributes to specify the trend lines are slope of each line, direction of the starting point of the line following the tail of the line, and change of gaps between two different types of lines. The slope can be classified by the 'intervals of angles'; shift direction 'up' or 'down'; and changes of 'wider' or 'narrower' gaps. The line and gap elements can be represented in frames as shown in Figure 13.6.

```
{ { TLP element
   LINE TYPE: [central line upper supporting line lower supporting line]
   TOLERANCE: value
   SLOPE: lower bound upper bound
   SHIFT AT TAIL: [up down]          } }

{ { TLP GAP element
   TLP UPPER: TLP element
   TLP LOWER: TLP element
   GAP: [narrower wider]          } }


Legend

Capital letters:  reserved words
[ ] :  one of the statements should be chosen
```

Figure 13.6 Syntax of elements of trend line of stock price

For instance, the example elements are as follows.

{{*TLP-1*
   LINE-TYPE: *lower-supporting-line*
   TOLERANCE: *20*
   SLOPE: *0 20*
   SHIFT-AT-TAIL: *up*}}
{{*TLP-2*
   LINE-TYPE: *upper-supporting-line*
   TOLERANCE: *15*
   SLOPE: *20 45*
   SHIFT-AT-TAIL: *down*}}
{{*TLP-GAP-12*
   TLP-UPPER: *TLP-2*
   TLP-LOWER: *TLP-1*
   GAP: *wider*}}

3.2   Moving Average Curves of Stock Price (MAP)

We use two moving average curves of stock price. One is relatively shorter-term moving average than the other. The n-day Moving Average (MA) of stock price at day t is defined as

$$\text{MAP}_n(t) = \sum_{j=t-n+1}^{t} \hat{P}(j)/n \qquad (13.4)$$

We consider five attributes from the moving average curves: slope of approximate derivative, slope of approximate second order derivative, number of data points n in equation (13.4) (length), gap between two moving averages, and relative topological position of two moving averages.

Formal definition of the attributes are as follows.

Slope of an Approximate Derivative

A derivative is the slope of a curve when the curve can be defined as a continuous function and is differentiable. Since the moving average curve of the stock price is a collection of discrete time points, the curve is not differentiable. Therefore we adopt the approximate derivative defined below instead of an exact derivative:

$$\text{Slope of approximate derivative at time } t = \frac{(\text{MAP}_n(t) - \text{MAP}_n(t-d))}{d}$$

$$(13.5)$$

where d is the time lag. The slope can be classified into intervals of angle.

Slope of Approximate Second-order Derivative

In the same way, the approximate second-order derivative is defined as

Slope of approximate second-order derivative

$$= \frac{\dfrac{\text{MA}_n(t) - \text{MA}_n(t-d)}{d} - \dfrac{\text{MA}_n(t-d) - \text{MA}_n(t-2d)}{d}}{d}$$

$$= \frac{(\text{MA}_n(t) - 2\text{MA}_n(t-d) + \text{MA}_n(t-2d))}{d^2}$$

$$(13.6)$$

Relative Topological Position

The topological position between the short-term moving average value and the long-term moving average value at time t is defined as

$$\text{Relative topological position} = \begin{array}{l} \text{above if } \text{MAP}_n(t) \geq \text{MAP}_m(t) \\ \text{below if } \text{MAP}_n(t) < \text{MAP}_m(t) \end{array}$$

$$(13.7)$$

where $n < m$.

Gap Between Two Moving Average Curves

The gap between two moving average curves is defined as

Gap between two MAPs

$$= \begin{array}{l} \text{wider} \quad \text{if } |\text{MAP}_n(t) - \text{MAP}_m(t)| \geq \gamma|\text{MAP}_n(t-d) - \text{MAP}_m(t-d)| \\ \text{narrower if } |\text{MAP}_n(t) - \text{MAP}_m(t)| < \gamma|\text{MAP}_n(t-d) - \text{MAP}_m(t-d)| \end{array}$$

$$(13.8)$$

where γ is a weight factor whose default value is 1.

The elements can be represented in frames by the syntax in Figure 13.7. An example of this representation is

```
{{MAP-1
    TIME-LAG: 1
    LENGTH: 25
```

```
          {{ MAP–element
             TIME–LAG: value
             LENGTH: value
             SLOPE: lower–bound upper–bound
             CHANGE–OF–SLOPE: [increase decrease] }}


          {{ MAP–POSITION–element
             MAP–SHORT: MAP–element
             MAP–LONG: MAP–element
             POSITION: [above below] }}


          {{ MAP–GAP–element
             TIME–LAG: value
             MAP–SHORT: MAP–element
             MAP–LONG: MAP–element
             GAP: [narrower wider] }}
```

Figure 13.7   Syntax of elements of moving average curve of stock price

  SLOPE: *20 45*
  CHANGE-OF-SLOPE: *decrease*}}
{{*MAP-2*
   TIME-LAG: *1*
   LENGTH: *75*
   SLOPE: *-20 20*
   CHANGE-OF-SLOPE: *increase*}}
{{*MAP-POSITION-12*
   MAP-SHORT: *MAP-1*
   MAP-LONG: *MAP-2*
   POSITION: *above*}}
{{*MAP-GAP-12*
   TIME-LAG: *1*
   MAP-SHORT: *MAP-1*
   MAP-LONG: *MAP-2*
   GAP: *narrower*}}

Moving Average Curves of Trading Volume (MAV)

This chart is the same as the moving average curve of stock price except the price $P(t)$ in equation (13.4) is replaced by the trading volume $V(t)$. Therefore we can use the element definition syntax in Figure 13.7.

4 DEFINITION AND RECOGNITION OF PRIMITIVES

To recognize the elements defined earlier in the charts we need to identify the duration that the elements subsist because the price change may be sensitive to duration. Take, for example, an element lower supporting line LOWER_45_10,

{{LOWER_45_10
  LINE-TYPE: *lower-supporting-line*
  TOLERANCE: *10*
  SLOPE: *45 90*}}

whose tolerance is 10, and the slope is between 45° and 90°. The relationship between the duration of the element occurrence and the mean price change is shown in Figure 13.8. In this case, if the line exists for less than 11 days, the price change after 30 days is greater than zero. Otherwise, the direction of price change is negative. Since there can exist two contradictory conclusions due to the duration, identifying duration additionally to the element is essential.

Therefore we define 'an element with duration' as a primitive because they become the basic components of patterns. In general, duration is represented as an interval of lower bound and upper bound.

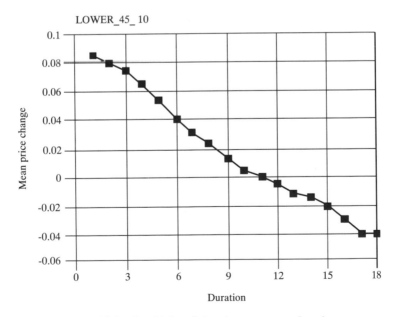

Figure 13.8 Sensitivity of duration to mean price change

5   COMPOSITIONAL OPERATORS: CONC AND SEQ

The primitives can be combined by the compositional operators to represent more complex patterns. We adopt two operators: CONC and SEQ. CONC means two primitives occur concurrently, while SEQ means two primitives occur in sequence. Let us define the operators formally:

Definition 1. Range(P) is the time range that the primitive P occurs.

Definition 2. CONC($P1, P2$) indicates the primitives $P1$ and $P2$ occur concurrently. That is,

$$\text{Range}(\text{CONC}(P1, P2)) = \{t | t\varepsilon \text{ Range}(P1) \text{ and } t\varepsilon \text{ Range}(P2)\} \qquad (13.9)$$

Definition 3. SEQ(P1, P2) indicates that the primitive $P1$ starts to occur at least one day earlier than the occurrence of primitive $P2$, and the gap between the ending point of $P1$ and starting point of $P2$ does not exceed g days. That is,

$$\text{Range}(\text{SEQ}(P1, P2)) = \{t | t\varepsilon \text{ Range}(P2), \text{Starting\_day}(P1) + 1 \leq t$$

$$\text{and Ending\_day}(P1) + g \geq \text{Starting\_day}(P2)\} \qquad (13.10)$$

We can represent patterns as compositions of primitives by using CONC and SEQ. Example of the patterns are as follows:

TLP-PATTERN = SEQ(*TLP-PRIMITIVE-1, TLP-PRIMITIVE-2*)

MAP-PATTERN = CONC(*MAP-PRIMITIVE-1, MAP-PRIMITIVE-2*)

TLP-MAP-PAT = CONC (SEQ (*TLP-PRIMITIVE-1, TLP-PRIMITIVE-2*),

CONC (*MAP-PRIMITIVE-1, MAP-PRIMITIVE-2*))

The patterns such as *TLP-PATTERN* and *MAP-PATTERN* are intra-chart patterns which are defined by the primitives in the same chart respectively. On the other hand, the pattern *TLP-MAP-PAT* is an inter-chart pattern which is defined by the primitives from multiple charts.

6   DEFINITION OF IMPACT OF PATTERNS

A pattern can be constructed out of the syntactically organized primitives, and the pattern with its corresponding impact can make a rule. Therefore it is necessary to define the impact of patterns. The criteria of measuring the impact may vary depending upon the purpose of investment. In this study, we consider the time lag and price change as evaluation criteria:

(1) Time lag: The time lag between pattern occurrence and impact evaluation should be determined according to the investment time horizon. The patterns relevant to

the long-term investment may not be relevant to the short-term investment and vice versa.

(2) Price change: We may compare either the actual or the normalized price. Let us denote the time of pattern occurrence t_p; the time of impact evaluation t_e; and price change ΔP. The definitions of price change are defined as follows:

(i) $\Delta P = P(t_e) - P(t_p)$ (13.11)

(ii) $\Delta P = MAP_n(t_e) - MAP_n(t_p)$ (13.12)

(iii) $\Delta P = (MAP_n(t_e) - MAP_n(t_p))/MAP_n(t_p)$ (13.13)

Expression (13.11) is a special case of (13.12) with $n = 1$. The degree of price change can be classified into several groups such as 'Up', 'Sustained' and 'Down'.

Our goal is the construction of rules whose conditions are patterns and conclusion is the impact. To begin with, we need to collect primitive-based instance data set as represented in equation (13.14) below. Primitive-based instance means that the occurrence of a single primitive with its impact class. However, a potential problem among the primitive-based instances is the inconsistent conclusions under the same primitive. Thus the eventual rule generated from the instances should be represented with a 'credibility' measure which assesses the degree of conformity.

{{*Instance-TLP1-081287*
  PRIMITIVE: *TLP1*
  IMPACT: *Up*
  DATE: *08/12/87*}}   (13.14)

7   SYNTACTIC PATTERN-BASED INDUCTIVE LEARNING

Our ultimate concern is the syntactical synthesis of primitive-based instances into more sophisticated rules with the highest accuracy. To attain this goal, we propose an algorithm called SYNPLE (SYNtactic Pattern-based LEarning). We have two versions of the algorithm. The first version (SYNPLE-0) is the conceptual framework of the algorithm, while the second version (SYNPLE-1) pursues computational efficiency.

SYNPLE-0 algorithm

Step 1. Set the OPEN and CLOSE rule set null.

Step 2. Detect the primitive-based instances chronologically. Denote the instances as a pair of primitive and conclusion impact.

$$INSTANCE_u = (PRIMITIVE_v, IMPACT_w)$$

Step 3. Group the instances with the same primitives as follows:

Group	Instances	Frequency	Credibility
w_1	$(\text{PRIMITIVE}_v, \text{IMPACT}_{w_1})$	f_{w_1}	$f_{w_1}/\sum_{i=1}^{k} f_{w_i}$
w_2	$(\text{PRIMITIVE}_v, \text{IMPACT}_{w_2})$	f_{w_2}	$f_{w_2}/\sum_{i=1}^{k} f_{w_i}$
...	...	...	...
w_3	$(\text{PRIMITIVE}_v, \text{IMPACT}_{w_k})$	f_{w_k}	$f_{w_k}/\sum_{i=1}^{k} f_{w_i}$

Step 4. For each primitive, select the group with the highest credibility $CR_v = \max_{w_i}\{CR_{w_i} \geq CR_{\text{threshold}}$ and $f_{w_i} \geq f_{\text{threshold}}\ i = 1, \ldots, k\}$. Construct a rule set by the selected primitive-based rules, and include the rule set in the OPEN set.

Step 5.
5.1 For each impact class in conclusion, compose syntactically legitimate pairs of primitives (or subpatterns) in the OPEN set toward higher credibility.
5.2 Include the newly generated rules in the OPEN set. Move the overridden rules into the CLOSE set.
5.3 Repeat Steps 5.1 and 5.2 for all impact classes in conclusion.

Step 6. Continue the synthesis of patterns in Step 5 with the rules in OPEN set until no further improvement of credibility is possible. The final rule set in OPEN is the rule base generated.

Since Step 5 of SYNPLE-0 is a combinatorially expanding computation, we propose a heuristic that can prevent the full search at the cost of approximate pursuit of maximum credibilities. The modified algorithm is called SYNPLE-1

SYNPLE-1 Algorithm
Steps 1–4. The same as the corresponding steps in the SYNPLE-0 algorithm.
Step 5.
5.1 For each impact class in conclusion, order the primitive- (or subpattern-) based rules by the level of credibility. If the level of credibility is the same, order by the magnitude of mean price change. Let us denote n ordered primitives (or subpattern) by $V_1, \ldots, V_n$.
5.2 Pair the primitives (or subpatterns) according to the following rules. Let us denote i and j the first and second components of a pair respectively, k the number of rules generated, and $K_{\text{threshold}}$ the maximum number of rules desired.
    5.2.1   Set $i = 1$, $j = i + 1$ and $k = 0$.
    5.2.2   Make a pair (V_i, V_j) via the compositional operators CONC and SEQ.
    5.2.3   If $CR(V_i, V_j) \geq CR'_{\text{threshold}}$ and $k < K_{\text{threshold}}$, reset $j = j + 1$. Go to Step 5.2.2.

5.2.4 If $CR(V_i, V_j) < CR'_{threshold}$ and $k < K_{threshold}$, reset $i = i+1$. Go to Step 5.2.2.

5.2.5 If $i > n$ or $k \geq K_{threshold}$, stop the iteration.

5.3 Include the newly generated rules into the OPEN set. Move the overridden rules into the CLOSE set.

5.4 Repeat Steps 5.1–5.3 for all impact classes in conclusion.

Step 6. The same as Step 6 of the SYNPLE-0 algorithm.

8 CASE STUDY

This section evaluates the performance of the rules generated by the above method. Five chronological data series containing daily price and trading volumes for 43 Korean companies were used for the experiments. The first data set was between 22 April 1987 and 22 October 1987; the second between 23 October 1987 and 22 April 1988; the third between 23 April 1988 and 22 October 1988; the fourth between 23 October 1988 and 22 April 1989; and the fifth between 23 April 1989 and 22 October 1989. Each data set has a six-month interval. In Experiment I, the first data set is used for learning, while the following four data sets are used for testing. In Experiment II, the second data set is used for learning while the following three data sets are used for testing.

8.1 Definition of Impact Classes

As a measure of price change, we have adopted the formula defined in equation (13.13) with $n = 5$ and 30 days' evaluation time lag. The impact belongs to one of the following classes: Up, Sustained or Down. The class Up means that the price change of the individual stock is higher than the overall mean price change of the data set by 2.0%; and the class Down means the price change is lower than the overall mean price change of the data set by -2.0%; the other cases belong to the class Sustained.

8.2 Element Definition

We have prepared 208 elements which are composed of the attributes and values listed in Table 13.1.

8.3 Primitive Detection

211 primitives and 257 primitives are identified from the first and second data sets respectively. The number of instances detected are 117,121 and 204,311 from the first and second data sets respectively. Examples of primitives detected are as follows:

{{*TLP-UPPER-10-4590*
  LINE-TYPE: *upper-supporting-line*
  TOLERANCE: *10*
  SLOPE: *45 90*
  DURATION: *1 27*}}

{{*MAV-SLOPE-12-2020*
  LENGTH: *12*
  SLOPE: *−20 20*
  DURATION: *24 45*}}

Table 13.1 Charts, attributes, and values used in the experiment

Chart	Attribute	Values
Trend line of stock price	LINE-TYPE	Central-line, upper-supporting-line, lower-supporting-line
	TOLERANCE	40, 60, 80 (for central-line) 10, 15, 20 (for upper-supporting-line and lower-supporting-line)
	SLOPE	$(-90\ -45)$, $(-45\ -20)$, $(-20\ 0)$, $(0\ 20)$, $(20\ 45)$, $(45\ 90)$
	SHIFT-AT-TAIL	Up, down
	GAP	Narrower, wider (between upper-supporting-line and lower-supporting-line)
Moving average of stock price	LENGTH	3, 12, 25, 50, 75
	SLOPE	$(-90\ -20)$, $(-20\ 20)$, $(20\ 90)$
	CHANGE-OF-SLOPE	Increase, decrease
	POSITION	Above, below (between two moving average lines of different length)
	GAP	Narrower, wider (between two moving average lines of different length)
Moving average of Trading Volume	LENGTH	3, 12, 25, 50, 75
	SLOPE	$(-90\ -20)$, $(-20\ 20)$, $(20\ 90)$
	CHANGE-OF-SLOPE	Increase, decrease
	POSITION	Above, below (between two moving average lines of different length)
	GAP	Narrower, wider (between two moving average lines of different length)

{{*TLP-ABOVE-10*
  LINE-TYPE: *upper-supporting-line*
  TOLERANCE: *10*}}

{{*TLP-LOWER-10*
  LINE-TYPE: *lower-supporting-line*
  TOLERANCE: *10*}}

{{*MAP-25-DAY*
  LENGTH: *25*}}

{{*MAP-50-DAY*
  LENGTH: *50*}}

{{*TLP-GAP-WIDER-10*
  TLP-UPPER: TLP-ABOVE-10
  TLP-LOWER: TLP-LOWER-10
  GAP: *wider*
  DURATION: *19 26*}}

{{*MAP-POSITION-25-50-BELOW*
  MAP-SHORT: *MAP-25-DAY*
  MAP-LONG: *MAP-50-DAY*
  POSITION: *below*
  DURATION: *13 45*}}

Table 13.2 Performances of primitive-based rules

Data-set		1st (10/23/87–4/22/88)	2nd (4/23/88–10/22/88)
Overall mean of price change		−0.00627	0.07671
Overall variance of price change		0.01407	0.02314
Class Up	Number of primitives	100	129
	Number of instances	54 350	104 270
	Mean of normalized price change[a]	0.3792	0.4112
	Variance of normalized price change	0.96312	1.09527
	Credibility	0.554	0.555
Class Down	Number of primitives	111	128
	Number of instances	62 771	100 041
	Mean of normalized price change	−0.3794	−0.3576
	Variance of normalized price change	0.74643	0.67093
	Credibility	0.670	0.681
z-value		139.40	185.32
p-value		<0.0001	<0.0001

[a]Normalized price change $= \dfrac{\text{Price change} - \text{overall mean price change}}{\text{Overall standard deviation of price change}}$

The performance of primitive-based rules are evaluated and summarized in Table 13.2. For the case of the first data set, the credibilities of Up and Down classes are 0.554 and 0.670 respectively. For the case of the second data set, the credibilities are 0.555 and 0.681 respectively. The means of normalized price changes are 0.3792 and −0.3794 for the Up class, and 0.4112 and −0.3576 for the Down class. Two groups are significantly different with the probability of error less than 0.0001.

9 RULE GENERATION BY THE SYNPLE-1 ALGORITHM

To enhance the effectiveness of the primitive-based rules, we have synthesized more sophisticated patterns using the SYNPLE-1 algorithm. We have used the compositional operators CONC and SEQ (with $g = 1$). The maximum number of rules for each class is set 300. The generated inter-chart patterns for class Up include the following:

(1) *PAT-1350* = SEQ(SEQ(*TLP-GAP-WIDER-10, MAV-SLOPE-12-2020*)
     SEQ(*MAV-SLOPE-12-2020, TLP-UPPER-10-4590*))

(2) *PAT-6229* = SEQ(SEQ(*TLP-GAP-WIDER-10, MAV-SLOPE-12-2020*)
     CONC(*MAP-POSITION-25-50-BELOW, TLP-UPPER-10-4590*))

Table 13.3 Experiment I results

Data-set		1st 4/22/87– 10/22/87	2nd 10/23/87– 4/22/88	3rd 4/23/88– 10/22/88	4th 10/23/88– 4/22/89	5th 4/22/89– 10/22/89	Average (2nd–5th)
Overall mean of price change		−0.00627	0.07671	0.03513	0.07743	−0.06764	0.03053
Overall variance of price change		0.01407	0.02315	0.01283	0.01303	0.04993	0.02461
Class Up	Number of patterns	300	300	300	300	300	
	Number of instances	1885	681	447	608	1118	
	Mean of normalized price change	2.2682	0.7375	0.5171	0.2879	0.2787	0.4275
	Variance of normalized price change	0.21667	0.70636	1.04089	1.14306	0.48683	0.7657
	Credibility	1.000	0.812	0.617	0.461	0.851	0.722
Class Down	Number of patterns	300	300	300	300	300	
	Number of instances	1167	461	583	2573	1060	
	Mean of normalized price change	−1.6519	−0.5160	−1.1909	−1.0651	−0.8009	−0.9668
	Variance of normalized price change	0.03160	1.31996	0.32778	0.56958	3.53602	1.2857
	Credibility	1.000	0.638	0.962	0.896	0.324	0.749
	z-value	328.94	20.07	31.76	29.51	17.58	
	p-value	<0.0001	<0.0001	<0.0001	<0.0001	<0.0001	

The above patterns can be easily transformed into rules such as in the following example:

IF pattern = *PAT-1350*
THEN stock price will be Up after *30* days.

After having executed the SYNPLE algorithmic procedure, the performance is enhanced significantly as shown in Tables 13.3 and 13.4. For the case of the first data set, the credibilities of the Up and Down classes are 1.0 and 1.0 respectively (Table 13.3). For the case of the second data set, the credibilities of the Up

Table 13.4 Performance by Experiment II

Data set		2nd 10/23/87– 4/22/88	3rd 4/23/88– 10/22/88	4th 10/23/88– 4/22/89	5th 4/22/89– 10/22/89	Average (3rd–5th)
Overall mean of price change		0.07671	0.03513	0.07743	−0.06764	0.01534
Overall variance of price change		0.02315	0.01283	0.01303	0.04993	0.02509
Class Up	Number of patterns	300	300	300	300	
	Number of instances	3996	423	171	1396	
	Mean of normalized price change	2.4432	0.6133	−0.0160	0.3393	0.3670
	Variance of normalized price change	0.66335	1.20884	1.10582	0.51153	0.7108
	Credibility	1.000	0.586	0.292	0.972	0.832
Class Down	Number of patterns	300	300	300	300	
	Number of instances	995	444	969	193	
	Mean of normalized price change	−1.5851	−0.9608	−1.1895	−1.1434	−1.1207
	Variance of Normalized price change	0.03754	0.26283	0.43374	4.23060	0.8427
	Credibility	1.000	0.997	0.911	0.399	0.873
	z-value	282.22	26.80	14.11	9.93	
	p-value	<0.0001	<0.0001	<0.0001	<0.0001	

and Down classes are also 1.0 and 1.0 respectively (Table 13.4). The means of normalized price changes are 2.2682 and 2.4432 for the Up class and −1.6519 and −1.5851 for the Down class. The two groups are statistically different with p-value <0.0001. The significant enhancement in credibilities and mean of normalized price changes shows the effectiveness of the SYNPLE algorithm.

10 PERFORMANCE TESTS

To test the performance of the generated rules for the following periods, we have performed two experiments:

(1) Experiment I: The rules generated from the first data set are tested on the following four data-sets. The result is summarized in Table 13.3. The average credibilities on the following four periods are 0.722 for the Up class and 0.749 for the Down class. The mean of normalized price changes for the periods 2nd–5th is 0.4275 for the Up class and −0.9668 for the Down class. To determine whether the mean price changes of the Up class are significantly higher than that of the Down class, the z-values are considered. The p-values are less than 0.0001 for the entire test periods. The results prove that the rules are quite reliable.

(2) Experiment II: The rules generated from the second data set are tested on the following three data-sets. The results are summarized in Table 13.4. This table shows that the average credibilities on the following three periods are 0.832 for the Up class and 0.873 for the Down class. The mean of normalized price changes for the periods 3rd–5th is 0.3670 for the Up class and −1.1207 for the Down class. The p-values are less than 0.0001 for the entire test periods.

11 ANALYSIS OF RESULTS

The means of normalized price changes by the Experiments I and II are graphically shown in Figures 13.9 and 13.10 respectively. Compare the result with that of the primitive-based rules which have not applied the SYNPLE algorithm. We can observe that the prediction power of the rules generated by the SYNPLE algorithm outperform the primitive-based rules except in the fourth data set. We can also observe that the effects of the rules fade as the test time becomes further from the rule generated time. This observation can also be supported by the decreasing z-values as the test time becomes further except the second period, at which time the Seoul Olympic Games and the presidential elections in Korea had boosted the market exceptionally. Therefore we suggest updating the pattern set periodically to maintain the best performance.

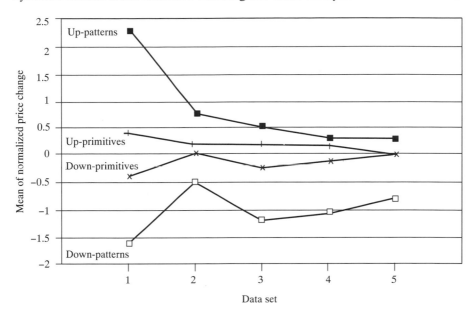

Figure 13.9   Mean of normalized price change by the experiment I

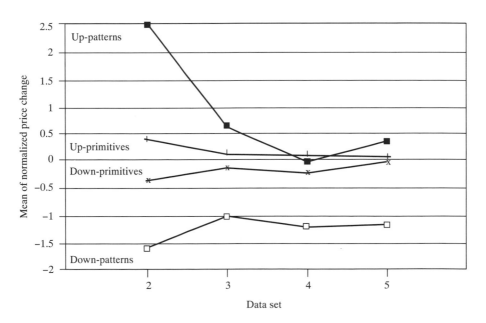

Figure 13.10   Mean of normalized price change by the experiment II

12 CONCLUSIONS

We have developed an algorithm called SYNPLE which can synthesize accurate pattern-based rules. The experimental results show very good performance and demonstrate its applicability as a general-purpose method for stock market prediction. Further, this approach can also be applied to many other graph-based business analysis tasks. Currently, we are developing methods that can discover the best primitive sets, which may further improve the performance of the SYNPLE algorithm.

ACKNOWLEDGEMENTS

This material is a revision of 'Security trading rule synthesis: A syntactic pattern-based learning approach' (Jae K. Lee, Hyun S. Kim and Robert R. Trippi (1992) *Heuristics*, **5**(4), 47–61).

REFERENCES

Basu, S. (1977) 'Investment performance of common stocks in relation to their price-earnings ratio: a test of the efficient market hypothesis', *Journal of Finance*, **32**, 663–82.

Braun, H. & Chandler, J.S. (1987) 'Predicting stock market behavior through rule induction: An application of the learning-from-example approach', *Decision Sciences*, **18**(3), 415–29.

Buchanan, B.G. & Feigenbaum, E.A. (1978) 'DENDRAL and Meta-DENDRAL: Their applications dimension', *Artificial Intelligence*, **11**(1,2), 5–24.

Chung, J.R. (1987) 'Trading volume and stock price changes: theory and empirical evidence', *The Journal of the Korean Securities Association*, **9**, 309–336.

De Bonnt, W. & Thaler, R. (1985) 'Does the stock market overreact?', *Journal of Finance*, **40**, 793–805.

De Mori, R. (1972) 'A descriptive technique for automatic speech recognition', *IEEE Trans. Audio Electroacoust.*, **AU-21**(2), 89–100.

Dietterich, T. & Michalski, R. (1981) 'Inductive learning of structural descriptions', *Artificial Intelligence*, **16**, 257–94.

Forsyth, R. & Rada, R. (1986) *Machine Learning: Applications in expert systems and information retrieval*, Ellis Horwood, Chichester.

Fu, K.S. (1982) *Syntactic Pattern Recognition and Applications*, Prentice Hall, Englewood Cliffs, NJ.

Gibes, D.A., Bourne, J.R. & Ward, J.W. (1979) 'Syntax analysis of electroencephalogram', *IEEE Transactions on Systems, Man, and Cybernetics*, **SMC-9**, 429–34.

Granville, J.E. (1976) *A Strategy of Daily Stock Market Timing for Maximum Profit*, Prentice-Hall, *Englewood Cliffs*, NJ.

Joint Research (1988) 'A study on the overreaction of stock prices in the Korean stock market', *The Journal of the Korean Securities Association*, **10**, 1–15.

Kamijo, K. & Tanigawa, T. (1990) 'Stock price pattern recognition — A recurrent neural network approach', in *Proceedings of International Joint Conference on Neural Networks*, IEEE Neural Networks Council, **1**, 215–21.

Kandt, K. & Yuenger, P.A. (1988) 'Financial investment assistant', in *Proceedings of the 21st Annual Hawaii International Conference on Systems Sciences*, IEEE, 510–17.

Kim, C.S. (1987) *Stock Investment Strategy*, Stock Institute, Seoul, Korea.

Kim, H.S. (1987) *Generating rules by inductive machine learning: Exploratory application to stock investment*, unpublished master's thesis, Korea Advanced Institute of Technology and Science, Department of Management Science, Seoul.

Kimoto, T. & Asakawa, K. (1990) 'Stock market prediction system with modular neural networks' in *Proceedings of International Joint Conference on Neural Networks*, IEEE Neural Networks Council, **1**, 1-6.

Langley, P. (1979) 'Rediscovering physics with BACON.3', in *Proceedings of the 6th International Joint Conference on Artificial Intelligence*, 505-7.

Lee, J.K., Chu, S.C. & Kim, H.S. (1989) 'Intelligent stock portfolio management system', *Expert Systems*, 6(2), 74-87.

Lee, J.K., Kim, H.S. & Trippi, R.R. (1992) 'Security trading rule synthesis: A syntactic pattern-based approach', *Heuristics*, **5**(4), 47-61.

Lee, J.K., Trippi, R.R., Chu, S.C. & Kim, H.S. (1990) 'K-FOLIO: Integrating the Markowitz model with a knowledge-based system', *Journal of Portfolio Management*, 17(1), 89-93.

Lee, J.K., Kim, H.S., Chu, S.C., Shin, J.C., Kwon, S.B., Kim, W.J. & Gwag, K.Y. (1991), *Application of K-FOLIO at Lucky Securities: BRAINS*, In Lee, J.K. (ed.), *Operational Expert System Applications in the Far East*, Pergamon Press, New York.

Lenat, D.B. (1976) 'AM: An artificial intelligence approach to discovery in mathematics as heuristic search', *Rep. No. STAN-CS-76-570*, Stanford University, Department of Computer Science, California.

Le Roy, S. & Porter, R. (1981) 'The present-value relation: test based on implied variance bounds', *Econometrica*, **49**(3), 555-74.

Levy, R.A. (1966) 'Conceptual foundations of technical analysis', *Financial Analysis Journal*, **22**(4), 83-92.

Michalski, R.S. (1980) 'Pattern recognition as rule-guided inductive inference', *IEEE Transactions on Pattern Analysis and Machine Intelligence*, **PAMI-2**(4), 349-61.

Michalski, R.S. (1983) 'A theory and methodology of inductive learning', in Michalski, R.S., Carbonell, J.G. & Mitchell, T.M. (eds), *Machine Learning: An artificial intelligence approach*, Tioga Publishing, Palo Alto, CA.

Michalski, R.S. & Chilausky, R.L. (1980) 'Learning by being told and learning from examples: An experimental comparison of the two methods of knowledge acquisition in the context of developing an expert system for soybean disease diagnosis', *Journal of Policy Analysis and Information Systems*, **4**(2), 125-60.

O'Keefe, R.A. (1983) 'Concept formation from very large training sets', in *Proceedings of the 8th International Joint Conference on Artificial Intelligence*, 479-81.

Pring, M.J. (1985) *Technical Analysis Explained*, McGraw-Hill, New York.

Quinlan, J.R. (1979) 'Discovering rules by induction from large collections of examples', in Michie, D. (ed.), *Expert Systems in the Micro Electronic Age*, Edinburgh University Press.

Quinlan, J.R. (1987) 'Decision trees as probabilistic classifier's, in *Proceedings of the 4th International Workshop on Machine Learning*, Morgan Kaufmann, Los Altos, CA, 31-7.

Rao, K. & Balck, K. (1980) 'Type classification of fingerprints: A syntactic approach', *IEEE Transactions on Pattern Analysis and Machine Intelligence*, **PAMI**-2(3), 223-31.

Shiller, R. (1981) 'Do stock prices move too much to be justified by subsequent changes in dividends?' *American Economic Review*, 421-36.

Stockman, G., Kanal, L. & Kyle, M.C. (1976) 'Structural pattern recognition of carotid pulse waves using a general waveform parsing system', *Communications of the ACM*, **19**(12), 688-95.

Tou, J.T. & Gonzalez, R.C. (1974) *Pattern Recognition Principles*, Addison-Wesley Reading, MA.

Trippi, R.R. & Lee, J.K. (1992) *State-of-the-art Portfolio Selection*, Probus, MA.

Winston, P.H. (1970) 'Learning structural descriptions from examples', *Rep. No. TR-231*, AI Laboratory, Massachusetts Institute of Technology.

Yoon, Y. & Swales, G. (1991) 'Predicting stock market performance: A neural network approach', in *Proceedings of the 24th Annual Hawaii International Conference on Systems Sciences*, IEEE Computer Society Press, Los Alamitos, CA: **4**, 156–61.

You, K.C. & Fu, K.S. (1979) 'A syntactic approach to shape recognition using attributed grammars', *IEEE Trans. Syst. Man Cybern.*, **SMC-9**(6), 334–45.

Part V
Economic Modelling

14

Genetic Programming for Economic Modeling

JOHN R. KOZA

1 INTRODUCTION

The problem of discovering the mathematical relationship between the empirically observed variables measuring a system is an important one in economics and other areas of science (Langley et al., 1987). In practice, the observed data may be noisy and there may be no known way to express the relationships involved precisely. Problems of this type are sometimes called symbolic system identification problems, black box problems, *data mining* problems, or *modeling* problems. When the model that is discovered is used in predicting future values of the state variables of the system, the problem is called a *forecasting* problem.

Mathematical relationships can be expressed by means of formulae and ordinary mathematical equations; however, computer programs offer greater flexibility in the way that they express an arbitrary mathematical relationship. Computer programs start with one or more inputs (the independent variables of the system), perform various operations on the variables (including arithmetic operations and conditional decision-making operations), and produce certain outputs (the dependent variables). Thus, the problem of finding a mathematical model for empirical data can be viewed as one of finding a computer program that produces the observed value of the single dependent variable as its output when given the values of the independent variables as input. We call problems of this type symbolic regression because we are seeking a mathematical expression, in symbolic form, that fits, or approximately fits, a given sample of data.

Intelligent Systems for Finance and Business. Edited by S. Goonatilake and P. Treleaven

Symbolic regression differs from conventional linear regression, quadratic regression, exponential regression, and other types of regression wherein the nature of the model is specified in advance by the user. In conventional linear regression, for example, one is given a set of values of various independent variable(s) and the corresponding values for the dependent variable(s). The goal is to discover a set of numerical coefficients for a linear expression involving the independent variable(s) that minimizes some measure of error (such as the square root of the sum of the squares of the differences) between the values of the dependent variable(s) computed with the linear expression and the given values for the dependent variable(s). Similarly, in quadratic regression the goal is to discover a set of numerical coefficients for a quadratic expression that minimizes the error. In employing a conventional regression technique, the user must select, as a preparatory step, whether to try to fit to a linear model, a quadratic model, or some other model. But often, the real problem is deciding what type of model most appropriately fits the data, not merely computing the appropriate numerical coefficients after the model has been preselected. Symbolic regression searches for both the functional form and the appropriate numeric coefficients that go with that functional form. Finding the functional form and the appropriate numeric coefficients of a model can be viewed as being equivalent to searching a space of possible computer programs for the particular individual computer program which produces the desired output for given inputs.

The desired computer program can be found by means of the recently developed genetic programming paradigm originally developed for solving problems of Artificial Intelligence, automatic programming, and machine learning. In genetic programming, populations of computer programs are bred using Darwinian competition and genetic operations. The Darwinian competition is based on the principle of survival and reproduction of the fittest. The genetic crossover (sexual recombination) operator genetically mates computer programs so as to create potentially more fit new offspring programs. The best single individual computer program produced by this process after many generations may be a satisfactory solution to the problem.

In this chapter we illustrate the process of formulating and solving a problem of econometric modeling using genetic programming. We focus on the non-linear econometric exchange equation $P = MV/Q$ relating the price level, gross national product, money supply, and velocity of money in an economy. The problem of modeling requires finding the computer program, in symbolic form, that fits given numeric data. The numerical value of the velocity of money is one of the elements of the to-be-discovered computer program.

In genetic programming the individuals in the population are compositions of functions and terminals appropriate to the particular problem domain. The set of functions used typically may include arithmetic operations, mathematical functions, conditional logical operations, and other functions appropriate to the problem domain at hand. The set of terminals typically includes the inputs to the as-yet undiscovered computer program and various numerical constants. The search space is the space of all possible computer programs that can be recursively composed of the available functions and terminals. The crossover operation appropriate for mating two parents from this space of programs creates new offspring programs by exchanging subtrees between the two parents.

As will be seen, the computer program required to solve the problem described above will emerge from a simulated evolutionary process. This process will start with an initial population of randomly generated computer programs composed of functions and terminals appropriate to the problem domain.

The fitness of each individual computer program in a population at any stage of the process will be measured as to how well the program grapples with its problem environment (i.e. of producing the observed outputs from the given inputs). In particular, fitness will be measured by the sum of the squares of the distances (taken for all the fitness cases) between the point in the solution space created by the program for a given set of inputs and the correct point in the solution space. The closer this sum is to zero, the better the program.

Predictably, the initial random individual programs will have exceedingly poor fitness. Nonetheless, some individuals in the population will be somewhat more fit than others. Then, a process based on the Darwinian principle of reproduction and survival of the fittest and genetic recombination will be used to create a new population of individuals. In particular, a genetic process of sexual reproduction among two parental programs will be used to create offspring programs. Both participating parental programs are selected in proportion to fitness. The resulting offspring programs will be composed of subexpressions (building blocks) from their parents. Finally, the new population of offspring (i.e. the new generation) will replace the old population of parents and the process will continue.

At each stage of this highly parallel, locally controlled, and decentralized process the state of the process will consist only of the current population of individuals. Moreover, the only input to the algorithmic process will be the observed fitness of the individuals in the current population in grappling with the problem environment.

As will be seen, this process will produce populations which, over a period of generations, tend to exhibit increasing average fitness in dealing with their environment, and which, in addition, can robustly (i.e. rapidly and effectively) adapt to changes in their environment.

The dynamic variability of the computer programs that are developed along the way to a solution is also an essential aspect of genetic programming. We do not specify the size and shape of the eventual solution in advance. The advance specification or restriction of the size and shape of the solution to a problem narrows the window by which the system views the world and might well preclude finding the solution to the problem.

2 GENETIC ALGORITHMS

Genetic algorithms are highly parallel mathematical algorithms that transform populations of individual mathematical objects (typically fixed-length binary character strings) into new populations using operations patterned after natural genetic operations such as sexual recombination (crossover) and fitness proportionate reproduction (Darwinian survival of the fittest). Genetic algorithms begin with an initial population of individuals (typically randomly generated) and then, iteratively, evaluate the individuals in the population for fitness with respect to the problem environment and perform genetic operations on various individuals in the population to produce a new population.

John Holland presented the pioneering formulation of genetic algorithms for fixed-length character strings in *Adaptation in Natural and Artificial Systems* (Holland, 1975). Holland established, among other things, that the genetic algorithm is a mathematically near-optimal approach to adaptation in that it maximizes expected overall average payoff when the adaptive process is viewed as a multi-armed slot machine problem requiring an optimal allocation of future trials given currently available information.

In this work Holland demonstrated that a wide variety of different problems in adaptive systems (including problems from economics, game theory, pattern recognition, optimization, and Artificial Intelligence) are susceptible to reformulation in genetic terms so that they can potentially be solved by the highly parallel mathematical genetic algorithm that simulates Darwinian evolutionary processes and naturally occurring genetic operations on chromosomes.

Genetic algorithms differ from most iterative algorithms in that they simultaneously manipulate a population of individual points in the search space rather than a single point in a search space. The current increasing interest in genetic algorithms stems from their intrinsic parallelism, their mathematical near-optimality in solving problems, and the availability of increasing parallel computers. An overview of genetic algorithms can be found in Goldberg's *Genetic Algorithms in Search, Optimization, and Machine Learning* (1989). Additional information on current work in genetic algorithms can be found in Forrest (1993), Davis (1987, 1991), Michalewicz (1992), Bauer (1994), Whitley (1992), Maenner & Manderick (1992), Schaffer & Whitley (1992), Albrecht, Reeves & Steele (1993), and Langton (1994).

The classifier system (Holland, 1986) is a cognitive architecture into which the genetic algorithm is embedded so as to allow adaptive modification of a population of string-based if–then rules (whose condition and action parts are fixed length binary strings). Marimon, McGrattan & Sargent (1990) have applied genetic classifier systems to describe the emergence of a commodity in a simulated trading environment as a medium of exchange among artificially intelligent agents. Holland (1990) discusses the global economy as an adaptive system.

3 GENETIC PROGRAMMING

Genetic programming is an extension of the genetic algorithm in which the genetic population consists of computer programs (that is, compositions of primitive functions and terminals). The book *Genetic Programming: On the Programming of*

Computers by Means of Natural Selection (Koza, 1992) demonstrated a surprising and counter-intuitive result, namely that computers can be programmed by means of natural selection. Specifically, genetic programming is capable of evolving a computer program for solving, or approximately solving, a surprising variety of problems from a large number of fields. To accomplish this, genetic programming starts with a primordial ooze of randomly generated computer programs composed of available programmatic ingredients and genetically breeds the population using the Darwinian principle of survival of the fittest and an analog of naturally occurring genetic crossover (sexual recombination) operation. In other words, genetic programming provides a way to search the space of possible computer programs to find a program which solves, or approximately solves, a problem.

Genetic programming is a domain-independent method that genetically breeds populations of computer programs to solve problems by executing the following three steps:

(1) Generate an initial population of random computer programs composed of the primitive functions and terminals of the problem.

(2) Iteratively perform the following substeps until the termination criterion has been satisfied:
(a) Execute each program in the population and assign it a fitness value according to how well it solves the problem.
(b) Create a new population of programs by applying the following two primary operations. The operations are applied to program(s) in the population selected with a probability based on fitness (i.e. the fitter the program, the more likely it is to be selected).
  (i) *Reproduction*: Copy an existing program to the new population.
  (ii) *Crossover*: Create two new offspring programs for the new population by genetically recombining randomly chosen parts of two existing programs. The genetic crossover (sexual recombination) operation (described below) operates on two parental computer programs and produces two offspring programs using parts of each parent.

(3) The single best computer program in the population produced during the run is designated as the result of the run of genetic programming. This result may be a solution (or approximate solution) to the problem.

The use of automatically defined functions in genetic programming is discussed in Koza (1994a). Recent advances in genetic programming are described in Kinnear (1994). A videotape visualization of numerous applications of genetic programming can be found in Koza & Rice (1992) and Koza (1994a).

3.1 Preparatory Steps in Applying Genetic Programming

In applying genetic programming with automatic function definition to a problem there are five major preparatory steps. These steps involve determining

(1) The set of terminals
(2) The set of functions
(3) The fitness measure
(4) The parameters and variables for controlling the run
(5) The criterion for designating a result and terminating a run

3.2 Terminal Set and Function Set

The set of terminals and functions are the ingredients from which the yet-to-be-evolved computer program will be composed. Consider the well-known econometric exchange equation $P = MV/Q$, which relates the money supply M, price level P, gross national product Q, and the velocity of money V of an economy. In particular, suppose we are given the 120 quarterly values (from 1959:1 to 1988:4) of four econometric time series.

- GNP82 is annual rate for the US Gross National Product in billions of 1982 dollars.
- GD is the Gross National Product Deflator (normalized to 1.0 for 1982).
- M2 is the monthly value of the seasonally adjusted money stock M2 in billions of dollars, averaged for each quarter.
- FYGM3 is the monthly interest rate yields of 3-month Treasury bills, averaged for each quarter.

In attempting to rediscover the exchange equation using genetic programming paradigm, we might use the function set for the problem

F = {+, -, $*$, %, RLOG, EXP}.

The first four functions in this function set are arithmetic operations. The protected division operation % produces a result of one if division by zero is attempted. RLOG and EXP are protected versions of the mathematical functions for the logarithm and exponential. The protected logarithm function RLOG is the logarithm of the absolute value and is equal to zero for an argument of zero. These definitions allow arbitrary compositions of the functions in the function set.

GNP82, GD, FM2, and FYGM3 are functions of time, T, measured in quarters. However, if the time variable, T, is made implicit, these four functions become zero-argument functions and are regarded as terminals (i.e. endpoints of the parse tree) so that the terminal set for the problem

$T = \{$GNP82, GD, FM2, FYGM3, $\mathbf{R}\}$.

Here $\mathbf{R}$ is the ephemeral random constant allowing various random floating point constants to be inserted at random amongst the initial random computer programs as described in detail in Koza (1992). The terminals GNP82, FM2, and FYGM3 provide access to the values of the time series. In effect, these terminals are functions of the unstated, implicit time variable.

The actual long-term historic post-war value of the M2 velocity of money in the United States is relatively constant and is approximately 1.6527 (Hallman, Porter & Small, 1989; Humphrey, 1989). Thus, a correct solution for the price level P in terms of M, V, and Q is the multiplicative (non-linear) relationship

$$P = \frac{MV}{Q} \tag{14.1}$$

or, alternately,

$$GD(T) = \frac{(M2(T) * 1.6527)}{GNP82(T)} \tag{14.2}$$

As it happens, the monthly interest rate yields of 3-month Treasury bills (FYGM3) is extraneous in this equation.

In this chapter we will present programs in the LISP programming language. In LISP, everything is expressed in terms of functions operating on some arguments. In LISP programs, the function appears just inside an opening (left) parenthesis and is then followed by its arguments and a closing (right) parenthesis. Thus, for example, (+ 1 2) calls for the function of addition (+) to be applied to the arguments 1 and 2. In other words, the computer program (+ 1 2) is equivalent to '1 + 2' in ordinary mathematics and evaluates to 3. In LISP, any argument can itself be an program. For example, (+ 1 (* 2 3)) calls for the addition function to be applied to the argument 1 and the argument (* 2 3). That is, the addition function is to be applied to 1 and the result of applying the multiplication function (*) to the arguments 2 and 3. The result is 7.

Thus, in LISP, one correct computer program for the price level of an economy in terms of the exchange equation would be

(% (* FM2 1.6527) GNP82)

Any computer program can be depicted graphically as a rooted point-labeled tree in a plane whose internal points are labeled with functions, whose external points (leaves) are labeled with terminals, and whose root is labeled with the function appearing just inside the outermost left parenthesis. The tree corresponding to the computer program above for the exchange equation is shown in Figure 14.1.

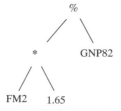

Figure 14.1　The exchange equation represented parsimoniously as a tree

In this graphical depiction, the two internal points of the tree are labeled with functions (% and ∗). The three external points (leaves) of the tree are labeled with terminals. The root of the tree is labeled with the function appearing just inside the outermost left parenthesis of the computer program (i.e. %). Note that two lines emanate from the multiplication function ∗ and the % because they each take two arguments. Note also that no lines emanate from the terminals at the external points (leaves) of the tree.

It is not necessary to use LISP programming for genetic programming. In fact, most implementations of genetic programming employ other computer languages. However, LISP makes it clear that all computer programs are applications of functions to arguments and can be represented as a parse tree such as Figure 14.1.

3.3 The Fitness Measure

Each individual in a population is assigned a fitness value as a result of its interaction with the environment. Fitness is the driving force of Darwinian natural selection and genetic algorithms.

Fitness cases provide a basis for evaluating a particular program. For example, for the exchange equation, the fitness cases consist of the set of 120 cases listing, for each quarter between 1959:1 and 1988:4, the values of GNP82, FM2, and FYGM3 along with the associated value of GD.

The raw fitness of any computer program is the sum, over the fitness cases, of the squares of the distances (taken over all the fitness cases) between the point in the solution space (which is real-valued) returned by the individual program for a given set of arguments and the correct point in the solution space. In particular, the raw fitness $r(h, t)$ of an individual computer program h in the population of size M at any generational time step t is

$$r(i, t) = \sum_{j=1}^{N_e} |S(i, j) - C(j)|^2 \qquad (14.3)$$

where $V(h, j)$ is the value returned by program h for fitness case j (of N_e fitness cases) and $S(j)$ is the correct value for fitness case j. The closer this sum of distances is to zero, the better the program.

Thus, the raw fitness of an individual computer program for the exchange equation problem is computed by accumulating, over each of the 120 values of time T from 1959:1 to 1988:4, the sum of the squares of the differences between the actual value of GD and whatever value the individual computer program produces for that time.

Each raw fitness value is then adjusted (scaled) to produce an adjusted fitness measure $a(h, t)$. The adjusted fitness value is

$$a(i, t) = \frac{1}{(1 + r(i, t))} \qquad (14.4)$$

where $r(h, t)$ is the raw fitness for individual h at time t. Unlike raw fitness, the adjusted fitness is larger for better individuals in the population. Moreover, the adjusted fitness lies between 0 and 1.

Each such adjusted fitness value $a(h, t)$ is then normalized. The normalized fitness value $n(h, t)$ is

$$n(i, t) = \frac{a(i, t)}{\sum_{k=1}^{M} a(k, t)} \qquad (14.5)$$

The normalized fitness not only ranges between 0 and 1 and is larger for better individuals in the population, but the sum of the normalized fitness values is 1. Thus, normalized fitness is a probability value.

3.4 Parameters for Controlling Runs

The population size is 500. The maximum number of generations, G, to be run is 51 (i.e. an initial random population, called generation 0, and 50 additional generations). Crossover is performed on 90% of the population. That is, if the population size is 500, then 225 pairs of individuals from each generation are selected (with reselection allowed) from the population with a probability equal to their normalized adjusted fitness. In addition, fitness proportionate reproduction is performed on 10% of the population on each generation. That is, 50 individuals from each generation are selected (with reselection allowed) from the population with a probability equal to their normalized adjusted fitness. Note that the parents remain in the population and can often repeatedly participate in other operations during the current generation. Several minor parameters are used to control the computer implementation of the algorithm as described in Koza (1992).

3.5 Result Designation and Termination Criterion

The single individual with the best value of fitness over all the generations (the so-called best-so-far individual) is designated as the result of a run. Each run is terminated after running $G = 51$ generations.

3.6 The Reproduction and Crossover Operations

The two primary genetic operations for modifying the structures undergoing adaptation are Darwinian fitness proportionate reproduction and crossover (recombination). They are described below.

The operation of fitness proportionate reproduction for the genetic programming paradigm is the basic engine of Darwinian reproduction and survival of the fittest. It is an asexual operation in that it operates on only one parental program. The result of this operation is one offspring program. In this operation, if $s_i(t)$ is an individual in the population at generation t with fitness value $f(s_i(t))$, it will be copied into the next generation with probability

$$\frac{f(s_i(t))}{\sum\limits_{j=1}^{M} f(s_j(t))} \tag{14.6}$$

Note that the operation of fitness proportionate reproduction does not create anything new in the population. It increases or decreases the number of occurrences of individuals already in the population. To the extent that it increases the number of occurrences of more fit individuals and decreases the number of occurrences of less fit individuals, it improves the average fitness of the population (at the expense of the genetic diversity of the population).

The crossover (recombination) operation for the genetic programming paradigm is a sexual operation that starts with two parental programs. Both parents are chosen from the population with a probability equal to its normalized fitness. The result of the crossover operation is two offspring programs. Unlike fitness proportionate reproduction, the crossover operation creates new individuals in the populations.

Every computer program can be depicted graphically as a rooted point-labeled tree in a plane whose internal points are labeled with functions, whose external points (leaves) are labeled with terminals, and whose root is labeled with the function appearing just inside the outermost left parenthesis. The operation begins by randomly and independently selecting one point in each parent using a specified probability distribution (discussed below). Note that the number of points in the two parents typically are not equal. As will be seen, the crossover operation is well defined for any two programs. That is, for any two programs and any two crossover points, the resulting offspring are always valid computer programs. Offspring contain some traits from each parent.

The crossover fragment for a particular parent is the rooted subtree whose root is the crossover point for that parent and where the subtree consists of the entire subtree lying below the crossover point (i.e. more distant from the root of the original tree). Viewed in terms of lists in LISP, the crossover fragment is the sublist starting at the crossover point.

The first offspring is produced by deleting the crossover fragment of the first parent from the first parent and then impregnating the crossover fragment of the second parent at the crossover point of the first parent. In producing this first offspring the first parent acts as the base parent (the female parent) and the second parent acts as the impregnating parent (the male parent). The second offspring is produced in a symmetric manner.

Because entire subtrees are swapped, this genetic crossover (recombination) operation produces syntactically and semantically valid computer programs as offspring regardless of which point is selected in either parent. For example, consider the parental computer program:

(% (**+ 0.85 GNP82**) GNP82)

The % function above is the division function defined so that division by zero delivers zero as its result. Now, consider the second parental program:

(- FM2 (* **FM2 1.65**))

These two computer programs can be depicted graphically as rooted, point-labeled trees with ordered branches. The two parental computer programs are shown in Figure 14.2.

Assume that the points of both trees are numbered in a depth-first way starting at the left. Suppose that the second point (out of six points of the first parent) is randomly selected as the crossover point for the first parent and that the third point (out of six points of the second parent) is randomly selected as the crossover point of the second parent. The crossover points are therefore the + in the first parent and the * in the second parent.

The two crossover fragments are two subtrees shown in Figure 14.3. The places from which the crossover fragments were removed are identified with a #. The remainders are shown in Figure 14.4. These two crossover fragments correspond to the bold, underlined subexpressions (sublists) in the two parental computer programs shown above. The two offspring resulting from crossover are shown in Figure 14.5. Note that the first offspring above is a perfect solution for the exchange equation, namely

(% (* FM2 1.65) GNP82).

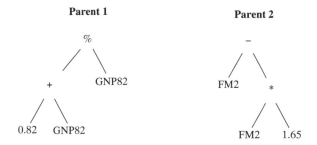

Figure 14.2 Two parental computer programs for the crossover operation

Figure 14.3 The two crossover fragments

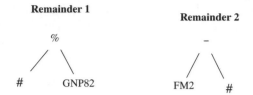

Figure 14.4   The remaining computer programs

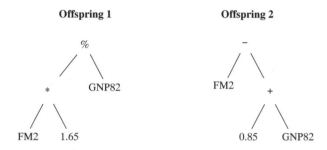

Figure 14.5   The two offspring from the crossover operation

4   REDISCOVERING THE EXCHANGE EQUATION

The problem of discovering empirical relationships from actual observed data is illustrated by the well-known econometric exchange equation $P = MV/Q$, which relates the price level P, money supply M, the velocity of money V, and the gross national product Q of an economy. Suppose that our goal is to find the relationship between quarterly values of the price level P and the three other elements of the equation. That is, our goal is to rediscover the multiplicative (non-linear) relationship

$$GD = \frac{(M2 * 1.6527)}{GNP82} \qquad (14.7)$$

from the actual observed time series data given the 120 quarterly values (from 1959:1 to 1988:4) of the four econometric time series GNP82, GD, FYGM3, and M2. The four time series were obtained from the CITIBASE_ database of machine-readable econometric time series (Citibank, 1989).

The sum, over the entire 30-year period involving 120 quarters (1959:1 to 1988:4), of the squared errors between the actual gross national product deflator GD from 1959:1 to 1988:4 and the fitted GD series calculated from the above model for 1959:1 to 1988:4 was 0.077193. The R^2 value was 0.993320. A plot of the corresponding residuals from the fitted GD series calculated from the above model for 1959:1 to 1988:4 is shown in Figure 14.6.

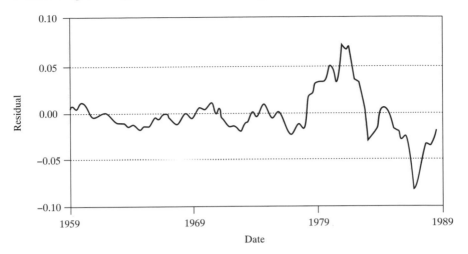

Figure 14.6 The corresponding residuals from the fitted GD series calculated from the model for 1959:1 to 1988:4

4.1 Model Derived from First Two-thirds of Data

We first divide the 30-year, 120-quarter period into a 20-year, 80-quarter in-sample period running from 1959:1 to 1978:4 and a 10-year, 40-quarter out-of-sample period running from 1979:1 to 1988:4. We are not told *a priori* whether the functional relationship between the given observed data (the independent variables) and the target function (the dependent variable GD) is linear, multiplicative, polynomial, exponential, logarithmic, or otherwise. We are not told that the addition, subtraction, exponential, and logarithmic functions as well as the time series for the 3-month Treasury bill rates (FYGM3) is irrelevant to the problem.

The initial random population (generation 0) was, predictably, highly unfit. An example of a randomly generated individual that appeared in generation 0 is

(RLOG (+ 0.27 (EXP 0.65)))

In one run of the genetic programming paradigm, the sum of squared errors between the single best program in the population and the actual GD time series was 1.55. The value of R^2 was 0.49.

After the initial random population is created, each successive new generation in the population is created by applying the operations of fitness proportionate reproduction and genetic recombination (crossover). In generation 1, the sum of the squared errors for the new best single individual in the population improved to 0.50. In generation 3, the sum of the squared errors for the new best single individual in the population improved to 0.05. This is approximately a 31-to-1 improvement over the initial random generation. R^2 improved to 0.98. In addition, by generation 3, the best single individual in the population came within 1% of the actual GD time series for 44 of the 80 in-sample points. In generation 6, the sum of the squared errors for the new best single individual in the population improved to 0.027. This is approximately a 2-to-1 improvement over generation 3. R^2 improved to 0.99. In generation 7, the sum of the squared errors for the new best single individual in the population improved to 0.013. This is approximately 2-to-1 improvement over generation 6. In generation 15, the sum of the squared errors for the new best single individual in the population improved to 0.011. This is an additional improvement over generation 7 and represents approximately a 141-to-1 improvement over generation 0. R^2 was 0.99.

A typical best single individual from a late generation of this process had a sum of squared errors of 0.009272 over the in-sample period and is shown below:

(% (+ (* (+ (* −0.402 −0.583)
   (% FM2(−GNP82 (−0.126
   (+ (+ −0.83 0.832)

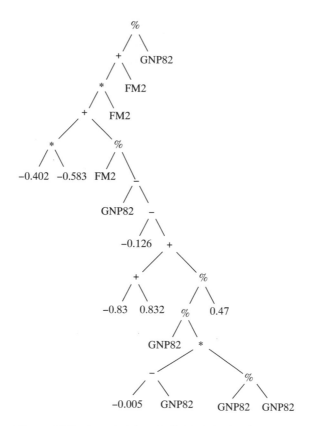

Figure 14.7 A typical best individual depicted as a tree

(% (% GNP82 (* (−0.005 GNP82)
(% GNP82 GNP82)))
0.47)))))) FM2) FM2) GNP82).

This individual is equivalent to

$$GD = \frac{(M2 * 1.634)}{GNP82} \tag{14.8}$$

This individual can be graphically depicted as a rooted, point-labeled tree with ordered branches as shown in Figure 14.7.

Table 14.1 shows the sum of the squared errors and R^2 for the entire 120-quarter period, the 80-quarter in-sample period, and the 40-quarter out-of-sample period.

Figure 14.8 shows both the gross national product deflator GD from 1959:1 to 1988:4 and the fitted GD series calculated from the above genetically produced model for 1959:1 to 1988:4. The actual GD series is shown as a line with dotted points. The fitted GD series calculated from the above model is a simple line. A

Table 14.1 The sum of the squared errors and R^2 for the 120-quarter period, the 80-quarter in-sample period, and the 40-quarter out-of-sample period

Data range	1–120	1–80	81–120
R^2	0.993480	0.997949	0.990614
Sum of squared error	0.075388	0.009272	0.066116

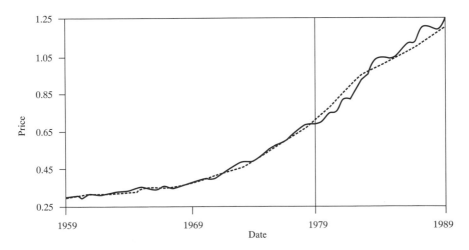

Figure 14.8 The gross national product deflator GD from 1959:1 to 1988:4 and the fitted GD series calculated from the genetically produced model for 1959:1 to 1988:4. The actual GD series is shown as line with dotted points while the fitted GD series calculated from the model is the plain line

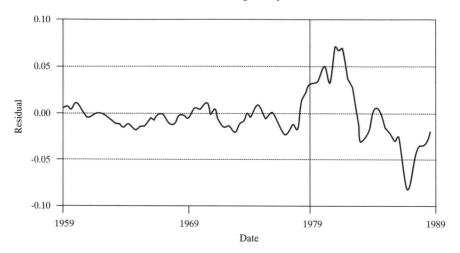

Figure 14.9 A plot of the residuals from the fitted GD series calculated from the model for 1959:1 to 1988:4

plot of the residuals from the fitted GD series calculated from the above model for 1959:1 to 1988:4 is shown in Figure 14.9.

4.2 Model Derived from Last Two-thirds of Data

We now divide the 30-year, 120-quarter period into a 10-year, 40-quarter out-of-sample period running from 1959:1 to 1958:4 and a 20-year, 80-quarter in-sample period running from 1969:1 to 1988:4. A typical best single individual from a

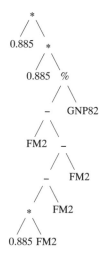

Figure 14.10 The individual graphically depicted as a rooted, point-labeled tree with ordered branches

late generation of this process had a sum of squared errors of 0.076247 over the in-sample period and is shown below:

(∗ 0.885 (∗ 0.885 (% (−FM2
  (− (− (∗ 0.885 FM2) FM2)
  FM2)) GNP82)))

This individual can be graphically depicted as a rooted, point-labeled tree with ordered branches as is shown in Figure 14.10. This individual is equivalent to

$$GD = \frac{(M2 * 1.6565)}{GNP82} \tag{14.9}$$

Table 14.2 shows the sum of the squared errors and R^2 for the entire 120-quarter period, the 40-quarter out-of-sample period, and the 80-quarter in-sample period.

Figure 14.11 shows both the actual gross national product deflator GD from 1959:1 to 1988:4 and the fitted GD series calculated from the above genetically

Table 14.2 The sum of the squared errors and R^2 for the 120-quarter period, the 40-quarter out-of-sample period, and the 80-quarter in-sample period

Data Range	1–120	1–40	41–120
R^2	0.993130	0.999136	0.990262
Sum of squared error	0.079473	0.003225	0.076247

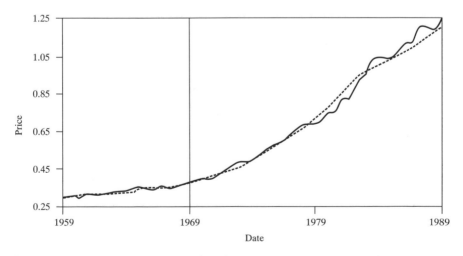

Figure 14.11 Both the gross national product deflator GD from 1959:1 to 1988:4 and the fitted GD series calculated from the model for 1959:1 to 1988:4. The actual GD series is shown as a line with dotted points while the fitted GD series calculated from the model is the plain line

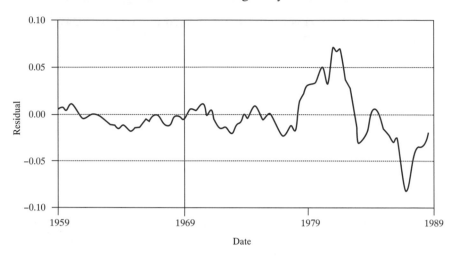

Figure 14.12   The residuals from the fitted GD series calculated from the model for 1959:1 to 1988:4

produced model for 1959:1 to 1988:4. The actual GD series is shown as a line with dotted points. The fitted GD series calculated from the above model is a simple line. A plot of the residuals from the fitted GD series calculated from the above model for 1959:1 to 1988:4 is given in Figure 14.12.

5   CONCLUSION

We have shown how genetic programming can be used to create an econometric model by rediscovering the well-known non-linear econometric exchange equation relating the price level, gross national product, money supply, and velocity of money in an economy. The genetically evolved program representing the exchange equation included an appropriate evolved numerical value for the velocity of money.

ACKNOWLEDGEMENTS

James P. Rice of the Knowledge Systems Laboratory at Stanford University made numerous contributions in connection with the computer programming of the above. Christopher Jones of Stanford University helped in analyzing the results.

REFERENCES

Albrecht, R.F., Reeves, C.R. & Steele, N.C. (1993) *Artificial Neural Nets and Genetic Algorithms*, Springer-Verlag, New York.
Bauer, R.J., Jr (1994) *Genetic Algorithms and Investment Strategies*, John Wiley, New York.

Citibank, N.A. (1989) 'CITIBASE: Citibank Economic Database (Machine Readable Magnetic Data File), 1946–present', Citibank NA, New York.

Davis, L. (ed.) (1987) *Genetic Algorithms and Simulated Annealing*, Pitman, London.

Davis, L. (1991) *Handbook of Genetic Algorithms*, Van Nostrand Reinhold, New York.

Forrest, S. (1993) 'Genetic algorithms: Principles of adaptation applied to computation,' *Science*, Vol 261, pp. 872–878.

Goldberg, D.E. (1989) *Genetic Algorithms in Search, Optimization, and Machine Learning*, Addison-Wesley, Reading, MA.

Hallman, J.J., Porter, R.D. & Small, D.H. (1989) *M2 per Unit of Potential GNP as an Anchor for the Price Level*, Board of Governors of the Federal Reserve System. Staff Study 157, Washington, DC.

Holland, J.H. (1975) *Adaptation in Natural and Artificial Systems*, University of Michigan Press, Ann Arbor, MI.

Holland, J.H. (1986) 'Escaping brittleness: The possibilities of general-purpose learning algorithms applied to parallel rule-based systems', in Michalski, R.S., Carbonell, J.G. & Mitchell, T.M. (eds), *Machine Learning: An Artificial Intelligence Approach*, Volume II, pp. 593–623, Morgan Kaufman, Los Altos, CA.

Holland, J.H. (1990) 'The global economy as an adaptive system', in Anderson, P.W., Arrow, K.J. & Pines D. (eds), *Santa Fe Institute Studies in the Sciences of Complexity: The Economy as an Evolving Complex System*, Addison-Wesley, Redwood City, CA.

Humphrey, T.M. (1989) 'Precursors of the P-star model', *Economic Review*, Federal Reserve Bank of Richmond, July-August, 3–9.

Kinnear, K.E. Jr (ed.) (1994) *Advances in Genetic Programming*, The MIT Press, Cambridge, MA.

Koza, J.R. (1990) 'A genetic approach to econometric modeling', paper presented at Sixth World Congress of the Econometric Society, Barcelona, Spain.

Koza, J.R. (1992) *Genetic Programming: On the Programming of Computers by Means of Natural Selection*, The MIT Press, Cambridge, MA.

Koza, J.R. (1994a) *Genetic Programming II: Automatic Discovery of Reusable Programs*, The MIT Press, Cambridge, MA.

Koza, J.R. (1994b) *Genetic Programming II Videotape: The Next Generation*, The MIT Press, Cambridge, MA.

Koza, J.R. & Rice, J.P. (1992) *Genetic Programming: The Movie*, The MIT Press, Cambridge, MA.

Langley, P., Simon, H.A., Bradshaw, G.L. & Zytkow, J.M. (1987) *Scientific Discovery: Computational Explorations of the Creative Process*, MIT Press, Cambridge, MA.

Langton, C.G. (ed.) (1994) *Artificial Life III*, Addison-Wesley, Reading, MA.

Maenner, R. & Manderick, B. (eds) (1992) *Proceedings of the Second International Conference on Parallel Problem Solving from Nature*, North-Holland, Amsterdam.

Marimon, R., McGrattan, E. & Sargent, T.J. (1990) 'Money as a medium of exchange in an economy with artificially intelligent agents', *Journal of Economic Dynamics and Control*, **14**, 329–73.

Michalewicz, Z. (1992) *Genetic Algorithms + Data Structures = Evolution Programs*, Springer-Verlag, New York.

Schaffer, J.D. & Whitley, D. (eds) (1992) *Proceedings of the Workshop on Combinations of Genetic Algorithms and Neural Networks 1992*, The IEEE Computer Society Press, Los Alamitos, CA.

Whitley, D. (ed.) (1992) *Proceedings of Workshop on the Foundations of Genetic Algorithms and Classifier Systems, Vail, Colorado 1992*, Morgan Kaufmann, San Mateo, CA.

———— 15 ————
Modelling Artificial Stock Markets Using Genetic Algorithms

PAUL TAYLER

1 INTRODUCTION

Historically, the study of economics has been advanced by a combination of empirical observation and development of theory. The analysis of mathematical equilibria in theoretical economic models has been the predominant mode of progress in recent decades. Such models have provided many powerful insights into economic processes, but have usually employed restrictive assumptions, making them appear to be overstylized simplifications of their complex subject matter. However, the advent of massive, cheap computing power and new intelligent technologies makes it possible to delve further into some of the complexities inherent in the real economy. It is now feasible to create a rudimentary form of 'artificial economic life'.

The following describes the creation of an artificial 'stock market' in which computerized traders compete with one another to buy and sell a stock for profit. The objectives were twofold: first, to create a miniature economic laboratory in which to study some aspects of behaviour in real markets; and, second, to make a practical investigation of how machine-learning techniques might be applied to financial trading.

Intelligent Systems for Finance and Business. Edited by S. Goonatilake and P. Treleaven
© 1995 John Wiley & Sons Ltd

The artificial stock market consisted of a computer model in which simulated traders updated an array of trading rules over time. At intervals, the traders attempted to discover better sets of rules using a genetic algorithm (GA) learning technique. The price of the 'stock' in the market was entirely endogenously produced (i.e. it was completely determined by the buying and selling decisions of the traders). Over time, the traders did indeed evolve better rule sets, and the endogenously generated market behaviour displayed many of the complex features attributed to the real stock market.

The work described here was done while I was visiting the Santa Fe Institute (SFI), New Mexico, USA, forming part of an ongoing collaborative project at SFI, involving Brian Arthur (Stanford University and SFI), John Holland (Michigan), Blake LeBaron (Wisconsin), Richard Palmer (Duke) and the author. (A full description of further developments in the SFI stock-market model is given in Arthur et al., forthcoming.) The usual disclaimer applies, however — errors or misconceptions expressed herein are purely my responsibility, as are the speculations.

2   ECONOMIC MODELS, STOCK MARKETS AND ARTIFICIAL ECONOMIC LIFE

Traditional economic models of financial markets incorporate the assumption that markets are 'efficient'. This assumption takes different forms, but essentially includes the idea that the current price takes account of all relevant available information, and is basically a 'rational' reflection of value. The significance accorded to rationality in financial markets paints a picture of cool deliberation and deep calculation, of heroic foresight and instantaneous adaptations.

The reality, as anyone on a securities dealing floor during the crash of October 1987 could testify, is very different — at least, it *feels* very different. Massive sums are risked at startling speed, and amid a chaotic cacophony of shouted orders (and expletives) traders often have literally only seconds in which to make decisions. An old adage has it that markets are driven by a combination of fear and greed; in a typical *Financial Times* report of events in markets around the world we might read of 'hopes' of interest rate cuts, or 'fears' of a fall on Wall Street, contributing to major market changes. Anecdotal evidence from market participants suggests that the analysis of mathematical equilibria in textbook economic theory plays no part whatever in trading decisions (see e.g. Lewis, 1989, p. 25). J. M. Keynes famously compared stock market investing to judging a beauty contest, remarking that the objective was not to select the (objectively) most attractive contestant but to identify the one (subjectively) most likely to be favoured by the other judges. Profits would be made by anticipating market demand for a stock, for its price would rise if others wished to buy it, but fall if they chose instead to sell.

A useful and natural partitioning of different kinds of economic models is based on their purpose. A model may be developed with the intention of providing the most accurate possible numerical predictions. Such a model might consist of a number of abstractions (such as econometric equations) which are not intended to directly mimic economic transactions but to serve as an approximation to behaviour in aggregate; most macro-economic models fall into this category. This kind of model is 'good' to the extent that it delivers forecasts (e.g. of inflation or economic growth) with tolerably small average errors.

An alternative approach is to build a model to illustrate and illuminate understanding of its subject by providing a realistic account of economic processes. Although it need not be a full simulation, the purpose of such a model is to incorporate intuitions of the key aspects of micro-behaviour into a model from which macro-behaviour will then emerge. If the emergent system behaviour does correspond in significant features with the macro-behaviour of the economic system being modelled, then that increases confidence that it is a 'good' model.

Traditional economic models of this second kind have tended to be very simple in scope, assuming, *inter alia*, economic actors with perfect foresight and complete knowledge of their (stable, linear) environment acting in a totally 'rational' fashion. However, Nelson & Winter (1982) have pioneered an alternative approach, developing a series of models dealing with inter-firm competition, technological change and economic growth. (See also Tayler, 1990, for some extensions, including phenomena such as economies of scale and more detailed representations of technological change.)

Even these evolutionary models, however, only dealt with the behavioural aspects of economic systems in a rudimentary way. If the emotional factors ('fear and greed') are important in modelling markets, then a much richer description of economic actors' decisions and behaviour will be needed. In this sense, the SFI stock market model is much closer to the 'Artificial Life' approach than to other contemporary economic models. The A-Life school has married biology and computation in a fascinating synthesis which is helping to advance understanding of evolutionary processes in general. Levy (1992) is recommended as a very readable general survey; more detailed accounts are given in Langton (1989) and Langton et al. (1992). Indeed, Alfred Marshall, often cited as the father of modern equilibrium economic theory, wrote that 'The Mecca of the economist lies in economic biology' (Marshall, 1920, Preface).

3 APPLICATIONS OF GENETIC ALGORITHMS

The preceding intuitions suggest that a good descriptive model of a market must include an account of participants' micro-level decision making, and of how it adapts and changes over time. We therefore needed an 'intelligent' approach to modelling our computerized traders. They would have to be capable of handling a wide range of decision variables, and of learning how to improve them over time. There might be significant non-linearities in the trading environment, which would not necessarily be time-invariant. For all these reasons, the Genetic Algorithm seemed a promising candidate. Additionally, the question of whether GAs could be employed to 'learn' time series such as financial prices is interesting for its own sake.

The Genetic Algorithm is a relatively new way for computers to 'learn' to solve problems. It is a search procedure inspired by the mechanics of natural selection in biology. It uses 'survival of the fittest' in a population of decision rules (or problem solutions, or function values). Successful 'creatures' (rules encoded as logical strings of information) in the population have the opportunity to 'mate' and produce offspring, whose structure combines features inherited from their parent strings. The evolution of the population of strings is randomized, but its rate of improvement is vastly superior to that of a simple random walk. The GA (as in biological evolution) exploits past experience (represented by relative fitness) to yield an efficient search for improved performance.

GAs have now been successfully applied to a wide range of problem domains. Further extensions and developments are being made all the time; the following is only a partial list (see Goldberg, 1989, for some further details):

- One of the classic early applications of the GA was a system which 'learned' to control a gas pipeline. Pressure and temperature at different points in the pipeline were monitored, and the system learned both to optimize normal behaviour and to respond appropriately to rare events such as sudden leaks.

- Other control problems successfully tackled with the help of GAs include controlling a blast furnace, and (at least in a computer simulation) helping US Navy aircraft escape from surface-to-air missiles.

- GAs have been applied to 'textbook' Operational Research domains, such as the classic travelling salesman problem. GA performance is said to be comparable to other known heuristic techniques. Job-shop scheduling problems have also been successfully solved with GAs.

- Engineering problems such as designing turbine blades and airframe parts have yielded incremental improvements to GAs, often when combined with other intelligent technologies (e.g. expert systems).

- GAs, often in combination with neural networks and other hybrid systems, are known to be in use in a number of securities and currency trading institutions, although their users are understandably reluctant to reveal too many details of the implementations.

- At Nuclear Electric, GAs have been used to analyse ways of improving fuel cycle efficiency in nuclear power stations (Poon, 1990).

4 BACKGROUND AND INTRODUCTION TO GAs

The basic Genetic Algorithm has four stages:

(1) An initial population (of rules or solutions) is generated, usually at random.

(2) The fitness of each member of the population is determined.

(3) A number of members of the population with low relative fitness is eliminated.

(4) The population is replenished with new individuals produced by combining information from high-fitness members of the population. The algorithm returns to step 2, evaluating the fitnesses of the members of the new population.

4.1 A Simple Example

A simple example might be the problem of finding the maximum value of the function $y = x^2$ on the range [0, 1]. One way of tackling this is to use a rule string with bits representing binary 'decimals'. Suppose we use five bits (more could be deployed to find a solution to any required degree of accuracy); then

$$
\begin{aligned}
(0, 0, 0, 0, 0) &= 0 & &= 0.0 \\
(1, 0, 0, 0, 0) &= 1/2 & &= 0.5 \\
(0, 1, 0, 0, 0) &= 1/4 & &= 0.25 \\
&\quad\cdots & &\cdots \\
(0, 0, 0, 0, 1) &= 1/32 & &= 0.03125 \\
(1, 1, 0, 0, 0) &= 1/2 + 1/4 & &= 0.75
\end{aligned}
$$

and so on. We might choose a population size of twenty rules, which can be generated completely at random.

The first step is to evaluate the *fitness* of each string. In this case, the fitness is the value of x^2 corresponding to the logical string, so that

$$
\begin{aligned}
\text{fitness of } (0, 0, 0, 0, 0) &= 0.0 * 0.0 &= 0.0 \\
\text{fitness of } (1, 0, 0, 0, 0) &= 0.5 * 0.5 &= 0.25
\end{aligned}
$$

etc.

The next step is to discard a fraction of the population — in this case, we will remove half of the strings (ten) from the population. They will be replaced by ten new rules, which are created by 'mating' between the other ten rules with superior fitness. Pairing of parents is random again.

Typically, two genetic operators are used to produce 'children' — *crossover* and *mutation*. To perform crossover, a random point on the string is selected, and the child string is produced by copying genetic material from one parent up to the crossover point, and from the other after the crossover:

parent 1   (1, 1, 1, 1, 1)
parent 2   (0, 0, 0, 0, 0)

crossover   ⌒

child   (1, 1, 1, 0, 0)
or
child   (0, 0, 0, 1, 1)

Mutation is easily understood; with some (usually very low) probability, a single bit on the string is switched from 0 to 1 (or vice versa).

Mating is repeated to produce ten new 'child' strings to replenish the population. The GA progresses by successively evaluating the fitnesses of new populations of strings, removing the weakest, and replacing them with new strings derived from the more successful.

In this simple case, it is easy to see what happens. Strings with a 1 at any location will be favoured over strings with a 0. Moreover, strings with 1's in the leftmost locations will be favoured over those with their 1's to the right. The outcome is very likely to be that, after a few generations, the population will be dominated by strings with lots of 1's. Eventually, the population will consist of many copies of the optimal string (1, 1, 1, 1, 1), with a few transient mutants appearing and disappearing.

4.2 Why Does It Work?

The success of the GA in this 'toy' example could be attributed to 'random variation' — the algorithm checks the fitness of many randomly generated possibilities until it happens upon the best solution. This interpretation would be mistaken, however; random sampling alone might work on this tiny problem, but for more difficult tasks, the string-space (number of bits) rapidly becomes so large that a random walk through it would have little hope of success.

A clue to the success of the GA in the $y = x^2$ example can be found by noticing that there is something special about the leftmost bit in the string; it gives the largest single contribution to fitness. If we watched the evolution of successive generations of the string population, we would see that strings with '1' in the leftmost position (which makes the largest single contribution to fitness) would dominate the population quickly, and that strings with a '1' in the next-to-left position as well would also prosper.

The power of the GA comes from its ability to select strings with useful blocks of information (such as the high fitness contribution of the leftmost bit), and to concentrate its search on variations which include those blocks. In more complex problems, finding a good solution often depends upon putting together several such useful blocks (which may in themselves each consist of more than just one bit) in the right combinations. The GA is an effective search procedure because it is an efficient way of processing many blocks in parallel. The so-called *implicit parallelism* result states that a population of size N strings implicitly processes of the order of N^3 blocks per generation. This surprising theorem shows that the GA employs considerable computational 'leverage', without requiring the storage of any information about past attempts to solve the problem, apart from what is stored in the genetic material of the current population. (See e.g. Goldberg, 1989, for a discussion of implicit parallelism.)

5 STRENGTHS AND WEAKNESSES OF GENETIC ALGORITHMS

Almost any function-optimization problem can be coded up for the GA to tackle. For many 'normal' and well-behaved functions (with only one or few optima) there is no practical advantage in using GA methods. However, GAs can be a powerful tool for searching mathematical spaces defined by functions of multiple variables, particularly if they involve non-linear interactions. For example, GAs are well suited to exploring functions of genuinely discrete variables. GAs also represent a superior approach to problem domains in which the contribution to fitness resulting from two 'blocks' of information combined is much greater than the sum of the influence of the blocks on their own.

There is, as may be deduced from the absence of any convergence criterion from the description of the basic algorithm given above, a difficulty with the GA: how do we know that it has found the optimum solution to a problem? The answer is that we don't. There is in fact no guarantee that the GA will find the globally optimum solution. However, in practical applications it is often satisfactory just to find a better solution than the one we already knew about, so this is not be a fundamental objection to employing GAs in most cases.

It is also often true that, for any *particular* problem, the GA is not necessarily the best optimization technique available. In many cases (e.g. OR scheduling tasks) there is another approach that will deliver equally good or better performance. However, the interesting thing about the GA is that it seems to deliver acceptable to good performance in very many different problem domains. It is thus a relatively robust algorithm.

As an intuition as to why that is, reflect on the biological parallels for a moment. We ourselves are essentially the product of something like a huge GA. (Biological evolution involves some other quite complex processes too, but the central principles do seem to be similar.) The survival and diversity of life itself is a testament to the robustness and power of the GA, and its capability to adapt to a continually changing environment.

In common with other leading-edge techniques such as neural nets, there is an element of 'black art' in the successful application of GAs. There are many parameters to be tuned (population size, replacement rate, mutation rate, etc.), and often considerable experimentation is needed before the best performance is obtained.

6 THE SFI STOCK MARKET MODEL

6.1 Overview

The artificial market consists of a number of simulated traders, each possessing a unique array of decision rules. At each successive time period, traders consult their decision rules and select the most appropriate one upon which to act, choosing whether to buy or sell stock. Those transactions which can be matched by willing buyers and sellers are then performed. As a result of the relative balance of buying and selling pressure, the stock price is adjusted, and the market prepares to trade for the next period. As experience is gained in applying the trading rules, a GA is introduced to improve each individual trader's decision rule set.

6.2 The Participants

There are 60 trading agents in the simulated market, buying and selling units (or fractions of units) of a homogenous 'stock'. At the beginning of any trading period a trader may hold either a long or a short position in the stock (i.e. traders may sell stock which they do not possess). There is a limit to the size of position (long or short) which a trader may adopt. Each trader possesses an array of 60 classifiers — trading rules — from which it selects to make trading decisions.

6.3 The Market and Stock Prices

Depending upon the prompting of their trading decision rules (see below) traders choose whether they wish to be long or short of stock, and in what size. Having selected a desired position, comparison with their existing holdings indicates whether the traders wish to add to or reduce their positions, and each then accordingly make bids to buy or offers to sell.

Bids and offers are made at the current ruling market price. If the aggregate bids and offers are exactly equal, then all orders are fulfilled by trading between the agents at the current price. Usually this does not happen; there will be a surplus either of bids or of offers. In this case, supposing that there are more bids to buy than offers to sell at time t, then all desired sales are executed, and purchases are partially fulfilled (pro-rated by bid size between all bidders). The market price is then adjusted for the next trading period $t + 1$ according to:

$$\text{Price}_{t+1} = \text{Price}_t * [1 + K * (\text{sum of bids} - \text{sum of offers})] \qquad (15.1)$$

where K is a constant. In the next period $t + 1$ the updated price is used, and traders will seek to trade at this new level. The new stock price will be re-evaluated by the traders' updated rule sets, and hence their desired stock positions may change; the bids and offers made at the next round of trading are unlikely to be the same as the 'residual' demand from the previous period.

6.4 Dividends and Interest

The stock pays a notional dividend each trading period, which varies over time. (The dividend is the only exogenous input to the market.) Repeated experiments showed that the most interesting behaviour in our stock market was produced when the dividend followed combined cycles of varying lengths (e.g. the dividend time series was produced as a sum of sine waves of widely differing frequencies), with a small 'noise' term, plus occasional major random shocks. It seemed that the computerized traders (perhaps like their real-life counterparts) needed some variety before they became sufficiently 'interested' in the market to evolve more complex decision rules.

A constant interest rate R is also assumed in the market. It is used for comparison with the earnings from dividends — in other words, the traders face an opportunity cost in holding stock. The interest rate is important because it allows the 'true' fundamental value of the stock to be assessed (see below).

6.5 Classifiers and (Short-run) Learning

In complex environments, economic agents are unlikely to have just one decision rule. They are likely to have several or many, and they may under some circumstances conflict. In the stock market model each trader has an array of 60 trading rules. A rule consists of two elements: a condition string, which describes a state or set of states of the trader's environment, and an action string, which determines the consequences of selecting the rule. A constantly updated strength is associated with each rule, which estimates the reliability or usefulness of the rule. When the state(s) described in a condition string matches the present state of the environment, the condition is satisfied, and the rule is said to be active. The action string then specifies the desired market position (long or short).

The condition string contains about 80 "bits" (not quite binary — see below). The bits code observations about the market and its recent past, such as:

- Recent price movements (up or down)
- Recent changes in the dividend
- The relative positions of moving averages of different periods of the price and dividend time series (e.g. whether the 10-period moving average is above or below the 20-period average)
- The current market price, expressed as a multiple of the dividend
- Logical indications of whether there have been recent market 'shocks'

These condition string bits take true/false values (1/0). However, with 80 bits of information, an astronomical number of trading rules would be required to cover the whole universe of different possible market states. To avoid this constraint, each bit is also permitted to take the value 'don't care', represented as '#'. If the condition bit for a particular logical state of the market variable is '#', then the condition is satisfied by both true and false values. A condition string might, for example, just encode information about recent price trends, with all other bits set to '#'. (For further discussion of the use of classifiers and the '#' operator, see Holland et al., 1989, Chapter 4.)

The strength of a rule reflects its past forecasting performance, and is updated using a moving average of the rule profitability over the past 25 periods for which the rule was active (i.e. for the last 25 trading periods in which the condition string was satisfied). The contribution to strength, dS, from each activation of the rule is given by:

$$dS = X * [P_t - P_{t-1} * (1 + R) + D_t]/P_{t-1} \qquad (15.2)$$

where

D = dividend at time t

R = interest rate

X = position (long or short) taken as a result of adopting action

P_t = market price at evaluation of rule

P_{t-1} = market price at activation of rule

dS is thus the normalized price change in the stock, adjusted for the interest that the trader could have notionally earned by putting its money in the bank instead, plus the dividend earned by holding the stock for a period.

6.6 Fundamental Value

The fundamental value of the stock at any trading period is given by D/R (the dividend divided by the interest rate; this assumes that the trader believes that the current price is the best estimator of the future price, and that the dividend will remain constant). To verify this, substitute D/R for P_t and P_{t-1} in equation (15.2) — this price provides an equilibrium reference point for the market. That is, a price higher than D/R should make it profitable to sell the stock and hold cash to earn interest instead (*if* we ignore everything else that may be going on in the market), and a price lower than D/R should make it profitable to hold the stock. In this sense, D/R is the fundamental value of the stock; since the interest rate is constant at 10% in this simulated stock market, the fundamental price/dividend ratio should therefore always be 10.

6.7 Selection and Activation of Rules

At any trading period each trader is likely to have several rules active. They may all suggest the same course of action, but it is quite possible that they are in conflict (the price/earnings multiple might be low, suggesting a buying opportunity, but recent price movements indicate strong selling pressure, warning the trader to hold firm). In such cases, the rule used for trading is chosen on a random basis, weighted by the current strength of each rule multiplied by the 'specificity' of the rule. The specificity is the number of non-'don't care' bits in the condition string. This means that traders will choose rules which have performed well in the past, biased towards those which give the best correspondence to the current market situation and discriminating against those which are merely vague generalizations.

6.8 The Genetic Algorithm

Rule strengths reflect short-term performances. In the long run, GA recombination of rules with high strength (fitness) is used to evolve better families of rules.

Rules are initially generated by giving traders random strings. The development of the market was aided, however, by seeding the non-'#' parts of the condition strings in bunches in particular areas, so that (while rules are still randomly produced) there is a better chance of producing 'interesting' schemas early on.

GA recombination of trading rules is performed after every 250 periods (to allow time for activation of a good proportion of each trader's rule array). Crossover is performed on 10 out of each agent's 60 rules, using tournament selection of 'parents' (Davis, 1991). Mutation with a probability of 1% is applied to bits in the new 'child' rules.

6.9 Special Genetic Algorithm Characteristics

In order to facilitate continuing learning in what was often a changing and evolving market, special consideration was given to maintaining a diverse and robust rule set. (This is a generic issue in the application of genetic algorithms. Over-rapid convergence sacrifices richness — there is a trade-off between on- and off-line performance.) The following three enhancements were successfully introduced to the standard GA:

- *Reversal*: A new GA operator was devised to exploit a special feature of the stock market 'problem'. If a trading rule has below-average strength then that means that it tends to lose money over time. The market is symmetrical, however, in the sense that doing the opposite would have yielded profits on average. For this reason, a 'bad' rule in each trader's repertoire is reversed at each GA generation, i.e. the instruction to go long or short attached to the condition recognition string is simply changed in sign.

- *Crowding*: When new rules are introduced as 'children' of superior trading rules, preference is given to discarding inferior rules which are as similar as possible to the new offspring. This has the benefit of maintaining a more diverse 'gene pool' of trading rules. (The crowding technique and its merits are described in Goldberg, 1989.)

- *Generalization*: If a rule remains inactive for a long time, the chances are that it has become too specialized — its condition part is difficult to fulfil. After a rule has been dormant for a long time, a single 1 or 0 bit from the condition string is picked at random and changed to '#', i.e. the condition for activation of the rule is relaxed somewhat.

6.10 Implementation

The artificial stock-market was programmed in C on a Sun workstation. Runs of many hundreds of thousands of trading periods (and several thousand GA generations) would take up to a day of real time.

7   RESULTS

The foregoing has described in detail how the micro-level behaviour of the modelled entities is constructed. All model outputs are the result of their complex interactions. What are the key emergent features of the stock market model?

7.1   Price Behaviour

First, the artificial traders are able to learn about their artificial market sufficiently well that for much of the time the market price tracks the fundamental 'fair value' with some accuracy. This is no small achievement, and amounts to more than the GA 'learning' to track an exogenously determined price series. The traders

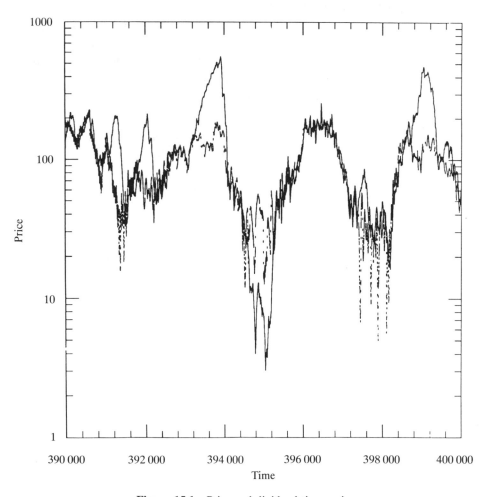

Figure 15.1   Price and dividend time series

constitute their own environment, and their decision rules were initially randomized. All behaviour has been 'bootstrapped' up from an initial 'soup' of random binary trading rules. Hence, the market's evolution to states in which prices track fundamental value is an example of *self-organization*.

Second, however, it is noticeable that there are also periods when prices depart radically from fair value. Figure 15.1 plots an excerpt from a market price which illustrates this clearly. (The dashed line represents fundamental value.) Price and value are congruent at the beginning of the excerpt ($t = 390\,000$), but part company temporarily a couple of times ($t = 392\,000$) before prices drive upwards in a huge 'speculative bubble' ($t = 394\,000$). A fall in dividends then seems to prick the bubble, and prices collapse, in fact overcompensating with a great 'crash' ($t = 395\,000$). Normal behaviour then reasserts itself, but there is a still further 'bubble' later ($t = 399\,000$).

These episodes, which can last for hundreds of trading periods, are examples of self-reinforcing behaviour, in which expectations of a rise (or fall) in prices lead to anticipatory buying (selling). The behaviour thus induced has a self-fulfilling effect upon the market price, at least until it goes so far out of line that more 'fundamental' valuations gain enough weight to reverse the process.

In general, price sequences are volatile. There are periods when prices follow consistent trends up or down, but there are also times when the price simply oscillates without moving in any particular direction. The time series do not statistically resemble the idealized 'random walk' behaviour predicted by economic theory (because of the occasional periods of steady price trending in one direction or the other). However, to the eye, the graph of prices in the artificial stock market often resembles real stock price movements.

Much of the time, prices are close to the theoretical fundamental value — Figure 15.1 was chosen to illustrate the extremes. Moreover, there is a strong tendency for the market price to respond to significant moves up or down in the fundamental value (caused by changes in the dividend).

7.2 Rule Development

Over time the specificity (descriptive power) of the traders' rule sets increases steadily (Figure 15.2). Once some useful schemas have been 'discovered' by the GA, specificity increases even after hundreds of GA generations. Typically an average specificity of 15 is reached after about 1500 generations. Of course, some rules are developed with an individual specificity much higher than this. This reinforces the conclusion that traders are learning something useful about their environment, and finding it useful to create more detailed 'maps' in their decision space.

In the same way, the diversity of the rule set for each trader tends to decrease steadily over time (Figure 15.3). Diversity is defined as the average Hamming distance between the classifier strings (the sum of the absolute difference between the individual elements of the string). Decreasing diversity is partly a reflection of

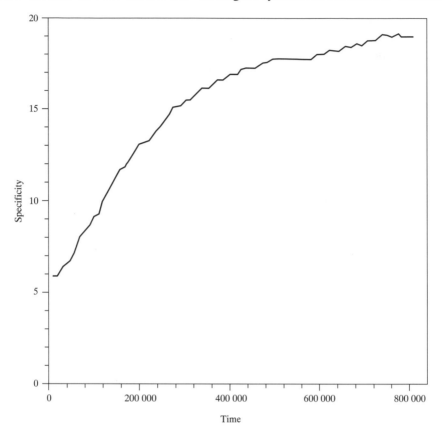

Figure 15.2 Traders' rule specificity over time

the reduction in the number of 'don't care' logical statements in traders' condition strings, but it is also indicative of a tendency for individuals to specialize in particular rule types.

Rules of the kinds which might be expected do indeed form in some well-defined categories. These involve e.g. combinations of recent price movements; buy and sell triggers at low or high values of price/dividend multiples; complex combinations of the moving average indicators (suggesting some learning of the deeper long-term structure of the dividend time series); and combinations of the 'shock' indicators with recent price or dividend changes.

Those rules which base trading decisions on recent price movements are perhaps the most interesting, since they seem to provoke the 'trend-chasing' behaviour which leads to bubbles and crashes in the artificial market. These rules are, of course, self-fulfilling if enough traders employ them, reminding us of Keynes'comparison with a beauty contest: it doesn't matter whether the rule is 'true', so long as sufficient market participants are likely to act on it.

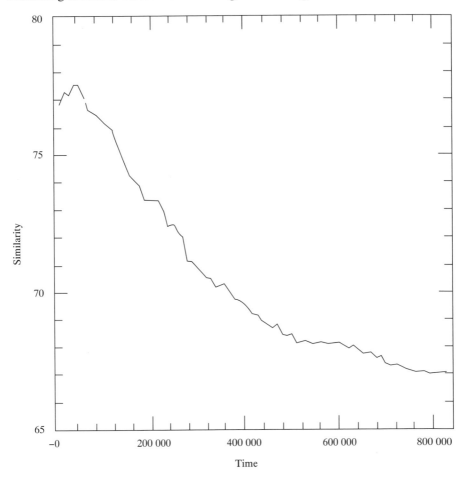

Figure 15.3 Traders' rule similarity over time

7.3 Differentiation of Traders

Traders do not, in general, develop comprehensive rule sets. That is, each tends to evolve a fairly specialized group of rules. Typically, a trader becomes either a 'bull' or a 'bear', in the sense that it evolves a rule set which predominantly looks just for signals to buy or for indications to sell.

Moreover, traders tend to specialize in variants of the same effective rules, rather than maintaining a wide variety of rule types. For example, one trader may 'look' mainly at price/dividend multiples (a 'fundamentalist'), another may be 'interested' in recent price movements ('trend chaser'), while a third tracks the relative positions of different moving averages ('chartist').

8 CONCLUSIONS

Our first objective in undertaking this project was to create an economic micro-cosm to illustrate properties of stock markets. In this I believe we were successful, creating 'artificial economic life' which self-organized from random initial conditions. The traders evolved in competition, their combined behaviour leading to market prices usually in agreement with the theoretical equilibrium, but occasionally lapsing into speculative episodes of overvaluation or pessimistic bouts of market depression.

Our second interest was to enhance understanding of how genetic algorithm techniques might be applied to learning about market behaviour. Clearly, the market described here is purely artificial. However, I believe that the results are encouraging from the perspective of the further application of GAs, suggesting that they may be harnessed to learn useful things about complex time series like stock prices. This artificial stock market is much simpler than the real thing, of course, but it still contains considerable complexity; the computerized traders succeeded in mastering concepts like fundamental value and significant price trends.

In conclusion, the experience of building this stock-market model suggests that applying the genetic algorithm is still as much art as science. Patience and improvization are both essential; small changes to the learning 'recipe' can have surprising results in the long run. The key to success is to find ways of maintaining a sufficiently diverse rule set for long enough to allow the GA to select on important information. This is particularly important in a problem domain with as much 'noise' in the data as a market (either real or simulated).

9 FUTURE DIRECTIONS

A number of variations to the stock-market model are possible, and indeed the work is still ongoing. Other decision variables can be introduced, and there is scope for introducing other techniques (such as neural nets) to improve the traders' abilities to recognize and respond to market events. Introducing limited exchanges of information — successful rules — between the traders would turn the entire market into a 'Parallel Genetic Algorithm'.

The potential for economic artificial life ('E-Life') may be quite considerable. Many issues in economic theory are being re-examined using game theory approaches, and GAs may be well suited to developing understanding in these areas. For example, a GA has been used to evolve excellent strategies for playing the so-called 'Repeated Prisoner's Dilemma', a simple two-player game economists consider important as a metaphor for many problems involving cooperation or collusion — see Axelrod (1987).

A case in point is the problem of oligopolistic competition, in which a market is dominated by a small number of firms. Traditional analysis says that the market price should fall to marginal production costs, yet this is by no means a guaranteed outcome in the real world. An E-life model of the problem might examine how alternative market regimes can exist. This is a problem with real importance not just to theorists but also to business decision makers and public policy makers. Other related examples include issues around new entry to markets, barriers to trade, and problems of social cooperation over public goods.

ACKNOWLEDGEMENTS

I would like to thank both the Santa Fe Institute and the Decision Systems Group at Coopers & Lybrand Deloitte who granted me a sabbatical, for making my involvement in this research possible. Neither of these bodies, nor my current employer Brunel University, is responsible for the opinions contained herein.

REFERENCES

Arthur, W.B., Holland, J.H., LeBaron, B., Palmer, R., & Tayler, P.J. (forthcoming) Provisional title: *An Artificial Stockmarket*.

Axelrod, R. (1987) 'The evolution of strategies in the iterated prisoner's dilemma', in Davis, L. (ed.) *Genetic Algorithms and Simulated Annealing*, Morgan Kaufmann, Los Altos, CA.

Davis, L. (1991) *Handbook of Genetic Algorithms*, Van Nostrand Reinhold, New York.

Goldberg, D.E. (1989) *Genetic Algorithms in Search, Optimization and Machine Learning*, Addison-Wesley, Reading, MA.

Holland, J.H., Holyoak, K.J., Nisbett, R.E. & Thagard, P.R. (1989) *Induction: Processes of Inference, Learning, and Discovery*, MIT Press, Cambridge, MA.

Langton, C.G. (1989) *Artificial Life*, Santa Fe Institute Studies in Complexity, Vol. 6, Addison-Wesley, Reading, MA.

Langton, C.G., Taylor, C., Farmer, J.D. & Rasmussen, S. (1992) *Artificial Life II*, Santa Fe Institute Studies in Complexity, Vol. 10, Addison-Wesley, Reading, MA.

Levy, S. (1992) *Artificial Life: The Quest for a New Creation*, Cape, London.

Lewis, M.M. (1989) *Liar's Poker: Rising Through the Wreckage on Wall Street*, Penguin, Harmondsworth.

Marshall, A. (1920) *Principles of Economics* (8th edition — first published 1890), Macmillan, London.

Nelson, R. & Winter, S. (1982) *An Evolutionary Theory of Economic Change*, Harvard University Press, Cambridge, MA.

Poon, P.W. (1990) 'Genetic algorithms and fuel cycle optimization', *The Nuclear Engineer*, 31(6), 173–7.

Tayler, P.J. (1990) *Problems of Scale: An OR/Systems Approach*, PhD thesis, University of Warwick.

16

Intelligent, Self-organizing Models in Economics and Finance

PETER M. ALLEN

1 INTRODUCTION

Understanding the emergence and evolution of structure and pattern in natural and human systems is one of the most important and complex questions that can be addressed. Indeed, intelligence itself concerns the capacity to perceive and respond to pattern and structure, as well as the ability to act wisely when it is changing and uncertainty prevails. Anticipating the emergence of possible new structures or regimes is therefore one of the key factors in strategic 'intelligence'. Statistics and data cannot allow such foresight unless used to develop self-organizing models capable of spontaneous structural evolution. Without such models, one is locked into responding to the short-term dynamics, at the expense of an adequate preparation for the longer-term changes that may occur. The mathematical framework within which a real understanding of how structure and organization emerge and evolve began to be established with the study of dissipative structures (Nicolis and Prigogine, 1977; Prigogine, Herman & Allen, 1977) and synergetic systems (Haken, 1977). However, the new view took some time to be understood as it challenged the equilibrium and mechanistic paradigms which had reigned supreme for many years.

In this chapter we shall briefly describe the ideas underlying these advances and show how they provide a new basis for intelligent systems and an entirely new

Intelligent Systems for Finance and Business. Edited by S. Goonatilake and P. Treleaven
© 1995 John Wiley & Sons Ltd

view of risk and uncertainty. The traditional scientific approach was based on the mechanical paradigm emerging from physics (Prigogine and Stengers, 1987; Allen, 1990; Allen & Lesser, 1991), and sought to produce, wherever possible, *predictive* models of systems, based on the *causal* mechanisms underlying them. Sometimes this was softened by a statistical 'spread' around average behaviour, but this did not change the principle. It only provides an effective representation of a *fixed* set of mechanisms, for which the 'task' envisaged for the model, and its environment do not change.

Living systems, however, are not like this. Whatever the set of relations dominant at a given moment, evolution and intelligence ensure that innovations and changes occur as part of a co-evolutionary process between individuals and also with the physical environment. Simple systems representations of reality are just a reflection of the limited perceptions of those that conceive them. Any set of causal relations that are used to model reality will always turn out to be just a small subset of an expanding and much more complex web of interactions. Prediction on the basis of the simple system is therefore found to be illusory and we find that we are dealing with a future that is intrinsically uncertain.

In the face of this, a first reaction might be to base decisions purely according to the short-term advantages that are clear at present. But this runs the risk that they could be completely wrong over a longer term, and short-term success may be bought at the cost of long-term failure. In order to find a way forward, we must examine nature's way of dealing with uncertainty and change, and explore how we may imitate this procedure.

Let us briefly consider the basic framework of understanding and modelling human systems. If we examine a region, a city, a high street or a business and consider the evidence that remains of successive occupants, then after dating and classifying them, an *evolutionary tree* of some kind emerges, possibly with discontinuities suggesting disaster and invasion, but nevertheless suggesting a changing 'cast of characters' and behaviours, over time (Figure 16.1). If we want to understand how its future might be affected by some decision or policy, then traditionally, we try to build a mathematical model of the system as it is at present. This is based on the components and mechanisms that are present in the system. In other words, after making a choice of variables based on the perceived taxonomy of the system, we then account for the set of processes that increase or decrease the values of these variables over time. This is our model of the system which captures how the variables change over time as a result of the present mechanisms. However, in such a model there is no place for variables representing behaviours that are *not* present in the system at that time, and therefore there is no place for innovation, learning and adaptation. If we are to imitate the evolutionary process, then we need to put that back.

Clearly, the evolutionary tree represents the changing behaviours that are present in the system over time, but at any particular moment, we can identify the *components* of a system, and the *interactions* operating on these from the outside world

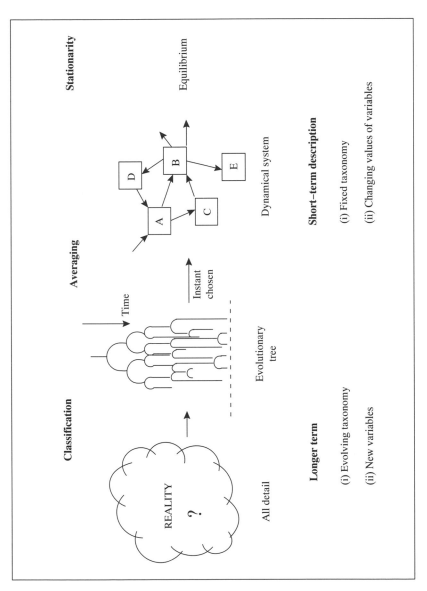

Figure 16.1 Classification of the data concerning the actors and artefacts present leads to the picture of a changing structure and taxonomy over time. Mathematical models however, have concentrated on the changes resulting from the mechanisms present at a given time

and from each other. This provides a traditional scientific understanding of the system at a given time, a mechanical representation of the system which can be run on a computer, to give predictions. However, as we see clearly from our broader picture of the 'evolutionary tree', the predictions that such a model can give can *only* be correct for as long as the taxonomy of the system remains unchanged.

Despite this, however, much attention has rightly been given to the interesting behaviours of non-linear dynamical systems. Their equations display a rich spectrum of possible behaviours in different regions of both parameter space and initial conditions. They range from a simple approach to a homogeneous steady state, characterized by a *point* attractor, through that of sustained oscillation of a *cyclic* attractor, to the well-known *chaotic* behaviour characteristic of a strange attractor. These can either be homogeneous or can involve spatial structure as well. This possibility of rich behaviours has proved to be of great significance for many fields of science (Nicolis and Prigogine, 1990; Thompson and Stewart, 1986; Holden 1986.)

However, here we are trying to understand the evolution and emergence of structure and the intelligence necessary to survive change, and this concerns models in which *adaptive* and *innovative* responses can occur as the individuals 'deal' with unexpected change. As has been shown elsewhere (Allen, 1988), in order to derive deterministic, mechanical equations for such systems, two assumptions are required:

- Events occur at their average rate
- All individuals of a given type, x say, are identical and of average type

The errors introduced by the first assumption can be addressed by using a deeper, probabilistic dynamics, called the 'Master Equation' in which events of different probabilities can and do occur. Therefore, sequences of events which correspond to successive runs of good or bad 'luck' are included, with their relevant probabilities (Allen & Ebeling, 1983). For systems with non-linear interactions between individuals, this destroys the idea of a *system trajectory*. However, learning and innovation really concern the second assumption, and we shall turn to this now.

2 MODELS OF LEARNING AND ADAPTIVE BEHAVIOUR

Returning to the general conceptual framework of Figure 16.1, the evolutionary tree is generated by a dialogue between the 'average dynamics' of an existing situation and the unpredictable, exploratory perturbations around this that result from the inevitable occurrence of non-average events and components. This dialogue leads to the new concept of 'evolutionary drive' (Allen & McGlade, 1987a, 1989), which is really about learning and adaptiveness.

In order to explore the behaviour of systems with *endogenously* generated innovations and selection we define a 'possibility space', a space representing the range of different strategies and behaviours that could potentially arise for the different actors present. This 'possibility space' will be explored by actors who experiment and try out new techniques.

Because players cannot all be winners some behaviours will always do better than others, and through imitation and growth, some strategies will be successful and others will fail and disappear. Possibility space can be seen as a 'landscape' of hills and valleys, of advantage and disadvantage. Through inherent underlying differences, incomplete information and just plain 'error making', evolution explores 'outwards' from any existing individual's behaviour, and some new behaviours are amplified, finding higher ground in the landscape, and some are suppressed. Evolution is shown therefore to select for populations with the ability to *learn* rather than for populations with optimal, but fixed, behaviour.

In the space of 'possibilities' closely similar behaviours are considered to be most in competition with each other, since they require similar resources, and must find a similar niche in the system. However, we assume that in this particular dimension there is some 'distance' in character space, some level of dissimilarity, at which two behaviours do not compete. Initially, a single population is placed at the centre of possibility space, and since it has adequate resources, it grows. However, error making in the transmission through time of the 'rules' underlying any specific behaviour or technique, means that there is a constant tendency for divergent behaviours to appear, and this operates just like a diffusion process, only instead of spreading outwards into geographical space, the diffusion represents the population behaviour spreading outwards to new behaviours and types (Figure 16.2).

During the initial phase of an experiment in which we start off with a single population in an 'empty' resource space, resources are plentiful, the centre of the

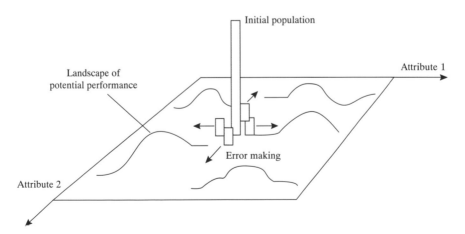

Figure 16.2 The effect of 'error making' in the reproduction of a population produces a diffusion into the surrounding 'character' space. The landscape shows the peaks and valleys of potential performance

distribution, the average type, grows better than the eccentrics at the edge. The population forms a sharp spike, with the diffusing eccentrics suppressed by their unsuccessful competition with the average type. However, any single behaviour can only grow until it reaches the limits set by its input requirements, or in the case of an economic activity, by the market limit for any particular product. After this, it is the 'eccentrics', the 'error makers' that grow more successfully than the 'average type', and the population identity becomes unstable. The single sharply spiked distribution spreads, and splits into new populations that climb the evolutionary landscape that has been created, leading away from the ancestral type. The new populations move away from each other, and grow until in their turn they reach the limits of their new normality, whereupon they also split into new behaviours, gradually filling the resource spectrum (Figure 16.3).

Instead of considering the evolution of techniques and behaviours in a fixed landscape expressing higher/lower pay-offs, we shall allow for the fact that the 'pay-offs', the adaptive landscapes, are really generated by the interactions of a population with the other populations in the system. In this way, instead of simply evolving towards the peaks of a *fixed* evolutionary landscape, through their inter-actions populations really create the landscape upon which they move, and by moving across it change it. So the different behaviours present grow, split off, and gradually fill the possibility space with an 'ecology' of activities, each identity and role being formed by the mutual interaction and identities of the others. The limit of such a process would be given by the amount of energy that is available for useful work that can be accessed by the 'technological' possibilities potentially open to the system. This means that evolutionary processes would explore and reinforce mutually consistent technologies and strategies that capture parts of the

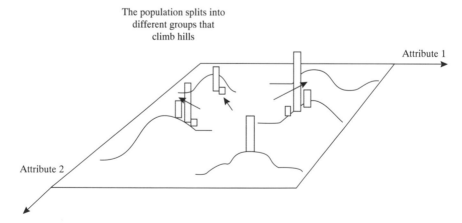

Figure 16.3 A single population splits into several different groups, which separate, and climb the hills of this fixed landscape. However, in general, the landscape will depend upon the populations in play

energy flows through the system and use them to build and maintain their necessary internal structure. The limit would be set by the amount of available energy.

In order to understand this more clearly, let us consider in detail a simple, one-dimensional character space, in which competition for underlying resources exists, but so also do other possible interactions. For example, for any two particular populations i, and j, practising their characteristic behaviours, there may be an effect of one on the other. This could be positive, in that side-effects of the activity of j might in fact provide conditions or effects that help i. Of course, the effect might equally well be antagonistic, or neutral. Similarly, i may have a positive, negative or neutral effect on j. If we therefore initially choose values randomly for all the possible interactions between all i and j, then these effects will come into play if the populations concerned are in fact present. If they are not there, then obviously, there can be no positive or negative effects experienced. For example, to be precise, let us consider 20 points, and between each of them a random number is used to choose a value for the potential interaction on i from j:

$$Interaction(j, i) = fr.(2.Random(j, i) - 1)$$

where $Random(j,i)$ is a random number between 0 and 1, and fr is the strength of the interaction. Each population that is present will experience the net effect that results from all of the other populations that are also present. Similarly, it will affect those populations by its presence.

$$Net\ Effect\ on\ i = \sum_j x(j) \cdot interaction(j, i)$$

The sum is over j including i, and so we are looking at behaviours that, in addition to interacting with each other, also feed-back on themselves. There will also always be a competition for underlying resources, which we shall represent by:

$$Crowding(i) = \sum_j \frac{x(j)}{(1 + \rho Distance(i, j))}$$

At any time, then, we can draw the landscape of synergy and antagonism that is generated and experienced by the populations present in the system. We can therefore write down the equation for the change in population of each of the x_i. It will contain the positive and negative effects of the influence of the other populations present, as well as the competition for resources that will always be a factor, and also the error making diffusion through which populations from i create small numbers of off-spring in $i + 1$ and $i - 1$.

$$\frac{dx(i)}{dt} = b(fx(i) + 0.5(1 - f)x(i - 1) + .5(1 - f)x(i + 1))(1 + 0.04.Neteff(i))$$

$$\times (1 - Crowding(i)/N) - mx(i)$$

where f is the fidelity of reproduction (0.99).

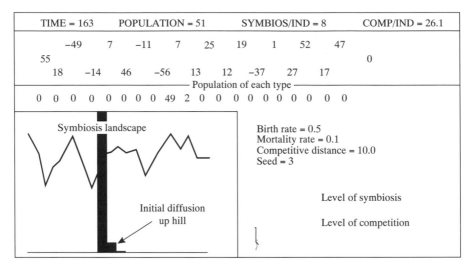

| TIME = 163 | POPULATION = 51 | SYMBIOS/IND = 8 | COMP/IND = 26.1 |

```
          -49    7   -11    7    25   19    1    52   47
    55                                                          0
       18   -14   46   -56   13   12   -37   27   17
                    ———— Population of each type ————
   0   0   0   0   0   0   0   0  49   2   0   0   0   0   0   0   0   0   0   0
```

Symbiosis landscape

Birth rate = 0.5
Mortality rate = 0.1
Competitive distance = 10.0
Seed = 3

Initial diffusion
up hill

Level of symbiosis

Level of competition

Figure 16.4 The initial population and evolutionary landscape of our simulation

In Figure 16.4 we show an early stage in a simulation with a single population of five individuals placed at 10. In other words, $x(10) = 5$ initially. The only population initially present is 10, and therefore the evolutionary landscape in which it sits is in fact the one it creates itself. No other populations are present yet to contribute to the overall landscape.

What matters then, is how the population 10 affects itself. This may have positive or negative effects depending on the random selection made at the start of the simulation. However, in general the population 10 will grow and begin to 'diffuse' into types 9 and 11. Gradually, the landscape will reflect the effects that 9, 10 and 11 have on each other, and the diffusion will continue into the other possible populations. Hills in the landscape will be climbed by the populations, but as they climb, they change their behaviour, and change the landscape for themselves and the others. Figures 16.4–16.7 show this process taking place over time.

Although, competition helps to 'drive' the exploration process, what is observed is that a system with 'error-making' explorations of behaviour evolves towards structures which express synergetic complementarities. In other words, evolution evolves cooperative structures. The synergy can be expressed either through 'self-symbiotic' terms, where the consequences of a behaviour in addition to consuming resources is favourable to itself, or through interactions involving pairs, triplets, and so on.

Several important points can now be made. First, a successful and sustainable evolutionary system will clearly be one in which there is freedom for imagination and creativity to explore at the individual level, and to seek out complementarities and loops of positive feedback which will generate a stable community of actors.

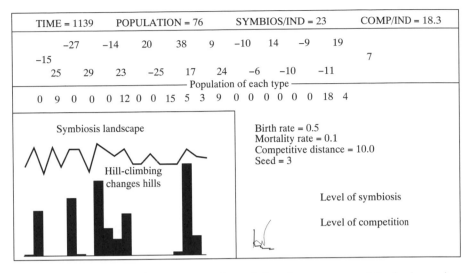

| TIME = 1139 | POPULATION = 76 | SYMBIOS/IND = 23 | COMP/IND = 18.3 |

Figure 16.5 After 1139 time steps several populations have grown, and the landscape has changed as a result

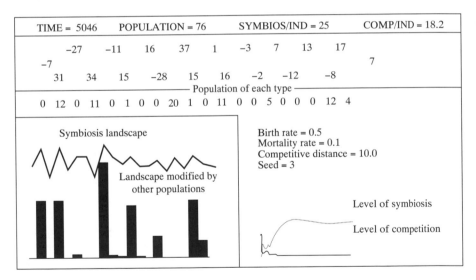

| TIME = 5046 | POPULATION = 76 | SYMBIOS/IND = 25 | COMP/IND = 18.2 |

Figure 16.6 After 5046 time steps the system has found a stable structure with a high degree of synergy. Single, pair and triplet step hypercycles have emerged

Second, the self-organization of our system leads to a highly cooperative system, where the competition per individual is low but where loops of positive feedback and synergy are high. In other words, the free evolution of the different populations, each seeking its own growth, leads to a system which is more cooperative than competitive.

Pair and self symbiots

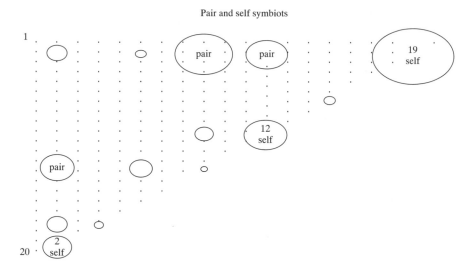

Figure 16.7 This shows the pair and self-symbiotic populations that emerge after the evolution. Triplets are 2-12-19 and 2-9-19

From our example, the discovery of cooperatives, and the formation of communities of players with a shared interest in each other's success, is the outcome of the evolutionary process. The other important point, particularly for scientists, is that it would be impossible to discern the 'correct' model equations even for our simple 20 population problem, from observing the population dynamics of the system. Because any single behaviour could be playing a positive, or negative role in a self, or pair or triplet interaction, it would be impossible to 'untangle' its interactions and write down its governing equations simply by noting the population's growth or decline. The system itself, through the error-making search process, can find stable arrangements of multiple actors, and can self-organize a balance between the actors in play and the interactions that they bring with them, but this does not mean that we can deduce what the web of interactions really is. This certainly poses problems for the rational analysis of situations, since this must rely on an understanding of the consequences of the different interactions that are believed to be present. It is also true that although we would not be able to 'guess' how to arrange the populations to form a stable community, evolution can find how to do this.

Clearly, if we cannot really know how the circles of influence are formed by looking at the data, the only choice would be to ask the actors involved, in the case of a human system. This in turn would raise the question of whether people really understand the roots of their own situation, and the influences of the functional, emotional and historical links that build, maintain and cast down organizations and institutions. The loops of positive feedback that build structure introduce a truly collective aspect to any profound understanding of their nature, and this will be beyond any simple rational analysis, used in a goal-seeking local context.

To summarize, the response of nature to the problem of future uncertainty is 'diffusion' in both geographical and strategic space. It provides a permanent capacity to generate and 'run' *parallel strategies* and this is the basis for resilience and long-term success for any player within a complex system. It tells us how nature 'deals' with the long term, and does not make the mistake that we do, which is to focus exclusively on the short-term dynamics.

3 SPATIAL EVOLUTION OF COMPLEX SYSTEMS — REGIONAL AND URBAN CHANGE

The first applications of these ideas to human systems (Allen & Sanglier, 1979, 1981) examined the question of self-organization in geographical space. A nonlinear dynamical system of equations underlying the patterns of supply and demand of different goods and services evolved as a result of the random occurrence of entrepreneurs at different points and times in the system. Consumer demand was assumed to reflect relative prices. The creative interplay of random exploration and rational selection resulted in the gradual emergence of self-consistent market structures and patterns of settlement as economic functions either prospered or declined at their locations.

Regional structure emerged as a result of the interplay of positive and negative feedbacks:

- Positive due to the urban multiplier, economies of scale and externalities
- Negative through spatial competition both for producers and for residential space

Studies showed that many futures are possible initially, but gradually systems may 'lock in' to a somewhat unsatisfactory market structure, as a result of a particular history. These simulations show us that a very large number of possible stable structures could potentially result, involving different numbers of centres in different locations, and necessarily not offering the same level of cost, utility or efficiency. In some ways they show rather clearly that a 'free market' system does not necessarily run to an 'optimal' solution, but just to one of many possible solutions. The 'invisible hand' of Adam Smith therefore, although ensuring that incompatible entities do not cohabit the space, can lead to a great number of possible structures — each with its own mixture of good and bad qualities. Real choices exist, but we can only successfully make these strategic choices if we can understand the qualitative evolution of the system over the long term, using this kind of model.

These models show many important principles: many final states are possible, precise prediction in the early stages is impossible, approximate rules appear (centre separations, etc.) but always with considerable deviation and local individuality present. The results are affected by the particularities of the transportation system, as well as by information flows affecting the mental maps of consumers (Gould & White, 1978). This approach leads, therefore, to the first integrated land-use/transportation models and showed how the strategic evolution of structure as a result of changing technology, transportation, resource availability, etc. could be explored, as the changing patterns of supply and demand affect each other in a complex dynamic spatial process.

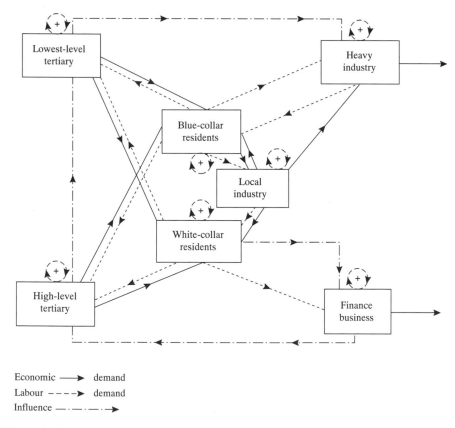

Figure 16.8 The intra-urban interaction scheme which leads to the development of urban structure

The fundamental basis for these models are the decisions of the different types of individual actors, which reflect their values and functional requirements. Although these are represented by very simple rules for each type of actor, when distributed among average and non-average individuals they give rise to very complex patterns of structure and flow, and to a structural emergence and evolution at the collective level. In turn, the macrostructures that emerge constrain the choices of individuals, and fashion their experience, so that without the knowledge afforded by such models there may not be any simple relation between the goals of actors, and what really happens to them. Each actor is co-evolving with the structures resulting from the behaviour of all the others, and surprise and uncertainty are part of the result.

The 'selection' process, on the other hand, results simply from the success or failure of enterprises in the competitive and cooperative dynamical game that is running. Models were developed showing the evolution of cities and regions as a result of these evolutionary processes. For example, the generic interaction scheme of Figure 16.8 was shown to successfully generate the emergence and evolution of the spatial structure of the city of Brussels.

In this model, the decisions of individual actors of different types is simulated as each of them changes the conditions which affect the others. As the city grows, so the demand for space changes the price of available land, and the different abilities of actors to pay, affects their responses (Figure 16.9). These differences reflect the particular spatial requirements of economic activities, where, for example, manufacturing industry may require twenty times the surface area as an insurance office, for the same 'value added'. Also, different actors will have different requirements concerning their location, such as either being very central for communication and contacts, or needing transportation infrastructure such as a port, rail and road access for the import of raw materials and the export of finished products. Residents too will have different locational needs depending on where they work, and on their age, family composition and socio-economic group. Through the spatial interaction of all these decisions, running over time, the city structures and generates business and administrative districts, industrial satellites, retailing centres, and areas of high- and low-quality residential housing. All the spatial choices of the different actors are made according to the networks of private and public transportation, which will themselves be changed according to the intensity of demand and congestion that occurs. The models therefore constitute a unique 'intelligence' about the possible evolution of a city, providing a basis for investment decision for housing, retail, office or industrial developments.

Similarly, regional models were developed which showed how the urban centres within the system interacted. This mutual interaction was both influenced by and in its turn influenced the flows of investment and of migrants. From this an evolutionary model of Belgium, for example, was developed and has been described in detail elsewhere (Sanglier & Allen, 1989). The overall effectiveness of a city is conditioned by the costs and benefits that result from its location within the national framework, and also from its internal structure. Therefore cities that suffer high

INDUSTRY

TERTIARY

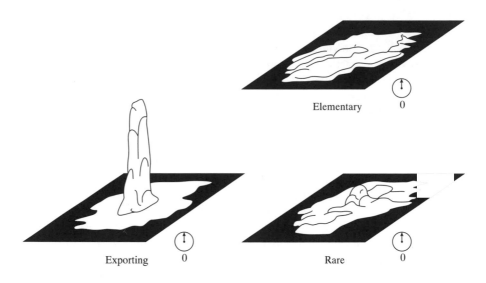

RESIDENTS

Figure 16.9   The city of Brussels that emerges from our interaction system after 20 units of time starting from a central seed

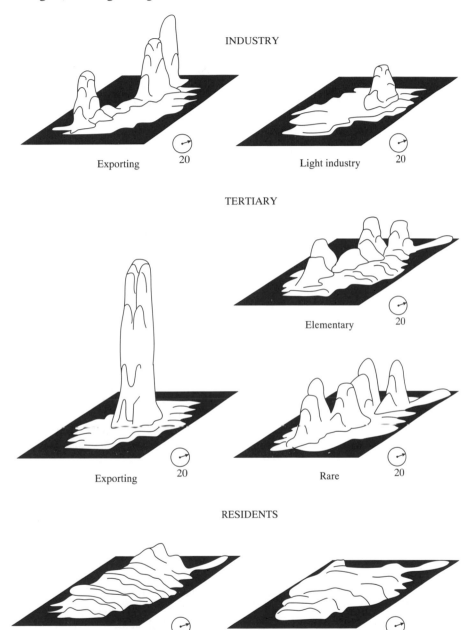

Figure 16.9 (*continued*)

levels of congestion have poor infrastructure, dissatisfied residents with poor educational and training levels, environmental problems and high taxes, for example, will not be characterized by the same parameters of 'functioning' as they would be if they had better internal structures and facilities. Because of this, the particularities of the internal structure, and the success or failure of urban centres with respect to their inhabitants, penetrates upwards to affect their capacity to attract investment and migrants, and hence their long-term growth.

The spatial models of urban and regional evolution therefore demonstrate the fact that what emerges are *ecologies* of populations, clustered into mutually consistent locations and activities, expressing a mixture of competition and symbiosis. This nested hierarchy of structure is the result of evolution. It is not 'optimal' in any way, because there are a multiplicity of subjectivities and intentions, fed by a web of imperfect information.

The total pattern emerges as a result of the interaction of imperfect patterns of behaviour for each type actor, and what this really means is that there is an intrinsic element of unpredictability in the system. Creativity and adaptive response are therefore powered by the degree of heterogeneity of the population and their microscopic diversity. Applications of these ideas have been made in the USA, Belgium, Holland, Senegal and France, as well as in understanding intra-urban evolution in cities of Belgium and France. Such models provide an 'intelligent' basis for decision support and policy exploration since they can show the complex, creative *responses* of a system, and not simply the directly imposed effects.

4   MANAGEMENT OF NATURAL RESOURCES

This evolutionary approach was also used to develop intelligent decision-support models for the management of natural resources. This work has been discussed elsewhere in detail (Allen & McGlade, 1987a), but it is worth mentioning briefly some of the main conclusions.

One essential and very general point that emerged was that success in fishing requires two almost contradictory facets of behaviour. First, the ability to organize one's behaviour so as to exploit the information available concerning 'net benefits' (to be rational) which we have called 'Cartesian' behaviour. More surprisingly, however, a second ability is required, that is, to be able to ignore present information and to 'explore' beyond present knowledge. We have called these kinds of fishermen 'Stochasts'. The first makes good use of information but the second generates it! At the root of creativity is always this second type.

In the short term it is always true that the more 'rational' actor will outperform the less, and therefore taking steps to maximize present profits must, by that yardstick, be better than not doing so. Nevertheless, over a longer period the best performance does not come from the most rational but instead from behaviour which is some complex compromise. For example, a fleet of Cartesians which goes where available information indicates highest profits will in fact lock into zones for much too long, remaining in ignorance of the existence of other more profitable zones simply because there is no information available concerning them. This underlines the important point that 'You don't know what it is you don't know'.

New information can only come from boats which have 'chosen' not to fish in the 'best' zones, or who do not share the consensus values, technology or behaviour, and hence who generate information. They behave like risk takers, but may or may not see themselves as such. They may act as they do through ignorance, or through a belief in some myth or legend. Whatever the reason, or lack of it, they are vital to the success of the fishing endeavour as a whole. It is their exploration that probes the value of the existing pattern of fishing effort, and lays the foundations for a new one.

As information is generated concerning the existence of new, rich fishing grounds, so the value of this starts to fall as the news spreads, and exploitation rates increase there. We see a cyclic pattern in the discovery of value in a zone, the spread of information and with it the saturation or exhaustion of the discovery, calling for fresh explorations.

The model can either be used as a simulator, for the overall management of the fishery, or for the benefit of any particular fleet wishing to improve its performance. The parameter values which appear in the mechanisms governing the decision making of fishing boats are calibrated so as to give realistic behaviour (Allen & McGlade, 1987). It is also possible to make a model which will run competing strategies against each other, and eventually discover for itself robust and successful sets of strategies — again generating an 'ecology' of fishing strategies (Allen, 1991).

5 DECISION SUPPORT IN ECONOMIC MARKETS

The idea that economics should be thought of in 'biological' terms occurred to authors as far back as Marshall (1927) and, of course, before that, Darwin himself was inspired partially by the ideas of Adam Smith. However, for various reasons, economics borrowed the inappropriate 'equilibrium' perspective of classical physics. Economists such as Schumpeter (1934) and, later, Goodwin (1951), who attempted to introduce dynamical considerations and non-linear effects were not followed by the mainstream. Nelson & Winter (1983) set out an evolutionary perspective, of competing firms subject to 'mutation'. This has helped to inspire much of the research that is going on concerning the evolution of technology, and of technical change (Dosi et al., 1988). A particularly interesting perspective was developed by Clark & Juma (1987), who clearly separated out the short-term picture of an economic system from the long-term processes that govern its evolution.

Self-organizing simulation models of economic markets similar to the regional, urban and natural resource management models described above have been built. These allow an exploration of the possible consequences of different product and pricing strategies in a changing market. The possible space of products may be multi-dimensional, concerning all the different possible qualities that the product could have. The customer characteristics are also diverse, and the model requires an analysis of how the products of one particular company will attract potential clients, compared to competing products. Sales strategies are realistically represented, with their costs and therefore the market changes as it matures. Clients which have just bought a product cease to be potential clients for some length of time. Clients are seeking the qualities important to them, at the lowest price, and so the relative competitivities of different companies leads to changing market shares, and this in turn to different economies of scale, and profits. As well as providing decision support for company strategy, the system shows how a market of possible products will self-organize, leading to an evolving pattern of supply and demand.

The screen shown in Figure 16.10 shows a simple competition between three firms, with different quality products, and different fixed and variable costs, and profits mark-up. In this case, the simulation corresponded to a 'new' market, and the program allows simulations of the strategies, and hence the possibility of learning what might or might not work successfully. A player can indulge in advertising campaigns, in research programmes or can change the quality and mark-up of a product. The other players can respond, and in this way, one can learn successful strategies that might be appropriate in different markets, or with different types of competitor. Similarly, it allows one to learn the change in strategy required when moving from an immature to an mature market, and indeed, the question of long-term survival with product portfolios and product life-cycles represented explicitly. Once again, this kind of model can be called 'intelligent' in that it allows users

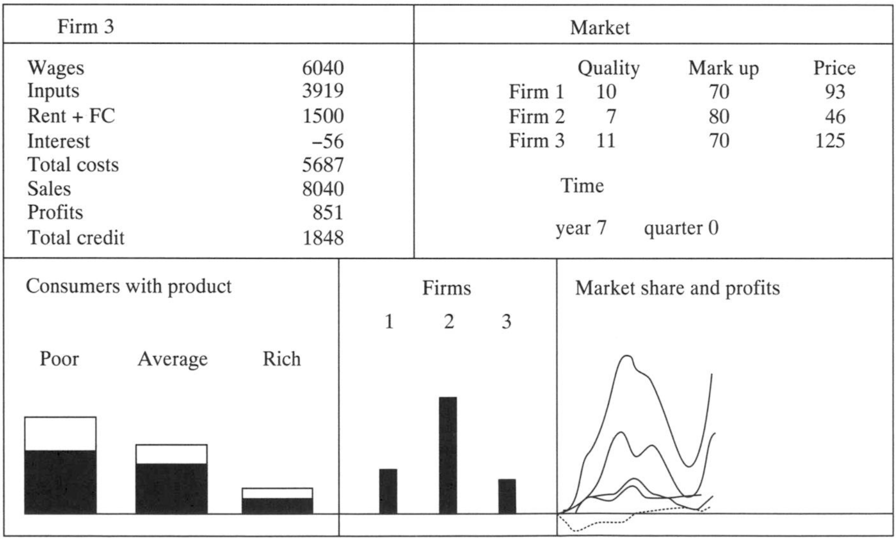

Figure 16.10 A system used to explore the strategic plans of companies in competition in a new market

to anticipate the complex consequences of their behaviour — which they could not anticipate without the model.

6 INTELLIGENCE AND LEARNING IN A FINANCIAL MARKET

Another area of applications concerns the development of trading and portfolio management systems. In conventional economics general *equilibrium* theory and the 'efficient market' hypothesis portray changes in the market as being due to external factors represented as a *random walk* (Osborne, 1964; Muth, 1961; Fama, 1970). The subsequent realization that equilibrium forms only a partial view and indications of the existence of instability through market crashes has motivated the search for alternative paradigms. Non-linear dynamics, in particular *chaos theory*, has been the focus of much recent research (Blank, 1991; Chen, 1988; Day, 1983; Grandmont & Malgrange, 1986; Hsieh, 1991; Kesley, 1988; Larrain, 1991; Peters, 1989, 1991a,b; Savit, 1988, 1989; Scheinkman & LeBaron, 1989). Of course, the value of such research would be to demonstrate the persistence of a particular chaotic attractor for some time, during which it could be used to trade successfully. However, this does not get around the problem that as soon as this 'persistence time' became known, then it, and the chaotic attractor, would change!

Clearly, if any trend or knowledge becomes apparent, traders react to it, and by their actions change what subsequently will occur in reality. This implies that markets will always drive themselves to the 'edge' of predictability and that it might be easier to learn how to survive uncertainty, rather than trying to predict the dynamics of future prices. In order to do this, an intelligent model has been developed which uses parallel strategies and an internal selection to choose behaviour which is sufficiently good to survive, despite the fact that we cannot know 'the' future. Intelligence in trading depends on maintaining a whole range of strategies in play, and in switching to those that are working well at any given time.

As a basis for our strategies, we have used the *moving average* method. It is one of the most simple, yet versatile and widely used of all technical indicators (Murphy, 1986). It does not pretend to anticipate events but only to respond to them. Successful trading depends on which moving average is chosen. Too short, and the system trades too often, losing money each time. Too long, and it comes in too late, and stays in too long so that money is lost while waiting for the signal. In addition, however, if the price produces a 'spike', cutting the moving average curve and then immediately cutting it in the opposite direction, then losses occur. A *bandwidth* can be added to the moving average method to act as a precaution against unnecessary trades.

Evolutionary intelligence then consists in comparing the performance of different strategies over a recent period, and using the best for some time. As the other players change their games, and as players enter and leave the market, so the price time series are affected, and our system adapts the parameters of its strategy in response. Our 'possibility space' for strategies has four dimensions: over what length of time to test the performance; how often to re-adapt, what moving average and bandwidth to use.

The trading model includes things like commission charges incurred in executing trades, fluctuations in exchange rates as well as slippage costs when transactions were not carried out at the expected price as a result of delays in communicating trades to the trading floor. These factors bring a sense of reality to the simulation results obtained.

The system has been developed at present to trade in the futures markets of various commodities, currencies and financial instruments (Allen & Phang, 1993). The trading in different commodities and currencies has been combined in a 'self-adapting' portfolio system. In this, the recent success of trading in different commodities affects the number of lots that are traded. This trading can be either long (buying what you don't have) or short (selling what you don't have), and the trading success encountered affects the weighting of the commodity within the

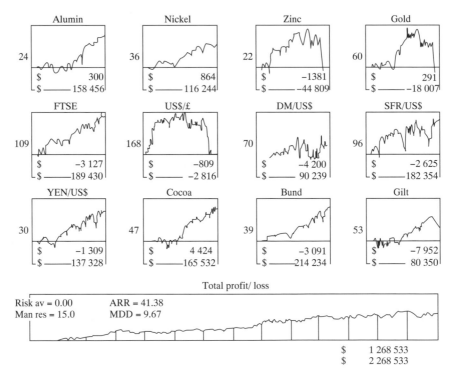

Figure 16.11 The final screen after 615 days trading of 12 futures contracts. An initial $1 million becomes $2 268 533 trading 10% of the fund, excluding interest on the 90% and management fees

portfolio. There is a parameter which the user is free to choose, which determines the 'strength' of the portfolio management. If it is set to zero, then whatever the trading has been like, there is an even spread of investment right across the portfolio, while if it is set high, then, in contrast the fund reacts strongly to the success for different contracts. Similarly, there is a parameter which concerns 'risk aversion', and this affects the fraction of the total fund that is traded. The system described here represents the performance of an ungeared fund, with only 10% being traded. In Figure 16.11 we show the result for 12 contracts over 615 days with a maximum drawdown of 10%, excluding the interest earned on the 90% of the fund.

7 DISCUSSION

In this chapter a range of applications of self-organizing models has been presented. These provide a new basis for 'intelligent' decision making by allowing the longer-term trajectories of the system — its possible futures — to be explored. Through the interplay of individual diversity and non-linear processes of amplification, complex human systems possess self-adaptive behaviour capable of surviving in the face of uncertainty. Survival therefore demands adaptability, and evolutionary intelligence is the means by which this is achieved. It consists of the permanent generation of multiple, parallel strategies and possibilities, and the ability to focus sufficiently on the successful ones. Our models of self-organizing systems provide a new basis for 'intelligence' and 'wisdom' when considering strategy and planning in the complex and changing world which we inhabit.

ACKNOWLEDGEMENTS

The urban and regional models were developed with the collaboration of Michele Sanglier, Guy Engelen and Francoise Boon. The financial trading and portfolio models were developed with Hoon Khing Phang and Mark Strathern. This work was partially supported by Toppan Moore Systems Ltd (Japan), by the Open Society Fund of New York, and by Futures Management Ltd, London.

REFERENCES

Allen, P.M. (1985) 'Towards a new science of complex systems', in *The Science and Praxis of Complexity*, United Nations University Press, Tokyo.
Allen, P.M. (1988) 'Evolution: why the whole is greater than the sum of its parts', in *Ecodynamics*, Wolft, W., Soeder, C.J. & Drepper, F.R., Springer-Verlag, Berlin.
Allen, P.M. (1990) 'Why the future is not what it was', *Futures*, July/August, 555–70.
Allen, P.M. (1994) 'Evolution, sustainability and industrial metabolism', in Ayer, R. & Simonis, U.E. (eds), *Industrial Metabolism*, United Nations University Press, Tokyo.
Allen, P.M. & Ebeling, W. (1983) 'Evolution and the stochastic description of simple ecosystems', *Biosystems*, **16**, 113–26.

Allen, P.M. & Lesser, M. (1991) 'Evolutionary human systems: learning, ignorance and subjectivity', in Saviotti, P.P. & Metcalfe, J.S. (eds), *Evolutionary Theories of Economic and Technological Change*, Harwood Chur, Switzerland.

Allen, P.M. & McGlade, J.M. (1987a) 'Modelling complex human systems: a fisheries example', *European Journal of Operations Research*, **30**, 147-67.

Allen, P.M. & McGlade, J.M. (1987b) 'Evolutionary drive: the effect of microscopic diversity, error making and noise', *Foundations of Physics*, **17**, No. 7, July.

Allen, P.M. & McGlade, J.M. (1989) 'Optimality, adequacy and the evolution of complexity', in Christiansen A. & Parmentier, J. (eds), *Structure, Coherence and Chaos in Dynamical Systems*, Manchester University Press, Manchester.

Allen, P.M. & Phang, H.K. (1993) 'Evolution, creativity and intelligence in complex systems", in Haken M. & Mikhailov A. (eds), *Interdisciplinary Approaches to Nonlinear Complex Systems*, Springer-Verlag, Berlin.

Allen, P.M. & Sanglier, M. (1979) 'Dynamic model of growth in a central place system', *Geographical Analysis*, **11**, No. 3.

Allen, P.M. & Sanglier, M. (1981) 'Urban evolution, self-organization and decision making', *Environment and Planning*, A., 181, **13**, 167-183.

Blank, S.C. (1991) 'Chaos in futures markets? A nonlinear dynamical analysis', *Journal of Futures Markets*, **11**, 711-28.

Chen, P. (1988) 'Empirical and theoretical evidence of economic chaos', *System Dynamics Review*, **4**.

Clark, N. & Juma, C. (1987) *Long Run Economics: An evolutionary approach to economic change*, Pinter, London.

Day, R. (1983) 'The emergence of chaos from classical economic growth', *Quarterly Journal of Economics*, **98**, 201-13.

Debreu, G. (1959) *Theory of Value*, John Wiley, Chichester.

Dosi, G., Freeman, C., Nelson, R., Silverberg, G. & Soete, L. (eds) (1988) *Technical Change and Economic Theory*, Pinter, London.

Fama, E.F. (1970) 'Efficient capital markets: a review of theory and empirical work', *Journal of Finance*, **25**, 383-423.

Goodwin, R.M. (1951) 'The non-linear accelerator and the persistence of business cycles', *Econometrica*, **19**.

Gould, P. & White, R. (1978) *Mental Maps*, Penguin Books, Harmondsworth.

Grandmont, J. & Malgrange, P. (1986) 'Non-linear economic dynamics: Introduction', *Journal of Economic Theory*, **40**.

Gustave, Le Bon (1922) *Psychologie des Foules*, reprinted as *The Crowd*, Macmillan, New York.

Haken, H. (1977) 'Synergetics', in *Synergetics*, vol.1, Springer-Verlag, Berlin.

Holden, A. (1986) *'Chaos'*, Princeton, NJ: Princeton University Press, 1986.

Hsieh, D.A. (1991) 'Chaos and nonlinear dynamics: application to financial markets', *The Journal of Finance*, **66**, 163-187.

Kesley, D. (1988) 'The economics of chaos or the chaos of economics', *Oxford Economic Papers*, 40.

Larrain, M. (1991) 'Empirical tests of chaotic behaviour in a nonlinear interest rate model', *Financial Analysts Journal*, Sept.-Oct., 51-62.

Marshall, A. (1890/1927) *Principles of Economics*, 8th edition, Macmillan, London.

Murphy, J.J. (1986) *Technical Analysis of the Futures Market*, New York Institute of Finance, New York.

Muth, J.F. (1961) 'Rational expectations and the theory of price movements', *Econometrica*, **29**, 315-35.

Nelson, R. & Winter, S. (1983) *An Evolutionary Theory of Economic Change*, Bellknap Press, Harvard University, Cambridge, MA.

Nicolis, G. & Prigogine, I. (1977) *Self-Organization in Non-Equilibrium Systems*, Wiley Interscience, New York.

Nocolis, G. & Prigogine, I. (1989) *Exploring Complexity: an Introduction*, Freeman, W.H., New York.

Osborne, M.F.M. (1964) 'Brownian motion in the stock market' in Cootner, P. (ed.), *The Random Character of Stock Market Prices*, MIT Press, Cambridge, MA (originally published in 1959).

Peters, E. (1989) 'Fractal structure in the capital markets', *Financial Analysts Journal*,

Peters, E. (1991a) 'A chaotic attractor for the S & P 500', *Financial Analysts Journal*,

Peters, E. (1991b) 'R/S analysis using logarithmic returns: a technical note', *Financial Analysts Journal*,

Prigogine, I., Allen, P.M., & Herman, R. (1977), 'The evolution of complexity and the laws of nature', in Laszlo, E. & Bierman, J. (eds), *Goals in a Global Community*, **1**, Pergamon Press, Oxford.

Prigogine, I. & Stengers, I. (1987) *Order Out of Chaos*, Bantam Books, New York.

Sanglier, M. & Allen, P.M. (1989) 'Evolutionary models of urban systems: an application to the Belgian provinces', *Environment and Planning*, A, **21**, 477–98.

Savit, R. (1988) 'When random is not random: an introduction to chaos in market prices', *The Journal of Futures Markets*, **8**, 271–89.

Savit, R. (1989) 'Nonlinearities and chaotic effects in options prices', *The Journal of Futures Markets*, **9**, 507–18.

Scheinkman, J. & LeBaron, B. (1989) 'Nonlinear dynamics and stock returns', *Journal of Business*, **62**, 311–37.

Schumpeter, J. (1934) *The Theory of Economic Development*, Harvard University Press, Cambridge, MA.

Soros, G. (1988) *The Alchemy of Finance*, Weidenfeld & Nicolson, London.

Thompson, J.M.T. & Stewart, H.B. (1986) *Non-Linear Dynamics and Chaos*, John Wiley, Chichester.

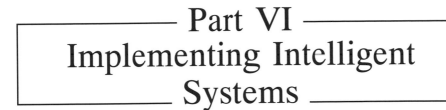
Part VI
Implementing Intelligent Systems

17

Software for
Intelligent Systems

PHILIP C. TRELEAVEN

1 INTRODUCTION

Previous chapters in this book have presented the *applications* of intelligent systems in banking, insurance and retail. This final chapter reviews software environments for building intelligent systems applications.

The emergence of each new intelligent computing technique — expert systems, fuzzy logic, neural networks and genetic algorithms — follows a predictable metamorphosis. Initially the technique is poorly understood, literature is scarce, and applicable application domains unclear. 'Proof of concept' applications are then handcrafted by researchers using a programming language such as C or FORTRAN. Next operational systems are built again using a language like C. Then as the intelligent technique becomes better understood, textbooks emerge and specialist consultancies are established. Finally, software environments and tool kits begin to emerge. Initially these environments are rudimentary stand-alone or educational tools. But they rapidly progress to sophisticated domain-specific or general-purpose environments, that interface to industry standard spreadsheets and databases.

At maturity, software for intelligent systems fall into one of three broad categories:

- *Application-oriented* — dedicated to a specific application domain (e.g. finance)
- *Algorithm-oriented* — supporting one or more important algorithms (e.g. Back-prop) or

---

Intelligent Systems for Finance and Business. Edited by S. Goonatilake and P. Treleaven
© 1995 John Wiley & Sons Ltd

- *General-purpose* — comprehensive tool kits supporting a range of algorithms and applications.

Recently, 'hybrid' applications combining two or more intelligent techniques have become a popular way of harnessing the strengths of individual techniques (Goonatilake & Khebbal, 1995). This in turn has led to the emergence of 'hybrid' environments (Rocha, Khebbal & Treleaven, 1993) integrating neural networks, genetic algorithms and rule-based systems.

This chapter reviews environments for neural networks, genetic algorithms, and fuzzy logic, concluding with a discussion of hybrid programming environments.

2 TAXONOMY

Our review of intelligent systems software environments utilizes the three-category taxonomy (Recce, Rocha & Treleaven, 1992): application-oriented, algorithm-oriented, and general-purpose.

2.1 Application-oriented

Application-oriented environments are aimed at specific business domains, such as finance, engineering, marketing, or medicine. They are designed for professionals who have little expertise (or even interest) in the actual intelligent technique, other than wishing to apply it to their business.

Software environments in this class trade off generality for ease of use, and attempt to hide the implementation details from the user. This software can be viewed as 'black boxes', offering a domain-specific range of facilities, and usually having excellent interfaces to spreadsheets, databases, data feeds and statistical packages. Increasingly the environments are OLE compatible. An example is BehavHeuristics' *Airline Marketing Tactician* which is used to make predictions on the availability of airline seats.

2.2 Algorithm-oriented

Algorithm-oriented environments support one or more specific, popular algorithms. For neural network environments this might be Back-propagation or Self-Organizing Maps. The major strength of algorithm-oriented environments is their flexibility and ease of use. Algorithms are typically supplied as parameterized libraries and often in source code form, allowing easy integration with user applications.

Algorithm-oriented software can be further subdivided into:

- *Algorithm-specific*, supporting a single algorithm that can be applied to a broad range of applications and
- *Algorithm libraries*, which offer a number of parameterized algorithms or models in a standard language such as C.

Algorithm-specific environments, by specializing in a single algorithm like Back-propagation, can provide simple interfaces and highly tuned algorithms. Likewise, algorithm libraries have powerful capabilities for integrating algorithms with systems written in the same language. Again drawing on neural network environments: classic examples are BrainMaker supporting Back-propagation and the OWL Libraries supporting over 21 C-encoded algorithms.

2.3 General-purpose

General-purpose software environments are comprehensive tool-kits comprising algorithm libraries, simulators, graphical user interfaces (GUI) and other programming tools. These environments are designed for experienced programmers and offer a great deal of flexibility in their interfaces, algorithms and execution control mechanisms. However, this may involve trading off performance for flexibility and generality. To boost algorithm performance, some software provide hardware support either through accelerator boards or compilers to parallel computers.

3 NEURAL NETWORK ENVIRONMENTS

Of all the intelligent techniques, software for neural networks is by far the most extensive. A recent survey of neural network software environments for the UK Department of Trade and Industry (DTI, 1993) listed over 50 commercial products. Worldwide many hundreds of products are now available. In this section we review some influential neural network software, such as BrainMaker and NeuralWare's NeuralWorks. As a case study we examine Europe's major neural network environment called Galatea which was developed at University College London (UCL).

3.1 Application-oriented

One of the earliest applications-oriented neural network tools was the Decision Learning System (DSL) marketed by Nestor (Nestor Inc., 1988) and targeted at financial applications such as mortgage underwriting, car insurance and credit card transaction risk assessment. A host of excellent systems have followed (DTI, 1993). Companies typically offer a family of products, each tailored to a specific business application domain. For example, Recognition Systems sell Customer Predict for data mining applications, Data Builder for marketing and sales forecasting, and Time Series Predictor for forecasting financial time series. Table 17.1 provides an extensive list of application-oriented products and their domains (DTI, 1993).

These application-oriented environments typically are PC based, running under Microsoft Windows, and have interfaces to industry-standard spreadsheets and databases like Excel and Paradox. Next we will examine Algorithms-oriented systems.

Table 17.1 Application-oriented neural network software

Product	Company	Application area
EAGLE	HNC Software	Credit card fraud detection
FALCON	HNC Software	Credit card fraud detection
FDS	Nestor	Fraud detection system
Gem	Forvus Forecasting	Electricity industry
Gist	EDS-Scicon	Classification and segmentation of images
HyNet	Green R&D International	Fault detection and corrective action
Lucid	Logica	Image processing and remote sensing
Matchfinder	AEA Technology	Gas chromatography and pattern recognition
NeuForecast	Neural Computer Sciences	Time series forecasting
Nestorwriter	Nestor	A handwriting recognition system
NeuMan	Sension Advanced Computing	Machine maintenance monitoring and inspection
Neural Crosswire	EDS-Scicon	Artillery muzzle velocity prediction
Sentinal	EDS-Scicon	Intelligent scene monitoring
TADS -X100	Domain Dynamics	Machine maintenance monitoring and fault analysis
Trainable Patt Clssifer	Domain Dynamics	Intruder detection and recognition
Wisard	Computer Recognition Systems	Adaptive image recognition
XDR Netwk reader	Advanced Recognition	Hand and machine print recognition

3.2 Algorithm-oriented

Algorithm-oriented software aims for *flexibility* and has the great advantage of easy integration with user applications. Two pioneering examples are the algorithm-specific system BrainMaker, optimized for the Back-propagation model and marketed by California Scientific Software; and Owl an algorithm library offered by Omlsted & Watkins (Omlsted & Watkins, 1988).

BrainMaker, by California Scientific Software, consists of three packages. The core of the environment comprises a tutorial, control routines, and eight complete sample networks. It has a graphics interface which displays histograms for each layer and associated connection weights, and produces predefined plots which show the effect of varying network parameters. The environment's preprocessor is used to define the network structure (connections, activities, etc.) with arrays, and through entry of data in a spreadsheet-like style.

The Owl algorithm library is written in C and targeted at the experienced programmer. Owl supports over 19 different models, all seen by the programmer as a data structure and a set of service calls that operate on the data structures. The

Table 17.2 Algorithms-oriented neural network software

Product	Company	Comments
Autonet Windows	Recognition Systems	Windows based systems that automatically configures networks
BrainMaker	California Scientific Software	Comprehensive package built around Back-propagation
Braincell	Promised Land Technologies	Neural network that links to Excel and Lotus 1-2-3
ExploreNet	HNC Software	20 architectures for building neural applications
KnowledgeNet	HNC Software	Explains decisions made with ExploreNet
Neuralyst	Epic Systems Group	A neural network add-on program for Excel
NeuroWindows	Ward Systems Group	A tool that can easily integrate with most spreadsheets and databases
Miminise	Mimetics	Extensive neural network library from Galatea project
Matlab	Mathworks Inc	Neural network toolbox to use with Matlab products
OWL Libraries	Hyperlogic	Olmsted & Watkins library of 21 algorithms

data structure specifies the properties of the networks and the service calls invoke entry points within the network objects. To deploy the network, the user specifies the object and library modules, and an 'include' file corresponding to the required model. The user specifies the parameters needed during creation time (instantiating the network), and during execution time. The execution time parameters are defined on a per-network basis and can be altered dynamically.

Table 17.2 provides a list of some Algorithm-oriented software products (AI Expert, 1992; DTI, 1993).

3.3 General-purpose

General-purpose programming software aim to be *comprehensive* and span a range of algorithms and applications. Pioneering examples include SAIC ANSpec (Science Applications International Corp., 1989), NeuralWare NeuralWorks (NeuralWare Inc., 1991) and the Esprit II Galatea (Recce, Rocha & Treleaven, 1992). Other well-known examples include IBM's Neural Network Utility providing both development and runtime environments.

These general-purpose environments, like NeuralWorks and Galatea, typically provide: a graphical interface, an algorithm library, a specialized programming language, a simulator and often a hardware accelerator board. The algorithm libraries are the core component. The libraries incorporate popular models such as Back-propagation, in various flavours, and Self-Organizing Maps, etc. (Table 17.3).

Table 17.3   General-purpose neural network software

Product	Company	Comments
ANSpec	SAIC	DBaseIII & Lotus 1-2-3 compatible. Has 13 neural models
Galatea	Mimetics, UCL	Includes a graphic monitor and a neural programming language
IBM Neural Net utility	IBM	Environment supporting Backprop, SOM, constraint satisfaction
Anza/Axon	HNC	Has a graphical user interface; description language and a parallelizer
NeuModel...NeuRun	Neural Computer Sciences	Range of utilities called 'Neu...' for neural applications
NeuralWorks	NeuralWare	Comprehensive neural network development tool-kit

As a case study we examine Galatea, and its precursor the Pygmalion environment, built around industry standards such as X-Windows and the C and C++ programming languages to make tools easily extendible.

3.4   Case Study: The Galatea System

The structure of Galatea, built as part of a large European Commission-funded project on neural networks, is typical of that found in the other general-purpose environments providing a GUI, an algorithm library and execution environments on a range of workstations and special neural hardware. The Galatea System comprises two interdependent domains (Figure 17.1): an execution environment and a programming environment. The execution environment offers hardware platforms for the simulation of any neural network model and for the integration of application-specific chips. To integrate these heterogeneous platforms, Galatea introduces the concept of a Virtual Machine (VM): a hardware abstraction that isolates any special characteristic of the actual execution platforms. The programming environment integrates with the execution environments through the native code of a virtual machine: the VM Language (VML), an optimized low-level neural network representational language.

VML constitutes a set of arithmetic operations that reflect the inherently parallel nature of neural network algorithm calculations. VML is machine-independent and addresses parallelism by implementing operators over a matrix representation of network data.

The programming environment of Galatea supports tasks such as: (1) the definition, programming, customization and development of algorithms; (2) the control of the simulation of a model or the execution of an application; and (3) debugging. The environment comprises (Taylor, Recce & Mangat, 1993) a

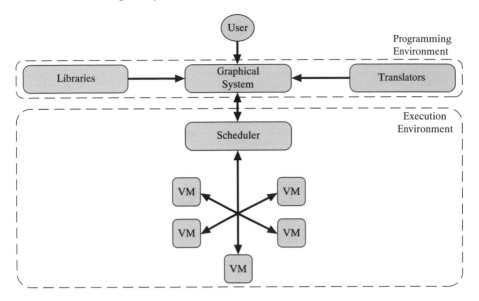

Figure 17.1 The Galatea system

high-level programming language based on C++, algorithm and preprogrammed application libraries, language translators to VML, and four key graphical tools:

- A systems application builder, a tool for graphically constructing neural network algorithms that are then automatically converted into executable code
- An executable monitor, a tool for neurocomputer developers that measures and displays the load distribution and the traffic between the components of the neurocomputer
- An algorithm debugger, perhaps the most common and desired component of a programming environment, that lets the user change at any level of the network hierarchy
- An application monitor, a windowing system that can be customized to display versions of the key parameters, inputs and outputs that are of interest to the end-user.

Having reviewed neural network software, we next examine tools for genetic algorithms.

4   GENETIC ALGORITHM ENVIRONMENTS

Interest in Genetic Algorithms (GAs) is expanding rapidly with their applications domain spanning areas as diverse as chemistry (e.g. protein folding), finance (e.g. credit assessment), and manufacturing (e.g. production scheduling). GAs have emerged much more recently than neural networks, hence the volume of GA

Table 17.4 Genetic algorithm software

Product	Company	Application area
Application-oriented environments		
Evolver	Axcelis	Spreadsheet-oriented GA business tool
Omega	KiQ and CAP Volmac	Software for applying GAs to financial applications
PC/Beagle	Pathway Research	Extracts decision rules from a database of examples
XpertRule GenAsy	Attar Software	Expert systems shell with embedded genetic algorithms
Algorithm-oriented environments		
EM	Technical University Berlin	Library supplying a range of 'Evolutionary Algorithms'
Escapade	University of Dortmund	Environment supporting $(\mu, +\lambda)$ 'Evolutionary Algorithms'
GAGA	University College London	Task independent GA targeted at minimizing difficult cost functions
Gaucsd	UC San Diego	GA software allowing most C functions as evaluation functions
Genesis	The Software Partnership	Widely used set of GA routines written in C
Genitor	Colorado State University	Software package implementing Whitley's Genitor algorithm
OOGA	The Software Partnership	Davis' LISP-based GA software
General-purpose environments		
EnGENEer	Logica	General-purpose C-based applications environment
Game	University College London	General GA environment, enhanced with parallel GA facility
GA Workbench	Cambridge Consultants	Educational GA system with powerful graphical interface
Micro GA	Emergent Behaviour	A software framework of GA objects written in C++
Pegasus	German National Research Center	Tool kit written in ANSI-C
Splicer	NASA Johnson & Mitre Corp.	Comprehensive GA software: kernel, libraries + fitness modules

software is significantly less. However, an increasing number of powerful GA environments are becoming available (Ribeiro Filho, Alippi & Treleaven, 1994). Table 17.4 lists some example systems.

4.1 Application-oriented

Professionals wishing to use GAs without having to acquire detailed knowledge can choose from a growing number of Application-oriented GA software (see

Table 17.4). Some environments have interfaces to a spreadsheet utility, while others employ a mixture of techniques.

PC/BEAGLE, in particular, is a 'rule finder' program that turns data into knowledge by examining a database of examples and using machine-learning techniques to create a set of decision rules for classifying those examples. The system is composed of six executable blocks that are run in sequence. The GA component is a so-called Heuristic Evolutionary Rule Breeder that generates the decision by 'Naturalistic Selection'. The system runs on PC compatibles and accepts data in ASCII format. Rules are produced as logical expressions.

4.2   Algorithm-oriented

In the algorithm-oriented category, a well-known software environment, is the GENEtic Search Implementation System — Genesis (Grefenstette, 1984). It has been used to implement and test a variety of new genetic operators. Genesis is now at Version 5.0 and runs on Sun Workstations and PCs (The Software Partnership, 1992).

Genesis provides the basic procedures for natural selection, crossover, and mutation, and provides a highly modifiable environment and a large amount of statistical information on outputs.

4.3   General-purpose

General-purpose GA software environments provide users with facilities to fully customize the algorithms and systems. The number of these environments is growing, stimulated by the increasing interest in the application of GAs in many domains. Two major systems in Europe are EnGENEer (Robbins, 1992), developed by Logica Cambridge Ltd, and Game (Kingdom, Ribeiro Filho & Treleaven, 1992), part of the European Community Papagena project.

EnGENEer helps the developer to apply GAs to new problem domains by offering: a *Genetic Description Language* for the description of the structure of the genetic material (i.e. its genes, chromosomes, etc.); an *Evolutionary Model Language* for the description of options such as population size, structure and source, and mutation and crossover types; *Graphical Monitoring Tools*; and a *Library* of routines for the representation and interpretation of the genetic solutions such as grey-coding, permutations, etc.

As a case study of GA software we will briefly examine the Game environment.

4.4   Case Study — The Game Environment

Game is an object-oriented environment for programming sequential and parallel GA applications and algorithms. The environment comprises five major parts (see Figure 17.2): Virtual Machine, High-Level GA language, GA Libraries, Graphical Monitor, and Compilers.

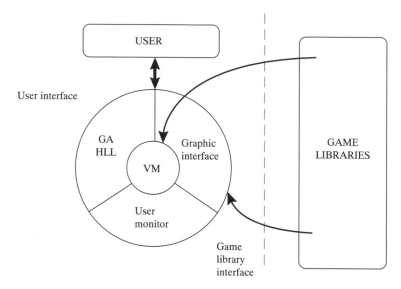

Figure 17.2 The Game software environment

The *Virtual Machine* is the machine-independent low-level abstraction representing the code responsible for the management and execution of a Genetic Algorithm application. The *High-level Language* GA-HLL is an object-oriented programming language for defining new GA models and applications. The *Genetic Algorithm Libraries* stores parameterized algorithms, applications, and operator libraries, constituting validated models written in the high-level language. The *Graphical Monitor* is the software environment for controlling and monitoring the execution of a GA application simulation. Lastly, *Compilers* are provided to the various target machines, ranging from parallel hardware to PCs.

Game is designed to allow a single application to use many (and possibly different) algorithms running in parallel, or a single parameterized algorithm to be configured for many applications.

To develop a Genetic Algorithm application, the user first loads the required modules from the library. With the high-level language it is then possible to configure, modify and extend the GA software. To execute the application, the user can invoke the graphical monitor command language for interactive monitoring and control of the simulation.

The environment is being offered in plain C++, with the ultimate goal being its development in a parallel language derived from C++, for execution in parallel machines. A preliminary version of Game — in source code form — is available free from University College London.

A sample list of GA software is given in Table 17.4. Next we will review fuzzy logic software.

5 FUZZY LOGIC SYSTEMS

The rise of fuzzy logic must be largely credited to Japan. Japan's launch of a new generation of fuzzy logic-based consumer products (Schwartz et al., 1994) has caused an explosion of interest in fuzzy logic, and stimulated a growing range of software tools (Cox & Schwartz, 1993).

In contrast to the previous intelligent techniques we have examined, fuzzy logic applications are frequently supported by hardware. Thus in Table 17.5 we have listed both major software and hardware suppliers.

We will now briefly review a few key products that illustrate the types of software available.

Table 17.5 Fuzzy logic software and tools

Product	Company	Application area
Application-oriented environments		
A-B Flex	Allen-Bradley	Fuzzy applications software
AIS	Adaptive Information Systems	Fuzzy information retrieval and flexible querying systems
C500-FZ001	Omron Corp.	Fuzzy logic processor and application-oriented controllers
FuziCalc	FuziWare	Spreadsheets-based environment for financial applications
MB94100	Fujitsu	Fuzzy single-chip controllers
MSM9U111	Oki Electrics	Single-chip 8-bit fuzzy controller
NLX110, NLX230	American NeuraLogix	Fuzzy chips and hardware
Algorithm-oriented environments		
C-Fuzzy	Byte Craft	Fuzzy preprocessor that generates C code
CubiCalc	Hyperlogic's	Targeted at control and information modelling problems
FMC	TransferTech	Fuzzy shell
FRIL	Fril Systems Ltd.	Fuzzy Relational Inference Language
Fuzzle	Modico	Fuzzy shell generating C
FuzzySoft	FuzzySoft AG	Fuzzy simulation system
Manifold Editor	Fuzzy Systems Engineering	Fuzzy systems editor
Metus Fuzzy Library	Metus Systems	C/C++ library of fuzzy processing routines
NeuFuz	National Semiconductor	Combines fuzzy logic and neural networks
General-purpose environments		
Fide	Aptronics	Complete development system for microprocessor-based fuzzy systems
FuzzyTECH	Inform Software	Leading fuzzy development environment
SieFuzzy	Siemens	Extensive software–hardware tools developed jointly with Togai
TILShill…TILGen	Togai Infralogic	Extensive software–hardware tools developed jointly with Siemens

5.1 Application-oriented

An illustration of application-oriented fuzzy tools is given by FuziCalc (Cox & Schwartz, 1993). FuziWare's FuziCalc supports fuzzy calculations within a spreadsheet format, and is therefore good for financial applications like budgeting. FuziCalc supports Microsoft's DDE. The user enters the fuzzy set as a *belief function*, and then selects a representative function from a menu of five predefined shapes. FuziCalc also provides a use of predefined standard formulas such as *sum*, *average*, *max* or *min* fuzzy operations.

5.2 Algorithm-oriented

For Algorithm-oriented software, two tools that seem to be "algorithm-oriented" are CubiCalc and NeuFuz. HyperLogic's CubiCalc provides powerful fuzzy algorithmic features: operators (*not*), hedges (*somewhat*, *very*), arithmetic, logical and trigonometric functions, and explicit rule weights. The system operates through windows, with a fuzzy editor used to build a fuzzy vocabulary and enter rules in a text file. This file is then loaded, compiled and executed, with the simulation system displaying the output of the model on a two-dimensional grid.

In contrast, National semiconductor's NeuFuz is a combined neural network and fuzzy product, using a back-propagation-based seven-layer net. It takes a neural net training set and outputs fuzzy rules and membership functions. All the user needs to specify are the learning rate, training error, and the inner layer learning rate modifier. Neufuz outputs C and COP-8 for the NSC microcontrollers.

5.3 General-purpose

In the general-purpose area, four important companies marketing software are Aptronix, Inform Software, Siemens, and Togai Infralogic. Each supplies a complete fuzzy logic system development environment.

Using Aptronix's Fide, a system is created of multiple fuzzy inference units, each define by a text file. This file contains the definitions of the input and output variables, their associated fuzzy sets, and the rules. Facilities exist for specifying (in the file) the types of fuzzy representations required, and a range of common operators (e.g. *min*, *max*). In addition, a *Membership function* editor is available to help create fuzzy sets. The source text file is then compiled into an executable unit. A notable feature of Fide is the *Composer*, an integrated analyser and system simulator, providing two- and three-dimensional views of the fuzzy control surface.

A second major supplier of general-purpose tools is Inform Software. Its FuzzyTECH centres on a flexible set of editors for creating: input/output variables, membership functions, and rules. It generates C or assembly language for microcontrollers such as the Intel 8051 MCU. For instance, using the Rule Input/Output Editor a user can select the form of rule aggregation (e.g. *and*, *or*, *min-avg.*) on a global level, then using the Rule Editor rules can be modified on an individual basis. FuzzyTECH also provides graphical tools for displaying: variables and outputs as two-dimensional representations, time and transfer plots of simulated systems, and a three-dimensional picture of the rule matrix.

As the case study we will examine the jointly developed Siemens-Togai Infralogic range of fuzzy logic tools marketed, respectively, as SieFuzzy and TILGen.

5.4 Fuzzy Logic Products

Siemens-Togai Infralogic have an extensive environment comprising five software tools. The Togai names (Cox & Schwartz, 1993) are: TILShell, Fuzzy-C development system (FCDS), MicroFPL system, FC110 system, and TILGen; and six hardware products: FC110 digital fuzzy processor, FCA10AT FC110 Board for the IBM PC, FC10SA development module, FC10SB FC110 single-board fuzzy controller, FCD10SBus board for Sbus, and the FCA10VME board for VME.

TILShell is a Windows-based graphical CASE tool for supporting the building of fuzzy expert systems, which interacts with all other TIL software and hardware. TILShell — the heart of the system — provides rule and membership function (fuzzy set) editors. In addition, variables created can be associated with a range of storage classes, and can be grouped into a number of fuzzy sets. The TILShell editor is claimed (Cox & Schwartz, 1993) to be very simple to use. The user selects the basic fuzzy set shape and places it in the editor window at any position in the range of possible values. In addition, windows are provided for *equations* to create fuzzy sets from a variety of mathematical expressions, and for repeating a series of standard (triangular) fuzzy sets across the set's range.

The FCDS system is a set of tools that compile a fuzzy expert system specified in the Fuzzy Programming Language (FPL) into C. Other tools include the MicroFPL development system which contains an FPL compiler that generates an internal form for a FPL fuzzy expert system, plus a runtime module to interpret this internal form on embedded microcontrollers. Associated with this tool is the FC110 system which provides an assembler, linker and loaders for the FC110 proprietary fuzzy processor.

Finally, having examined neural network, genetic algorithms and fuzzy logic software, we look at *Hybrid* software that allow two or more intelligent techniques to be exploited in a single application. Hybrid intelligent applications are becoming increasingly popular, and software environments are being enhanced to encompass not just intelligent techniques but also advanced statistical techniques.

6 HYBRID SYSTEMS

Researchers and application builders are beginning to realize that a combination of two or more intelligent technologies is often the best strategy for tackling complex real-world problems such as those in Finance, Language Processing, and Automated Manufacturing (Goonatilake & Khebbal, 1995). Pioneering examples include: combining a neural network for pattern recognition with an expert system for decision support as in the Kobe Steel Blast Furnace control system and the London Stock Exchange's Insider Dealing Detection system which uses a combination of neural networks, genetic algorithms and statistical techniques (*Economist*, 1994).

Software for programming hybrid systems is at an early stage of development, therefore a review based on our three-category taxonomy is premature. However, there are a few notable systems (Khebbal & Shamhong 1995), such as Prodeas' Synergy, Visix's Galaxy, InferOne's IntelliSphere, which are briefly reviewed below, and UCL's Hansa system, used as the case study.

Synergy is a visual programming environment that aids inter-utility integration. Synergy comprises four major elements: *Packages* — define interconnections of utilities, with the utilities represented by icons and the information flows by arrows; the *Library* — is a Packet storage manager; the *Variable Server* — provides 260 predefined global variables used for communication between Microsoft's DDE and OLE, and the utilities; and the *Application Service Database* — records utility information such as name location, type and key functions.

Galaxy is a distributed system supporting development of distributed hybrid applications across heterogeneous platforms including MS Windows, Macintosh, VMS, OS/2 and Unix. The environment consists of a set of Libraries, Services and Tools providing a so-called Applications Programming Interface (API). The API supports graphics facilities including rendering, and colour/image management, as well as I/O, file and directory services.

IntelliSphere is a graphical development environment for integrating symbolic and neural processing based on so-called *neurOagents*. A neurOagent is an assembly of neurons that operates as a knowledge base. Various symbol-neural mechanisms are supportable, including deductive reasoning using backward, forward and mixed propagation between neurOagents, and constraint satisfaction with 'fuzzy' information.

As a case study of Hybrid software we will examine the European Community-funded Hansa framework.

6.1 Case Study: The Hansa Framework

The Hansa (Heterogeneous Application geNerator Standard Architecture) Project has developed an object-oriented cross-platform framework to allow developers to rapidly configure industry standard utilities and artificial intelligence shells, and is targeted at business applications for marketing, banking and insurance (Rocha et al., 1993).

The Hansa Framework (Figure 17.3) utilizes the object-oriented paradigm through C++ and a communication protocol to allow the exchange of information between modules within an application. The framework hides platform-related implementation details, promoting software re-use and rapid prototyping. On each of the target platforms (PCs running MS-Windows 3.1 or Windows NT, and UNIX/X-Windows workstations) the framework implements a services interface

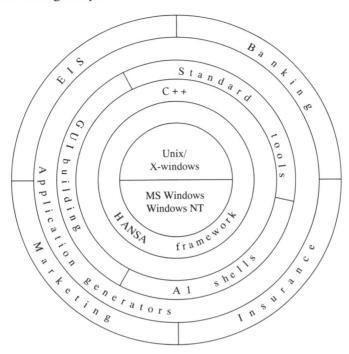

Figure 17.3   The Hansa framework

inspired by, and compatible with, Microsoft's OLE protocol. For UNIX/W-Windows systems, Hansa is developing an OLE-like interface following closely the philosophy of the Object Management Architecture (from Object Management Group Consortium), and builds the framework on top of the services supplied by the Object Request Broker. The common OLE-like interface allows an easy port of the application code, from one platform to the other.

For each of the application domains targeted by the project (Executive Information Systems, Direct Marketing, Banking and Insurance) there is at least one application generator in charge of controlling the configuration and execution of cooperating Hansa Tools selected from the Hansa Tool kit. This Tool kit includes: expert systems such as Pamela; neural networks development environments such as Mimenice, derived from the Pygmalion and Galatea Projects and commercialized by Mimetics; the GA programming environment Game; as well as industry-standard utilities that comply with the Hansa-OLE protocol on PCs or Unix Workstations.

For allowing the integration of such a diverse range of Tools, Hansa constitutes a natural programming environment for the implementation of hybrid applications. Moreover, the possibility of utilizing off-the-shelf Tools, putting them together in an intuitive environment, allows the user to configure and tune the application by utilizing the most appropriate utilities for each task involved in the application execution.

7 CONCLUSIONS

The past few years has witnessed a veritable explosion of interest in the application of neural networks, genetic algorithms and fuzzy logic, no more so than in financial services, and we expect this to continue. However, as complex real-world problems are tackled, the strengths and limitations of these new intelligent technologies become clear. To capitalize on the individual techniques' strengths, hybrid systems are being increasingly developed, integrating the adaptive, symbolic and even numeric approaches. These new systems are growing in number and acceptance as the most effective solution.

There is, however, currently no comprehensive environment for Hybrid Systems. It is to be expected that neural network, genetic algorithm and fuzzy logic software will increasingly be enhanced with additional techniques, intelligent and statistical. This trend is illustrated by software we have examined such as NeuFuz with neural networks and fuzzy logic. For Hybrid software to reach the state of the art of neural network, GA and fuzzy logic software environments in terms of graphic interfaces, libraries, and high-level languages, there is still a long path to follow. One attempt is the Hansa Framework, which aims to offer facilities for integrating rule-based systems, neural networks and GAs, allowing the rapid configuration and prototyping of hybrid applications. We believe this is the way forward for software of intelligent systems.

ACKNOWLEDGEMENTS

We would like to acknowledge our ESPRIT Partners for the above projects:

Galatea: Thomson-CSF, Philips, Siemens AG, Mimetics, SGS-Thomson, INPG, IS, CRAM, INESC and CTI.
Papagena: Brainware, IFP, Telmat Informatique, CAP Gemini Innovation, GMD, KiQ. University of Grenoble, GWI and Institut für Kybernetic & Systemtheorie.
Hansa: CRL Ltd, O.Group, Promind, J&J Financial Systems, IFS Brainware and Mimetics.

REFERENCES

AI Expert (1992) *Neural Network Resource Guide*, June.
Cox, E. & Schwartz, T.J. (1993) 'Software review: around the world with fuzzy products', *AI Expert*, March, 44–8.
Dekker, L. & Ribeiro Filho, J. (1993) 'The GAME Virtual Machine Architecture', in *Parallel Genetic Algorithms: Theory and Applications*, IOS Press, Amsterdam, pp. 93–110.
DTI (1993) *Neural Computing Learning Solutions*, Directory of Neural Computing Suppliers, Products and Sources of Information, UK Department of Trade and Industry.
The Economist, The World in 1995, 'A neural network is watching you', p. 140
Goonatilake, S. & Khebbal, S. (1995) *Intelligent Hybrid Systems*, John Wiley, Chichester.

Grefenstette, S. (1984) 'GENESIS: A system for using genetic search procedures', in *Proceedings of the 1984 Conference on Intelligent Systems*, pp. 161-5.

Hecht-Nielsen Neurocomputers Inc. (1991) ExploreNet 3000, KnowledgeNet Balboa 860, 5501 Oberlin Drive, San Diego, CA 92121, USA.

Khebbal, S. & D. Shamhong (1995) 'Tools and environments for hybrid systems', in Goonatilake, S. & Khebbal, S. (eds), *Intelligent Hybrid Systems*, John Wiley, Chichester.

Kingdom, J., Ribeiro Filho, J. & Treleaven, P. (1992) 'The GAME programming environment architecture', in *Parallel Genetic Algorithms: Theory and Applications*, IOS Press, Amsterdam, pp. 85-92.

Nestor Inc. (1988) *Learning Systems Based on Multiple Neural Networks*, One Richmond Square, Providence, RI 02906, USA.

NeuralWare Inc. (1991) NeuralWorks Explorer, Penn Center West, Building IV, Suite 227, Pittsburgh, PA 15276, USA.

Olmsted & Watkins (1988) OWL Neural Network Library, 2411 East Valley Parkway, Suite 294, PO Box 3751, Escondido, CA 92025, USA.

Pathway Research Ltd (1992) PC-BEAGLE, 59 Cronbrook Rd, Bristol BS6 7BS, UK.

Recce, M.L., Rocha, P.V. & Treleaven, P.C. (1992) 'Neural network programming environments', in International Conference on Neural Networks, Brighton, UK.

Ribeiro Filho, J., Alippi C. & Treleaven, P. (1994) 'Genetic algorithm programming environments', *IEEE Computer*, **27**, No. 6, June, 28-45.

Robbins, G. (1992) 'EnGENEer — The evolution of solutions', in *Proceedings of 5th Annual Seminar on Neural Networks and Genetic Algorithms*.

Rocha, P.V., Khebbal, S. & Treleaven P. (1993) 'A framework for hybrid intelligent systems', in *Proc. ANNES'93*, 1st New Zealand International Conference on Neural Networks and Expert Systems, November 1993, pp. 206-9.

Schartz, D.G., Klir, G.J., Lewis, H.W. & Ezawa, Y. (1994) 'Applications of fuzzy sets and approximate reasoning', *Proc. IEEE*, **82**, No. 4 April, 482-97.

Science Applications International Corp. (1989) SAIC Product Information — Delta Processors, ANSpec, ANSim, CARL/BP, 10260, Campus Point Drive, Mail Stop 71, San Diego, CA 92121, USA.

The Software Partnership (1992) GENESIS, PO Box 991, Melrose, MA 02176, USA.

Taylor, J., Recce, M. & Mangat, A. (1993) 'Flexible operating environment for matrix based neurocomputers', in *Proc. Int. Workshop on Artificial Neural Networks IWANN'93*, June 1993, pp. 382-7.

Treleaven, P. & Goonatilake, S. (1992) 'Intelligent financial technologies', in Workshop on Parallel Solving from Nature: Applications in Statistics and Economics, by the Statistical Office of the European Communities (EUROSTAT), 1992.

Index